THE

STORY OF ROYAL ELTHAM

No 1.

R. R. C. GREGORY.

THE

STORY OF ROYAL ELTHAM

BY

R. R. C. GREGORY

Head Master of the Eltham National School, People's Warden of Eltham Parish Church,
Member of the Council of the Woolwich Antiquarian Society, Author (with H. B. M. Buchanan)
of "Lessons on Country Life," and "Junior Country Readers," (Macmillan), Editor of
"The Ludgate School Books," including "Story Readers," "Standard Author Readers,"
etc., etc.

WITH ILLUSTRATIONS FROM OLD PLATES

AND PRINTS, SKETCHES

By R. W. GREGORY AND W. H. BROWNING,

AND PHOTOGRAPHS SPECIALLY TAKEN

By F. W. NUNN

(Vice-President of the Greenwich and the Woolwich Antiquarian Societies),

TOGETHER WITH AN INDEX

By W. H. BROWNING.

KENTISH DISTRICT TIMES COMPANY, LTD.,
HIGH STREET, ELTHAM.

1909.

THE STORY OF ROYAL ELTHAM.

PREFACE.

⊕ HE chapters which go to make up this book are the outcome of a number
of simple addresses which the writer had prepared to interest the older children
of his school in the history of their ancient village.

It was suggested that these addresses might be re-written and amplified for
the benefit of "children of older growth," and thus came about their publication in
weekly instalments, in the local Press, for the space of twenty months. It is in
response to a very general request from all sorts and conditions of readers, not only of
Eltham, but of the neighbouring districts, that the chapters are now presented in
book form

It has been the aim of the writer to tell simply and clearly the story of a
village that is brim full of historic interest, to recount as vividly as may be the many
romantic incidents that have been associated with it, and to recall from the depths
of the past, the noble and distinguished personages, who, from time to time through
the long centuries, have trod our Eltham fields and lanes, and helped to make our
village story.

Local historians do not always recognise sufficiently that each village, however
small or remote, has played and is playing its part in the greater drama of national
history. Nevertheless, it is the fact which makes the investigation of local history
a matter of great importance in any scheme of historical study. The Church, the
Manor, the Tithe Barn, the Parish Records, the Cross, the Field names, the Lanes,
the Pound, and many another old-time relic, all have their tale to tell of the life and
progress of the village community, and very often reveal the part which it has played
in the nation's destinies.

Eltham's rôle in this respect has been a notable one, so, as opportunities have
arisen, the writer has taken advantage of them, to get glimpses, from the village
stand-point, of passing national events, of the changes in manners and customs, and
other circumstances which seemed to lend an interest to the narrative

The general plan of work is shown by the table of contents The parish possesses antiquities of a tangible character which date back to the earliest periods of
history These have been taken, as far as possible, in the order of their antiquity,
and the story written round them The Dover Road, the Common, the Manor, the
Church, the Palace, and the many other landmarks are thus made to tell their own
tale. This method of treatment seemed the most appropriate, not only from an
educational point of view, but from that of the general interest of the casual reader.

The self-imposed labour of research and writing which the book represents has occupied the leisure hours of upwards of four years It has been a labour of love; the result, however, would never have been obtained but for the kind help, encouragement, and advice, which have been so readily given by many old residents, and others, in Eltham and elsewhere, interested in the study of local history.

Special thanks are due to Mr. F W. Nunn, of Lee, a Vice-president of the Woolwich, and also the Greenwich, Antiquarian Society, not only for his personal assistance at the British Museum Library, but for his long and patient labours in the field of photography. With the exception of the plates that have been kindly and specially lent by Messrs. Macmillan and Co., for the purpose of this book, nearly all the photographs, whether from old prints and pictures, or originals, are the production of his camera, and represent the work of more than a year.

Grateful thanks are also accorded to Dr E A Baker, M A, the Borough Librarian, and his Assistants at the Public Libraries of Eltham, Woolwich, and Plumstead, for their ready co-operation and advice in the use of the fine collection of Kentish records which the Borough possesses; to Miss Lewin, who has herself kept records of Eltham for the latter portion of the nineteenth century, for much valuable information; to Miss Bloxam, for many facts regarding the Palace; to Mrs Dobell, for permission to photograph her copy of "Hortus Elthamensis," for the use of her copies of the Sherard Letters, and for other assistance; to Miss May, of Avery Hill Training College, for her kind help in construing the old French poem of Froissart referring to Eltham, and published now in English for the first time; to Miss Moore, who also has made studies of Eltham history, for kind criticism and assistance; to Miss Edith Anderson, also an enthusiastic student of local history, to Mr. W. H. Taffs, our Eltham numismatologist; to Mr T. W. Mills, the Treasurer of the Eltham Charities; to Dr J Jeken, a fifty year's resident of Eltham; to Mr. C. H. Athill, F.S.A., to Mr. W. J. Mortis, who, for upwards of half a-century, held public offices in the parish, and whose local knowledge of the period is unique, to the Rev T N Rowsell, former Vicar of Holy Trinity Church, for permission to quote extensively from his history of the "Golf Club House", to the Rev. E. Rivers, Vicar of Eltham, for permission to photograph the Parish Registers; to Mr R. Whittaker Smith, Mr W B Hughes, and Mr W G Thame, for much useful information; to Mr. W. H. Browning, for so kindly undertaking the compilation of the index; to Mr Geo Bishop (Pope Street), Mr T. H. Bartlett (The Gordon), and Mr. D. Waters (Mottingham), for information respecting their respective Schools; to the Rev. H. A. Hall (Holy Trinity), Rev Father MacGregor (S Mary's Roman Catholic), Rev. E. J. Penford (Congregational), Rev. A. C. Chambers (Baptist, Westmount Road), Mr. G. W. E Dowsett (Wesleyan), and Mr Alfred Smith (Baptist, Balcaskie Road), for notes respecting their several Churches; to Mr. F J. Furnivall, LL D, for special permission to use the plate of "Chaucer on Horseback"; and to many others who have so kindly placed their knowledge at the writer's disposal.

November, 1909   R.R.C.G.

CONTENTS.

LIST OF HALF-TONE ILLUSTRATIONS.

(For the list of Old Prints, Sketches, Tail-pieces, etc., see last pages of index).

ELTHAM PALACE FROM S.W.
Showing thatched sheds on what is now lawn.

No 5.

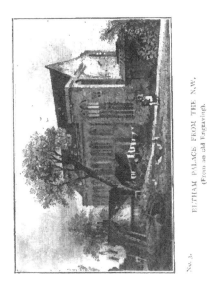

ELTHAM PALACE FROM THE N.W.
(From an old Engraving).

No. 3.

TO THE YOUNG FOLKS OF ELTHAM

November, 1909.

JULIUS CÆSAR (from a Copper Coin in the British Museum.)

CHAPTER I.

IN CÆSAR'S DAYS.

The dwellers in Eltham hardly need to be reminded that the place in which they live, at one time a quiet Kentish village, has a very interesting history.

Every place, of course, has a history of some sort, more or less interesting, when traced back to the beginning. But Royal Eltham has seen so many stirring times, has had so many great and interesting people associated with it, and has so much of its history written down in old books, and scattered about here and there in national records, that we may quite truly say there are few villages in the whole of England which can reveal a more romantic story. Though we may find, however, a great deal told us about Eltham in these old and musty records, and in books that are very learned, or very expensive, or very rare, it is doubtful whether one in a hundred of our young people will care to hunt for the story in those quarters, because old tomes are usually so tiresome to read, and n d n h patience to understand.

So, it has been suggested that it would be a good thing to write the story of Eltham, right down from the earliest times, in such a way that even the children may read and comprehend; and that it would be a particularly good thing to do so now, before the old village loses all its rustic features; for, alas, its green fields are gradually disappearing, and its quaint buildings are being removed, one by one, to make way for modern needs. This, then, is the excuse for the following chapters.

Now, it is quite likely, when you caught sight of the heading to this chapter, that you may have exclaimed, "Cæsar, indeed! Surely Cæsar never came to Eltham!" You are right. Cæsar never came to Eltham, for when the Romans invaded the land, and subdued the Britons, Eltham had not come into existence. But it is very probable, nay, the probability is so great that we may regard it as a fact, that the great Julius himself, he who

Br a d m r r an   e l me Po u ,
Wh e r e ms   1 l neral x r fll,—

passed with his victorious troops within the bounds of what afterwards became the parish of Eltham

We will consider presently what grounds there are for such an assertion as this, but, in the meantime, let us walk up the Well Hall-road, to the point where the great highway runs, right and left, past the Herbert Hospital, and over Shooter's-hill Here we find ourselves face to face with something which the old Roman conquerors did for us, something that was so useful and so permanent that it has remained to this day, a memorial of their industry and skill That something is the fine road itself, the Old Dover-road, which runs straight from London to the sea For more than eighteen hundred years this old road has been a highway for traffic! What a tale it might tell us if it could only relate the many great events of history with which it has been associated!

In the course of these chapters we shall have to consider some of those events—the most important of them To tell the whole tale of the Old Dover road would need a book all to itself. That is not our purpose For the present, our attention is directed to Cæsar and the Romans, and their associations with what is now Eltham

As you know quite well, there were two Roman invasions First of all, Julius Cæsar came, 55 years before Christ, and again in the following year He then went away with his host of warriors, only stopping just long enough to make it quite plain to the Britons that it was little use to resist the Roman arms From the time of Julius Cæsar's departure the Britons were not again molested by the Romans until a hundred years had passed, and the great Cæsar and all the host that came with him had long been dead Then, 47 years after Christ, in the time of another Cæsar, came other Roman legions, and they conquered the land and made the Britons Roman subjects. It was after this second invasion that the old road on which we stand was constructed according to the ideas of the Roman engineers.

Let us have a look at it, and see what history we can make out of it. In the first place you will notice how straight it is. As far as you can see, right to the top of the hill in one direction, and beyond the Brook Hospital in the other

direction it is almost a straight line Now, follow it here upon this map of Kent From London all the way to Canterbury it is perfectly straight At Canterbury it breaks off at an angle where it runs south-east to Dover That portion, too, is quite straight

Now let us examine this large map which shews all the Roman roads of Britain in thick black lines Notice the directness of them all Straightness, directness, this seems to have been one of the objects of those old road makers You will notice, too, that the road is called Watling-street. How it came by that name does not appear to be quite certain "Watling" is not a Roman name, and it must have been applied long after the Roman times One authority tells us that it is a mispronunciation of the Roman name "Vitellina Strata," which means "Street of Vitellius," who, at the time of its construction, was the Emperor of Rome But this interpretation seems rather far-fetched Another writer says that it is derived from the "Wætlings," but nobody seems to know who or what the "Wætlings" were, though it has been said that they were a "craft," possibly "basket makers," which is very likely This we do know, however, that in Anglo Saxon days it was called "Wætlinga Stræt"; in the middle ages, it had become "Watling Strete," and it has come down to us as "Watling Street"

Look at the length of it Here is where it touches Eltham, you see. On it goes westward till it crosses the Thames a little above London Then it strikes a north-westerly direction to St. Alban's, and on right through the midlands. At Gailey, which is a small village in Staffordshire, it branches off in two directions. The branch to the left crosses the Severn at Wroxeter, and then runs south. The right hand branch continues north-west from Gailey until it strikes Chester It then takes a north-easterly course, passes Manchester, and joins a continuation of Ermine-street at Aldborough By a direct northerly course it thence intersects the Wall of Hadrian, winds through the Cheviots, crosses the Tweed just below Melrose, and eventually strikes the Wall of Antonine, at the head of the Firth of Forth.

It is a great and noble road Space it out by means of the compass and scale and you will find that it is nearly 500 miles in length. You must not think, however, that all the roads made by the Romans were perfectly new at the time of their construction. Very often old British trackways already existed, and, when convenient, the Roman road-makers would make use of these, merely re-modelling them according to Roman methods.

Most of you remember how, a few years ago, the Woolwich Borough Council transformed the winding and rather narrow road from Eltham into the wide, straight, and up-to-date Well Hall-road.

towards the sea the Cenimagni, from Cambridge, Suffolk, and Norfolk, the Ancalites, from Berks and Wilts, the Cassi from Herts.

They passed this way, bands of grim and fearless fighters—chieftains, in rude chariots, painted blue, with scythes protruding from the axle trees, tended by horse and foot, some bearing blue-stained shields, some wearing plumed helmets, many with their bodies stained with woad, armed with pike, or dart, or broadsword, or with that terrible three-pronged spear, the trident— all pressing onward to foregather on the coast,

BRITISH WAR CHARIOT, SHIELD AND SPEARS.

In a similar way, the Romans, when it suited their purpose, brought the old British trackways "up-to-date," and this is what actually happened to the highway here. It is the opinion of antiquarians that, even before the first coming of Julius Cæsar, a British road ran from London to Dover, upon the line of the present Old Dover-road. A knowledge of this fact makes the spot upon which we stand all the more interesting. When the news spread among the tribes that Cæsar was coming, and that a vast fleet of Roman galleys was preparing to bring across from Gaul another host of warriors in greater numbers, and better prepared, than those who came a year before, it was along this primitive track that the Trinobantes, from Essex, hurried

under the gallant Cassibelan, once more to dispute the landing of the invading host.

You know the end of it. They were beaten.

Many of the defeated Britons fled to the dense forests, many more retraced their steps along this old track way, hastening to get beyond the river before the Roman soldiers should overtake them. A few miles above London there was a spot where the river could be forded. It was towards this point that the trackway led, and thither hastened the retreating Britons, where they crossed the stream and, on the other side, fortified their position as best they could. Presently came along the pursuing legions of Rome, led by the most famous of all Roman Generals

—" immortal Cæsar." It was a well disciplined army that marched past this point, every man armed with the most effective weapons that civilisation could then devise, and trained in the art of warfare by the experience of a hundred fights under the most successful leader Rome had ever known.

The Britons stuck great pointed stakes in the river to prevent the Romans from crossing, and the spot was known as Cowey Stakes for many years.

But it was of little avail. The Roman Eagle triumphed, and it must have been along this trackway that the victors passed once more. It was the return of a victorious army, bearing with them the trophies of war, and many a wretched British captive fated to be dragged through the streets of Rome, to grace the triumph of the conqueror.

So, although we cannot definitely say that thus and thus the things occurred, taking all matters into consideration, there seems to be sufficient evidence to warrant the presumption that this part of Eltham parish came within Cæsar's line of march.

ROMAN SOLDIERS.

Chapter II.

FROM AUGUSTA TO THE SEA.

It is not from books only that we may read history. There are other means of obtaining information about the doings of our forefathers. The printer is a useful man, and by means of his art he is able to record, and to distribute broadcast, the thoughts of men, wise and otherwise. But there have been occasions when a man with a pickaxe has revealed historical facts which all the books in the world had failed to recognise. If we walk about Eltham with our eyes open, our wits alert, and our thinking cap properly adjusted, we may perhaps pick up many a bit of history which has escaped the ken of other people. The works of Nature are an open book, and happy is he who knows how to read it. But the same may be said of those other works which are the result of man's art and industry.

A few years ago some workmen were making a trench along Edgware-road for the purpose of putting down a telephone tube. In the course of digging the men who wielded the pick-axe and spade came upon the . . . . pavement of the Roman road, over which the present Edgware-road runs. It lay beneath some six to twelve inches of ordinary soil, which came below the wood paving and concrete of the present road. The Roman pavement " was found to consist of large black nodular flints, weighing from four to seven pounds each, on a bed of rammed reddish-brown gravel of thickness varying according to the inequalities of the clay surface below." In T. Codrington's book, dealing with " Roman Roads in Britain," you will find the particulars of this interesting discovery, together with other information which the discovery revealed as to how the Roman road-makers did their work. From this, too, we may deduce some knowledge of the construction of the part of Watling-street upon which we now stand.

We may safely say that it was paved, because it was the general custom of the Romans to pave the roads. Sometimes, too, the roads lay along embankments which were thrown up and prepared by great . . . . . Such embankments are still to be seen in some parts of the country Most of them, however, have been levelled in the course of farming operations, or for the sake of the stone and other materials they contained Sometimes the road had a causeway erected along its side The methods of construction seem to have varied according to the needs or the resources of the locality, but the paving, the embankment, the causeway, and the directness of the course, were common features of the Roman roads in Britain. So we may almost imagine what this Old Watling street was like after the Roman workmen had completed it We might, perhaps, have said "British" workmen, for there can be little doubt that the Britons had to take their share in the labour. It is easy to think of the skilled work being done by the more experienced Roman workmen, and much of what we now call unskilled labour being done, under Roman direction, by the subjugated Briton

Before we go any farther let us have another look at the map Let us see if we can make out any other interesting facts about those ancient times Here is a modern map It shews the great railways of England Now look at those great trunk-lines Where do they run to? They all run to one centre, and that centre is London And why do they do this? The reason is, that London is not only the greatest city of England, but it is also the greatest mart, and the greatest port Now here again is this other map, that of "Britain in Roman Times" Look at those black lines indicating the Roman roads What do you notice? Yes, you notice that, just as the great trunk railways run to London, or radiate from London, like the spokes of a wheel, so did those old Roman roads

Here is our own Watling-street, you see, whose course we have already described Then there is Stane street, running from London to Chichester in the south, Ermine-street, from London to the north, and that great highway, whose name seems to have been lost, which runs from London south-west as far as Exeter, and north-east into the Eastern Counties There are six great roads, radiating from London as a centre Does not that suggest to us that London must have been a place of considerable importance even in those remote days? That it was so is also borne out by the fact that the Romans

called the city Augusta, in honour of their Emperor of that name.

But, under the Roman rule, you may be pretty sure that London increased in importance, and as it did so, this very road, which now forms the northern boundary of Eltham parish, became of greater and greater importance By an examination of the map you will see that it was the direct course between London and Dover, and that was the nearest way to Gaul, which was the route to Rome Rome ruled Britain through its Governors, somewhat in the way that England rules India at the present time There were, however, no means of rapid communication —no telegraph, no railway Imperial troops, imperial despatches, in fact every communication between the imperial rulers in Rome and the ruled in Britain, had to go by road, and the one great highway along which they travelled must have been this part of Watling street.

Now, the reading of history, even in a superficial sort of way, is a dull and dreary pastime, unless you exercise a little imagination, so, standing as we do now in this interesting part of Eltham, let us look back in imagination across the intervening nineteen centuries, and try to picture what those earliest Roman invaders saw when they passed this way When immortal Cæsar climbed the hill on the other side, following the old British trackway along which the Britons had but lately fled in hasty retreat, he looked out upon an expanse of country, even as we can look now

But the face of the country was very different From suitable vantage points we may look down upon the slated roofs of Well Hall, and on to Eltham village, with its two spires pointing upwards, further away in the hazy distance we may discern Sidcup and Chislehurst and other places, and in the intervening spaces cultivated fields and market gardens, or park-like meadows, characteristic of modern Kent. What Cæsar looked down upon was an expanse of forest, consisting mainly of oak, ash, holly, or yew There the red deer, wild oxen, and wild hogs found cover The beaver and water fowl were common to every stream, affording ready prey to such beasts as the wild cat, the wolf, and the bear He probably saw but few natives, for, in the first place they were not very numerous It has been said that their number right through the country did not exceed two millions. In the second place, they were not likely to expose themselves to view, seeing that they had only recently suffered defeat.

But the land was not all forest, nor were the " wild wood wanderers," as the natives have been called, quite the savages that they are sometimes described. There were clearings in the forests, where the natives cultivated their wheat, barley, millet, and even roots and fruit trees. They tilled the land with wheeled ploughs, and knew the use of loam and chalk as manures. Upon these open spaces might have been seen the primitive huts, circular, wattled,

merchandise. Upon its banks are thickly-populated towns, Woolwich, Greenwich, Deptford, and other places, now component parts of the great city of London, busy hives of men, from which arises the buzz of industry. Cæsar looked on no such scene as this. The old river was there, but it had not then been made to confine its waters within its banks. Far away to the right and left it spread itself out in swamps and lagoons. When the tide was up it covered the land for many miles, almost like a sea. When it returned the swampy islands revealed themselves, and we may imagine that among its many channels, or over the surface of the main stream, the native fishermen plied their coracles, or

ROMAN EAGLE.

and thatched. It needs no great stretch of imagination to picture such a settlement hereabouts, in this sunny valley, say, below Shooters'-hill, where the natives kept their tiny breed of cows, and in those intervals of time, when the demands of agriculture were not imperative, worked at basket making, sending the hand-made articles to foreign markets for sale. The osier beds of the great river so near at hand would have supplied ample materials for the industry. An old Roman writer has recorded that basket making was peculiarly a British industry, and that British baskets were exported to the Continent.

Then, what about the prospect on the other side of the hill? There we see the Thames, with its procession of mighty ships bearing

other primitive boats, in search of daily food.

Well, may we say, as we survey the scene at our feet, " Look on this picture—and on this." Then, after four hundred years, there came those last dramatic scenes, when Rome was humbled, and was obliged to withdraw her men from Britain, to protect their fatherland in Italy. Four hundred years is a very long time when compared with the usual span of a man's life. During those centuries of Roman occupation, immense changes had taken place in the condition of the people, their habits of life, their industries, their religion. Even the face of the land, too, had undergone a change. New towns had sprung up upon the great roads, new methods of building had been introduced. Roman villas were familiar objects upon the landscape. You may see the floor of such a villa, in Greenwich Park, exposed to view at the present day, and it is quite within the bounds of possibility that some such Roman residences existed about here too. Who knows?

But to Roman rule and influence there came an abrupt end. Rome was in danger. Home was the word. The exodus began. Along those great highways that converged upon London—the Augusta Trinobantum of the Cæsars—there commenced the great retreat. And from Augusta to the sea, there passed, this way, the main bulk of those who were bound Rome-ward. Surely it was a tragedy which the old road witnessed in those last days of Rome in Britain; a tragedy of such a character that its ultimate effect was to change the course of our National history.

No. 7. BANQUETING HALL, WEST END,
(From Engraving in "Archæologia," 1782).

No. 9. BANQUETING HALL, EAST END,
(From Engraving in "Archæologia," 1782).

No. 8. MOAT BRIDGE FROM N.E.
(From old Engraving)

No. 10. BANQUETING HALL, USED AS A STABLE.
(From an old Engraving)

No. 11.   THE MOAT BRIDGE.
                          (1908).

No. 12.   INTERIOR OF BANQUETING HALL, WITH SCREEN.

ARMS AND COSTUME OF AN ANGLO-SAXON KING AND ARMOUR BEARER.
(From an old Print).

CHAPTER III.

ELTHAM IN THE MAKING.

Now, although Eltham is singularly rich in relics which are memorials of one or the other of the recognised periods of English history, we seem to have nothing left to us to look at—— no old road, no old ruin that we can touch and say of it "This was, certainly, the handiwork of those fierce fighting folk from oversea, who came and settled here and first started Eltham and gave the place its name."

But there is a stretch of land on the side of Shooter's-hill—"Eltham Common"—where the furze bushes grow, and where we have a right to take a stroll if we like; and there is the fact recorded in the encyclopœdia, or the guide book, that "Eltham is in the Hundred of Blackheath," and, moreover, there is the very name itself, "Elt-ham'; all of which associate the village with what we call the "Saxon period."

Though these plain and obvious facts may seem rather dull and uninteresting, they are luminous enough, if we know how to use them, to throw a light across the long fifteen centuries and enable us to discern something of Eltham in the making.

We need not dwell at any length upon the troubles endured by the Britons when their protectors, the Romans, had left them for ever. You may read all about that in your history books—how the Jutes came over and landed in Kent to help the British to fight the barbarians from the north, the Picts and Scots—how, when they saw that the land was fair and fertile, these very Jutes turned against the Britons themselves and drove them out—how there followed fellow tribes of Jutes, and English, and Saxons, who, landing on the eastern and southern coasts, continued the great struggle which lasted more than a hundred years, and did not cease until the Britons had been driven away westward into Cornwall and Wales, and the intruding tribes had established themselves in the land and laid the foundation of this nation of ours which we call England

But, to get an idea of how Eltham came into existence we must know something of these fierce people who came with fire and sword and devastated the land, burning Christian churches, razing to the ground the beautiful Roman villas, and wiping out whatever was left of Roman civilization, for they were our forefathers, and it was they or their immediate descendents, who settled "here about," and gave their settlement the name of Eltham.

Let us have a look at them as they lived yonder on the bleak shores of the Baltic, for, by knowing something of their habits of life over there, we may better understand the new kind of social life they set up here—new, at any rate, to this land

They were a fine race of people, tall, fair-haired, gray-eyed, brave, and adventurous, and they lived together in clans or families Note that fact particularly. Family life was the basis upon which their social system was built up Each family lived by itself and took all the necessary measures for the benefit and protection of its members.

Each little village community lived apart from all the others, and around it there lay a stretch of appropriated land, sometimes it was a broad belt of virgin forest, and sometimes moorland, and this belt was called a "mark" It was the boundary, and very jealously was it guarded by the "marksmen" A well-known writer says of it —"Whoever crossed the 'mark' was bound to give notice

of his coming by blowing a horn, or else he was cut down at once as a stealthy enemy The 'marksmen' wished to remain separate from all others, and only to mix with those of their own kin. *In this primitive love of separation we have the germ of that local independence and that isolated private home life which is one of our characteristics as a people at the present day."*

Can we wonder that tribes living like this found the rich wooded vales of Britain a great attraction ? Kent must have appeared to them as well suited for 'such a mode of life There were wide clearings in the forests which had been already applied to farming purposes by the British, ideal spots in which to establish their villages communities The temptation was irresistible To secure so fair a land was worth the sacrifice of blood So hither they came, tribe after tribe. They fought and bled, but made the land their own

You may fairly ask, was the first settlement at Eltham early in the English conquest, or did it spring up in later years, when the country had, to some extent, settled down ? But it is hard to fix the exact time All that we can be sure about is that it came into existence in Saxon times, but in which century is a matter of doubt, and will remain so until further evidence is brought to light to help us to decide.

But let us try and picture the first beginning of a typical English village, and see to what extent the conditions may be applied to Eltham

A tribe of Angles, or Saxons, or Jutes, suddenly swoop down upon a district and find that it will suit their needs exactly If Britons are already in possession, out they have to go There is a fight, may be, great shouts and the clash of arms. In the end, the Britons are driven away, or put to the sword, or made slaves Then the new comers set to work to establish themselves. They destroy the British huts, and construct others of their own, and after a while there arises a village of rude dwellings surrounded by a wooden stockade Each family puts up a little homestead, consisting of a small wooden shanty, a court-yard, and a cattle-fold, and the land upon which this homestead stands becomes their own. Here, you see, is the beginning of private property in land.

The forest and pasture land outside the stockade become the common property of the community. Every householder can turn his stock upon it—his cattle into the pasture land, his pigs into the ring of forest. But to keep the too selfish person within bounds, and to be sure that he does not encroach upon the rights and privileges of his neighbour, and so, by an act of injustice disturb the harmony of the us as the "common-land." Its uses have not been entirely diverted to other purposes. There are no Anglo Saxon buildings left to us. The early Saxons were not good builders. Their structures were mostly of wood. They were not of a character to last many years. So the hall of the headman, with the dwellings of the churls, and the huts of the serfs, have long since passed away. But we have Eltham Common still left to remind us of the conditions under which our ancient forefathers lived.

In those rustic homes what an important person was the head of each family. The Eltham

RESIDENCE OF A SAXON NOBLEMAN (from old M.S.)

community, an officer is appointed to see that no man trespasses or turns more than his proper share of cattle into the common ground.

Besides the woodlands and the common lands which belong to the tribe as a whole, a certain part of the land is set apart for tillage. Three large fields fulfil this purpose, one field being allowed to lie fallow each year. Every householder is allotted a portion of each of these fields, which he and his family are expected to cultivate.

Eltham Common. Yes. Here we have what is left of the "Common lands," set apart by the earliest Eltham community. Through all these long centuries it has come down to churl was, truly, the king of his household. He made the laws for the government of his family, and he enforced them sternly, too. But, his duties were not limited entirely to his family. He had public responsibilities. As the head of a house, it was his right, and his duty, to attend the "Moot," or Village Council, to help in the management of the affairs of the community as a body.

Now-a-days we still have our "Moot" but it has a different name. Our fathers, or grandfathers, will recollect the village "moot" as the "Vestry." In all country villages it is now the "Parish Council." Mottingham, for instance, has such a "moot." But, as Eltham has been made part and parcel of Woolwich.

our "moot" goes under the dignified name of "Borough Council." Indeed, our "moot," at the present time, is resisting an attempt of the War Office to encroach upon our rights in the "common land" of Eltham

It would not be possible, in these times for the head of every family to be a member of the "moot." The number would be too large. So we elect special members to look after the business for us. Notice, however, that the electors are mainly composed of householders. Therefore, you will notice, our present system of local government is based upon those principles which were first applied by our adventurous ancestors when they came over and took possession.

We are considering these matters here because they had so much to do with "Eltham in the Making," and, unless you keep them well in your mind you will never get a really intelligent idea of the history of Eltham, nor, indeed of the history of your country.

In course of time, the families of the original communities increased, and branches of the old stock went farther afield and set up new communities. To enable these communities to act together in resisting a common foe, it is said that "hundreds" first came into existence. A hundred families supplied a hundred warriors——a chosen champion for each family

A writer says that "these hundred families recognised a bond of union with each other, and a common inheritance, and arranged themselves under one name, for a general purpose, whether for defence, administration of justice, or other reasons."

The common name of the hundred was sometimes derived from that of some chieftain or from some tree or familiar place where it was the custom of the hundred to meet. For this district the meeting place was on that bleak open country now called Blackheath. So it was called the "Hundred of Blackheath."

If Eltham found its origin in the early period of the Saxon occupation, and it may have done, although we cannot be certain about it, we may picture in our minds a meeting of the hundred. On the appointed day,

a hundred champions mounted their horses and proceeded to Blackheath, there to meet the acknowledged chief of the "hundred." There they gathered about him. When he dismounted from his steed and planted his spear in the ground, each warrior in his turn touched the leader's spear with his own, in token of the compact that existed between them, and as a solemn pledge of loyal support. Then would they confer together, in their vigorous Anglo-Saxon speech. If a speaker said something that the meeting did not agree with, they made loud exclamations of dissent, but if they approved of what he said, they knocked together their spears as a sign of agreement.

A hundred would meet somewhat in this way in its very earliest days. In course of time, as the population increased and the conditions of social life gradually changed, the work of the hundred increased more and more, and took in the trial of criminals, settlement of disputes, bargains of sale and such like matters.

Then, in the course, of a long time, the "hundred" ceased to be known as a hundred families, but came to mean a hundred "hides" of land, and a division of a county, even as we recognise it now. It is said that Alfred the Great divided the land up into counties, hundreds, and tithings. It would, perhaps, be more likely that he took the 'hundreds" as he found them, combined them to form counties, and divided them to form tithings. At any rate, we should bear in mind that in the first instance the "hundred" referred to "persons," and, subsequently, the name got to be applied to "land."

It would be a satisfaction to be able to fix the exact date of the birth of Eltham. But, at present, it is a matter of doubt. The earliest records of the "Hundred of Blackheath" do not seem to mention Eltham. This suggests that the village was not in existence at the time. On the other hand, there is the "common land." There it is pointing distinctly to antiquity. Then there is the name. Elt-ham, by which it has been known from the beginning.

"Eltham" is generally regarded as a modified form of "Eald-ham." This is Anglo-Saxon, and, therefore, it would have been applied to the place by the stranger folk—the English.

"Eald" means "old," and "ham" is the same word as the German "heim," meaning "home." So, "Eald-ham" means "Old-home," or "Old place of abode."

Does it not seem a little strange that the term "old" should have been used in the first place? Why "old"? The question gives rise to several interesting theories.

One of these is that there was, originally only a residence here, perhaps a royal residence. That in the course of years a village grew up around it, and it came to be named after the residence or "old-home." This theory seems to fit in with the fact that we find no mention of Eltham in the earliest records of the "Hundred of Blackheath."

Another suggestion is that a British settlement may have existed here, and that when the Saxon came and founded a new colony, he named it "old-place of abode" as a consequence.

Another theory casts a doubt upon the generally accepted meaning of the name. It suggests that "Eald" may have been the name or the corruption of the name of some clan, and, as was often the case, the clan name was given to the place, just as Billing-ham is the "home of the Billings," and Wokingham, is the "abode of the Wokings."

But there is uncertainty about it all. What we may be pretty sure of is that Eltham came into existence somewhere, in the misty past, long anterior to the coming of the Normans. When we tread the soft turf of the "common land" on Shooter's-hill, we may feel some satisfaction in being in direct contact with a relic of those distant ages, and, as we have been doing to-day we may find a pleasant exercise for our imagination in trying to estimate the possibilities and probabilities of what took place when Eltham was in the making.

SAXON WHITE HORSE.

GREAT SEAL OF EDWARD THE CONFESSOR.

CHAPTER IV.

WHEN ALWOLD WAS LORD.

One of the earliest bits of really authentic written history about Eltham is to be found in Domesday Book, that remarkable document which was compiled by order of William the Conqueror, and completed about 1086, A.D. Here we are told that "Alteham" was held by Alwold under the King. "Alteham," of course, means "Ealdham," or "Eltham," and we must suppose that the Norman scribe who wrote the name in this way, was not particularly good at the spelling of English. This was excusable, under the circumstances, so we may forgive him.

But the statement thus set forth throws much light upon what had been happening in the ancient village. It reminds us of the many changes that had been taking place, in social life, since those very early days of "Eltham in the Making," alluded to in the last chapter.

Six hundred years had passed away since the Saxons first came and settled here. Six hundred years since Hengist founded the Kingdom of Kent, and during that long period many small Saxon kingdoms had risen, and existed for a time, to finally disappear, as by degrees they were all wrought into one kingdom and ruled by one king.

When Alwold, the lord of "Alteham," gathered his friends about him in his manorial hall,—for we may suppose that he had one, although no mention seems to have been made of it anywhere—when the ale was quaffed, and songs were sung, and the jests went round, if by chance the talk turned upon lore, and the doings of their forefathers, as it sometimes would, very ancient history must have seemed the beginning of England, just as to-day "the Wars of the Roses," "the Battle of Agincourt," or the Norman Conquest, seem to us very far away in the past.

Alwold's over-lord was the King, Edward the Confessor. You know something about him, how he was a man of saintly character, living a strict religious life, and how, on account of this, he has been known ever since as Edward the "Confessor." It was he who brought over the expert Norman workmen to build the beautiful abbey at Westminster.

On a clear day we can see the old Abbey from our playground It may be that the boys and girls of Alwold's days looked out from our Eltham fields at the distant Abbey, and watched it slowly rising up, or listened to their elders when they talked about its building It may be, also, that a few of those older folk had some grumbles to make about the king's fondness for foreigners, and his bringing over these workmen to do his work. It is most likely, however, that complaints of this kind were only made in whispers, for was not Alwold lord of "Alteham," and did he not hold "Alteham" under the king himself?

We are apt to forget the children when we read history unless they happen to be young princes or young noblemen We are so taken up by the deeds of the heroes, and men of action, and noble ladies, that we think but little of the multitudes that made up England, and of the merry lads and lasses who were to be the future builders of the kingdom, just as you young folks of to-day will be the future citizens of the Empire There were interesting boys and girls in "Alteham," when Alwold held it under the King, just as there are interesting boys and girls now But they lived under very different conditions. Let us give them a thought, now and then, when we consider those conditions

Who was Alwold? We do not know anything about him or his family. But we may assume that he was a rather important person, or the king would never have entrusted him with one of his own manors He paid the king sixteen pounds a year for the use of the manor It does not sound much in these days. But in the time of the Confessor, and for a long time afterwards, a pound was worth a great deal more than it is now, and sixteen pounds then was a good large sum

Alwold may have been a soldier, or a great hunter, or a statesman, or he may have been one of those "lore thanes," as they called them, who, unlike thanes in general, were fond of study and the reading of books. The king was of this kind of habit Alwold, who held "Alteham" under the king, may have been a man of his kind, too. We do not know.

But as the chroniclers have not been good enough to tell us what sort of a man he was, there is no reason why we should not make a kind of fancy picture of him in our mind's eye

Imagine you see him, then, on a bright summer day, when the fields and meadows of "Alteham" were dressed in their fairest garb, riding forth from his huge wooden manor house, upon his favourite horse. He wears no covering to his head, save the natural covering of thick, fair hair, which hangs down to his shoulders, and a full, fair beard adds dignity to his intellectual face.   He wears a red woollen tunic, which reaches to his knees, and around his waist is a leathern belt, untanned Breeches of similar material reach to his knees, while the lower parts of his legs are clothed in linen hosen, laced or bandaged with cross garters, called shank guards. His shoes are of leather, untanned, and from his shoulders there is suspended a square mantle, which hangs in graceful folds behind.

There! Don't you think our Alwold is a handsome fellow, as he sits easily his noble steed, which canters gracefully across the Alteham greensward?

The Domesday scribe tells us nothing about the house of Alwold. But it was no uncommon thing for Domesday scribes to leave out all mention of a Manor House or a Church. Indeed the survey of Churches and Churchyards seems to have been outside the scope of Domesday Book. So, because we find no mention of a Manor House, nor yet of a Church, at "Alteham," at that time, we must not jump to the conclusion that there was no Manor House and no Church The probabilities are that there were both.

And although Domesday really refers to the period immediately *after* the Saxon thane had gone, and a Norman Lord had taken his place, it may be taken to fairly represent the condition of the village in the late Saxon times and Alwold's day The social condition of the classes below that of the lord was not greatly changed at first, except in name   The "ceorls" were now called "villans," the "cotters" were "lordars," and the "thralls" wore "slaves." Otherwise the change was not so very great at first.

Domesday says that 'Alteham' answered for "one suling and a half. There is the arable land of twelve teams. In demesne there are two teams. And forty two villans with twelve bordars have eleven teams. Nine slaves there. And twenty-two acres of meadow. Wood of fifty hogs. In the time of King Edward it was worth sixteen pounds. When he received it twelve pounds. And now twenty pounds. Alwold held it of the King."

"What queer words!" you will exclaim. They are old English words that have gone out of use. Let us read it again, giving, as near as we can the interpretation of those strange words.

"Alteham" answered for, "about 240 acres, for a suling was as much land as a team of eight oxen could plough in a year, together with the pasture land that was required for the feeding of the oxen.

"There is arable land of about 1,800 acres.

"In that portion of the land around the Manor and cultivated by the lord himself there are about 320 acres.

"There is nothing 'villianous' about the forty-two villans. They are called villans only because they live in the villa or village. They are respectable men, who are tenants of the lord, and farm the land of the manor, except the lord's own land, or demesne as it is called. They pay rent for their land to the lord, and sometimes, in place of rent, help in the tilling of the lord's land. They have to provide one or more oxen for the manorial plough. They are freemen, though they may not give up their farms without the special permission of their lord.

"The twelve bordars, are also called cottiers, or cottagers. They sometimes had small allotments, but they kept no oxen. They helped in the cultivation of the lord's land, and also worked some days of the week on the farms.

"The nine slaves were attached to the lord's land. Their lot was not a happy one. They were of a class that were supposed to have descended from the British who were kept in

thraldom. They were born in slavery, and generally died in that state. They were attached to the Manor, and were bought and sold with the land and cattle. They could be scourged and branded, as the lord pleased, and even if one was killed, the punishment was only a small fine. Saxons who were captured in war, or those who were unable to pay fines for offences committed, were often made slaves or serfs. Occasionally a lord would set a slave free. He would give him a lance or sword, and tell him that he was at liberty to go where he pleased. The slaves had to do the hardest work—they were the ploughmen, shepherds, and swine herds.

So, from all this, we may picture in our minds what life in "Alteham" was like when Alwold was the lord. The great house, built of wood, low, one storied, and around it clustering the huts of the serfs who wait on the lord. Further afield the cottages of the villans and the thralls—with mud walls and roofs thatched with reed.

The great house of the lord has its hall and chapel. The hall is the principal apartment; it is there that Alwold feasts his guests. It has a fire in the centre and a smoke-hole in the roof, and on the clay floor rushes are strewn and changed from time to time. It is furnished with a heavy clumsy table set upon tressels, along the sides of which the guests sit upon benches and stools.

What feasts they have, for these Saxon forefathers of ours, love eating and drinking. The table is covered with a cloth, and upon it are set the platters, bowls, dishes, horns, and knives. Swine's flesh is the usual meat, and when the joint is roasted, it is carried round the table on the spit, and each one cuts off a slice for himself. The usual vegetable is colewort, and the usual drink is ale, though a rich man may afford wine and mead. Table manners are sometimes rather slovenly.

They eat and drink far into the night, and on very festive occasions through successive days and nights. As the flowing bowl is going its round, so also is the harp, which is handed from one to another, as each contributes his song to the minstrelsy of the evening. And when it is time to sleep, many of the men

No. 13.

PART OF OLD WALL—ELTHAM PALACE (1909).

(From the Moat, South-East).

No. 14.

WATER GATE TO MOAT.

South Side.

No. 15.

OLD GABLE, ELTHAM COURT.

From a local Sketch.

No. 16.

NORTH DOORWAY TO HALL.

(From old Engraving).

No. 17.

ELTHAM COURT—SHOWING THE OLD GABLED BUILDING.

Residence of Mr. C. D. Wilson.

On the right the part erected by Mr. Bloxam, which connects the older building with the Great Hall.

No. 18.

MOAT HOUSE AND BRIDGE.

Residence of Mr. Newton Dunn.

throw themselves upon mattresses in the hall, upon the floor. The lord retires to his bed, which is a sort of crib or trough filled with straw, with a coverlid of skin, and so they sleep off the effect of their carouse.

But apart from their less praiseworthy habits, those ancient Elthamites, contrived to get a good deal of real enjoyment out of life. They lived a great deal in the open air, and their amusements were often found in such manly sports as running, leaping, wrestling, riding and fighting. There was plenty of hunting, hawking and fishing, for the lord could hunt on his own grounds, and boars, deer, hares, and even wild goats were sometimes to be found.

The tradesmen of the village were very important persons then. The smith had to look after the iron-work of the ploughs, and to shoe the horses. Then there were the carpenter, the stone-mason, the constable, the steward of the manor, who had to look after the interests of the lord and the tenant, and among many others, that important person, the bee-keeper. Bee-keeping was a great business in those days, for you must remember that there were no colonies to send them sugar, and those who liked sweets had to depend for the luxury upon the bees. Moreover, was not honey wine sweet to the tooth of those old forbears of ours? No wonder, the bee-keeper was an important person.

The great blot upon the social life of the time was "serfdom." Here is a little dialogue, written at the time by an old Saxon writer. Does it not bring the condition of the serf vividly before our minds? :—

"'What sayest thou, ploughman? How dost thou do thy work?'

"'Oh, my lord, hard do I work. I go out at daybreak, driving the oxen to field, and I yoke them to the plough. Nor is it ever so hard winter that I dare loiter at home, for fear of my lord, but the oxen yoked, and the ploughshare and the coulter fastened to the plough, every day must I plough a full acre, or more.'

"'Hast thou a comrade?'

"'I have a boy driving the oxen with an iron goad, who also is hoarse with cold and shouting.'

"'What more dost thou in the day?'

"'Verily then I do more. I must fill the bin of the oxen with hay, and water them, and carry out the dung. Ha! Ha! hard work it is, hard work it is! *because I am not free.*'"

Let us hope that the lot of the slaves that were attached to the Manor of Alteham was happier than that of this poor thrall, seeing that their lord was Alwold who held the Manor under the good king Edward

FEAST AT A ROUND TABLE (Bayeux Tapestry.)

WHEEL BED (Cotton M S.)

THE SICKNESS AND DEATH OF EDWARD THE CONFESSOR (Bayeux Tapestry.)

CHAPTER V.

THE SIGN IN THE SKY.

The year 1066 was a fateful year for Eltham, as it was for the whole of England. In its earlier days the Royal House was over-shadowed by death, an event which had a direct effect upon the conditions of life in our village. Then, just after Eastertide, appeared the strange sign in the sky fore-boding the over-throw of a kingdom, and filling the hearts of men with fear. Summer brought wars and rumours of wars. The fall of the year witnessed the great fight and England stricken beneath the heel of a foreign foe, and, ere its eventful months had run their course, Eltham had passed into other hands, and Alwold was no longer to hold its Manor under the King. Surely, it was a terrible year, and it left its mark upon our history, national and local, as no other year has ever done.

When the New Year was born, Edward the King lay dying. For many weeks he had battled with disease. In those latter days he uttered strange words, and his people, filled with reverence and awe, declared that he had the gift of prophecy. On January 5th, 1066, the "Confessor" passed away.

We may be sure that the folk of Eltham, especially Alwold, who held the Eltham lands of the King, were distressed by this event, for, though the English people were not well pleased by his liking for foreigners, Edward the Confessor was held, generally, in esteem and love by his subjects. He had been spared to see the completion of his own new Church at Westminster—the noble Abbey, which, with its additions, is the pride of all Englishmen to day. But he was too ill to be present at its consecration on December 28th. "Holy Innocents' Day." A week or so later he died, and, the very next day, January 6th, they solemnly conveyed his body to the beautiful minster, and gently laid him to rest. There is something sad and pathetic about this incident, yet it seems consistent and beautiful that he, who conceived the building of that majestic edifice, who watched it lovingly through the years of its erection, should have been the first of that long array of kings and heroes who have been buried within its walls

King Edward's death was the beginning of the end of Saxon rule in England, as it was the beginning of the end of Alwold's tenure of Eltham

There was a great gathering at the funeral, for that year the dead king had called together the assembly of wise men—the Witan—in London, instead of at Gloucester as was usual, and immediately after the solemn ceremony of interment was over—Professor Freeman says, that in all probability it was on the same day,—the Witan proceeded to elect a new king. Was Alwold of Eltham present on that occasion? There is no record to say that he was, but, one can well believe that the Lord of Eltham, being so near at hand, whether he took part in the important deliberations or whether he did not, would not have been absent on an occasion which was fraught with so much of importance to Eltham and himself

The Witan selected Harold, the son of Earl Godwine, and he was duly installed as King and the Crown lands of Eltham passed into his hands. But Harold had rivals for the Kingship. There were some Englishmen who thought the youthful Atheling, Edgar, had a stronger claim But the Atheling was young and weak, and the Witan wanted a strong man Tostig, the brother of Harold, also set up a claim, but the most formidable rival was William, the Duke of Normandy. William declared that the Confessor had promised him the crown. But the Confessor had no legal power to do this. He also accused Harold of breaking an oath that he had made to support the claim of the Norman Duke to the throne But Harold said that the oath was obtained from him by unfair means, and was therefore not binding

And, after all, Harold's claim was the strongest of all, for, not only was he specially recommended by the Confessor himself, before he died, as the most suitable man for the office, but he was duly and regularly elected by the Witan In quaint language the old Chronicler of the time puts it thus

" Nathless, that wisest man,
Dying made fast the realm
To a high-risen man,
Even to Harold's self,
Who was a noble earl:
He did at every tide
Follow with loyal love
All of his lord's behests,
Both in his words and deeds:
Naught did he e'er neglect
What e'er of right belonged
Unto the people's king "

And he further says, " Now was Harold hallowed as king, but little stillness did he there enjoy, the while that he wielded the kingdom."

We may well imagine that the men of Eltham took their proper share in these national events, and it is quite likely that the Eltham ceorls, or villans, as Domesday Book calls them, who farmed the manor lands were amongst the crowds who assembled about the new minster to look upon the great men and to see what they could of the ceremonies But notwithstanding that Harold, the great warrior and the wise councillor, had been made king, and most people seemed pleased, there was in the air a feeling of uncertainty, a feeling that something was going to happen. This feeling was increased and intensified by the appearance of a strange sign in the sky. It was a comet of unusual dimensions, and, superstitious as the people were, they were easily led to believe by those who thought they understood such matters, that this strange " star" with the monster tail which seemed to sweep the sky, was a portent sent to warn them that a terrible disaster was about to overtake the kingdom

When you read Tennyson's Play, " Harold," which you should all do, you will see, in the first act, how the poet vividly describes the effect of this great comet upon the terror-stricken people

"It glares in heaven, it flares upon the Thames,
The people are as thick as bees below,
They hum like bees—they cannot speak—for awe,
Look to the skies, then to the river, strike
Their hearts, and hold their babies up to it.
I think that they would Molochize them too,
To have the heavens clear."

Aldwyth: Gamel, son of Orm,
What thinkest thou this means ?
Gamel: War, my dear lady !

* * *

One of the pictures shown upon the Bayeux Tapestry is that of six men pointing fearfully "towards a star which trails a rudely drawn streamer of light behind it." It is explained that "These men are marvelling at the star." We do not marvel so much at comets now, and you will be interested to know that the comet which so alarmed the English in the spring of

and had sailed up the Ouse to the City of York. Then Harold the King of England gathered around him his trusty men of London and of Kent and marched northward, and gave them battle. The invaders were routed, and Tostig and the giant Harold, King of the Northmen, were slain in the fight. This was on September 25th. Four days later Duke William of Normandy landed with an army in Sussex.

" While the Normans were yet at Pevensey, an English Thane had seen them land, and

CORONATION OF HAROLD (Bayeux Tapestry.)

1066, is one which comes our way once in about every seventy-five years. They tell us that it will be here again in three years' time—in 1910. When it comes, if we are alive, we may be able to look upon it and think of Harold the King, and Alwold of Eltham, and the stirring scenes of those old days, but it is not likely to bode disaster, or to fill men's hearts with fear, as it did when it swept the sky eight centuries ago.

But, as the Chronicler has told us, " Harold had but little stillness " during his short reign. The late summer brought the news that his brother Tostig, and Harold King of the Northmen, had come to England with a great host,

he went and mounted his horse, and rode northwards, and rested not day or night, where King Harold and his host were resting after their great fight. So the Thane came to King Harold, and said, ' My Lord O King, Duke William and his Normans have landed in Sussex, and they have built them a fort at Pevensey, and they are harrying the land, and they will of a truth win thy kingdom from thee, unless thou goest speedily and keepest thy land well against them !'

" And presently there came a churl also who had come from Hastings, and he told King Harold how that the Normans had marched from Pevensey to Hastings, and how they had built them a castle at Hastings and how they were harrying the land far and wide.

"Then King Harold answered and said, 'This is evil news indeed; would that I had been there to guard the coast, and Duke William never should have landed; but I could not be here and there too!' So the King hastened with all speed to London."

Now, would it not be interesting if we could only slip back, somehow, over those eight hundred and sixty years, and peep into some of the

with him against the Duke of Normandy. Kent and all the southern counties quickly responded to his call, and we may be sure that the men of Eltham were foremost amongst the men of Kent, for, apart from the patriotic spirit which was strong in men's hearts at that time, it must be remembered that Eltham was one of the Royal Estates, and Alwold would be expected to come up with his full force of fighting men.

Yes, they had stirring times in the village for those few days. Harvest was over and men

A SHIP OF THE FLEET OF DUKE WILLIAM TRANSPORTING TROOPS
FOR THE INVASION OF ENGLAND (Bayeux Tapestry.)

Eltham homes of the time—into the huts of the cottiers and the houses of the churls, and actually hear what the folk themselves had to say about all these happenings? It is most likely that one would find those simple villagers full of gloomy forebodings. The strange star with the sweeping tail had gone away in the early summer, but they had not forgotten it, and in these risings against their lord the King, and in this coming of the Norman Duke, they saw, only too plainly, the realisation of the message brought by that awful sign in the sky.

The King abode for some six or seven days in London, and word was sent forth bidding all men to gather under his banner and to march

could be better spared. Every available horse was got out and made ready. What a busy man was the blacksmith! There were coats of mail to put into order, shields and helmets to make good, to say nothing of the trappings of the horses, and the weapons for the men. Every axe, and sword, and spear, and bow, was brought out for use, and in every house that sent forth a fighting man there was all the bustle of preparation.

In the old wall that bounds our Church-yard a stone is fixed, upon which is graven the names of those Eltham heroes, who, a few years ago, fell fighting for their Queen and country in the far South Africa. It is right that we should keep them in memory. The great Empire of which we are proud has been built up by the sacrifice of life and labour on the part of individuals. And we should remember that there is a long line of heroes whose names have never been recorded upon the roll of fame. The sturdy Eltham cottiers and churls, who, in those fateful days, strode forth to fight for King and Fatherland, who fought and fell at Senlac and never returned to gladden aching hearts in those simple Eltham homes, are of a great host who have kept aglow that fire of patriotism which has made the British nation what it is

You know well the story of the fierce fight at Senlac on Saturday, October 16th, 1066—the death of Harold and his great Earls fighting to the last, the rout of the English army, the triumph of William. It is a thrilling story. The English were defeated, but not disgraced. But it brought about a new order of things. Then passed Eltham into other hands, and Alwold the Englishman, goes out of the story. We know not whither he went, or what was his fate. And the new lords of Eltham were strangers who spoke a foreign tongue

BISHOP ODO, THE LORD OF ELTHAM MANOR, PRONOUNCING A BLESSING.
(From an old Print).

CHAPTER VI.

THE WARRIOR BISHOP.

Let us refer once more to Domesday Book. These are the words of the scribe:—

"Haimo holds of the Bishop, Alteham . . . . In the time of King Edward it was worth sixteen pounds. When he received it twelve pounds. Now twenty pounds."

Notice. There is no mention of King Harold. Domesday Book ignored his very existence as King. It was William's policy to impress upon the English that Harold was an impostor, an adventurer who had no right to the throne at all. He wanted them to forget Harold and to recognise that he, William, was the only true successor to Edward the Confessor. So you get no mention of Harold, the King, in Domesday. There is a story concerning the burial of Harold, which shews how relentless was the spirit of William in this respect. It

is so beautifully and simply told by Professor Freeman, that we really must read it in his words:—

"The great battle being over, Duke William came back to the hill and stayed there all night. He had the dead bodies swept away around where the Standard had stood, and there he pitched his tent and did eat and drink. The next day he had the dead among his own men buried, and he gave leave that the women and people of the country might take away and bury the bodies of the slain English. Many women, therefore, came and took away the bodies of their husbands and sons and brothers. Then the two Canons of Waltham, who had followed the army, came to the Duke and craved that they might take the body of their founder,

King Harold, and bury it in his own minster at Waltham. And Gytha, the King's mother, also craved the body of her son . . . . . She offered the Duke King Harold's weight in gold if she might have his body to bury at Waltham. But the Duke said nay; for that Harold was perjured and excommunicated, and might not be buried in holy ground. Now, there was in the Norman army one William Malet, a brave knight, who was in some way or other a kinsman or friend of King Harold's; so Duke William bade William Malet take the body of his friend and bury it on the sea coast, under a heap of stones, which men call a cairn. For Duke William said: 'He guarded the shore when living, let him guard it now that he is dead.' But no man could find the body, for it was all defaced and mangled, and it had been thrown aside when the bodies were cleared away for William's tent to be pitched. But there was a lady called Edith, whom, for her beauty men called 'Swanneshals,' or the Swan's Neck, whom Harold had loved in old times when he was Earl of the East Angles." She was able to point out the dead King, so they buried him under a heap of stones beside the sea. "But after a while, when Duke William was crowned King of the English, his heart became milder, and he let men take up the body of King Harold from under the cairn, and bury it in his own minster at Waltham."

There. We have read this story, although it is not exactly Eltham history, because it shews that hard, harsh nature of William which was responsible, among other things, for keeping the name of Harold out of the Domesday record. But for all that, Harold was not forgotten, and to this day, in the memory of his countrymen, he stands for all that is noble and great in an Englishman.

"Haino holds of the Bishop, Alteham."

The Bishop was Odo, a half brother of William. Let us consider some of the history of Odo, and see how it was that he became possessed of Eltham. When Odo was about twelve years of age he was made Bishop of Bayeux, which is a town in Normandy. Rather young to be a bishop, you will say, but we do sometimes read of foolish and inconsistent things in history. Odo has not left a very good name behind. He was ambitious and selfish. Indeed, his ambition led to his loss of Eltham, and, for a time, to his undoing. He is, however, credited with one very good thing, and that is with getting the famous Bayeux Tapestry made. If it had not been for this wonderful piece of needlework we should not have known so much of the Norman invasion of England as we do.

It is two hundred and fourteen feet long and twenty inches wide, and the pictures worked upon it represent scenes of the invasion and of the Battle of Hastings. There are on it six hundred and twenty-three persons, seven hundred and sixty-two horses, dogs, &c., thirty-seven buildings, and forty-one boats. It must have taken a long while to make, but one great historian says that it is the best and most reliable account of the Conquest that exists. It is said that Odo had this work done for the ornamentation of his Cathedral Church at Bayeux. So we may give him credit for one useful piece of work, at least.

When William decided upon the invasion of England, he had much trouble in persuading the Norman barons to join with him in the expedition. They did not like the idea. They thought it would be doomed to failure. But when William told them that if they helped him to success, he would divide amongst them the estates of the English nobility, they began to think better of the matter, and ultimately agreed to go with him.

Odo, who was quite a young man at the time, was very active in bringing round the barons to William's side. So was Robert, his brother, and, of course, another half brother of William. Though Odo was a bishop, and a young one, he was a warrior, and well acquainted with the ways of fighting men. It must have been a fine sight at Hastings to see this young bishop riding into battle. When the order was given to the Norman troops to advance, William the Duke rode at their head, and on one side of him rode Odo, on the other side rode Robert. The sight of these three brothers on their chargers, leading the army to battle, must

N... 3   ELTHAM PALACE FROM THE SOUTH.
(1905).

No. 21.   PALACE FROM THE SOUTH LAWN, SHOWING BAY
(1905).

No. 2.   A BIT OF OLD WALL, ELTHAM PALACE, SHOWING LOOP-HOLES.
It overlooks the Moat on the East.   Taken 1905.

No. 20.   THE GREAT HALL OF PALACE AS SEEN FROM THE SOUTH-WEST.
(1905).

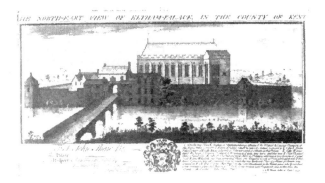

THE NORTH-EAST VIEW OF ELTHAM-PALACE, IN THE COUNTY OF KENT

No. 23.   FROM THE OLDEST KNOWN PICTURE OF ELTHAM PALACE.
(Engraved by S. & N. Buck. 1735).

No. 24.
"MY LORD CHANCELLOR'S LODGING"
The portion now occupied by Mrs. Alexander Milne.
(See plan page 89).

No. 25.
WOODEN HOUSE ADJOINING CHANCELLOR'S
LODGING.
Residence of the Misses Brookes,
(See plan page 89).

have been an inspiring one to those who followed.

Odo did not carry a sword, because the laws of the Church forbade a priest to shed blood. But he wielded a heavy mace, and, when the right moment came, no doubt he used it pretty stoutly. He could not run his opponents through with a mace, but he probably did serious damage to some of their skulls.

It is recorded that at one moment of the battle, the Normans were getting the worst of it. The horsemen in retreating got into a fosse, or ditch, and rolled about, trampling upon one another, and they were all a confused and struggling mass. Some of the Normans started to run away. Then up rode Bishop Odo, swinging his mighty mace, laying about him, and shouting reproof and encouragement to the bewildered Normans. He stayed the panic and probably saved the day.

William was as good as his word. The Conquest completed, he divided the land amongst his knights and nobles. Odo and Robert came in for most liberal rewards. Together with estates in other counties, Odo was given two hundred manors in Kent, that of Eltham being one of them, and he was given also the English title of Earl of Kent. He had immense power, too, in the government of the country. When William, a few years later, found it necessary to return to Normandy for a time, Odo ruled in his name. But he was so harsh and tyrannical that the men of Kent rose against him, and sought aid from Eustace, Count of Boulogne.

Ambition led to the fall of Odo, as it has to the ruin of other men. William found that his great Earls were getting a little too powerful for him. So he took measures to keep their power within bounds. Some of them resented this, and scheming and plotting went on for resisting the will of the King. Odo was one of the schemers. He collected much money and men, making believe that he wanted to get himself made Pope. But William was too wide awake. He was not to be taken in. One day at Court, there was a surprise for Odo. The King was there and his courtiers all around. Quite unexpectedly William ordered the arrest of the Bishop. So taken back was everybody that no officer moved to carry out the King's command. They feared to touch a Bishop. So William walked up to Odo, and seized him with his own hands, exclaiming, with a grim laugh, " I arrest not the Bishop, but the Earl of Kent." And Odo was kept a prisoner till the Conqueror died.

At the death of the King, William Rufus, his second son, as you know quite well, was given the crown. The Conqueror, at his death, let Odo out of prison, and Rufus allowed his uncle to be once more Earl of Kent. After a while the Norman barons rose against the Red King. They said that they wanted to make his brother Robert King, but their real object was to increase their own power and influence. Odo was their leader. It looked as if the cause of the King was hopeless. But the English stuck loyally to him, and, the pride of ambitious Odo suffered another shock.

There was fighting in the north and the west, but Odo and his chief followers were at Rochester Castle, and William knew that if he wanted to crush out the revolt, he would have to march against his uncle at Rochester and destroy his power once and for all. So he gathered his fighting men round him in London, and the English came to his banner in force, for he promised to grant them good laws, to levy no unjust taxes, and to allow men the freedom of their woods and of hunting.

In the short struggle that ensued, our hero Odo did not cut a very heroic figure. On hearing of the Red King's advance, he hastened to Pevensey, where he expected to meet his brother Robert with additional troops from Robert of Normandy. But the Red King was too strong for them and Odo was obliged to give in.

Then the King did a rather foolish thing. The English would have been glad to see Odo put to death. But Odo promised to get the surrender of Rochester Castle, and then to leave the country for good, if the King, his nephew, would let him go. So William sent him on to Rochester to make arrangements for its surrender. But it did not come off as was expected, and the unhappy Odo was placed in a rather awkward predicament. When he came near to the castle, and explained the circumstances of his coming, the guards seized him and took him within the castle, and then said they would not give it up to the King. So, on the arrival of Rufus and his men, it was subjected to a siege. It was a considerable undertaking, and the King had to appeal to the English for more help. The Men of Kent responded to the call, and those who refused were given the dreaded name of "nithing," which was the vilest name in the language.

After a long siege, during which the garrison suffered from great sickness and privation, the castle surrendered, and when the prisoners were led out between the ranks of the royal troops, the English cried with a loud voice,

"Halters! Bring halters to hang up the traitor Bishop and his friends!" But the halters were not applied, and most of the rebels were spared execution. Many were banished from the country for ever. Among these was the Bishop of Bayeux.

Such, then, briefly told, is the story of Odo, half brother of the King, and the Bishop of Bayeux, who, through the grace of his royal master, became possessed of the broad acres of Eltham, who amassed great wealth and used it wrongfully, who, by ambition, fell. When he went into exile, he passed out of the history of England. Few tears were shed, we may be sure. And it is not with much regret that we now dismiss him from the Story of Eltham.

DUKE WILLIAM ADDRESSING HIS SOLDIERS AT THE FIELD OF HASTINGS (Bayeux Tapestry.)

DEATH OF HAROLD (Bayeux Tapestry.)

CHAPTER VII.

HAIMO THE SHIRE-REEVE.

When William the Conqueror proceeded to distribute the English estates among his Norman Barons he used a certain amount of discretion. He was anxious to win over to his side as many of the English nobility as he could, so he did not take away the estates of all of them. In districts where they were not particularly active in resisting William, many of the English nobles were allowed to keep their lands and manors. But in those quarters whence the bulk of the fighting men had come who had fought against him at Senlac, or who had subsequently opposed him in his conquest of England, William was heartless in his confiscations. Kent suffered especially. Not an English nobleman was allowed to retain his property in Kent. William had good reason for this. Kent was specially loyal to England and to Harold. So two hundred manors of Kent were given to Odo alone, and he ruled them with an iron hand. The Eltham Manor was allotted to Haimo, who held it under Odo.

This Haimo was, for more reasons than one, a rather distinguished personage. In the first place he was a kinsman of the King himself. Although he could not claim so close a relationship as Odo, the Earl and Prelate, who was the King's half-brother, he could claim to have descended from the same old stock— from that fierce Norse pirate, Rolf or Rollo, who was driven from his own land, Norway, as an outlaw, and who came to Normandy and founded the settlement there which afterwards became the Duchy, and of which William was the Duke. So, you see, Haimo, the new Lord of Eltham, was of royal blood.

And, otherwise, he was a very important man. He was the Shire Reeve of Kent. This was a very high office. In the old Saxon days the Reeve of the Shire was elected by the people, and, next to the Earldorman or Earl, he was the chief man in the County. But Haimo was appointed by the King, and it was his duty to preside, as the representative of the King, at the Shire Court or Leet, where he had to settle all sorts of disputes that were brought before him from among the people of the Shire. If he was unable to settle them to their satisfaction then they could take their disputes to the King   That was how some of the Courts of Law came to be formed, such as the King's Bench, Court of Common Pleas, &c. It must have been strange to have men who spoke a foreign tongue to do this kind of business, and it must have been the cause of a good deal of trouble in meting out justice The Eltham churls, probably, did not much like having a lord over their manor who could not speak to them in their own language and who could not understand them when they wanted to speak to him.

But it is very likely that these Norman Barons had very little to do with the English villagers They held themselves aloof from them, and, perhaps, thought themselves quite superior to them   This feeling would be shared by the retainers and foreign servants who waited upon the Baron in his hall, and the lot of the Eltham villagers could not have been so happy under Haimo as it was under Alwold, who was an Englishman and could speak their own tongue Not that we have any reason to think that Haimo was particularly hard or tyrannical, though the Norman Barons did not bear a very good character in this respect Haimo's own relative, Odo, for instance, has left behind him a very bad name. In his case " his evil deeds live after him," as Mark Anthony says in the play But Haimo could not have been quite the same sort of man as Odo

Odo was turned out of his Earldom by the King because of his wrong doings, but Haimo remained as Shire Reeve until his death, which shows, at any rate, that the King never suspected him of being mixed up with the scheming and plotting which led to Odo's un-doing. So, as we cannot find out anything against Haimo, we may as well put him down as a straight-forward Lord of Eltham, al-though, being a foreigner, speaking a foreign language, and obliged to carry out the strict laws of the King, the simple Eltham folk could hardly like him well, especially as his presence always reminded them that they were a conquered people.

One day, at the time when Haimo was the lord, there was commotion among the

Eltham farmers.   All the villans, as they were now called, were summoned to appear before the Hundred Court over at Blackheath, and there was no doubt a good deal of talk amongst them on the farm, or at the forge, or wherever they were in the habit of getting together for a gossip, as to the meaning of this summons   When they got to the Hun-dred Court, there they saw four stern looking persons, called commissioners, and near them were their clerks with quill pens, and ink, and parchment, all looking very wise, we may be sure, and ready to write down whatever they were told   Haimo was there, too, not only because he was Lord of Eltham, but because he was the Shire Reeve   There were also a number of folk from other Manors within the Hundred, priests too, and six villeins from each township   These farmers were not at all pleased to be called up in this way, and, on the quiet, there was a lot of grumbling going on amongst them

It was explained that at a great Council held at Winchester it was ordered by the King that commissioners with their clerks should be sent out into the shires, hundred by hundred, to make enquiries about the manors, and to set it all down in writing So Haimo himself, and the " villans " from the Eltham Manor were made to take a solemn oath that they would tell the truth, and then the stern Norman lawyers questioned them about the estate, how much land it contained and what sort of land it was, how many men there were upon it, and what kind of men they were, what it was worth in Edward's time and what it was worth now, how many cattle and swine each freeman kept, whether the rents could be raised, and other questions besides.   The villans had to give correct answers to these enquiries, whether they liked it or no, and the clerks worked away with their quill pens, set-ting it all down " in black and white " as they say, just as the King had commanded. When one town-ship was done with, another town-ship was treated in the same way till the whole Hundred was completed, and so the Commissioners went on right through the other Hundreds of the County. The clerks wrote these things down upon separate scrolls or leaflets, and when they had finished them, they were taken away to Winchester, where other clerks copied them all out again, in a form that had been already arranged

That was how Domesday Book was made up

Yes! Englishmen regarded this as a grievous day Deeply did they resent the humiliation of having to answer these searching questions. Bitter were the words used by the villagers against inquiry, although, perhaps, they were only muttered protests, for men feared to speak their minds aloud An old writer of the times says "It is a shame to tell what he thought it no shame for him to do Ox, nor cow, nor swine, was left that was not set down upon his writ" In some places men spoke their protests loudly There were disputes, which led to fighting and bloodshed But it was of no avail to resist The mailed fist of the Conqueror prevailed By Easter Day, April 5th, 1086, the day appointed as the time limit by the King, the work was finished, and Domesday Book was added to our National Records

Domesday Book! The name seems very appropriate. "Men called the book Domesday," says a writer, "for to the English the inquest seemed searching, and terrible as that of the Last Judgment"

We have styled Haimo, at the head of this chapter, as Shire Reeve, because that was the old Anglo-Saxon name for the office which he filled Now-a-days, we cut the name short and call the officer a Sheriff The duties of the Sheriff of the present day are not the same as those of the olden time, but many of those duties are similar. The interesting point to bear in mind is that the office was really first established long ago in early Saxon times, and that the present High Sheriff of Kent is on the long roll of Sheriffs which included Haimo, the Lord of Eltham, and many other Shire Reeves before him.

But in the Domesday page which refers to Eltham and to Haimo, he is not described as a "Shire Reeve." The word "Vicecomes," has been put in just above his name, which looks as if the clerk, in the first instance, omitted the title, and that it was afterwards inserted Domesday is written in Latin, and "Vicecomes"

is merely the Latin equivalent of Shire Reeve William found that the office of Shire Reeve in England so much resembled that of a "Viscount" or "Vicecomes" in Normandy that he introduced the Norman title to England, and that is how it comes about that Haimo is described as "Vicecomes" in Domesday. You will notice, however, that the old English name has survived after all, for we still call the important officer "Sheriff" and not "Viscount." Haimo seems to have lived to a good old age, for in the year 1111, forty-five years after the Norman Conquest, we read of his giving back to the Abbey of St Augustine at Canterbury the remaining portion of the Manor of Fordwich Haimo had a niece named Maud, or Mabel, and she married Robert Fitz Roy, Earl of Gloucester, who was a son of Henry I When Haimo died his lands were inherited by his niece, and that is how it came about that the Manor of Eltham, after Haimo's death, became one of the estates of the Earl of Gloucester, or, as the book tells us, "became appended to the honour of Gloucester"

We must now say good-bye to Haimo, for the hand of death has taken him out of our story. For many years the Eltham Manor was held by the Earl of Gloucester, and his descendants and heirs A hundred years slip away, in the course of which there seems to have been a dispute as to whom the "vill," or village of Eltham rightly belonged

This dispute led to a legal inquiry and a scrutiny of the Rolls This was in the seventh year of the reign of King Edward I As a result of this scrutiny we get an account of Eltham at that particular time, which is so interesting that we may as well read it in the quaint language in which it was written In reading it you would do well to read through the lines, as they say, and see if you can picture for yourselves, some of the conditions of life in our old village at that time

"Extent of the Manor of Eltham in the county of Kent made by precept of our Lord the King, on the death of Richard de Clare, formerly Earl of Gloucester and Hereford, before William de Axmouth and William de Horton thereto assigned

"By the oath of . . . . . . , who say on their oath that in demesne there are 206 acres of arable land, of which 111 acres are worth 4d. per acre; and the amount is 59s. 6d.

"And they say that there are two acres of meadow worth 3s. per acre; and the amount 6s. The pasture thereof, after the hay is carried, is extended (estimated) at 4d.

"And they say that there are 13 acres of pasture extended at 4s. 6d.

"The Court Lodge and the pasture of Court Lodge, and of a certain lane towards the church, are extended at 2s.

"And there is a certain enclosed wood containing 200 acres, and the pasture thereof is extended at 20s., and the pannage thereof is extended at half a marc.

"And they say that the sale of the underwood is worth 57s. per annum.

"The rent of the Free Holders (i.e., the quit rents) is extended at 24s. 9d.

"And they say that in Villenage (i.e., the lord's land not cultivated by himself) there are 28½ virgates of land, and the fourth part of a virgate, and half an acre; and the virgate contains seven acres and a half, and the rent thereof is 71s. and 8½d.

"And they say that the rent of the Cotters is 6s. 7½d. The rent of certain tenants, who are called Plocmen (i.e., tenants holding by plough service) is extended at 3s. 5d.

"And they say there are 245¾ acres which are let to the Villans of the new laud, at the lord's will; and the rent thereof is four pound and twenty-three pence, at 4d. per acre. The works of the Villans are extended at 30s. 1d.

"And they say that the assised aid of the Villans is 18s. 11d. per annum, &c., &c."

Such was the Manor of Eltham in the year 1263, when Edward I. reigned. This document reveals to us, in some degree, what life in our village was like, after the Normans had ruled for close upon a hundred years. If you will carefully read the national history of this eventful period, you will find it a pleasant exercise for your mind to consider what part the men of Eltham would in all likelihood have played in the national story.

For a while we shall now leave the Manor to consider, in the next chapter, another relic of antiquity of equal, if not even greater, interest.

BATTLE OF HASTINGS (Bayeux Tapestry).

CHAPTER VIII.

"GOD'S ACRE."

To-day we will take our position here, within the shadow of the Parish Church, upon this little plot of ground where sleep the "fore-fathers of the hamlet"

The Roman road over Shooter's-hill tells a story of life and strenuous activity through many centuries "The Common" recalls the pastoral life and field labours of our distant ancestors The crumbling palace speaks of royal pageants, of parliaments, of courtly festivals, and brilliant scenes of pomp and chivalry They all tell of "life" This patch of greensward, with its mouldering mounds and monuments, has another tale to tell—"Death"

Often, perhaps, you have witnessed the solemn ceremony of burial here It may be that many of you have taken part in that ceremony when someone near and dear has been laid to rest The scene in which you took part was only one of a countless number, whose chain goes so far back into the ages that we cannot see the beginning. The one you lost was but a unit of a countless host, all sleeping here beneath the grass awaiting the great day.

We cannot tell the age of Eltham Church-yard We know of three churches, but it is probable that the churchyard is older than the most ancient of them. Those grave stones there are crumbling away with age So old and weather-worn are they that you cannot read what was engraved upon them When they were set up, long ago, all fresh and clean and new, and sorrowing villagers in quaint old world garb came to scan the epitaphs, the churchyard was still of age beyond reckoning

Such thoughts should make us pause when we enter these hallowed precincts—pause, to reflect in seriousness, perhaps in awe Careless and flippant speech is out of place amid such surroundings Our talk and deportment should be in harmony with the scene, lest we should seem to desecrate the abode of the dead

There was a church here in Norman times It is the first about which we can find a record We shall have something to say about it another day But Eltham, even in Norman times, was still an old place It was bound to possess its burial ground, and it may be assumed that it had its church long before the time when we find it first mentioned. It would have been a Saxon church and built of wood, as Saxon churches mostly were

You know what your history book tells you, how Hengist and Horsa and all the tribes of the Saxons were pagans, fierce and unyielding heathen, who lifted their heart and voice to the gods—Wodin and Thor—who assailed the Christian churches they found in Britain, burning them and killing the Christian priests Christianity was quite strong amongst the British, before the Saxons came, and there were many churches in the land

Sometimes the Saxons spared a Christian church, and turned it into a heathen temple for their own use. It is said that the old church of St. Martin's, at Canterbury, was used in this way But, in course of time, Augustine came and preached Christianity to the heathen Saxons, and even they were converted Slowly, but surely, Christianity made its way among them They ceased their worship of Wodin and Thor, and, in place of heathen temples, the village communities set up their little Christian churches. Such a building may have existed at Eltham before the church about which we have the earliest record, and to the little churchyard that surrounded it the early Eltham villagers would have brought their dead.

In their heathen days it is said that the Saxons did not bury their dead in the vicinity of their temples, as we do now in the vicinity of a church. It was unlawful even to bury within the walls of their towns, and the dead were carried to the fields without St Cuthbert, the great preacher and teacher of the north of England, is credited with being the first to obtain permission to have yards to the churches proper for the burial of the dead So the churchyards of England may be regarded as memorials of the famous Bishop of Lindisfarne, who lived as early as the seventh century.

Let us now walk round our old churchyard and see what it has got to tell us

Some of those who remember the building of the present church will tell you that when the workmen were digging the foundations for the tower they came across a strange coffin made entirely of stone It had been buried beneath the earth for so long a time that no engraving could be distinguished upon it, and the body which it had once contained had long since changed to dust

This coffin shews that the churchyard is very old, because the custom of using stone coffins has long since passed away Such coffins were used in the Norman times, and right down through the middle ages We may assume that it was the coffin of some rich person, for a poor person could hardly afford such a form of burial in those old times There was probably much pomp and ceremonial when it was committed to the earth But that has all been forgotten Even the name of the individual is lost Nought remains but the stone itself, which is built into the basement of the tower

There stands the old yew tree It is not so large as some yew trees, but it has been grow-

ing there many, many years, perhaps centuries. You will see it represented in the very oldest pictures of the old church. Yew trees grow very slowly, but they live to a great age Some people say that they live longer than any other tree, and that in some churchyards the yew tree is nearly a thousand years old Many generations have come and gone since this tree was a sapling There used to be another yew tree on the other side of the church, but that died It is thought to have been killed by the lime that was lying about when the new church was built

It would be a hard matter to find any old churchyard without a yew tree People often wonder why they should have planted a yew tree in every churchyard in this way, and curiously enough, even those who have inquired into the matter cannot agree as to the reason.

Some of them seem to think that, in the olden times, before guns were used, the yew was planted for the purpose of supplying wood for the making of the bows. It was planted in the churchyard because it was fenced round, and the cattle would be thus prevented from getting at the yew and eating it, for it is poisonous But, from all accounts, it would appear that other woods were used for the same purpose, and that when yew was used, it was generally Spanish yew, and not English yew, which "was of inferior goodness." An old statute of the eighth year of Elizabeth requires "each bowyer always to have in his house fifty bows made of elm, witch, hazel, or ash " By an older act of Edward IV., we find that "every Englishman was obliged to have a bow in his house of his own length, either of yew, witch, ash, or auburn" (probably alder)

Another writer says that "the venerable yew trees still to be seen in our churchyards were planted for the purpose of furnishing *palms* for Palm Sunday, which, he thinks, were simply *branches of yew trees*" He holds to this, he tells us, "from the fact of those in the churchyards of East Kent being to this day universally called *palm* "

No. 27.   CONTINUATION OF DWELLINGS ATTACHED TO
"CHANCELLOR'S LODGINGS."
Residence of Mr. W. H. Hollis.
Originally part of "My Lord Chancellor's Butery."
(See plan page 89).

No. 29.   HOUSE NEAR TILT-YARD GATE.
Residence of Captain Holbrooke.   Stands on site of "The Great Bakery."
(See plan page 89).

No. 26.   "MY LORD CHANCELLOR'S LODGINGS."
Portion occupied by the Misses Bloxam.
(See plan page 89).

No. 28.   LANGERTON HOUSE.
Residence of Mrs Gordon.   Stands on the site of the old "Chauntry."
(See plan page 89).

No. 3.　WELL-HALL.　(1909).　Seen from the Paddock.

The Lawn and Gardens in foreground formed site of the old Mansion.

No. 34　TUDOR BUILDINGS AT WELL-HALL　(1909).

As seen from Moat Island.

WELL-HALL.　(The Front).　1909.

Residence of Mr. Hubert Bland.

No. 52.　THE MOAT, WELL-HALL.　(1909)

No. 34.   A BIT OF THE OLD COTTAGES, WELL-HALL ROAD,

Showing Caravan, 1909.

The Site is said to have been the resort of caravans for several centuries.

THE TUDOR FARM BUILDINGS, WELL-HALL.   (Date 1380).

With a part of the Moat.

(1909).

No. 38.

THE PARISH CHURCH.

From the North.   1870.

No 39.

INTERIOR OF OLD CHURCH.

Th k y l \rı... r the left, an n v prc ervd in Rochester Museum.

Another student of the subject does not agree with this. He "looks upon the yew as being too funereal to be substituted for the joyful palm." He rather thinks that the solitary yew is a relic of the times when many more trees existed round the church "for protecting the fabric of the church from storms." He refers us to a law of Edward I., "whereby leave was given to fell trees in churchyards for building and repairs," and the yew trees "would be the only trees left standing as unfit for such purposes," and thereafter he thinks "an *evergreen* would be thought *an emblem of the resurrection,* and even acquire some degree of regard and veneration."

There was a time when the yew was much used on the occasion of funeral ceremonies, and other writers suggest that it might have been planted in the churchyards to meet needs of this kind. There is a quaint old rhyme, which runs thus:—

"Yet strewe
Upon my dismall grave,
Such offerings as you have,
Forsaken cypresse and *sad yew,*
For kinder flowers can take no birth
Or growth from such unhappy earth."

In another old book, printed nearly three hundred years ago, and called "The Marrow of Complements," we get this sad lay, "A Mayden's Song for her dead Lover," which shews that the yew, like the cypress was regarded as a funeral plant—

I.

"Come you whose loves are dead,
And whilst I sing,
Weepe and wring
Every hand, and every head.
Bind with Cypresse and *sad Ewe,*
Ribbands black and candles blue;
For him that was of men most true.

II.

"Come with heavy moaning,
And on his Grave
Let him have
Sacrifice of Sighes and Groaning,
Let him have faire Flowers enough,
White and Purple, Green and Yellow,
For him that was of Men most true."

These lines are very quaint, and, perhaps, the expressions seem to our ears a little emotional and extravagant, but they serve to illustrate the fact that the yew was used for funereal purposes to express sadness.

The antiquarian, Sir Thomas Browne, in writing of the use of evergreens at funerals suggests, "that the planting of yew trees in churchyards derives its origin from ancient funeral rites," and conjectures, "from its perpetual verdure, that it was used as an emblem of the resurrection."

The mysterious yew in the churchyard, you will therefore notice, has been the cause of much thought and inquiry by learned men. But they cannot agree as to the reason of its presence. There it stands lonely, silent, sphinx-like, keeping its own secret. We shall probably never know the truth of it all.

The lich-gate there, at the entrance to the churchyard from the street, is not old. It is quite modern, so far as its construction is concerned. But the lich-gate, as an institution, is very ancient. Its name suggests that. It is Anglo-Saxon, and means, literally, "corpse-gate." It is only opened on the occasion of funerals, and it is said to have been the ancient custom for the corpse to rest there for a while, during the reading of the sentences at the beginning of the burial services.

PAUL'S CROSS (from an old Print).

CHAPTER IX

ELTHAM CROSSES.

The handsome Cross which was erected only a few years ago to the memory of an Eltham resident whose name will be long remembered here, like the Lich-gate to which we alluded last week, is of quite modern construction.

But a cross of this kind, whether it be ancient or modern, is a feature of special interest, because it points to a custom which was common in the middle ages, a custom which was so closely associated with national life that it needed an Act of Parliament to kill it.

There was a time, when, as an able writer tells us, "the face of the land bristled with crosses." Sometimes they were set up near the south door of the church. Very often they were in the market places of the villages and towns. Frequently they were by the wayside. Sometimes they were simple of construction; often they were elaborate and very beautiful.

Comparatively speaking, only a few of the original crosses are now to be found. Pro-bably you will come across most relics of them in districts remote from London. In Somerset and Dorset, and in Cornwall, for instance, it is quite a common thing to find the broken remains of these old stone crosses in the villages.

In some places, men who have a deep regard for the past history of our national life are having these old crosses restored. We read in the papers, not long ago, that a model of the notable one which used to stand in St. Paul's Churchyard, and was known in history as "Paul's Cross," will shortly be built upon the well-known spot. It is a good plan to do this kind of thing. Though such crosses can never have quite the same significance to the present generation as they had to our forefathers, it is good to have, before our eyes, such eloquent reminders of the past.

So we will take this modern cross in Eltham Churchyard as the excuse for our talk to-day.

Let us see if we can in some measure realise the part which the village cross played in the life of those old times And, let us see if we can find any direct evidence that Eltham itself possessed a village cross of its own

You know that the early Christians adopted the cross as the emblem of the Christian faith, and it was used by the first preachers and teachers to remind men that the founder of that faith was Christ the Crucified

The earliest missionaries used to set up crosses where they preached, that the natives might be always reminded of their teaching. "We are told that St Wilfred, who was Archbishop of York at the beginning of the eighth century, travelled about his diocese with a large body of monks and workmen attending him, amongst whom were cutters in stone, who made crosses and erected them on the spots which St Wilfred consecrated to the worship of God"

So you see that in the first instance, the cross was intended to fulfil a religious purpose.

There were many kinds of crosses, such as memorial crosses, churchyard or preaching crosses, market and village crosses, weeping crosses, pilgrim crosses, and boundary crosses.

The best examples of memorial crosses are those that are left of that line of crosses erected by Edward I , in memory of Queen Eleanor Only three of the original nine or twelve now exist, namely, at Geddington, Northampton and Waltham Crosses of this kind were usually erected by the wayside, or in a city, town or village, to commemorate some memorable circumstance. Those mentioned marked the resting place of the funeral procession which brought the remains of the Queen from the North to London.

"Preaching crosses" were generally set up in churchyards, and very often near the south door of the church. From their steps, preaching friars frequently addressed the people

"Market crosses" were usually erected in the market place of the village or town They were often elaborate in construction, having

arches and vaulted structures, sometimes of great size. "Often on market and fair days, a preaching friar would address the people from the market cross, reminding them of the sacredness of their bargains, and telling both buyers and sellers to be true and just in all their dealings"

"The village cross" was found generally on the village green, and was of more simple construction. Not far from it was the maypole, and, very often, the village stocks From the village cross, public proclamations were made, banns of marriage were published and tolls and market dues collected.

"Boundary crosses" marked the limits of parishes and manors, and owing to the superstitious reverence with which they were regarded in the middle ages, they were rarely tampered with.

"Weeping crosses" were put up for the use of those who were called upon to do penance for their wrongdoing

"Pilgrim crosses" were erected by the side of the highways They served as guide-posts to the different monasteries, oratories, and other religious foundations. Sometimes a rich traveller would deposit alms at the foot of a "pilgrim cross," for the help of the poor distressed wayfarer who might be coming along

From this brief description of the crosses that were common in those old times, we may discern in some degree the part which they played in the social life of the times, and the question naturally arises to one's mind—did Eltham possess any such cross as one of these, and, if it did, where did it stand and what has become of it ?

There does not seem to be any relic of an old cross, either in the churchyard or in the village, nor does one hear of any tradition of such a cross Curiously enough, evidence has just recently come to light, from an unexpected quarter, which bears out one's natural suspicion that one of these mediæval crosses must have existed at some time in such an historical village as Eltham

The well-known antiquarian, Mr. Leland L. Duncan, has been making researches, for the St. Paul's Ecclesiological Society and the Kent Archæological Society, amongst the "wills" of persons who died in the County of Kent in ancient times. Copies of these curious wills have been made and printed, and amongst them are quite a number relating to persons who have been buried in our Parish Church or churchyard of St. John the Baptist.

Two of these wills allude, incidentally but, most distinctly, to Crosses—one at Shooter's-

been written then, and people had a sort of free and easy way of spelling, which would not be tolerated in our enlightened days.

This is the will of one Roger Leche, and it is dated 1517. Good Master Leche would have been alive when Henry VII. was king. He would have been at Eltham when handsome Prince Harry was crowned. He might have been a witness of those gay May-day festivals which the young King Henry VIII., organised in the woods of Shooter's Hill. We cannot be sure, but we do know that he left sufficient property

DESTRUCTION OF CROSS IN CHEAP-SIDE (from an old Print).

hill and the other in Eltham itself. The Shooter's-hill cross may, in all probability, have been a "Pilgrim Cross," for the Old Dover road was the highway from London to Canterbury, and could have been used by the many pilgrims to the tomb of St. Thomas Becket in the Cathedral city. The Eltham cross might have been a "market cross," or a "village cross." One cannot tell. It will be a nice problem for those interested in lore of this kind to try and solve.

But let us read the wills referred to. You must not be shocked by the bad spelling. Doctor Johnson's dictionary, which first laid down how words should be spelled, had not

to bring in yearly two separate sixpences to be expended upon bread and ale for the poor. Truly, a considerate man was Master Robert Leche. These are his words:—

"I will Rauff Letham shall kepe or cause to be kept yerly the Wedynsday in the crosse weke *at the crose before his dur* when the procession cw'myth in brede and ale vjd, and vpon Seint Thomas nyght after the fest of Seint John Baptyst at the bonefyre in brede and ale vjd. Roger Leche, 1517."

What a light this quaint will throws upon the social life of the period! We could spend much time in pondering over the old time customs which it refers to—"the procession," the distribution of "bread and ale," and particularly to the "bonfire" at the time of the feast of "St John the Baptist." Another day, we may have something to say upon some of these features of the life and customs of old Eltham

To-day we are more interested with the "cross before the door" of Rauff Letham. Who was Rauff Letham? Whereabouts in Eltham did he live? And the cross which stood in front of his door, was it the Market Cross? Was it an ordinary village cross? Did the children play upon its steps? Did a poor mendicant priest occasionally preach from those steps to the gaping rustics, or for the edification of the stable men from the Palace, or even for the soul's welfare of Rauff Letham himself, who looked out upon the scene from his own respectable doorway? Rauff was a respectable man, or, is it at all likely that good master Roger Leche would have entrusted him with the responsible duty of distributing every year two separate sixpences in "brede and ale?" Did Rauff collect the market tolls at the Cross? There does not seem to be any record left of the life and doings of this man Rauff Letham But we are quite sure, now, that there was a *Cross* standing in front of his door, and it would be worth more than "two sixpences" to know where in Eltham that doorway was

We will now look at the other "will" It is that of John Browne, gentleman, and it was signed in 1533 That was just about the time when Henry VIII., who often came to Eltham Palace, was making up his mind to shake off the authority of the Pope and set up himself as head of the Church. It is quite likely that Master John Browne, gentleman, was an old Elthamite, who had seen the great Cardinal Wolsey, or the great Chancellor, Sir Thomas More, or the scholar Erasmus, at one time or another, on the occasion of their visits to Eltham Master Browne lived in stirring times

Here is the extract from his will Let us read it

"I will that John and Antony my sonnes and Sir Edward, William Bowen, and their heires or to whose handes or possession the foresaid landes and tenements doo com, dis-

cent, sale or otherwise enjoye the same that they and their heires shall every yere yerely for ever more fynde or cause to be founde alweys yerely upon Tewesday in the Rogacion weke at the Procession tyme *at the Cross vpon Shoters Hill* a fyrkyn of Ale, xijd in bred to be disposed and gyven amonge pour people coming wt the same procession and also shall geve and paye vnto the preest then reding the gospell, jd. and the clerk there being jd John Browne, gent , 1533 "

You will notice that Master Browne was liberal with his ale, giving as much as a firkin, which is, nowadays, nine gallons Twelve pence was also spent in bread for the poor But the priest who had to attend the procession to the Cross at Shooter's Hill, there to read the Gospel, and the faithful Parish Clerk who followed at his heels, had to be satisfied each with a penny for their services We may hope, however, that they had a reasonable share of the ale

But the point of this will which interests us most, at the moment, is the allusion to the "Cross at Shooter's Hill" From these old documents, only recently unearthed, we may therefore learn that mediæval crosses, of some sort, actually existed in Eltham, though, unfortunately, they have been destroyed

How came they to be destroyed, you will ask? It was done by an ordinance of Parliament in the year 1643

"Die Lunæ 28 Augusti 1643.

' An Ordinance of the Lords and Commons, assembled in Parliament, for the utter demolishing, removing, and taking away of all monuments of Superstition or Idolatry out of all Churches and Chapells and Open Places, within the Kingdom of England and Dominion of Wales.

"Before the 1st November, 1643 "

It was ordained that this destruction should be carried out within the period of some three months "It was further ordained that all and every such removal, taking away, and defacing such crucifixes and crosses as aforesaid should be done at the expense of the Churchwardens of every such parish for the time being respectively, and in the case of default for the space of 21 days after the said 1st day of November, 1643, under a penalty of 40s. to the use of the poor of the said Parish, and if default should be made after the 1st day of December, 1643, then the destruction was done by the Justice of the Peace, and the Churchwardens had to pay the cost. Poor Churchwardens!

It would seem that the Churchwardens did the work effectively in Eltham. "Paul's Cross" was destroyed at the same time, as well as thousands of others. In the western counties, however, the ordinance appears to have been only partially carried out. Many of the village crosses were defaced, but not destroyed entirely. When we read of this wide-spread destruction, in these days, we wonder at its severity, perhaps, and we appreciate the words of John Ruskin, when he deplores the loss of the beautiful examples of early architec-

ture. "The feudal and monastic buildings of Europe," he writes, "and still more the streets of her ancient cities, are vanishing like dreams; and *it is difficult to imagine the mingled envy and contempt with which future generations will look back to us, who still possessed such things, yet made no effort to preserve and scarcely any to delineate them.*"

So has it been with the beautiful examples of mediæval crosses which once were an ornament to our land. They can never be replaced. "Paul's Cross," new and spick and span, however closely it may be made to resemble its predecessor, can never speak to us with the voice of the one that was so ruthlessly destroyed. But it will be good to see it there. So we value this new Cross in Eltham church-yard, for it not only serves as a monument to a good man, but it reminds us of another age, and of social life and associations of our village which might otherwise be forgotten.

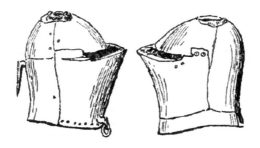

CHAPTER X.

CHURCHYARD SCENES.

There is at least one old churchyard custom that has not died out. It is that of placing flowers upon the graves There they lie, some of them choice and costly flowers, many of them simple flowers from the cottage garden, but all placed there by loving hands—for remembrance.

The practice interests us to-day because it is of ancient origin It is to be associated with the earliest days of Christianity, and it has been practised in varying degrees, by Eltham people, through the long centuries of this churchyard's existence.

As early as the fourth century we have an allusion to this custom of putting flowers upon graves in a funeral oration of St Ambrose, one of the Fathers of the Latin Church. "I will not sprinkle his grave with flowers," he says, "but pour on his spirit the odour of Christ. Let others scatter baskets of flowers Christ is our Lilly, and with this I will consecrate his relics."

Then, again, St Jerome, of about the same period, in the Epistle to Pammachius upon the death of his wife, says, "While other husbands strewed violets, roses, lillies and purple flowers upon the graves of their wives, and comforted themselves with such-like offices, Pammachius bedewed her ashes and venerable bones with the balsam of Alms "

An old writer, referring to this ancient practice, in England and especially in Wales and the West, says —
"None but sweet-scented flowers or evergreens are allowed to be planted upon graves, such as pink and polyanthus, sweet-william,

gill flower, and carnation, while mignonette, thyme hyssop, camomile, and rosemary, complete the pious decoration The turnsole, peony, African marigold, anemone, and others, though beautiful, are excluded for their want of odour. Sometimes, however, the tender custom is perverted into satire, and where persons have been distinguished for their pride, vanity, or other unpopular quality, the neighbours whom they have offended, plant these also by stealth The white rose is confined to the maiden's tomb, and the red denotes the grave of one distinguished for goodness, especially for benevolence of character.

"In Easter week," he continues, "the graves are generally newly dressed and manured with fresh earth At Whitsuntide, or rather during the preceding week, the graves are again attended to, and, if necessary, replanted A popular saying of those who employ themselves in this office of regard for departed friends is, that they are cultivating their own freeholds, explained by the fact that the nearest relations of the deceased invariably work with their own hands, never by servants or hired labour. Should a neighbour assist, he or she never expects remuneration, indeed, the offer would be resented as an insult "

Much more could be said about this beautiful old practice of putting flowers upon the graves of our friends, and many allusions to it could be gathered from the poets of the past. But we have said enough to show its antiquity, and to help us to realise, that in our practice of it to-day, we are doing what those before us have done for centuries.

Let us now consider some of those church-yard customs which no longer exist. Yes, there is the Church Clock striking the hour, and a very convenient thing it is to have a clock in the church tower to give us the time of day. Our forefathers had to content themselves with a sundial, and the Churchyard was the place where the village sundial was nearly always kept.

Eltham had its sundial, for in the Church-warden's accounts, we find the following entry. "1572 Received from Sir John Car-nicke, Vicar, towards making of *the dialle of* his own' free gifts, iijs "

You may see these old-fashioned denoters of the hour in many an old village churchyard, even in the present day. They are most commonly placed upon the south wall of the church, though sometimes they stand upon a pedestal away from the building. The Eltham sundial no longer exists.

But, the Churchyard has been the scene of practices, in the far away past, which we should regard in these days, as rather strange, and, some of them, even shocking. There are records which show that in the early English days, and even at a latter time, the Church-yard was used as a sort of Court of Justice.

"What better place than this," writes Mr. John Nicholson, "could be found in the whole township for the hearing of disputes and the settling of cases? Here, the bishop sat with the sheriff, the clerics were lawyers, where oaths could be taken on everything that was holy, and round which all a man's sacred associations clustered. The churchyard was a court of justice, but in later times, the ecclesiastical authorities discouraged the hold-ing of secular pleas in churches and church-yards."

"In 1287," continues the same writer, " a synod held at Exeter, said, 'Let not secular pleas be held in Churchyards,' but as late as 1472, we find from the York Fabric Rolls, that at Helmsley and Stamfordbrig, all the par-ishioners there hold pleas and other temporal meetings in the Church and Churchyard "

Such proceedings as these seem strange to us now. But we will notice now some that were discreditable. Though there does not seem to be any documentary evidence that these things occurred in our churchyard, there is no great reason for thinking that Eltham would have been different from other villages in this respect.

The great Church festivals were strictly ob-served in old days, and it should be remem-bered that the Church was the great centre at which people congregated on such "holy-days" These "holy-days," were really and truly "holi-days," and it seems that traders of all sorts used to assemble in the church-yards for the purpose of doing business with the people who thronged up to worship.

"At these gatherings," we are told, "dealers in all kinds of goods appeared on the scene, spread their wares on the tombstones, and could with difficulty be kept out of the sacred edifice itself. Their noisy shouting, the as-semblage of pleasure seekers, and the tumult attending such gatherings, interfered seriously with the Divine worship proceeding inside the Church."

A record, dating 1416, referring to a north-country parish, states :—"The parishioners say that a common market of vendibles is held in the Churchyard on Sundays and holidays, and divers things, and goods, and rushes are exposed there for sale, and horses stand over the bodies of the dead there buried, and defile the graves, to the great dishonour and mani-fest hindrance of Divine worship, on account of the clamour of those who stand about."

With so much disregard for the sacredness of the place it is not surprising that the Church-yard became a sort of public playground. The instructions issued to the clergy by the Synod of Exeter, to which we have already referred, gives us some idea of the prevailing state of affairs at the time. It proceeds thus :—

"We strictly enjoin our parish priests that they publicly proclaim in their Churches, that no one presume to carry on combats, dances or other improper sports in the Churchyards, especially on the eves of the feasts of saints, or stage plays or farces, by which the honour of the churches is defiled and sacred ordin-ances despised "

Yet another record says:—"It is ordered; by the consent of the parishioners, that no one use improper and prohibited sports within the Churchyard, as, for example, wrestling, football, and hand-ball, under penalty of two-pence."

"The Whitsun Ales," or "Church Ales" as they were called, were a curious custom initiated for a good purpose, but ultimately so abused that they can be fairly described as disgraceful. They were so general, and so usually connected with churchyards, that we must allude to them here; and they were so characteristic a feature of English village life, that the story of Eltham would not be complete without some notice of them.

The name "Ale" does not here refer to that well-known drink which has always been so palatable to Englishmen, even from the time when they dwelt in their stockaded villages upon the shores of the Baltic. The word really means "festival." Shakespeare uses it in this sense:

"On ember days, and holy *ales*."
Pericles I. Introduction.

Near to the church there used to stand a curious building called a "church-house." There is probably none of these in existence now. They have long since passed away, and are only met with in churchwardens' accounts. The "church-house" was a large building in which could be stored wood, lime, timber, and other articles, and it was often let to pedlars, or wandering merchants, to deposit their goods during the fair.

Within it was a long low room with a large fireplace and hearth, and down the centre of the room was a large oak table. Here it was that our ancestors established the headquarters of the "ale," the centre of village festivities, which were celebrated, sometimes, as often as four times in the year.

The antiquarian, Aubrey, has described a "church-house" in the following words:—

"In every parish was a church-house, to which belonged spits, crocks, and other utensils for dressing provisions. Here the house-keepers met. The young people were there too, and had dancing, bowling, shooting at butts, &c., the ancients sitting gravely by, and looking on."

An old writer has left us a pretty full account of how a "church ale" was conducted. So we will have the description in his own words:—

In certaine townes where dronken Bacchus beares swaie, against Christmas and Easter, Whitsondaie, or some other tymne, the churche-wardens of every parishe, with the consent of the whole parishe, provide half-a-score or twenty quarters of mault, whereof some they buy of the church stocke, and some is given them of the parishioners themselves, every one conferring somewhat, according to his abilitie; which maulte being made into very strong ale or beere, is set to sale, either in the church or some other place assigned to that purpose.

"Then when this is set abroche, well is he that can gette the soonest to it, and spend the most at it. In this kind of practice they continue sixe weekes, a quarter of a yeare, yea, halfe a yeare together. That money, they say, is to repaire their churches and chapells with, to buy bookes for service, cuppes for the celebration of the Sacrament, surplesses for St. John, and such other necessaries. And they maintaine other extraordinarie charges in their parish besides."

More details of the doings of the "Whitsun-ale" are left by another old writer.

"Two persons are chosen," he writes, "previously to the meeting to be lord and lady of the 'ale'; who dress as suitably as they can to the character they assume. A large empty barn or some such building, is provided for the lord's hall, and fitted up with seats to accommodate the company. Here they assemble to dance and regale . . . . . The lord and lady honour the hall with their presence, attended by steward, sword-bearer, purse-bearer, and mace-bearer, with their several badges and ensigns of office. They have, likewise, a train-bearer or page, and a fool or jester, drest in a party-coloured jacket. . . . The lord's music, consisting of a pipe and tabor, is employed to conduct the dance."

From a sermon preached by one William Kethe, on the 17th January, 1570, we find that it was the custom at that time for the "church-ale" to be kept on the Sabbath Day, which holy-day, said the preacher, "the multitude call their revelying day, which day is spent in bulbeating, beare-beating, bowlings, dyeyng, cardying, daunsynges, drunkennes, and other sinnes, in so much, as men could not keep their servauntes from lyinge out of theyr owne houses the same sabbath day at night."

It is not to be wondered at that "Church Ales" fell into disrepute and ultimately were discontinued altogether. It is hard to believe that such practices could have gone on in our village churchyards. But our ancestors probably satisfied their conscience by the knowledge that the proceeds of these entertainments went to the benefit of the parish, sometimes for the maintenance of the church, sometimes for the relief of the poor. There is at least one record which shows that in a Wiltshire village, Kingston St. Michael, the proceeds of the "Whitsun Ale," enabled the parish to do without a "poor rate"!

Such, then, were some of the scenes which our churchyard witnessed in other days. We may take credit to ourselves, that the making of "God's Acre" a place for merchandise is quite out of harmony with our modern ideas of the respect and reverence due to such a locality, and that the scenes which often accompanied the holding of "Whitsun Ales" would be repulsive even to the callous minded of the present generation.

So our churchyard speaks to us, whispering of the ancient dead which it embraces, and, if we will take the pains to interpret its message, revealing to us many aspects of the daily life of our ancestors which, now, seem strange and unfamiliar.

CHAPTER XI.

SOME OLD-TIME BURIAL CUSTOMS.

We are all familiar with the ceremony of burial as it is performed now, so impressive in its simplicity and solemnity. Many of the customs connected with that ceremony are of great antiquity.

For instance, there is the custom of following the corpse, in procession, to the grave. This is of ancient origin, and is said to have been practised by the heathen. An ancient writer says:—

"In burials, the old Rite was that the ded Corps was borne afore, and the people folowed after, as one should saie we shall dye and folowe after hym, as their laste woordes to the corpse did pretende. For thei used too saie, when it was buried, on this wise, farewell, wee come after thee, and of the folowyng of the multitude thei were called Exequies."

Another writer says: "The Christian observance of the custom is founded upon the same reason as the heathen; and as this form of procession is an emblem of our dying shortly after our friend, so the carrying in our hands of ivy, sprigs of laurel, rosemary, and other evergreens, is an emblem of the soul's immortality."

Then there is the custom of dressing in black at funerals. This too, is of very early origin, although the custom was not universal.

"Black," wrote the "Athenian Oracle," "is the fittest emblem of that sorrow and grief the mind is supposed to be clouded with; and as Death is the privation of Life, and Black a privation of Light, it is very probable this colour has been chosen to denote sadness, upon that account; and accordingly this colour has, for mourning, been preferred by most people throughout Europe. The Syrians, Cappadocians, and Armenians use sky-colour, to denote the place they wish the dead to be in, that is, the Heavens; the Egyptians yellow, or fillemot, to shew that as herbs being faded become yellow, so Death is the end of human hope; and the Ethiopians grey, because it resembles the colour of the earth, which receives the dead."

As evidence that "black" was not altogether general even in heathen times, Polydore Vergil refers to Plutarch thus: "Plutarch writeth that the women in their mournyng laid aparte all purple, gold, and sumptuous apparell, and were clothed, bothe they and their kinsfolk, in white apparel, like as then the ded body was wrapped in white clothes. The white colour was thought fittest for the ded, because it is clere, pure, and sincer, and least defiled. Of this ceremonie, as I take it, the French Quenes toke occasion, after the death of their housebandes the Kynges, to weare only white clothyng, and, if there bee any such widdowe, she is commonly called the White Quene. Mournyng garments for the moste part be altogether of blacke colour, and they are to wear them a whole yere continually, onlesse it bee because of a generall triumphe or rejoysyng, or newe magistrate choosyng, or else when thei bee toward marriage."

If you peruse the wills of those who have been buried in or about our Parish church, you will find frequent allusions to "lights" and "tapers" in association with their burial. For instance:—

In 1468, Richard Tottnam left provision for 2lbs. of wax, and also for a torch to burn before the image of St. John the Baptist.

In the same year William Goffe left 8d each towards four lights in the church

In 1477, John Frances, yeoman, provided for two tapers of 5lbs. each

In 1484, John Adene, husbandman, not only left 8d to the light attached to the great beam before the Crucifix, but he also made provision for a torch of 8s. to burn in the Church of Eltham, around the bodies of six dead parishioners

In 1519 Ralf Wotton left means for his wife Joan to burn a taper before the image of St. Christopher during her life time, and to deliver to the churchwardens enough to continue the same for ever.

These are but a few instances Many more might be found were it necessary They refer to the old custom of lights at burials, which has now practically died out The custom was intended as a mark of honour to the dead, and to have a great number of such lights was a special mark of honour The torches and the wax to make them were usually provided by the churchwardens, and the sale of these articles was a source of profit to the church

The antiquary, Brand, commenting upon this practice, says —

"The custom of using torches and lights at funerals, or in funeral processions, seems to be of long standing The Romans anciently solemnised their funerals at night with torches, to give notice of their approach, so that they might not come in the way of their magistrates and priests, whose sanctity was supposed to be violated by the sight of a corpse, insomuch that an expiatory sacrifice was required to purify them before they could perform their sacred functions In later times public funerals were celebrated in the day time, not without the addition of torches, private funerals continuing to be restricted to the night

"Coming down to Christian times," he continues, "the learned Gregory maintains the harmless import of candles, as shewing that the departed souls are not quite put out, but, having walked on earth as children of the light, are now gone to walk before God in the light of the living "

The practice of "lights" is still carried out in the Roman Catholic churches in England, but in the Church of England the custom has died out

In the earliest days of Eltham, the method of interment was somewhat different from that used at the present day In the Christian period of Anglo-Saxon times, they did not use coffins of wood, which are a fashion of the last few centuries, but resorted to the simple process of wrapping the corpse in linen Thus concealed, it was carried to the grave by two persons, one of them holding the head, the other the feet. The body was then "censed " by the priest, who offered up prayers and benedictions while it was being lowered into the grave

On the occasion of the burial of an important person, the ceremonial was more imposing The priests would attend in a body, and sing hymns while walking solemnly in procession

We may rightly imagine such scenes as these in the early history of Eltham, for, as we have already said, there is every probability that this ancient churchyard existed as a burial ground long before the Anglo-Saxon period of history came to an end.

In later centuries, stone coffins were sometimes used for those who could afford them As we have already pointed out, a coffin of this kind was actually found when the builders were digging for the foundations of the present church It is built into the wall at the basement of the tower, and is visible just inside the south door, on the right hand side You may identify it by the large stone cross which had been engraven upon it

Then it was customary, in olden times, to bury within the church itself. In many of the wills of Eltham people who died in ancient days, we find instructions for their burial in the church.

Henry Shylman, 1526, wished to be buried "in the chauncell of the parish church of Saynt John Baptist in Eltham "

Sir Philip Carrok, 1527, left instructions that he was to be buried "in the Church of Saynt John Baptist in Eltham, where as I am now

Vicar in the chauncell at the pwe or sets ende."

In 1494, Richard Pemberton willed that he should be buried "in the Churche of Saynt Joone Bapte in Eltham afore our lady of Pyte (Pity), and to the light of our lady of Pytei xxd."

Many more such instances might easily be found. But the practice was stopped, within the memory of man, by act of Parliament. In most old churches we may find brasses, flat stones, and other indications of the position of such burial places. We can point to nothing of this kind in our present church, as the structure is comparatively new, and though built upon the site of the old church, the exact position of the tombs within the edifice has been lost.

When a person dies, we still have a custom of tolling a bell, which is usually called the "Passing Bell." This is a relic of a very ancient practice, but the bell, strictly speaking, is not the "Passing Bell." We now ring the bell *after* the person has died. In the days of old Eltham, the bell was rung just before death. It was, therefore, called the "Passing Bell," because it notified that a person was "passing" out of the state of life into death.

From an Order issued in the seventh year of Elizabeth we find the following notice:—

"When anye Christian Bodie is *in passing*, that *the Bell be tolled*, and that the Curate be speciallie called for to comforte the sicke person; and *after the time of his possing*, to ring no more, but one short peale; and one before the Buriall, and another short peale after the Buriall."

But the custom was observed long before the time of Queen Elizabeth. In fact, Bede alludes to it in his Ecclesiastical History. From him we learn that the bell should be tolled *before* the person's departure, that good men might give him their prayers. If these prayers do no good to the departing sinner, it is added, they at least shew the disinterested charity of the person who offers them.

There is an old English proverb alluding to this bell which is widely known :—

"When thou dost hear a Toll or Knell,
    Then think upon Thy Passing Bell."

It is easy to believe how, in the dark ages, when ignorance was wide spread, all sorts of superstitions were associated with the "Passing Bell." There were some who believed that the mere ringing of the bell "was helpful to the passage of the soul."

"The Passing Bell," says Grose, "was anciently rung for two purposes: one to bespeak the prayers of all good Christians for a soul just departing; the other *to drive away the evil spirits who stood at the bed's foot, and about the House, ready to seize their prey, or at least to molest and terrify the soul in its passage;* but by the ringing of that bell (for Durandus informs us that Evil Spirits are much afraid of bells), they were kept aloof; and the soul, like a hunted hare, gained the start, or had what is by sportsmen called law.

"Hence, perhaps, exclusive of the additional labour, was occasioned the high price for tolling the greatest bell of the Church; for that, *being louder, the Evil Spirits must go farther off to be clear of its sound, by which the poor soul got so much the start of them:* besides, being heard further off, it would procure the dying man a greater number of prayers."

It is most probable that the true purpose of the Passing Bell was to enable those who heard it to offer a prayer for a "passing soul." You will therefore see how inappropriate it is to describe the bell which we now ring immediately after death, as the "Passing Bell."

The antiquity of the custom is further shewn by the writings of Durandus, who lived in the twelfth century. He sets forth details of the ringing, which are interesting.

"When anyone is dying, bells must be tolled that the people may put up their prayers; twice for a woman and thrice for a man, if for a Clergyman, as many times as he had Orders, and at the conclusion a peal on all the bells, to distinguish the quality of the person for whom the people are put to their prayers. A bell, too, must be rung while the corpse is conducted to church, and during the bringing of it out of the church to the grave."

There are many other customs, curious and interesting, followed by our forefathers, in connection with the solemn function of the burial of the dead. But those we have considered briefly, are sufficient, perhaps, to enable you to catch a glimpse of Eltham life and habits when, in those far-off days, they brought their dead for interment in this old churchyard.

CHAPTER XII.

SOME DISTINGUISHED DEAD (1).

It is the dust of a great multitude which is mingled here with earth. Eltham folk—men, women, children, of all times, of all sorts and conditions, lie beneath this green grass; many and varied were their callings. Knights, warriors, courtiers, divines, yeomen, churls, serfs, all have been brought here at the last. They may have led active and strenuous lives. Their hopes, ambitions, disappointments, sorrows, were such as we know ourselves, for human emotions and passions have been the same in all ages. They may have lived in love or in enmity one with the other; by their words and works they may have added to the joys of their village community, or have contributed to its sorrows; they may have been brave and industrious, or idle and good-for-nothing; the philanthropic, the virtuous, the wayward, the mischievous, they have all lived their little day, even as we are living ours, and then, by the hand of remorseless Death have been duly gathered in to the abode of silence.

In a few cases, loving friends have set up stones to their memory, graving their names thereon, setting forth their virtues. But writing, even upon stone, becomes defaced by age, the stones themselves crumble away, and the names are soon forgotten.

In the later centuries we may find the names of the buried recorded in books. We may scan these lists, but it is little that we know of the individuals, except in the case of the few whose works have lived for awhile after them. Of the great host we can gleam nothing beyond the name.

There are a few instances where something is said of them which excites our interest, and

our imagination is stimulated by the little glimpse which we get thereby of the times in which they lived.

On August 28th, 1799, John Saunders, late coachman to the King, was buried here, having died at the advanced age of 89 years. The King at this time was George III., and it is quite likely that, in his declining years, good master John Saunders had many a good story for his neighbours concerning King George and his German Consort, Queen Charlotte.

In 1603, "One Will Bromeland, *alias* Bromfield," was interred under rather harsh conditions. He was a servant of Sir William Roper, who lived at Well Hall—in the mansion some remains of which still exist near the moat. From the old Parish Register we learn that wayward Will Bromeland was "excommunicated for not coming to churche, and was buried by soom of his fellowes in Caulves garden the 26th of October, and taken up by them the 28th of the same moneth, and then coffened and carried to Kedbroke, where was no chappel this many a yere, and there lyeth."

From which we may learn that regular Church going was very rigorously enforced in those days. Woe to the individual who neglected it. You may be sure that the circumstances attending the burying of Will Bromeland, who, you will observe, found not a place in this churchyard, gave rise to much serious talk and wagging of wise heads among Eltham folk at the time.

Then there was "Old Battan," as the register calls him, who was buried on March 19th, 1620. He, too, was excommunicated, although we are not told why. However, he found his resting place here, for he was "buried at the permission of Doctor Pope, Chancellor to the right reverend father in God, the Lord Bushop of Rochester."

In 1603, we are told that, that "three servants of Sir William Roper died of the plague." This, of course, was not the great plague so well remembered in history. That occurred some sixty years later. "The plague" recorded in the Register at this date was probably some kind of malignant fever. Medical knowledge was of a very crude kind in the seventeenth century, even at its close, and one form of disease was easily confused with another. There were many other deaths in Eltham at the time from the same disease.

On November 24th, 1615, we learn that "Hester Ashfield was buried, being an excommunicated person, in the churchyard, according to ye lxvii cannon therin provided." One may there find, perhaps, what was the sin of poor Hester that such a fate awaited her body after death.

We are told that it was on May 1st, 1621, there was buried "Master Cornelius Orts, a Hollander, servaunt unto the King, for providing haukes under Sir Anthony Pell." The King was James I., who would ride out to Eltham on sporting expeditions. Hawking was a great form of sport with the Court in those days, lords and ladies fair taking part in it. No doubt Master Cornelius Orts was a pretty well-known figure at the Royal hawkings. But, notice that his funeral was on May-day, which was a national holiday, devoted to maypole dancing and other pastimes, and in every village there was merriment. There was a tinge of sorrow, doubtless, that day in Eltham, for, following the merriment of the May-day morn, there came the solemn tolling of Master Orts' funeral bell.

There is just one more that we must notice. It is the entry regarding Roger Twist, who was buried on September 23rd, 1612, and is described as a recusant, about whom the register says that he was "excommunicated and com from Rome and repenting earnestly and hastely desired of the bisshop absolution and to be received into the Church of God, departed this lyfe after he had received ye comfortable absolution within five houers after."

We are not told the particular form of recusancy for which unstable Roger Twist was given this term of reproach. It was enacted in the reign of Elizabeth that a fine of twelve pence should be imposed on every one absenting himself from church or chapel (of course, those of the Establishment), without reasonable excuse. There were four classes of recusants. There were the Simple Recusants, who absented themselves but managed to escape conviction. "But sith our Church him disciplined so sore, He, rank *recusant* came to Church no more."

There was the Recusant who had been convicted, also the Papist Recusant who would refuse to acknowledge the King as head of the Church, and the Popish Recusant convict. Protestant Dissenters were relieved from the penalties of recusancy by the Act of Toleration in the time of William and Mary. In the reign of George III the "Catholic Relief Act" was passed, which relieved the Roman Catholics. But in 1844, the Recusancy Statute itself was repealed.

The name of Shaw takes a prominent place in the burial records of Eltham, during the seventeenth, eighteenth, and nineteenth centuries. The family possessed a vault which was constructed beneath the church on the north side. The Parish Register records a rather unfortunate incident in connection with the building of this family vault. This is the extract —

"That while the workmen were digging to make the vault under Sir John Shaw's aisle, he having obtained a faculty for building the said aisle on the north side of the Church, the roof of the great aisle in the Church fell down by reason of the carelessness of the workmen in not shoring up the roof, upon St. Bartholomew's Day, June 24th, 1667, which with the pulpit and pews were rebuilt at the cost of the said John Shaw."

It will be noticed that the clerk who made this entry has confused St. Bartholomew's Day with that of St. John Baptist, the patronal Saint.

No. 40.

THE OLD VICARAGE AS SEEN FROM WHAT IS NOW SHERARD ROAD.

In the distance the Church. On the right the old "Chequers Inn." (Date 1833.)
The old shops on the immediate right are still in existence.

No. 41.

VIEW OF STREET LEADING TO THE OLD CHURCH,

Showing the old "Chequers Inn" (Date 1870).
On the left hand the railing, etc., of the old Vicarage field.

SIR JOHN SHAW.

As the family of Shaw, who were descended from Sir Edmund Shaw, Lord Mayor of London in 1382, were associated with Eltham for nearly two centuries and played a prominent part in its history, we may well regard the founder of the Eltham family, who was buried beneath the old church, as one of our distinguished dead. Let us, therefore, briefly recall his history.

Mr. John Shaw was a banker in the time of the Commonwealth, and he carried on business in London and in Antwerp. When Prince Charles, the son of the unhappy Charles I., was living in exile in Brussels and Antwerp, he had the good fortune to meet with the rich banker, who relieved the poverty-oppressed Prince by a loan of money.

In the course of time, the Prince was offered the Crown of his father, and returned to England as Charles II. Then it was that Mr. John Shaw was made the recipient of royal favours, apparently upon the principle "that one good turn deserves another." He was made a baronet, and was trusted with so many offices of State that Pepys, the diarist, has left on record that he was "a miracle of a man, holding more offices than any man in England."

Amongst his many duties were those of surveyor of the King's woods and trustee of the lands of the Queen.

Eltham was one of the royal estates, and, attracted, no doubt, by its delightful position, as well as by its proximity to the metropolis, Sir John was desirous of acquiring it for his own use. The result was that he was granted the lease of the manor for himself and heirs, for ever, on condition that they renewed the lease from time to time and paid certain fines that were duly set out in the document.

The manor embraced the land from South End of Horne Park, Lee, together with the old Palace, and all the rights of fishing, hawking, hunting, &c. The rental was £9 per annum, together with 20 shillings for the old house, and a "fine" of £3,700.

From the Eltham Registers we find that on June 24th, 1663, which must have been soon after his acquisition of the Eltham lease, Sir John was married to Lady Bridget, the widow of Viscount Killmurray. This was his second wife.

His lease carried with it building rights, and about this time he was proceeding with the erection of the large house now standing in the Park, and at present occupied by the Eltham Golf Club.

At this mansion, Sir John lived the life of a country gentleman, visited from time to time by his friends of the metropolis, including, at least on one occasion, King Charles II. himself. The old baronet has left behind him a good name, notwithstanding the fact that he lived at a period when wild and dissolute living was the fashion.

On the one hand, we have been told by Bishop Morley that he was "a very zealous Churchman." On the other, Samuel Pepys has declared him to have been "a very grave and fine gentleman, and very good company."

He died at the age of 80 years, March 1st, 1679, and he was interred in the vault which he had had built beneath the church, and where rest many other members of his family.

Among the distinguished members of the Shaw family is the Rev. John Kenward Shaw Brooke, who was for the long period of sixty years Vicar of Eltham. He died on December 16th, 1849, in the 82nd year of his age. He was beloved in Eltham for his good works, and on the occasion of his jubilee in 1833, there were great rejoicings in the village. He left a bequest for the benefit of our schools. There is an oil painting of the old Vicar at the Church, which was presented to him by his parishioners on the occasion of his jubilee. An engraving from this picture hangs in our school.

The members of the Shaw family who have been interred in the great family vault beneath the church are :—

EAST SIDE.

Dame Margery Shaw, late wife of Sir John Shaw, Bart., died 2nd August, 1690.

Sr John Peake, Knt and Alderman of London Died 2nd June, 1688

Sr John Shaw, Knight and Bait Died 1st March, 1679, aged 80 years

Mrs Elizth Shaw Died 24th April, 1693

Dame Elizth Shaw Died February, 1750, in the 24th year of her age

Sr. Jn. Shaw, Bart, Collector of his Majesty's Customs of the Port of London Died December 8th, 1721 Aged 63.

Sarah Lady Shaw, Late wife of Sr John Shaw, of Eltham, Bart., died ye 2nd Jan'y, 1742 (3)

John Shaw, Esq, Eldest Son of Sr. John Shaw, Bart, died 16th May, MDCCLXI, in the 11th year of his age

Lewis James Shaw, Esq, died 15th May, 1807, in the 14th year of his age.

Dame Judith Peake (Relict of Sir Jno Peake, Knt, late Lord Mayor of ye City of London), died ye 10th Jan'y, 1723 (4), in ye 81st year of her age

Dame Anne Maria Seaw, died 29th Nov'r, 1755, in the 58th year of her age

The Right Hon'ble Bridget, Viscountess of Kilmurry Died 7th July, 1696

Dame Martha Shaw Relict of Sr Jno Shaw, Bart, died Oct'r 28th, 1794, in the 64th year of her age

Sr John Shaw, Bart Died 18 June, 1779, in the 51st year of his age

Sr John Shaw, Bart Died 4th March, 1738 (9), aged 53 years

The Son of Sir John Shaw, Bart, and Dame Martha April 2nd, 1755

Mastr Jno Barnardiston Shaw Died 4th December, 1757, aged 4 mo & 6 dys.

Theodosia Shaw, daughter of Sir Jno Gregy Shaw, Bart, and the Hon Dame Tha. Mar died Feb'y 3rd, 1785, aged 9 ms & 14 dys.

Theodosia Martha Shaw, daughter of Sr. Jno Gregy Shaw, Bart, and the Honble Dame Theoa Margt, born April 28th, 1792, died June 11th, 1794

Vincit Qui Patitur Sir John Gregory Shaw, Bart., Died 28 Oct, 1831 Aged 75 years

The Right Honble Theodosea Baroness Dowager Monson, relict of John, the 2nd Baron Monson, died Feby 20th, 1821, in the 96th year of her age.

The Honorable Dame Theodosia Margaret Shaw Died 24 Oct'r, 1847, aged 85 years.

Miss Emma Grace Hawley Died 18th May, 1819, aged 5 mons

John Shaw, Died Octr 30th, aged 2 weeks, 1717

Two small coffins without inscriptions

WEST SIDE

The Honble Mab Phil Mohun Died 31st Augst, 1703

The Honble. Mary Needham Died 31st August, 1701, in the 39th year of her age.

Mrs Sarah Gwilt. Eldest daughter of Wm Shaw, Esq, and relict of John Gwilt, of Cheshunt, Herts, Esq, died July 5th, 1784, aged 62 years

Mrs Elizth Shaw, wife of Wm Shaw, Esq, died Decr. 28, 1758, in the 58th year of her age

Wm Shaw, Esq, eldest son of Sr Jno Shaw, Bart, by Sarah, his 2nd wife, died Feby 5th, 1767, aged 70.

Mary Shaw, spinster Died 10th May, 1768 Aged 65

Paggen Shaw, Esq Died 23rd Augst, 1770 Aged 70

Mrs Camilla Shaw Ob. 30 Decr, 1759, Ætat 35

Mr Jno Parker Died 16th Oct, 1720, aged 24

Wm. Smith, M D, Died 28th Mar, 1744, aged 33 yrs

Sarah, the wife of Wm Smith, Esq, eldest daughter of Sr Jno Shaw, Bart., by Dame Margy, his wife, died July 22nd, 1722. Ætat 35

Mrs Elizth Ram Died Sept 3rd, 1760, in the 71st year of her age

Jno Shaw, Esq, eldest son of Wm Shaw, Esq., died May 2nd, 1772 Aged 51

Mrs Ann Trons. Died 3rd Jany, 1775, aged 66 years

Mrs Jane Jackson Died 11th Dec'r, 1767. Aged 61

Eliz'h, 2nd daughter of Wm Shaw, Esqr, died 14th Oct, 1769

Wm Hughes Died 26th Deo'r, 1786, aged 13 years.

Wm Hughes, Esqr Died 21st April, 1786, aged 36 years.

Frances Anne Shaw Died 11 Dec'r, 1872 Aged 84 yrs

The Revd John Kenward Shaw Brooke Died 16th Decr, 1840, in the 82nd year of his age.

AUGUSTA ANNE SHAW. Died 15 June, 1833. Aged 42 yrs.

CHARLES SHAW, Esqr., Captain of the Royal Navy. Ob. 2nd May, 1829, aged 43 years.

ANNE MARIA CHARLOTTE SHAW (daughter of the late Charles Shaw, Esq., R.N.), died 15th Jany., 1840, aged 11 years 11 months.

In a letter written by the Queen of Bohemia from the Hague, to Mr. Secretary Nicholas, Sept. 29, 1654, an interesting comment is made upon one of the ladies who now sleeps in this Eltham vault. The Queen writes:—

"Phil. Mohun is here; she is fled from England, fearing to be imprisoned by Cromwell. She's verie good company and talkes verie freely but handsomlie."

The honourable lady is believed to have been a maid of honour to the Queen of Bohemia. The allusion throws a vivid flash of light upon those troublous times. (Note Evelyn's Diary. Ed. 1895. Vol. iv., page 212.)

HELMETS, 1675.

Ne Sutor ultra
Crepidam

THOMAS DOGGET DANCING THE "CHESHIRE ROUND."
(This picture is taken from the original and only contemporary Print of the famous Actor).

CHAPTER XIII.

SOME DISTINGUISHED DEAD (2).

We will continue in this chapter some further observations upon the distinguished dead who found a resting place in the old churchyard or beneath the old church of Eltham.

THOMAS DOGGET (Comedian),
Interred in the Parish Vault, Sept. 27th, 1721.

The parish register records that the churchwardens received the customary fee for interment of Thomas Dogget in the church. Although Dogget was a capable comedian and a highly respectable and respected gentleman in his day, his name would not have been any more familiar to us now-a-days than that of the other capable comedians and respectable gentlemen of his time if he had not been an ardent politician. He lived at a time when political controversy raged round questions associated with the Hanoverian succession. Dogget was a very pronounced Whig, so pronounced, indeed, that he set by a sum of money to endow an annual waterman's race upon the Thames in memory of the advent of the Hanoverian kings, and it is really this waterman's race which has made Dogget's name so distinguished. How many of the people who flock to this annual event have any idea who and what Dogget was, and why he instituted and endowed the contest for the "Dogget Coat and Badge?" This race comes off every year on the 1st of August, or as near to that date as the conditions of the tide will allow. The course of the highly-popular race is from London Bridge to Chelsea, on the top of an ebb tide. The contest is usually keen, and is witnessed by large crowds.

Now, although Thomas Dogget was really an Irishman by birth, we may fairly claim him as one of our Eltham worthies, for, not only was he buried here, but he had lived amongst the Eltham people for years, and had married the grand-daughter of old Dr Owen, the Vicar of Eltham at the time.

Dogget was a man of mark in his day. He was a distinguished actor and also an author of plays. He played at Old Drury, and so original was he at his art that Congreve, the dramatist, wrote plays to suit his particular style. He also shared in the management of Drury, along with Wilks and Colley Cibber The latter has said of him that "Dogget was the most of an original and the strictest observer of nature of all his contemporaries, he was a pattern to others, whose greatest merit it was that they sometimes tolerably imitated him "

Anthony Ashton, a companion of Dogget, has left behind a little word portrait of our comedian which is worth reading It runs thus "Dogget, in person, was a lively little man, in behaviour, modest, cheerful and complaisant, he sang in company very agreeably, and in public very comically, he danced the Cheshire round full well as Captain George I travelled with him in his strolling company, and found him a man of very good sense, but illiterate, for he wrote me word thus 'Sir, I will have a *hole* share,' instead of a *whole* share. He dressed neat, and something fine— in plain cloth coat and a brocaded waistcoat. While I travelled with him each sharer kept his horse, and was everywhere respected as a gentleman "

From this we may picture in our mind's eye Thomas Dogget going to Eltham church on a Sunday morning, decked out in his brocaded waistcoat, knee breeches, and shoes with shiny buckles, looking every inch a gentleman. We may, perhaps, picture the jolly little man making an occasional call at The King's Arms, or one of the other old Eltham hostelries, and there, to the old gossips of the village, retailing, with rare wit, tales from his storehouse of jests, to their great amusement and edification

But Dogget was a strong party politician Sir Richard Steel, the friend of Addison, used to say that "Dogget was a Whig up to his very ears " It was, therefore, no great wonder

that he endowed the race which was to keep in memory the accession of George I

We are told that Dogget made a fortune, and retired to the pretty country village of Eltham to enjoy it.

SIR WILLIAM JAMES

Sir William James was interred here on December 22nd, 1783 His death had occurred under very painful circumstances, for he died quite suddenly on the occasion of the festivities in connection with the marriage of his daughter at Park Farm-place.

Sir William was a distinguished sailor of his day "He was born at Milford Haven in 1721, went to sea at the age of 12 years, and commanded a ship when he was twenty He served under Sir Edward Hawke, in the West Indies in 1738 While in the command of a trading ship he was captured by the Spaniards in the Gulf of Florida After being released, he suffered shipwreck in a storm, and, with seven of his crew, endured great hardships for twenty days in a small boat, Mr James's snuff-box serving to measure each man's daily allowance of water They drifted back to Cuba, whence they had parted from the Spaniards, and were received by them back again into captivity

The East India Company afterwards employed the gallant captain as commander of the Guardian, in suppressing piracy on the Malabar Coast Acting as convoy to seventy trading vessels, he was attacked by Angria, the pirate, and a large fleet of frigates, which he beat off

In 1751, he was appointed Commander-in-chief of the East India Company's marine forces, and, on April 2nd, 1755, he captured Severndroog, the chief fortress of the pirate Angria.

In 1756 he captured a French ship, his superior in men and guns, and carried her to Bombay; and in 1757 he showed his nautical skill by navigating a vessel through a contrary monsoon, and conveying 500 troops to Admiral Watson and Colonel Clive, and the intelligence of the outbreak of the war with France The capture of the chief French settlement, Chandenagore, was the result of this piece of seamanship.

Captain James returned to England in 1759, and the East India Company presented him with a handsome gold-hilted sword. He was chosen a director of the Company, and remained in that office for twenty years.

For fifteen years he was Deputy-Master of Trinity House; he was also a Governor of

feet high, or in all, 140 feet higher than St. Paul's, and was constructed from the design of Mr. Jupp.

It consists of three stages; on each of the upper stories is a room with two smaller rooms adjoining, and neatly fitted up. At one time its vestibule was ornamented with armour and trophies taken at Severndroog, whence its name, "Severndroog Castle."

HILT OF PRESENTATION SWORD TO SIR WILLIAM JAMES.

Greenwich Hospital, and Member of Parliament for West Looe. As a testimonial for his skill in planning the reduction of Pondicherry he was presented by the East India Company with a rich service of plate.

He rebuilt the house in Eltham, and gave it the name of Park Farm Place. He was created a baronet in May, 1778."

The tower which we see yonder peeping out from among the trees was erected by his widow, Dame James, in memory of her distinguished husband. This interesting landmark is of triangular form. It stands sixty

"This far-seen monumental tower
   Records the achievements of the brave,
And Angria's subjugated power,
   Who plundered on the eastern wave."
                          ROBERT BLOOMFIELD.

The body of the deceased baronet was, in the first place, interred within the parish vault beneath the church, but was subsequently removed by his widow.

DAME JAMES.

Buried in the family vault, August 9th, 1798, aged 56 years.

Dame James is a household word in Eltham, by reason of the charity which is called by her name She was the daughter and heiress of Edward Goddard, of Hartham, Wilts, and became the wife of Sir William James.

Their only son, Sir Edward William James, of Eltham, Bart , died, unmarried, November 16th, 1752, at the age of 18. Their only daughter Elizabeth Anne, married Lord Ranchffe in 1795 It was on the occasion of this marriage that the sad death of Sir William took place

We find that Dame James obtained a faculty to erect a tomb in the churchyard for the exclusive use of her family, and she was empowered to have removed from the parish vault and placed in the new tomb the bodies of her cousin, Brigadier General Thomas Goddard, her husband, Sir William James, her father, Edward Goddard, her son, Sir Edward William James, and her child who had died at birth This tomb may be seen in the churchyard

Dame James left a legacy of £500, the interest of which was to be distributed in coal to the poor inhabitants of Eltham some day in December before the 14th of that month.

LADY RANCLIFFE
Buried on Jan 28th, 1797

This lady, the only daughter of Sir William and Dame Anne James, whose married life began under such tragic circumstances, was exceedingly beautiful The artist, Hoppner, painted a three-quarter length portrait of her, and this was engraved by Wilkin in 1795

Her son, the last peer, died in 1850 One of her daughters, Maria Charlotte, married, first in 1817, the Marquess de Choiseul, and secondly, in 1824, the Prince de Polignac, Ministers of Charles X , the King of France

The parish register informs us that Lady Ranchffe was buried at Eltham with great pomp She was only 31 years of age

CHAPTER XIV

SOME DISTINGUISHED DEAD (3).

BISHOP HORNE.

On the north side of the church, within a few yards of the chancel door, are two square tombs, each surmounted by an urn, and surrounded by iron railings On the larger of these tombs, and upon the side facing the church, will be found the following record —

Here lie Interred
The earthly Remains of
The Right Reverend George Horne, D D
Many years President of Magdalen College in
Oxford,
Dean of Canterbury
and late Bishop of Norwich,
In whose Character
Depth of Learning, Brightness of Imagination
Sanctity of Manners, and Sweetness of Temper
Were united beyond the usual lot of Mortality
With his Discourses from the Pulpit, his
Hearers
Whether of the University, the City, or the
Country Parish
were edified and delighted
His Commentary on the Psalms will continue
to be
a Companion to the Closet
Till the Devotion of Earth shall end in the
Hallelujah of Heaven
Having patiently suffered under such
Infirmities
as seemed not due to his years
His Soul took its flight from this vale of misery
To the unspeakable loss of the Church of
England
and his sorrowing friends and admirers
Janry. 17th, 1792, in the 62nd year of his age.

This warmly expressed eulogy, though written by one   ʾy   ɟ   ! ı ᵗ   ⸗ ⁻y

associated with the good Bishop, and at the time of recent bereavement, when we are apt to dwell upon the virtues of those of whom we are bereft, is not by any means an over statement of the excellent qualities of this distinguished divine   History speaks well of him, who, a man of ripe scholarship, of consistent life, of singular gentleness of character, was revered by his contemporaries, and was a force for good in the land.

He had no official connection with Eltham, but he married the daughter of Philip Burton, Esq , of Eltham House—the dwelling which is now the residence of Dr St John—and that was how it came to pass that he found a resting place in our churchyard, close to the adjoining tomb already referred to, which is that of the Burton family.

George Horne was born at Otham, near Maidstone, on November 1st, 1730, and was the son of Samuel Horne, who was rector of the parish. He received his early education from his father, and so great was his progress under parental tuition, that when, at the age of thirteen years, he was presented for admission to the Maidstone Grammar School, the head master, the Rev Deodatus Bye, was surprised that he should seek to enter the school when he was fit enough to leave it.

At the age of sixteen, he won a "Maidstone Scholarship" at University College, Oxford, where he matriculated in March, 1745-6

It was during his undergraduate course that he became first acquainted with William Jones, who was destined to become, in future years, his chaplain and also biographer. Among other   r   ıᵗ ƒrıⁱ ɟᵉ ₒᵗ ᵗ   Ⲧ‿ıveɪ ıty werᵉ Charles

Jenkinson, afterwards Earl of Liverpool, and John Moore, who became Archbishop of Canterbury

He graduated B.A in October, 1749, and was elected to a Kentish Fellowship at Magdalen College in 1750 Here he spent the greater part of his life He graduated M A in 1752, and was ordained by the Bishop of Oxford in 1753 He was made junior Proctor in 1758, and in 1768 was elected "President of Magdalen"

From 1771 to 1781 he was Chaplain in Ordinary to the King (George III) In 1776 he became Vice-Chancellor of the University, an office which brought him into direct contact with Lord North, who was Chancellor of the University at the time

His biographer says—"With two such friends as Lord Liverpool and Lord North, and with his own intrinsic merits, he was clearly marked out for preferment. Accordingly, in 1781, he was made Dean of Canterbury" On receiving this appointment, he intended to resign his presidentship of Magdalen, and to take up his abode permanently in Kent But he was persuaded from this course of action, and submitted to the unsettled life of a pilgrim between the two situations of his college and his deanery. We are told that "with everything that lay between Oxford and Canterbury he was acquainted, but with little else besides"

In 1788 his health seems to have broken down prematurely, but in June, 1790, after some hesitation on this account, he accepted the Bishopric of Norwich He held this important post but a short time His health grew worse, and while on a journey to Bath he suffered a paralytic stroke, from which he never fully recovered He died at Bath on January 17th, 1792, whence his remains were brought to Eltham for interment

There is a marble tablet to his memory on a pillar on the north side of the choir in Norwich Cathedral

It was in 1709 that he married the daughter of Philip Burton, of Eltham, and three daughters were the result of the union

The Dictionary of National Biography, from which most of these notes are taken, commenting upon the life and work of Bishop Horne, says —

"Like many earnest men of the day, Horne fell under the imputation of Methodism. He adopted the views of John Hutchinson (1674-1737), and wrote in his defence, although he disagreed with that theologian in his fanciful interpretations of Hebrew etymology.

"Hutchinsonianism had some points in common with Methodism, notably its intense appreciation of Holy Scripture, and its insistence upon spiritual religion But Horne was distinctly what would now be called a High Churchman, and he publicly protested from the University pulpit against those who took their theology from the Tabernacle and the Foundry, instead of from the great divines of the church.

"Nevertheless, apart from his position as a Hutchinsonian, Horne personally shewed a sympathy with the Methodists He strongly disapproved of the expulsion of the Methodist students from St Edmund's Hall, Oxford

"He would not have John Wesley, an ordained minister of the Church of England, forbidden to preach in his diocese, and John Wesley thoroughly appreciated his action

"Horne was an active promoter of the Naval and Military Bible Society, which was founded in 1780 Towards the close of his life he espoused the cause of the Scottish Bishops, who, in 1789, came up to London to petition Parliament for the relief from penalties under which they had long suffered"

As might be expected from a man of such learning and intellectual vigour, he wrote a great deal, and issued many pamphlets upon theological and other subjects

We are told that from an early age he wrote against such antagonists as Newton, Hume, Adam Smith, and William Law, "all of whom he ludicrously under-rated"

His chief works are.—

(1) "A Fair, Candid, and Impartial Statement of the Case between Sir Isaac Newton and Mr Hutchinson," 1753.

Of this work, his friend and biographer, Mr Jones, says "Toward Sir Isaac the great merit of having settled laws and rules in natural philosophy, but, at the same time, he claimed for Mr. Hutchinson the discovery of the true physiological causes by which, under the power of the Creator, the natural world was moved and directed."

(2) "Cautions to the readers of Mr. Law, and with very few varieties to the Readers of Baron Swedenborg," 1758

(3) "A View of Mr Kennicott's Method of Correcting the Hebrew Text," 1760

(4) "A Letter to Dr. Adam Smith," 1777.

(5) "Letters on Infidelity."

(6) "Answer to Dr Clayton's Essay on Spirit "

(7) "Commentary on the Psalms," 1771.

"A Defence of the Divinity of Christ," which he proposed to write, in answer to Dr. Priestly, was not accomplished, on account of his illness and subsequent death.

The great work of his life was his "Commentary on the Psalms," which took him twenty years to write, and he tells us in his well-written preface to the work that it proved to him a most delightful occupation The "Commentary," which is partly explanatory and partly devotional, proceeds upon the principle that most of the Psalms are more or less Messianic, and cannot be properly understood, unless in relation to the Messiah

Dr. Richard Mant has transferred the preface almost en bloc to the pages of his annotated "Book of Common Prayer "

Hannah More, of whom Bishop Horne was a great friend, and who was in Bath at the time of his fatal illness, was much attracted by the "sweet and devout spirit" of the "Commentary "

Another work of a similar character was "Considerations on the Life and Death of St John the Baptist," 1769. This work was an expansion of a sermon preached by Dr. Horne on St John the Baptist's Day, 1755, from the open-air pulpit in the quadrangle of Magdalen College

On the occasion of this sermon, it is recorded that a green fence was put up all round the quad, in order that "the preaching might more nearly resemble that of St John the Baptist in the wilderness."

Dr. Horne had a great reputation as a preacher, and his earnest and scholarly sermons were frequently reprinted Many of them are often quoted to-day by devotional writers, but of all his works the "Commentary" is the only one that holds a really permanent place in our literature

When Dr. Johnson visited Oxford, with his friend, Boswell, they waited upon Dr. Horne, at Magdalen, and as throwing a little sidelight upon the subject of our sketch, we may quote from Boswell's Life of Johnson, the note he made on the occasion The chronicler says —

"We drank tea with Dr Horne, late President of Magdalen College, and Bishop of Norwich, of whose abilities, in different respects, the public has had eminent proofs, and the esteem annexed to whose character was increased by knowing him personally. He had talked of publishing an edition of Walton's Lives, but had laid aside the design, upon Dr Johnson telling him, from mistake, that Lord Hailes intended to do it I had wished to negotiate between Lord Hailes and him, that one or the other should perform so good a work "

In another part of Boswell's "Life" an allusion is made to Dr Horne, which is very interesting. He says.—

"This year (1778) the Rev. Mr. Horne published his 'Letter to Mr Dunning on the English Particle ' Johnson read it, and though not treated in it with sufficient respect, he had candour enough to say to Mr. Seward, ' Were I to make a new edition of my dictionary I would adopt several of Mr. Horne's etymologies ; I hope they did not put the dog in the pillory for his libel; he has too much literature for that ' "

ST AUGUSTINE (Royal M.S.)

Chapter XV

THE PARISH CHURCH (1).

We do not seem to have any record of the first church that was erected in Eltham. In Doomsday Book there is no mention made of a church at all, but we must not think from this that there was no church at that time. It was no part of the plan of the Doomsday Survey to include the churches, and you will find that it is quite an exception to the rule if a church is mentioned in that interesting compilation. This seems to show that it was not the policy of William the Conqueror to interfere with the temporalities of the Church, as he found it in England. And we may safely assume that there was already a Saxon or English Church at Eltham. Five hundred years had passed away since Saint Augustine had first preached the Gospel to the heathen Jutes at Canterbury, and during that period Christianity had spread in all directions, a great English Church had

grown up, and in every village community a prominent point of interest was its little temple of worship.

These Saxon churches were mostly constructed of wood, and that is the reason why so few remains of them are to be found now. Some of them, however, were built of stone, and here and there, about the country, you may still come across them, or what is left of them.

There were very seldom any aisles or pillars in these old Anglo-Saxon Churches, but the roof was pitched from the outside walls. A nave, a chancel, and a western tower seem to have been the usual forms. There are some old towers still standing, attached to more modern churches, and, sometimes, you will find old towers have been added, or perhaps re-built, to an ancient nave.

There is Greenstead Church, in Essex, and Sompting Church, in Sussex, which will give you a very good idea of what an Anglo-Saxon church was like Whenever you visit a country village, where an old church still remains, you will find it an interesting exercise to examine its architecture, and try and discover at what period of our history it was first made Young cyclists in these days have excellent opportunities for the reading of village history in this way

Unhappily we have no ancient church building in Eltham to which we can point, for the Parish Church has only been in existence a little over thirty years But we do know, of a certainty, of two other churches that stood upon the spot where the Church of St John the Baptist now stands, for there are records to prove it, and we may be pretty sure that there must have been an Anglo-Saxon church even before them, in so ancient a community as Eltham, though, as yet, no records have come to light to tell us anything about it

The first mention that we can find of an Eltham church is in 1166 This was a hundred years after the coming of William the Norman, and it was in the reign of Henry II

You will recollect that, in an earlier chapter, we noted that the Manor of Eltham, in the time of Haimo, the "Shire-Reeve," became a part of the "honor" of Gloucester. From this we may be able to understand how it was that "William, Earl of Gloucester, on his founding the priory within his manor, at Keynsham, in Somerset, about the year 1166" was able to give "to the Church of St Mary and St Paul, of Keynsham, and the canons regular there serving God, in free and perpetual alms, the Church of St John, of Hautham (Eltham), with its appurts."

This gift was subsequently confirmed by another Earl of Gloucester, Gilbert de Clare, who was a grandson of the William referred to above, and also, in 1242, by Richard de Wendover, who was Bishop of Rochester, to whose diocese the living of Eltham belonged

Now, this arrangement was the beginning of the plan which has been in operation ever since, namely, that of making the priest of the Church at Eltham a vicar, and not a rector. Let us see if we can understand the difference.

Our ancestors, when they formed a Christian Church, did what other Christian communities had done They set apart one-tenth of their yearly products or increases for the payment of those who ministered unto them religion, and for the maintenance of their churches These "tenths" are called "tithes"

It is most likely that they got the idea of "one-tenth" from what they had read in the Old Testament You will remember how Abraham gave one-tenth of the spoils he had taken in his battle with the kings to Melchisedek, the priest of the most high God, how Jacob, at Bethel, vowed to give "tithes" to Jehovah, if he were divinely permitted to return to his father's tent in safety and prosperity, how the Jews had to pay "tithes" to the Levites, according to the law of Moses, and how, on their part, the Levites had to pay "tithes" for the support of the high priest. As we have already said, it was probably in imitation of the Jewish plan that the early Christian Churches adopted the system of "tithes"

In olden days these tithes were paid in "kind", that is to say, not in money, but in corn, or hay, or wood, and other products, which went to make up the yearly income of a person To receive these contributions most parishes had, not far from the church, a barn, or barns, and these were called "tithe-barns" There are many people in Eltham who can recollect the old "tithe-barn," which stood close to the churchyard, at the west end of the old church. It was burned down in 1872.

There were three kinds of tithes

(1) There were tithes which arose from the production of the land, such as corn, grass, hops, wood, and the like. These made up what was called the "great tithe."

(2) There were tithes for the live stock upon lands, such as wool, milk, pigs, &c., natural products, nurtured and preserved by the care of man, also

(3) Tithes from the personal industry of the inhabitants, such as manual occupation, trades, fisheries, and the like. These two latter kind of tithes made up what was called the "small tithe."

We may be sure that they had a busy time of it at the tithe-barns, when the waggons brought in their tenths, and the tenths of the live stock and other things were brought together.

In course of time it was found to be a difficult thing to arrange for the payments of tithes in this way. So a law was made, by which the payment was made in money, and not in kind, and that is how it is done at the present day.

Now, when the priest of the parish received all the tithes, namely, the "great tithe," and the "small tithe," he was called a "rector," but when the "great tithe" was appropriated by a "religious house," or by some other person who was not the officiating clergyman, and the priest received only the "small tithe," he was then called a "vicar."

From this you will see that the Abbots of Keynsham were really made the "rectors" of Eltham, when the Earl of Gloucester granted to them the Church of St. John of Hautham (Eltham), and the priest who had to perform the duties here became a vicar.

This arrangement went on for more than three hundred years. Then, in 1538, there came about that great historical event, the Dissolution of the Monasteries, by Henry VIII. The Abbey of Keynsham shared the fate of the other Abbeys, and along with other possessions of that monastery, the rectory of Eltham and the right of appointing the vicar were appropriated by the Crown.

Some five years afterwards the King granted these rights to Walter Hendley, who was one of his great officers of State. This official, therefore, was the one to whom the "great tithe" was paid.

After his death the rights were sold by his daughter to the Provost of Oriel College, Oxford, William Roper, of Well-hall, and others.

The right of appointing the vicar of Eltham was then reserved to William Roper, and the rectory to Oriel College, "with the stipulation that, on paying £100 as a fine, and a yearly rent of £14, the College should grant a lease of the same, either for three lives, or 31 years, to Roper and his heirs."

At the present day the Provost and Scholars of Oriel College, Oxford, are the "rector" of Eltham, and the receivers of the "great tithe." The advowson of the vicarage was sold by the Roper family, many years ago, and has several times changed hands.

PATRONS, RECTORS, AND VICARS OF ST. JOHN'S CHURCH, ELTHAM.

PATRON.—*William, Earl of Gloucester.*
RECTORS.—Adam de Bromleigh (?Chesilhurst). 1160.
      Picard. 1176.
      Robert London. May, 1242, when the church was appropriated to the Abbey of Keynsham.
VICARS.—Robert (probably the late Rector). 25 Sept., 1242.
      Phillip.

PATRON. *Abbot and Convent of Keynsham.*
VICARS.—John Vassur.
      John Hugh de Brampton. 23 Dec., 1348.
      John le Hwyte. (Resigned 1359.)
      Richard Nozebroun. 1359.

PATRON.—*Bishop of Rochester, jure devoluto.*
VICAR.—John Noble. 1362. (Resigned 1366).

PATRON. *Abbot and Convent of Keynsham.*
VICARS.—Henry Wessely. 1366.
      John Byrston. 1393-4.
      William Tyrell. 1399.
      John Aleyn. 1403.
      John Buset. 1405.
      Thomas Brownshale.
      John Palmer. 1423.
      Richard Briggs. 1430.
      John Brenan. 1434.
      Robert Purcell. 1457.
      Thomas Cary. 1463.
      David Knyston. 1464.
      John Waryre. 1493.
      Thurston Anderton. 1493.

PATRON—*John Chokke, gent , for this turn*
VICAR.—Thomas Turnour 1503-4

PATRON—*Bishop of Rochester*
VICAR—Robert Makerell. 1506

PATRON—*William Draper*
VICAR—Robert Robson. 1513 .

PATRON—*John Chokk, Esq (By grant from Abbot of Keynsham)*
VICAR—Philip Carlok 1521

PATRON.—*Abbot and Convent of Keynsham.*
VICARS—Roger Grenehod. 1529
        Henry Underwood
        Thomas Hugley. 1556
        William Hamond

PATRON—*William Roper, Esq*
VICAR—John Carnecke 1588-9
PATRON—*John Griffithe, LL D*
VICAR—Thomas Thirlwynde 1576
        Richard Tyler. 1584-5
        James Twiste, M A 1585
        John Fourde, M A 1589.

PATRON—*House of Convocation, Oxford (Sir William Roper, the true patron, being a convicted recusant, the presentation fell to the University of Oxford)*
VICAR—Robert Forward, B D 1628.
PATRON—*Oriel College, Oxford*
VICARS—Edward Witherston, M A 1635
        Richard Owen, M A 1635-6 (A distinguished scholar and divine

Ejected from his living in 1643 on account of his adherence to the Royal Cause   Rector of North Cray, 1657 Made D D 1660 Died at Eltham 1682-3)
William Overton 1646 (Recommended by Com of House of Commons to have the "Care of the Parish Church of Eltham " Assembly of Divines directed to examine his fitness   Sequestered 1650 Ceded living in 1658)

PATRON—*Edward Roper*
VICAR—Clement Hobson, M A 1658 (Subscribed to Act of Uniformity, 15 August, 1662)

PATRON—*Charles Henshaw.*
VICAR—Richard Peter, B A 1726

PATRON—*Sir Gregory Page, Bart*
VICAR—Peter Pinnell, M A 1749 (Subsequently was made D D In 1775 was a Prebendary of Rochester Cathedral He lived in the house now occupied by Mrs Dobell)
PATRON—*Sir Gregory Page-Turner*
VICAR—John Kenward Shaw, M A

PATRON—*The Queen for this turn (By reason of the lunacy of Sir Gregory Osborne Page-Turner, Bart.)*
VICAR—Charles Gulliver Fryer, M A 1841

PATRON—*Thomas Berin Sowerby*
VICARS—Walter James Sowerby, M.A 1869
        Elphinstone Rivers, L Th 1895

CHAPTER XVI

THE PARISH CHURCH (2).

Of the churches, that is to say, the fabrics or structures which have stood on the site of the Parish Church, we have records of three. There was the old church, which probably dated from very early times, and which fell down on St. John the Baptist's Day (June 24th), 1667. The restored church which succeeded it was pulled down in 1873, and the present church was then built and opened on the 5th of August, 1875.

THE OLD CHURCH.

There is not much known of the first of these fabrics, beyond what can be gleaned from the parish records. In the churchwardens' accounts there are references to the old church, which enable us to get some idea of what it was like, and these accounts date back as far as 1554, which was the time of Queen Mary. Further information may be obtained also from the references made to the church in the ancient wills which have been alluded to in a previous chapter. From these records we may learn a good deal of the services of the church and of the ornaments, vestments, and other attributes of public worship which it possessed.

There does not appear to have been anything very special or imposing in its structure. There was probably, in addition to the nave and chancel, a south aisle, and at least one chapel, if not more. The wills reveal the fact that it possessed images of saints, and several altars, and the usual rood screen and beam. A north aisle was built by Sir John Shaw about the middle of the seventeenth century.

We might explain here that the "rood" was a representation of the Crucified Saviour, or very frequently, of the Trinity, placed in Roman Catholic churches over the screen which separated the chancel from the nave, and hence called the "rood screen." Generally the figures of the Virgin and St. John were placed at a slight distance on each side of the principal group, in reference to St. John xxix. 26.

In the churchwardens' account book, in 1556, there is an entry to the effect that a payment of 13s. 4d. was made to the churchwarden, named Wombey, for making the rood, and a payment of 8s. to a painter from London for painting the rood, and the Mary and John. also a further payment of 8d. to the said "paynter for canvas, and for fire to heat his collours."

You get frequent allusion to the "rood" in the older literature.

"Now by the 'rood,' my lovely maid,
Your courtesy has erred!" he said.
Scott: "Lady of the Lake," i. 22.

The "beam" referred to in the "wills" would be the beam across the entrance to the chancel. It was sometimes used for supporting the "rood."

John Hooman, of Eltham, by will, dated 26th August, 1466, bequeathed 16d. to the support of the light on the beam before the Holy Cross (rood). Philip Bryde, in 1457, gave 8d. to the same light.

One of the chapels was dedicated to St. Nicholas, and from the "will" of one John Brown, gent, who was buried here in 1533, it is pretty certain there was a "lady chapel" as well. This quaint will gives us so vivid a picture of the church furniture and ornaments in use at the time that we may well reproduce its terms as an example of the use of "wills" in learning history

This is how it runs —

"To be buried in the chappell of our lady in Elteham Churche, and I will that my twoo vestments, oon of chamlet and another of white satten powdred with flowres, an aulter cloth of white satten powdered wt flowers, a coppar crosse gilt wt the baner or cross cloth belonging to the same, with the crosse staffe, twoo surples, twoo masse bokes, a chales of siluer wt two corporas and the cases, two latten candllesticks and two cruetts of Peawter there remayn in the same chappell to the honour of our blissed lady for ever John Brown, gent, 1533 "

. . . .

The old church came to an end rather abruptly in the year 1667, on Midsummer's Day, through an unfortunate incident   Sir John Shaw, who had come to reside in the mansion which he had built for himself in the Park, was having a vault constructed for his family along the north side of the Church, underneath the north aisle. Through the carelessness of those who were responsible for the work, precautions were neglected for making secure the wall of the nave, and the fabric came down with a crash

Here is the record —

"Memo, that while digging to make the vault under Sir John Shaw's Ile, he having obtained a faculty for building the said Isle on the north side of the Church, the roof of the great Isle in the Church not being shored fell down upon St. Bartholomew's day, 24th June, 1667, which, with the pulpit and pews, were rebuilt at the charge of the said Sir John Shaw."

The scribe here makes a mistake as to the day. The 24th of June is St John Baptist's Day, not St. Bartholomew's

The old church possessed a clock in 1556, for there is a record in the accounts of the payment of 6s. 8d , "paid to the clocke maker for lokinge to the clocke and mending of her for this yeares eande at Cristmas "

It also possessed a spire, as the following payments show —

"Payment to Sillvester page the shingler, for the Reprashines of the Churche Steaple paid by Robert Stubbes and John Pette churchwardens of the Parrish of Elham in the yeare of or Lord God 1568

It'm paid to Sillvester page, 24 May, iijs iijd

It'm paid to Sillvester page, 28 May, iijl. iijs iiijd

It'm paid to Sillvester page for 200 shingelles, vjs.

It'm paid to Sillvester page for 7 days work and 3 men, xxxijs viijd

Sum viijl vs iiijd

To John Petley for fetchinge the shingles, ijs

For MMMM (4,000) of 4 peny naylles from London, viijd

For a payre of ropes for the shinglers, js ijd.

To Robert Willey for a dayes work, xd

For a huudred of naylles, vjd

To John Pette for haulf a days worke, viijd

To John Clarke for a dayes worke for gathering rede to make a Cradell for the Stepell, viijd.

Paid for a vaine of copper of the Church Steapell, ijs

For a bare for the Church Stepell of 25 li , ijd , ob a pound, vs ijd. ob

To John Sketes man for a dayes work xd

Sum, xiiijs , ixd ob."

. . . . .

From this interesting account it will be seen that the "shingling" of the spire was an important piece of work A close examination of the details also throws a good deal of light upon the conditions of labour in Eltham, in the days of good Queen Bess. Labour seems to have been paid at the rate of 10d a day. The entries also reveal the fact that the Clerk who made them was not fettered by cast-iron rules in the spelling of the "Queen's English" of the day You may notice that there is a pleasing variety in the spelling of the word "steeple."

The old church not only possessed a clock, but, like many old churches of the time, it had its sundial This, it seems, was the free gift of a Vicar of Eltham

Here is the record —

"1572 Received from Sir John Carnicke, vicar, towards making of the dialle of his own free gift, iijs "

No 46.

ELTHAM LODGE, NOW THE GOLF CLUB HOUSE.

Erected by Sir John Shaw (Bart), 1664.

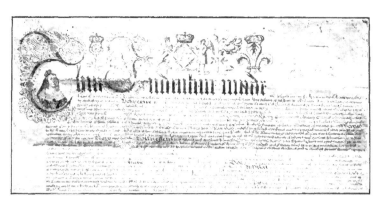

No 47

PORTION OF THE ORIGINAL LEASE GRANTED BY QUEEN HENRIETTA

TO SIR JOHN SHAW.

No. 48.　　STAIRCASE IN THE GOLF CLUB HOUSE.

No. 4.　　AN INTERIOR LYTHAM LODGE, SHOWING TAPESTRY.

In 1634 it seems that the church and churchyard were in need of renovation, so we find that a special rate was made to meet the expenses.

"An assesse made by the p'ishioners of Eltham for needful reparations towards the Churche and Churche yard, A.D. 1634. Sir Theodore Mayerne, Knyght, £11; Sir John Cotton, Knyght, 16s.; Anthony Rooper, Esq., £4 10s.; Pathrick Maule, £1; Wm. Withens, gen., 8s.; John Fletcher, gent, £1 10s., &c., &c."

A similar assesse for the needful "reparacion" of the church was made in the year 1636.

A few years after this we find evidence of the ascendency of Puritanism in Eltham. The Vicar of Eltham, the Rev. Dr. Owen, who has already been alluded to in a previous chapter, was deprived of his living on account of his devotion to the cause of the Royalists, and a Presbyterian divine was made his successor.

At this time, too, the interior of the church underwent great changes. The white-wash brush was very much in evidence. There is an entry in the accounts:

"Paid to James Guy for taking down the font and stopping up of the glass windows, iijs," which is eloquent testimony of the stern determination of those responsible for the new ordering of public worship to wipe out the associations of the past.

"Samuel Farnaby was paid £4 10s. for plastering and whiteing the church and chancel."

This, too, speaks volumes. Whatever there may have been in the way of decoration upon the walls was effectually obliterated, and we may be pretty sure that all the ornaments and symbols that had been placed in the church by former worshippers there were promptly removed.

We find that in place of the font, a pewter basin was provided for use at baptism, and a suggestion of what the pulpit discourses were like is afforded by the fact that the church-wardens, in 1656, found it necessary to provide the minister with an hour-glass to time his sermons by.

STATE CARRIAGE OF QUEEN ELIZABETH.

7

OLD ELTHAM CHURCH IN 1840 (from a Wood Cut).

CHAPTER XVII.

THE PARISH CHURCH (3).

THE RESTORED CHURCH.

It is only thirty-four years ago that the church which was restored in 1667, on the occasion of the catastrophe recorded in our last chapter, was pulled down. So there are plenty of people still living who can recollect the quaint old building, with its antiquated furniture and fittings, and its not too handsome exterior. The shock caused by the fall of the nave of the old church seems to have affected the whole of the edifice, for the south aisle had to be rebuilt. The chancel was probably rebuilt at the same period, or soon after, so that the restored church might almost be described as a new church. We have in the churchwarden's accounts a detailed statement of the costs of the building of the south aisle, which is worth perusing, for the sake of comparison with the modern costs of such works. It throws a good deal of light upon the conditions of life and labour in Eltham two hundred and fifty years ago:

"Imp. pd. for MMM new shingles ivl. vjs. vjd. Pd for trimming and laying MMMMDCCCC (4900) old ones, vijl. xvijs. vjd.

Pd for MMMM nails viijs.; use and carriage of ladders viijs.; pd Stubbs carpenter for work upon the steple, ijs.; paid more to ye shingler his boy, ijs. vjd.

Pd Mr. John Guy bricklayer as by an agreement for pulling down and rebuilding ye South Isle except the carpenters work, lxxvjl.; paid for drawing the agreement xs.

Pd to Ric. Greene carpenter for pulling down the old and putting up the new roof in the South Isle, xvl.

Pd John Guy for tiling the rest of the Church that was not pulled down and the vestry house xvjl. vs

Pd John Guy for pulling down the wall between the pillers in the gallery yt was formerly shaken by ye fall of ye church and for building it again and paving the Isle vijl vs

Pd Ric Waters for work and wainscott for Peter Stodders and ye rest of ye pewes in the church viijl vs.

Pd Tho Merifield for carriage of fower trees for the use of the church, xijs

From the steady increase in the yearly number of baptisms and burials, through the seventeenth and eighteenth centuries, we may gather that the population increased in like proportion, and this accounts for the fact that in 1819 it was found necessary to increase the seating accommodation of the church by the erection of two galleries at the west end, the further addition of a gallery in the south aisle being made some ten years later

The Parish Church of Eltham, as it appeared in 1830, has been briefly, but graphically, described in the "Churches of Kent" by Sir Stephen Glynne. The description runs as follows:—"A mean fabric, much patched and modernised, with scarce a trace of anything like good work, and from repeated alterations, the plan has become irregular The nave has a south aisle, cased in brick, and a north chapel of stone, bearing the date 1667, with square-headed, labelled windows, and a door of mixed Italian character. The chancel was wholly of brick. At the west end of the nave was a tower of flint, cased with brick, with large buttresses and pointed doorway It was surmounted with a spire of wood, covered with lead (shingle). Galleries were carried all round the interior of the church, and a double one at the west end, with an organ. The north chapel opened into the nave by three pointed arches, with octagonal pillars"

THE NEW CHURCH.

The building of the present Parish Church is a matter of quite modern history, and its story is pretty well-known to Eltham people. It is,

therefore, only necessary to deal with it briefly in these chapters, and those who would know more of the building of this fine structure should turn to the pages devoted to it in "Some Records of Eltham," by the Rev. E. Rivers, the present Vicar, published in book form, a few years ago Here will be found a most interesting account of how the present church came into existence, given in great detail. Although the necessity of a new church was recognised by most people, it was with some pangs of regret that they witnessed the demolition of the old one. Its historical associations were interesting Within its old walls many generations of Eltham people had worshipped. By long usage the older worshippers had become attached to the quaint interior, with its old-fashioned appointments, its antiquated pews, and its "three-decker" pulpit, where in olden times the black-gowned preachers thumped the cushions and thundered aloud their admonitions, until the hour-glass had been run out. But the end came, and old Eltham Church was only a memory.

The foundations of the new church were not made to coincide exactly with those of the old one The building stands about ten feet further north, which brings the Shaw vault, which was underneath the north aisle of the old building, below the nave of the present building. It was erected from designs of Sir Arthur Blomfield, the well-known architect, and son of the Bishop of London, and its style is Early English. The first stone was laid on the 27th November, 1873, and it was consecrated on August 5th, 1875, although it was not actually completed until 1880.

In the Eltham Parish Magazine for January, 1881, the Rev W. J Sowerby, who was Vicar of Eltham at the time, gives the following interesting account of the origin and completion of the undertaking —"I took advantage of the first issue of the Eltham Parish Magazine in 1872 to press upon your notice the great necessity there was for providing increased and improved accommodation in the Parish Church. The proposal to enlarge or rebuild the church having been almost unanimously carried at a large public meeting—there were, if I remember rightly, but three dissentients—the committee appointed to promote this object, had, after conferring with A W. Blomfield, Esq , the eminent church architect, recommended to the subscribers the rebuilding of the church, and obtained their concurrence This good work, then so auspiciously begun, has now been brought to a successful issue. On August 5th, 1875, those portions of the fabric which are used for divine worship were consecrated to the service of Almighty God, and last year the undertaking was crowned by the rebuilding of the tower and spire   On the Feast of the Nativity of St John Baptist, 1880, a service of thanksgiving for the completion of the work was held, in which the Bishop of St Albans, who was present when Sir Charles Mills, M P., laid the foundation stone, and who performed the consecration service in 1875, kindly took part   It was, indeed, a day of rejoicing throughout the village, and one which, judging from the great interest that was shown, will not soon be forgotten Most of the shops were closed, as on the day of consecration, five years before, that all might have the privilege of attending the service at the church.   I now avail myself of the opportunity offered by this first issue of a new Parish Magazine to express my deep gratitude for the blessing thus bestowed upon the people of Eltham, and to convey my thanks to all who have aided in this good work "

From the many interesting details referring to this great parochial work, given by the Rev. E Rivers, in his comprehensive book, we learn that the costs of the building were met by a variety of means On the occasion of the laying of the first stone the sum of £83 19s 10d was collected, while on the day of consecration £110 0s. 4d was contributed in a similar manner   The Crown gave £1,000.   The parishioners subscribed and collected £8,000. The cost of the erection of the south aisle was borne entirely by Mr F G Saunders Oriel College (The Rector), gave £300, and the Church Building Society contributed   £200   Then   many   private donors, a large proportion of whom are still living, made provision for the internal decoration, furniture and fittings of the sacred edifice, and their names and contributions are duly recorded in the book referred to   The fine organ, which is so important a feature of the church, was erected soon after the re-building of the church, at a cost of £1,200, which was raised by special subscriptions. It is interesting to learn that parts of the instrument which did duty at the old church were built into the new organ, which is the work of the well-known organ-building firm of Messrs Willis

Many more details of an interesting character might be added, but as it is the purpose of this story to deal with an older Eltham, this brief summary of the building of the new Parish Church, which is so familiar a feature to all of us, must here suffice. Its great interest in the Story of Eltham lies in the fact that it is the last of a succession of churches, which have existed upon the same site, and where the parishioners of Eltham have met together for the public worship of God, from a date so distant that it is lost in the mists of antiquity

Chapter XVIII

"THE BELLS OF ELTHAM."

It is rather a pleasant thing, on a summer evening, to get out in one or another of the Eltham fields, remote enough from the High-street to miss the noise of the traffic, but near enough to the Parish Church to catch the melody of the bells, as it comes floating upon the evening air It is the old melody which has greeted the ears of generations of Eltham folks, long past and gone

If you are disposed to reflection and love to ponder over the old customs that serve to link the Eltham of to-day with the Eltham of the past, and, in your waking dreams, to see again the life of those old villagers, to witness something of their joys and sorrows, their joustings and merry makings, their royal hunts and pageants, it is quite likely that the song of the bells may quicken your imagination, and help you to see these things more clearly

It has been said by those who have lived abroad in the distant Colonies, that one of the things they miss out there, almost more than anything else, is the chime of Church bells, which is so characteristic a feature in the Motherland. Some, perhaps, who read these lines, some of our old boys, who are living far away in Canada, New Zealand, or other far-off parts of the Empire, may still bear witness to the truth of this, knowing well how dear to them is the memory of the chimes so closely associated with the life at home

It is this close association with the village life, religious and communal, proclaiming, as they have done for centuries, its joys and sorrows, voicing the emotions of the people, and taking so prominent a part in the village story, that makes it necessary to devote a chapter to the bells of Eltham.

Although there does not seem to be anything left in the way of records of the "Bells of Eltham" until we come to the fifteenth cen-

tury, we may assume that the church had its bells long before that time, seeing that bells had been in use for Church purposes from a very early period of history

St Dunstan is said to have encouraged the art of bell-founding, and it is recorded that while he ruled over the see and province of Canterbury, from 954 A D to 968 A D, he not only provided the cathedral with bells, but also drew up a series of rules for their correct use

There is plenty of evidence to show a pretty general use of bells in connection with churches even at a period anterior to this, and, as a great authority upon the subject has written, "for fully a thousand years, we may feel certain that Christendom, and England as a part of it, has heard the far-reaching tones of the bells ring out, now gladly, now sadly, across broad acres of field and woodland, and over the busy hum of the bustling town. And in all that time there has been scarce an event of interest in the life of nations or of districts, not many even in the lives of private individuals, in which the tones of the bells have not mingled with the emotions that were aroused thereby "

" When the bells of Rylstone played
Their Sabbath music—"God us ayde"—
(That was the sound they seemed to speak),
Inscriptive legend, which, I ween,
May on those holy bells be seen "
(Wordsworth)

And the bells of Eltham have played their part in national and parochial events, sometimes sadly, sometimes gladly, as generations have come and gone

The earliest record that seems to be in existence referring to Eltham bells dates back to the time of Edward IV. (1467), when an inventory of Church goods in the county of Kent was made, where we find that at Eltham there were "Three great bells in the steeple, and saunts bell of brass"

We may explain that a "saunts" or "saunce" bell was the name sometimes used for the "sanctus-bell," or "sacring-bell." It was usually a small bell, used at the altar at that point in the celebration of mass, when the hymn, "Sancte, Sancte, Sancte, Domine Deus Sabaoth," was sung, and it was the signal to the people that the prayer of consecration was about to be said. It also gave notice that the priest was about to administer the Sacrament to the communicants And the "saunts" bell, such as that which was in Eltham steeple in 1497, was to give notice to people in the parish who were unable to be present at the celebration in the church. John Myric, a quaint author of this same period, amongst the many things he wrote for the religious edification of his fellows, has left the following lines upon the external use of the "saunts bell" —

"If thou may not come to church,
Wherever that thou do work,
When that thou hearest a Mass knell,
Pray to God with heart still,
To give thee part of that service
That in the church y-done is "

There is, of course, no relic of the "saunts bell of brass," in the steeple of Eltham Church at the present day, but we have a melodious peal of six bells, about which we shall presently have something to say.

In the "Booke of the accountes off the Churche Wardens called a Ledgere beginninge the xij day of July in the yeare of our Lorde Gode 1554," we find so many records of the expenses of the bells that to copy them all out would require many pages of a book. This cannot be done, so we will reproduce a few of them, from which you may judge of the interest in and care of its bells which the parish has always taken.

1554.—Paid to Robert Esbruke for takinge downe of the belle and hanginge of hir upe agayne and trussinge of the great bell, iiijs. iiijd.

1556-7.—Paid to John Bourne senr for making of the great bell clappir and the little bell clappr and spike for the carpinter for the dogge one the newe beame and ij forlocke for the great belle over and besides xiiijli. of ould irone that he had of the prishe for ij laye upon them, \

Item pd to Mills carpinter of Bexley for takinge downe of the great belle downe and new hanginge of hir vpe and mendinge of the bell whill, iijs iiijd.

Item geven to the men that did helpe take downe the bell and hang hir againe in bread and drinke, iiijd

1562.—Item paid for naylles for the belles. ijd

Item paid for greasse for the belles, jd

Two of the bells were re-cast in 1571 for £7, and again in 1610 we get the following account of another re-casting —

1610.—The carigge of the grete belle to be newe caste M Morrte bell founder dwellinge in white cappell wethe owte Allgate being agreed wethall for vl. and to deliver ett at the wate that he recefed itt att that wass ix hundred and a hallefe and att recessing of the bell back agane it waied iijxx and vij li. more than it ded before there was iijxx. and iiijli att viijd. the pownd and iijli. at ijs vid the pownd being called ten and tenglaes (bismuth) the holle som is vijli xs.

In 1618 the great bell was re-cast, and from the following entries we may gather that the peal consisted of three bells only —

1618.—Payed att the Warhoeues for waeing of the grett bell twies the firest waiett waes ixc iij quartres xxli ijli and a hallef more of the mettell waes at the Bell fownderes the second waiett or draeft waes viijo iij quarteres and vili. the ij April 1618, viijs

Payed the iijth day of Aprill 1618 tow Thomas Wode, bellwhele carpenter for tower ninge all the iij belles faisted in the stockes, xxs

Payed for all owre expenses there att Lowndone for three dayes attending one the belle and the fownder 1618, xxixs. iiijd

10 April 1618—Pd to Wm Land, belfounder in full payment of vl for casting the great bell. vls. pd to Mr Warren for making the bond from the belfounder and his surety for the warranting of the bell for a year and a day, ijs , payed for mending of the meddell belles clapper xd

By an examination of these latter entries it will be seen that a mention is made of "all the three bells," and also a further allusion to the "middle bell," from which we may infer that the number of the peal was no greater than three.

This number, however, was subsequently increased, and our present peal was the result of a re-casting which took place in 1794.

The firm of bell-founders that carried out the work was that of W. and T. Mears, which only a few years ago was carrying on business under the name of "Mears and Stainbank." It is one of the most famous firms of English bell-founders, having been established by one named John Mott, in the year 1570, and in the course of the three centuries and more of its existence it has supplied hundreds of bells for the churches of Kent.

The work was carried out while the Rev. J. Kenward Shaw (afterwards Shaw Brooke) was Vicar, and Thomas Noyes and William Glasbrook were Churchwardens. The dimensions of the six bells are as follows:—First, 27½in.; second, 29in.; third, 30½in.; fourth, 32½in.; fifth 34½in.; sixth, 37½in.

Upon each of the first five bells there appear the following names:—

THOS. NOYES & WM. GLAZBROOK CH. WARDENS 1794 THOS MEARS OF LONDON, FECIT.

The inscription upon the sixth bell runs thus:—

THE REV. I. KENWARD SHAW VICAR, THOS NOYES & WM. GLAZBROOK CHURCH WARDENS 1794. THOS. MEARS OF LONDON FECIT.

It is only to mention what is known to everybody in Eltham that the bells are chimed for Church services, are rung at the chief festivals of the Church, and on occasions of national or parochial rejoicing. The "death-knell" is tolled within twelve hours after death, and it is tolled again at the funeral. "Tellers" are tolled at the end only, on the occasion of the death-knell and also of the funeral, and consist of "three times three" for a male, and "three times two" for a female.

Such, then, very briefly told, is the story of the Eltham Bells. May the time be very distant when they will cease to perform the part in our village life which has been their function for long ages past.

* * *

The other churches of Eltham are provided with bells, which are used to proclaim the time of public worship. But none of them is of any particular historical interest, except the one at Holy Trinity. This was brought to England from the Crimea after the great war. Its original home was a turret in Sebastopol, where it witnessed the incidents of the terrible siege, and its voice was familiar to the British troops in the trenches. It was afterwards secured, found its way to Eltham, and was placed in the turret of Holy Trinity when the church was built, where it has done its part in proclaiming the message of Peace and Goodwill.

WATCHMEN (from Dekker).

QUEEN ELIZABETH HAWKING (from Turberville "Book of Falconrie," 1575.)
By permission of Messrs. MACMILLAN & Co.

CHAPTER XIX.

A PEEP INTO THE PARISH RECORDS (1).

The Parish Registers from which we have already taken many quotations are still preserved in the safe of the Parish Church. They have grown yellow with years, but most of the entries are still legible. They need, however, a practised eye to read them, and a great deal of patience and perseverance, for the style of writing employed by those old-time clerks was not the copy-book style of the present day, and their spelling, as we have already noticed, was not according to any fixed rule, so, as a consequence, it is of a varied character. It would seem, however, that the writers generally tried to spell a word as it was sounded, and from this we may sometimes come across words that were sounded quite differently then from the way they are pronounced now.

Another thing that strikes one is the wide parochial duties of the Churchwardens, as compared with their more limited responsibilities in the present day. Their duties now are practically confined to the maintenance of the fabric, and the arrangements for regular services in the church; but, in the olden times it would appear that they financially assisted many objects that could not be regarded as ecclesiastical. Some of the extracts we are going to consider will illustrate this.

"1562. Paid to the boys for the May-pole, vjd."

The purport of this simple line of cramped handwriting in a dingy old book that is seared and worn by the use of three and a half centuries is like a flash of light that reveals a landscape on a dark night. It illuminates the dark past, and shows us Eltham in the days of Merrie England.

Queen Bess is on the throne—Queen Bess, look you, who, when a child, played her childish games in Eltham fields. It is a time when the celebration of the May-day festival is in the height of its popularity. What preparations are made for it! How great is the excitement among the boys and girls of Eltham as the day draws near! Yes, and among the older folks, too, for the whole village turns out to take a part in or to witness the May-day revels. Eltham youth, enterprising then, as now, not only ply the rich for means to pay the expenses, but they go to the Church, and good Master Churchwarden gives them sixpence, and duly enters the payment in the account-book. Well done, Master Churchwarden. Did it occur to thee that thy entry and thy sixpence would be gossiped about three and a half centuries later?

May-day eve is come. Little sleep to-night. Companies go to the park, and the woods, and there spend the first hours of dawn. The girls bathe their faces in the morning dew, because it makes them beautiful. Then branches of the birch and other trees are collected, and carrying these, home they come again, singing loud, as Chaucer says, "against the sunne sheen." "But," says a writer of the time "the chiefest jewel they bring from thence is the May-pole, which they bring home with great veneration. As thus: They have twenty or forty yoke of oxen, every ox having a sweet nosegay of flowers tied to the tips of his horns; and these

oxen draw home the May-pole . . . . . . which they cover all over with flowers and herbs; bind round with strings from the top to the bottom: and sometimes it is painted with variable colours, having two or three hundred men, women, and children following it with great devotion. And, thus equipped, it is reared, with handkerchiefs and flags streaming on the top; they straw the ground round about it; they bind boughs about it; they set up summer halls, bowers, and arbours hard by it, and then fall they to banqueting and feasting, to leaping and dancing about it."

"Come, lasses and lads, get leave of your dads,
And away to the May-pole hie,
For ev'ry fair has a sweetheart there,
And a fidler standing by;
For Willie shall dance with Jane,
And Johnny has got his Joan,
To trip it, trip it, trip it, trip it,
Trip it up and down."

And where did these things happen? In the East Fields, the fields across which the new Archery-road now runs, were the village butts. It is very probable that these fields were also the scene of the May-pole.

What times they had! And what picturesque groups they made, dressed in their quaint Elizabethan dresses! How they enjoyed themselves! You must remember there were no railroads then, no newspapers, hardly any vehicles for travelling about. People were not in so great a hurry then. There was no rushing about from one place to the other. No excursions to the seaside. Every little village community was more or less self-contained. It found time for its village holidays, and its May-day romp was one of the brightest holidays of the year. Cannot you picture this May-dal scene in the East-fields in 1562? All Eltham was there, you may be sure—rich and poor. Master John Carnecke, the Vicar, no doubt, was there; he that had the sun-dial put on the church wall. And who shall deny that the Churchwardens themselves were there, looking on at the fun? Didn't they subscribe sixpence, as the accounts show?

* * *

There are other entries which give us pictures of Eltham under different conditions.

"1571. It'm paid to the becone on the xj. year, x ."

"1572. To mr bromhed the constapell of the hundreth for watchinge the beacone, vjs. 11jd."

1613. Pd to Wm leadsman Counstabell of the hundred the monie that the p'ishe of Eultham was sessed at for the Reperation of the beacon at Shuters hill and he to paie it to Ser tymothie lowe, 11js."

These entries refer to the beacon that was kept in readiness on the top of Shooter's-hill, to be lighted when it was necessary to warn the people that an enemy was approaching. It reveals the fact that the Churchwardens were also responsible for certain departments of the public defence It would appear from the first entry that the year 1571 was the eleventh year of the Shooter's-hill beacon. You will notice that the duty of watching the beacon fell to the constable of the Hundred, and that his expenses were met by means of a rate upon the parish, which was paid through the medium of the Churchwardens

Master Bromhed was the constable in 1572, and his duty of watching was no light one In some parts of the country such a duty was one of danger, as well as of great responsibility This was especially the case in the Border Land of the North of England. When the raiders were on the prowl, and desirous of making a descent upon the country without alarming the locality they would creep up stealthily in the dark, and woe to the watcher of a beacon who was not wakeful and alert then Many a poor constable was slain by these marauders before he had time to put his match to the pile There does not seem to be any mention of such a fate overtaking Master Bromhed, and let us hope that he escaped such an untimely end, and lived to a good old age.

But there was such a blaze of beacons in 1588 as never was known before. For centuries after it was the talk of the people, and the poet has given us so stirring an account of the incident that people are not likely to forget

it for many centuries to come It was the occasion of the Armada, when the King of Spain thought to do such wonders when he landed his army on the English shores He made a great mistake There was no telegraph then to flash the news of his coming throughout the land But the beacons of England flashed the warning from one end of the country to the other

When the Eltham constable, on that memorable night, saw the flames of the Blackheath beacon lighting the sky, he put a match to the pile on Shooter's-hill This was immediately followed by another fire at Erith. Then up shot the flames at Ruggen (Gravesend), then Halling, Coxheath, and Dungeness Seeing Gravesend alight, Allhallows followed suit, and then Egham, and so in a very short time the news of an approaching danger had spread throughout the county of Kent.

You may be sure that there was not much sleep at the village of Eltham that night, and many were the eager inquiries as to the meaning of this terrible night alarm How vividly has Macaulay described the spread of those beacon fires until the whole country was covered! You should read his stirring poem on the "Armada," from which the following lines are taken —

"From all the batteries of the tower pealed
    loud the voice of fear,
And all the thousand masts of Thames sent
    back a louder cheer,
And from the furthest wards was heard the
    rush of hurrying feet,
And the broad stream of pikes and flags rushed
    down each roaring street,
And broader still became the blaze, and louder
    still the din,
As fast from every village round the horse
    came spurring in,
And eastward straight from wild Blackheath
    the warlike errand went,
And roused in many an ancient hall the gallant
    squires of Kent"

LONG BOW ARCHERS (from an old Print).

CHAPTER XX.

A PEEP INTO THE PARISH RECORDS (2).

In an early chapter, in which we dealt with the old Saxon institutions, we alluded to the responsibility of the "hundred" in providing fighting men for the purpose of mutual protection. The Churchwardens' accounts show that in the days of Queen Elizabeth this old custom was revived, inasmuch as the parish had not only to provide its quota of soldiers for the "hundred," but had to equip them, and the expenses, which were met by a parish rate, were paid through the Churchwardens' accounts.

Look through the following list of sundries, which were paid in the year 1571, and notice how prominently the military equipments figure in the expenses:—

"1571. Paid for a bille, xvj*d*.

Paid for a sword girdell, xiij*d*.

To the soulderie at there goinge out at certayne times, viij*s*.

For matche and gunpowder, xvj*d*.

To John Rolt and Edd. Elliate for charges for goinge to London to bringe the harnesse, iiij*s*.

Pd. for frise sloppes and jerkinges, xxxv*s*.

for a couslette (corselet) and a pike, xj*s*.

for mending the harnisse, xviij*d*.

to Richard bore for the beacone in the xij. years, xxx*s*.

to the souldiers at Lewsham, xij*d*.

for ij. guns and ij. morindes (morions), liij*s*. vj*d*.

to the soulderie for a sworde and dager at his goinge to the shippes, iiij*s*.

pd to the counstapell for iij*li* of poulder, and ij*li*. of matche, and ij*li*. of shoute, v*s*. j*d*.

for laise for the flaske and touche boxe, vj*d*.

for conduct moni to the constapell and going to the mouster wth the soldirs, vlj*s*. vj*d*.

for scoweringe the p'rishe harnis, xij*s*. ij*d*.

for floweringe of swordes and dagers, xviij*d*.

for carige of a feline (felon) to Maidstone, iij*s*.

to quen Elizabethe for on fiftene the xiij yeare of hir raigen, xlv*s*."

We have pictured, in our mind's eye, the merrie Eltham folk, on May-day, dancing gaily about the May-pole in the East Fields. We listened, with our mind's ear to the songs, the sounds of the pipe and viol, and the peals of laughter from the youths and maidens at that festive time We have pictured the scene on that memorable night, when the sky was lighted by the beacon on Shooter's Hill, and tidings of the coming of the Spaniards was flashed from hill to hill Now we can imagine what the Eltham men looked like, when they were armed to the teeth, and ready to go out and fight for Queen and country

Let us examine the list of payments given above, and see how the picture may be lightened There is the reference to a "couslette" and a pike The "couslette" is Churchwarden spelling for "corselet," and it was a kind of breastplate, made of steel or iron, worn to protect the front of the body The wearer used to take a pride in keeping it clean and bright

"Many a scar of former fight
Lurked beneath his *corselet* bright"
        Byron · "Siege of Corinth."

It was kept securely in its place by means of a strap or band, buckled tightly round the waist.

"A moment now he slacked his speed,
A moment breathed his panting steed,
Drew saddle-girth and *corselet-band*,
And loosed in the sheath his brand"
        Scott "Lady of the Lake."

The "pike" was a very familiar weapon in these days, and, indeed, for centuries previous to the time, and quite a century later. It consisted of a lance-head fixed upon the end of a pole. The end of the staff had also a spike for insertion in the ground, thus enabling the musketeer to keep off the approach of cavalry while attending to his other arms In actual warfare the "pikemen" took up their position behind the "bowmen" If the battalion was on the defensive, and was being charged by mounted men-at-arms, it was the business of the "bowmen" to shoot as many horses of the foe as they could, and then to retire behind the line of "pikemen," who would present their "pikes" to receive the charge. In modern warfare, the bayonet has taken the place of the "pike."

The "bills," which, in the account quoted cost the Churchwardens 1s. 6d., was a formidable looking weapon, somewhat resembling the "pike" It consisted of a broad blade, with the cutting part hooked like a woodman's bill-hook, and with a spike, both at the top and at the back. It was mounted on a staff about six feet long. Sometimes the blade was varnished black to prevent it from rusting It was then known as "Black Bill" In 1584, that is, about thirteen years later than the time when this entry was made in the Churchwarden's accounts, we read, that out of a levy of 200 men for the Irish wars, one-fourth were ordered to be furnished with "good Black Bills" Who knows but some of our Eltham heroes carried these terrible weapons in the Irish wars The English "pikemen" and "billmen," like the English "bowmen," were famous as warriors Macaulay, in his "History of England," chapter I, says, "But France had no infantry that dared to face the English bows and bills"

Then two "morindes" are referred to These, no doubt, were "morions" They were a kind of helmet, or steel head-piece, shaped something like a hat with a brim that turned up at the front and the back. It was unlike the helmet of the previous and former centuries It had no vizor to protect the face

"'Tis meet that I should tell you now,
How fairly armed, and ordered how,
  The soldiers of the guard,
With musket, pike, and *morion*,
To welcome noble Marmion,
  Stood in the castle-yard."
        Scott · "Marmion"

We should bear in mind that there was no standing Army in the time of Queen Elizabeth, as there is at the present day The standing Army of England, that is, the permanent Army, really dates from Cromwell's time Before then, and at the period we are now considering, when the nation needed an Army, it was raised by means of levy, every "hundred" having to provide a certain number of armed men Hence the responsibilities of the parish of Eltham, to which these payments refer.

At the very time that our Churchwarden was setting down in this old book the records of expenditure, there was living a writer named

William Harrison, who has given us a clear and interesting account of England and its people, as it existed under his eyes From what he has told us, we can form an accurate idea of Eltham life, and we cannot do better, just now, than read that part of it which refers to the village soldiers which the parish had to provide

He tells us that in the previous reign—Mary's—there was much neglect of the provision of arms and soldiers, and that one of the greatest peers of Spain did espy our nakedness in this behalf, and did solemnly utter, in no obscure place, that "it should be an easy matter in short time to conquer England, because it wanted armour"

When Elizabeth came to the throne, and Spain had ceased to have great influence at the English Court, these words were remembered, and steps were taken to bring the national defence to a state of efficiency. Every "hundred" had to look to its duties, and every parish had to raise funds for the equipment of its fighting men So Eltham, as the accounts show, contributed its share to the purchase of arms, armour, and ammunition

"Our armour," writes William Harrison, "differeth not from that of other nations, and therefore consisteth of corslets, almaine rivets"—a light kind of armour introduced from Germany, having plates of iron for the defence of the arms—"shirts of mail, jacks quilted and covered over with leather, fustian, or canvas, over thick plates of iron, that are sewed in the same, and of which there is no town or village that hath not her convenient furniture. The said armour and munition is kept in one several place of every town, appointed by the consent of the whole parish, where it is always ready to be had and worn within an hour's warning"

Sometimes our Eltham fighting men came out on parade, for you will notice that 8s was paid "to the soulderie at there goinge out at certayne times," and also 7s 6d "for conduct moni to the constapell and going to the mouster wth the soldiis" No doubt the Eltham contingent made a brave show, decked out in bright corselet and morion, and arrsed

with pike or musket Hear what William Harrison says about these occasions of the musterings

"Sometimes also it is occupied when it pleaseth the magistrate either to view the able men, and take note of the well-keeping of the same, or finally, to see those that are enrolled, to exercise each one his several weapon, at the charge of the townsmen of each parish, according to his appointment Certes, there is almost no parish so poor in England (be it never so small) but hath not sufficient furniture in a readiness to set forth three or foui soldiers, as one archer, one gunner, one pike, and a billman, at the least

"No, there is not so much wanting as their very liveries and caps, which are least to be accounted of, if any haste required, so that, if this good order may continue it shall be impossible for the sudden enemy to find us unprepared"

Sometimes there would be a national muster of the forces Then, what a stir there was in every village! John Rolt, and Edd Elliate, Richard Bore, and other busy men of Eltham found plenty to do then What "scoweringe" there was of the "parish harnis!" What interminable drilling with the "bille" and the "pike!" What marching and counter-marching! What cleaning up of liveries, so that "frise sloppes and jerkinges" should appear quite spick and span for the inspection of the "counstapell," in readiness for the "mouster" at "Lewsham!"

It is really surprising how great an army could be raised at short notice by this method of levies On this William Harrison writes with some display of enthusiasm

"As for able men for service, thanked be God!" he says, "we are not without good store, for, by the musters taken in 1574 and 1575, our number amounted to 1,172,674, and yet were they not so narrowly taken but that a third part of this like multitude was left unbilled and uncalled" This was, indeed, a formidable army If the army of Spain, which came for our shores in the great Armada, had actually been able to land, they would have had a warm reception from the "bowmen," "billmen," and "pikemen" of old England that Spain would never have seen them again.

Not only did the "solderie" carry arms. The young men of Eltham who could afford to purchase a sword or dagger would wear such weapons every day. "Seldom shall you see," writes William Harrison, "any of my countrymen above eighteen or twenty years old to go without a dagger at the least at his back or by his side, although they be aged burgesses or magistrates of any city, who, in appearance, are most exempt from brabling and contention. Our nobility wear commonly swords or rapiers with their daggers, as doth every common serving man also that followeth his lord and master."

Very often this custom gave rise to trouble, for hot-tempered or quarrelsome fellows were apt to whip out their weapon upon the slightest provocation. Says Harrison:

"Some desperate cutters we have in like sort, which carry two daggers or two rapiers in a sheath always about them, wherewith in every drunken fray they are known to work much mischief."

It is a good thing that the custom of carrying weapons does not exist now. It is a habit of Elizabethan times, which we need not want to copy. But we may well admire, and even try to emulate, the patriotic spirit of her time. And we may derive satisfaction from the fact that Eltham, as the Churchwardens' accounts plainly show, took her proper share in the work of national defence.

CROSS-BOW AND QUARREL.

SHOOTING AT BUTTS (from an old Print).

Chapter XXI.

A PEEP INTO THE PARISH RECORDS (3).

The following is an interesting entry in the Churchwardens' accounts:—

"1566 A.D. It'm, geven at the Church dore ijs. for lj. yeres, at the bequeste of Henry Kightly according unto his last will and testament, the land lieth at popes streate in the custoditi of the parrish."

You will observe that there was a "Pope-street" in the time of Queen Elizabeth. The entry refers to a charity founded by Henry Keightley, who, by his will, dated 20th May, 1520, appointed that twelve honest men of Eltham should take his house and land at Pope-street, by estimation 13 acres 3 roods, for the use of the highway from Pope-street to Church Style, and thence to Mile Oak in Eltham, 12d. a year to be paid to the highways in Bromley, and the same sum to 12 poor men; a copy of his will on parchment to be hung up in the church at Eltham.

It would seem that the Churchwardens distributed the alms, under this will, to the 12 poor men at the church door. It had apparently been missed in 1565. So two years' allowance was paid in 1566.

"1566. Paid to Eddy Ellyat at the eating of the bucke that was geven to the parrish, xs."

It does not say who gave this buck to the parish. It no doubt came from the Royal Park, and "the eating" of the same provided the good folks of Eltham with a rare festive occasion. Why the Churchwardens paid Eddy Ellyat 10s. we do not know. We can only guess. Folks liked their ale in those days. Perhaps Eddy Elliat was a seller of good liquor.

"1569. Paid for drinke when the quene cam thorow the towne for the ringeres, vjd."

We get an entry similar to this, some years later, when King James visited the village, and

frequent reference to amounts paid to the
ringers for beer for the ringing of peals on
"coronation days" So far as we can find out,
there were only three bells in the peal—ding,
ding, dong, but loyal citizens, as the people of
Eltham always were, and none more loyal than
the bell-ringers, you may be quite sure that
the peal of three, when it tickled the royal
ears, rang out its welcome loudly and well.
The ringers received twopence each, you
observe. It does not seem a large amount, but
a penny went farther in Queen Elizabeth's
time than it does now. Twopence represented
more than a draught of ale

It is interesting to note that the writer of the
entry has spelt the word "through" as though
it were pronounced with two syllables,
"thorow." This was the pronunciation of the
time, for in Beaumont and Fletcher, two Elizabethan writers, we get

"On mountains, *thorow* brambles, pits and
floods."
"Philaster" IV

Shakespeare also in "Midsummer Night's
Dream," makes his fairies sing :—

"Over hill, over dale,
Thorough bush, *thorough* brier,
Over park, over pale,
Thorough flood, *thorough* fire."

Even at so late a period as that of Byron we
get it sounded in this way, for in his "Heaven
and Earth," Act I , Scene I , we get —

"No ! though the serpent's sting should pierce
me *thorough*."

" 1569 Geven to certayn boys at the com'on
beneath the tyll hous at the out boundes of
this p'rishe betwine this p'rishe, Wollwich,
and Charton, ijd "

This curious item of expenditure seems to
have reference to the old English custom of
" Beating the Bounds." At Whitsuntide, the
clergy, churchwardens, and the boys of the
parish school used to perambulate the boundaries of the parish.   At certain points the
boys would strike the boundary with willow
wands Sometimes, at the more important
places in the boundary line, the boys themselves would be whipped to impress the matter
upon their memories It is quite possible that

the "certayn boys" of Eltham here alluded to
had undergone this particular form of memory
exercise, and that the Churchwardens gave
them the twopence as some sort of compensation Let us hope that they always remembered the boundary line of Eltham, "Wollwich" and "Charton "

" 1569 Paid to roberte Allee for taringe
(tarrying) at Woolwiche one after none fore the
belles to bring them whome (home) and they
cam not, ijs."

It does not appear what bells are referred to
here, and why they came to be at Woolwich
There is a payment recorded in 1571 of £7, for
the re-casting of the bells. It is just possible
that Master Robert Allee was sent to Woolwich
to bring home the bells after the re-casting.
But he had a disappointing journey, for they
"cam not " Has it occured to you, by the
way, that the journey from Woolwich with a
load of heavy bells, in those days, was very
roundabout and troublesome? Master Allee
would not have come by way of the old Woolwich-road (now Well Hall-road), because in all
probability it was not in existence then as a
road for vehicles He must have gone round
by way of Kidbrook, and hence along Kidbrook-lane, down to Well Hall   It is more
than likely that this lane was the great road
which led from Eltham to Greenwich

" 1571 for carige of a feline to Maidstone,
iiijs "

The " feline" here referred to is not a " cat,"
but Churchwarden spelling for " felon." It
shows that the office of Churchwarden included
the duty of conveying criminals to the county
prison There are other entries of this kind

—1571 to quen Elizabethe for on fifteneth the
xiij yeare of her raigen, xlvs."

The word " on" means " one," and the entry
refers to a tax, known as the "fifteen penny"
tax, which the parish had to pay to the Queen
to meet the necessary expenses of the State
This tax probably owed its origin to the
ancient custom of setting apart " one-
fifteenth" of one's possessions for the use of
the King There are several references to the
payment of this money.

QUEENSCROFT.

Residence of Col. H. B. Lister.

No. 51.

KING'S GARDEN.

Residence of Mr. Stanley Clay.

No. 52.

OAKHURST.

Residence of Mr. G. Heath.

LANGERTON HOUSE. Residence of Mrs. Gordon.

Seen from King's Gardens.

No. 53.

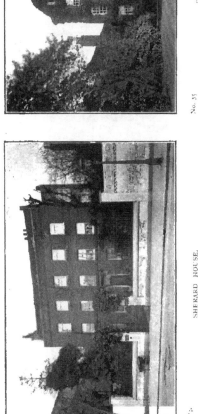

SHERARD HOUSE.
Residence of Mrs. Debell.

No. 55.

SHERARD HOUSE.
View from Garden.

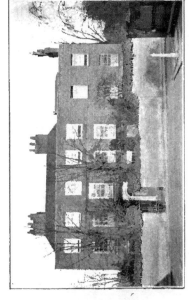

CLIEFDEN.
Residence of Mrs. Yeatman.

No. 57.

MERLEWOOD.
Residence of Mr. J. Roselli.

No. 56.

ELTHAM HOUSE.

Residence of Dr. St. John.

No. 60.

IVY COURT.

Residence of Mrs. Brown.

No. 59.

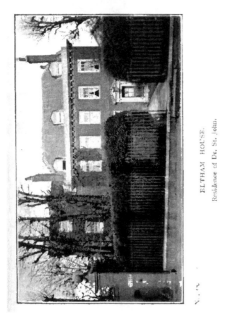

EAGLE HOUSE.

Residence of the Misses Scritton.

No. 62.

CONDUIT HOUSE.

Residence of Mr. W. H. Burman.

No. 61.

LEMON WELL.

Residence of Sir Harry and Lady North.

SOUTHEND HOUSE.

Residence of Mr. E. Warner.

"1602. Pd to Normington for the xxix of January for reeding servis in time of sickness when Mr. Fords hous was viasited, iijs."

Master Ford was the Vicar of the parish. The "sickness" was known as the "plague," a terrible and fatal disease which carried off a good number of Eltham people. The visitation, however, was not the "Great Plague," which did not occur till 1666, some sixty years

of the wolf, centuries before, a price was put on his head. But the badger was not nearly so harmful a creature as he was made out to be, and nowadays, people who understand his habits, will tell you that he does more good to the farmer than harm. He was always a good fighter, and the pleasure of hunting him down was all the greater, on account of the risks of being bitten. But it was cruel sport. No

PUBLIC WASHING GROUND, 1582 (Har. M.S.)

after. Here is another allusion to the "sickness," in the same year.

"For a bere to carry the dead uppon that died of the sickness, vjd."

1623. Sept. 4. Pd. for killing a badger, js."

"1660. Pd Philip Lock for a badger's head, js."

You will notice that the badger was regarded as an enemy of mankind, and, as in the case

doubt Master Philip Lock, when he brought the head of the victim to the Churchwardens, had a most exciting story to tell of its capture.

An interesting feature of this entry is that it suggests to our minds the rural character of Eltham in those days, for the badger loves the seclusion of the woods and forests. It is unlikely that we should be able to capture a badger in the woods of Eltham in our day. They are not numerous even in those places which are quite remote from the great centres of population, for the antipathy to the badger is still very strong, and men generally slay him if they get the chance. It is interesting to note, however, that the badger's first cousin, the weasel, has not yet been driven out of Eltham. One of these pretty little animals, a few years ago, ran along the platform of Well Hall station, and crossed the line. Only quite recently a gentleman walking along the Well Hall-road, on this side of the Herbert Hospital, counted six weasels, as they crossed the road just in front of him. Let us hope that these little habitués of the woodlands may remain with us for many a long year to come.

"1602. Paid to Borne for ringing the viij o'clock bell, vj$d$.

"1626, Sept. 24. To goodman Bankes for ringinge the eight a clocke bell for on quarter, iij$s$. iiij$d$."

There are frequent references to the ringing of this bell, which, as you know, was a relic of the old "curfew," introduced by William the Conqueror. This bell is still rung in many places in England.

"1614. Geven to a poore man that was robbed att Shoutershelle of all that he had and howndered miell home, vj."

Shooter's Hill, you will see, had a reputation for robberies, even as far back as the time of King James. The "poore man" was, indeed, in a parlous state. To be a hundred miles from home, without means, was a more serious matter than it would be now. He would have no way of getting over that hundred miles, except by trudging it on foot. No wonder the Churchwarden's heart was warmed, and that he gave him sixpence. But there are frequent items shewing payments on account of charity. Here is one relating to a rather horrible circumstance:

"1629, May 13. Geven to a poore man that had his tonge cut out by the Turckes, js. vj$d$."

There are many items referring to the maintenance of the church, and its services, and such matters as the provision of vestments, the purchase of " a communion cope and covere," "a boke called the omilles," "Elles of holland for to make surplies," and "the payment of goodwyfe Wington for makinge the surplies." But these things fall naturally within the sphere of a Churchwarden's business as we recognise it to-day. The selections we have given are intended to show how, in those early days, the church was in reality the centre of the parish, and its officers the servants of the parish.

INTERIOR OF AN OLD ENGLISH COTTAGE.

CHAPTER XXII.

A PEEP INTO THE PARISH RECORDS (4).

Here are more notes from the Church-wardens' accounts which are of special interest:

"1602. Paid to Goodman Borne and William the school master for keeping the clock that quarter that he rang the bell from St. Christmas to the Lady Day, vjs."

"1605. Paid to goodman Wyborne for charges of the cominge of the Kinges majestie into the towne and for ringinge one the byrthe daie of the younge prinse and for charges of Schoolmasters the xviiij of June 1605 latteses for the skole wyndowes, vjs."

These are the first references to a schoolmaster in Eltham. It is said that, as in the case of many other parishes, the school was held in a room over the porch of the church. In some village churches this room is still preserved, and on the walls may be sometimes found the alphabet, painted in old English characters, by means of which the ancient domine would teach the rudiments of reading.

The second entry, which refers to the cost of "latteses for the skole wyndowes," seems in some measure to suggest a separate building as the school. It will be seen that "William the Skolemaster" combined the profession of bell-ringer with that of pedagogue. If the truth were known, it is probable that his parochial work was even more comprehensive, for the parish school-master in olden days was often the parish letter-writer, the measurer of land, and the keeper of accounts for his neighbours.

There are occasional allusions to expenses in connection with "processions." For example:

"1629. May. Paid for the bread and beer for the parishenores that went in the presecione, iijs. lijd."

Then again:—

"1674. Apr. 14. Ordered in vestry in the parish church of Eltham that no churchwardens for the future shall expend more than fiftie shillinge in his precessioning but shall pay the rest out of his own purse (Clement Hodson, Vicar ")

In some of the ancient wills, such as those we have alluded to in an earlier chapter, we find mention of these "processions," and of sums of money being left for the purpose of providing bread or ale, or both, for the poor and others who took part in them These annual events were, therefore, rather notable occasions in the village history, and we might as well make some inquiry as to what they were, together with their object, in order that we may be able to form some mental picture of the scenes

The object of the processions which took place in "Rogacion Weke," that is, on one of the three days immediately preceding Ascension Day, is pretty well explained in the following quaint lines from an old book Let us read them —

"That ev'ry man might keep his owne possessions,
Our fathers us'd, in reverent *Processions*,
(With zealous prayers, and with praisefull cheeie),
To walke their parish-limits once a yeare,
And well knowne markes (which sacrilegious hands
Now cut or breake) so bord'red out their lands,
That ev'ry one distinctly knew his owne;
And many brawls, now rife, were then unknowne "

From this we may see that the "procession" was the more ancient form of the custom which subsequently became known as "Beating the Bounds " An old writer upon antiquities— Bourne—says that it was a general custom formerly, and was still observed in his time, in some country parishes, to go round the bounds and limits of the parish on one of the three days before Holy Thursday, of the Feast of our Lord's Ascension, when the minister, accompanied by his Churchwardens and parishioners, was wont to deprecate the vengeance of God, and, invoking a blessing upon the fruits of the earth, to pray for the preservation of the rights and properties of the parish

Shaw, in his history of Staffordshire, has left us a description of these interesting proceedings, as they were carried out at Wolverhampton. "The sacrist, resident prebendaries, and members of the choir, assembled at Morning Prayers on Monday and Tuesday in Rogation Week, with the charity children, bearing long poles, clothed with all kinds of flowers then in season, and which were afterwards carried through the streets of the town with much solemnity, the clergy, singing men and boys, dressed in their sacred vestments, closing the procession, and chanting, to a grave and appropriate melody, the Canticle, Benedicite, Omnia Opera, &c "

He describes the custom as of very ancient origin, adopted by the first Christians, and handed down, through a succession of ages, to modern times The idea was to give thanks to God, " by whose goodness the face of nature was renovated, and fresh means provided for the sustenance and comfort of His creatures "

So the procession was, in the first place, a distinctly religious ceremony At appointed places, generally at the crosses, the Gospel would be read. We have direct evidence in the wills alluded to that this was done in the Eltham procession, and we may easily picture to ourselves the Eltham villagers in those old times wending their way from point to point, Wyatt's Cross, the cross on Shooter's Hill, and other resting places

Hasted, in his "History of Kent," writes — "There is an old custom used in these parts, about Keston and Wickham, in Rogation Week, at which a number of young men meet together for the purpose, and with a most hideous noise, run into the orchards, and, in circling each tree, pronounce these words —

'Stand fast, root, bear well, top,
God send us a youling crop,
Every twig, apple big,
Every bow, apple enow.' "

For which incantation the confused rabble expect a gratuity in money, or drink, which is no less welcome, but if they are disappointed of both, they, with great solemnity, anathematize the owners and trees with altogether as insignificant a curse."

This old Kentish custom was probably a corrupted form of the Rogation ceremonies which we have been considering.

Although the processions were, in the first place, of a religious character, and designed for a good purpose, in the course of years they came to be abused and debased. It is to be feared that drunkenness and other excesses became common. When, on April 14th, 1614, the Rev. Clement Hodson, Vicar of Eltham, as Chairman of the Vestry, signed the minute which we have quoted, limiting the allowance to the Churchwardens for the processioning, to "fiftie shillings," we may well believe that so strong a course had to be taken for some good reason, not stated; but we may read between the lines It is more than likely that some straight talk took place at that Vestry meeting

In an old book called "Epistles and Gospelles, &c , London, imprinted by Richard Bankes," we get a sermon which throws great light upon the view taken of processions, just before they went out of fashion The preacher complains —

"Alacke, for pitie' these solemne and accustomable processions and supplications be nowe growen into a right foule and detestable abuse, so that the moost parte of men and women do come forth rather to set out and shew themselves, and to passe the time with vaigne and unprofitable tales and mery fables, than to make generall supplications and prayers to God, for theyr lackes and necessities I wyll not speake of the rage and furour of these uplandysh processions and goings about, which be spent in ryoting and belychere. Furthermore, the Banners and Badges of the Crosse be so unreverently handled and abused, that it is merveyle God destroye us not in one daye "

It is no wonder that "processioning" got into bad repute, and ultimately ceased to be recognised as being respectable Let us hope that in Eltham it was not so badly abused as to merit so stern a condemnation as that of the old preacher.

There is one writer in these Parish Records who wrote a good, firm "hand" This was John Fourde, who was Vicar of Eltham from 1598 to 1628—thirty years If hand writing be any key to the character of the writer, Master John Fourde would have been a man of very decided opinions. There are several entries

made by him which are of an interesting character. for they throw light upon the relations that existed between the Vicar and Sir William Roper, the Squire of Well Hall. Sir William was a Roman Catholic, and the Vicar was a Protestant of a very pronounced character. This is the Vicar's note —

"Memorand, that Mr Wm Rooper holdeth a certain parcel of wood, amongst his woods, called the Vicar's spring, containing by estimate 15 acres, and payed for the same 15s. a year, as a most ungodly lease expresseth more at large I leave a memorial to all Vicars succeeding after me, for there are yet so many years in the lease to come, being granted in the third of K. Edw VI by one Sir Henry Underwood, Vicar of Eltham, for four score and nyneteen yeers—by me, John Forde, Vic of Eltham, 44 Elizab A D 1602 "

But this "most ungodly lease" was not the only grievance which the Vicar had against Sir William Roper. The following note reveals another of quite a serious character Master Forde writes —

"The Vicar's diet at Mr. Rooper's table was dew to all Vicars for the aforesaid wood till Sir William Rooper came, but then denied to me, John Forde, Vicar, although justified unto me by his one moother John Forde."

And the Squire of Well Hall was not the only offender. Even King James wronged the Vicar, as the register shews:—

"It is said that the Vicar of Eltham should have the tithes of hay and corn on the south side of the town of Eltham, and that there is a hay and a door at the west end of the barn to enter and place the Vicar's hay and corn tithes, which is said to be lost "

"King James took in another parcel of ground into the Middle Park in 1615, about 22 acres, which are worth yearly to me John Forde, Vicar, 40s. the tithe of it, but with much ado I am allowed to me and my successors 20s a year."

The barn referred to in this note is, of course, the old tithe barn which abutted on the church yard at the west end of the church. It was destroyed by fire in the year 1872.

The bitter hatred, or perhaps prejudice, of Master Forde against the Roman Catholics is shewn in a note in which he describes an event in London in 1623. It has no connection with Eltham, and the fact that the Vicar thought fit to set it down in the Parish Register is some evidence of the strong opinions he held. He writes:—

"Let this be a pittifull remembrance to all posterityes, that in the yeare of our Lord 1623, the 26 day of October, in the 21 yeare of Kinge James his reigne, there lay a frenche imbassidor in the black friers in London, who beinge at masse the same saboth day in the afternoone with a multitude of blinde ignorant people, their fell in yt chappell in his house a gallery in the said chappell, yt crushed to deathe fower score and sixteen soules, besides a gret multitude yt had ther armes and legs broken, so muche was God offended with there detestable Idolatrie."

* * *

We will now close the Parish Registers for a while and proceed to the consideration of those associations which give to our village the right to be called "Royal Eltham."

QUEEN ELIZABETH'S COACH (from Braun's "Civitates Orbis Terrarum" 1572).
By permission of Messrs. MACMILLAN & Co.

YULE LOG.

CHAPTER XXIII.

AN ABODE OF KINGS.

We enter now upon a new phase of our story. Much that we have been considering in the last twenty-two chapters, although Eltham history, and the kind of history that must not be overlooked in the telling of the village story, is common in other country places which have their old churches and their parish records, their manors, and hundreds and moots. Now we come to the consideration of the great historical feature of Eltham, which specially distinguishes it from other villages, the Royal Palace, for three centuries the abode of the English kings, the scene of notable events that form part of the nation's story, the home of chivalry, the theme of many a poet's song.

It would be well, perhaps, at this point to explain briefly the plan we have followed, and propose to continue, in the telling of the Tale of Eltham. It was found to be impossible to tell the whole tale in chronological sequence; so we are taking it in sections. Eltham possesses features of interest that are associated

with the recognised periods of English history, from the British and Roman times to the present day. We have taken these features in the order of their antiquity. The "Old Dover-road" is a link with British and Roman days. The name of "Eltham," the "Common," the "Manor," the "Hundred," all associate it with the Saxon or earliest English period. Certain references in "Doomsday," shew our relations with the later Saxon or English period; other references from the same source shew the effect of the Norman Conquest upon the village. "The churchyard" probably dates back to a period long anterior to the Conquest. Though there may have been a Saxon Church—most likely there was—the first mention we get of a church was subsequent to the Conquest. That was why we dealt with the churchyard before we considered the church.

It may have been noticed that in the earlier chapters we have generalised considerably. This was necessary, in order to attain the

object we had in view. Our aim has been to interest the young people in the history of Eltham, and through that history to get an occasional glimpse of the history of their country. A mere record of names and events and statistics, however useful it may be to the well-read historian or antiquarian, would not alone do for this purpose So we have tried to excite the imagination, and, by the description of the old-time habits and customs, to help the reader to make a mental picture of some phases of life as it was lived in those by-gone times

Let us now proceed to the Court-yard, along the avenue of lime trees, and take up our position for a while upon the wonderful old bridge that spans the moat, and before we make any attempt to describe the many great events that took place here through these long centuries that the Palace was a royal residence, let us look around and examine as best we can the relics that are left to us from that distant age.

Perhaps these well-worn stones, the moat deep down here, or the old grey ruins yonder, if rightly appealed to, may quicken our perception and enable us to look backward and see some of the strange things that they have witnessed Look at the moat. You will notice that the water is not a great width On each side is a fresh, green lawn, and its sloping banks are richly covered with vegetation The brown autumn leaves are falling, and men are sweeping them from the lawn From this point of 'vantage we almost see the extreme ends of the water-way The scene is very beautiful Visitors from afar come and linger upon this old bridge, and feast their eyes upon the spectacle, and take away photographs to grace their albums at home It is a scene of quietude and peace, which is all the more effective, existing as it does almost within the hearing of the hum of the great city But this was not its character in its early days It encircled the whole of the area upon which the Palace stood, for it was made for the purpose of defence. It was made. There was little or no natural depression here for a moat It had to be dug out with spade and pick Military art of the time supplied the deficiencies of nature On its inner side there rose a wall,

difficult to assail, and th
was the work of great lab
an effective bulwark
formidable on the side w
—the side where we n
western side It's watei
within narrow limits, a
lawn then It was deej
and its breadth varied
hundred and fifteen fe
know how the moat w
It comes from the s
where the golfers pla
ducted to the conduit
Trinity Church, and
down to the moat.
had to be called in
of nature.

The approach te
bridge on which
gateway which st
Notice what a he
is, with its strong
served arches. I
of all lovers of
for the elegance
and soundness
vary in dimens
piers are susta

But this wa
may assume
Palace put a
was the cust
did, a surer
would not, o
though the
for the sec
Eltham, as
gave way
military m
found tha
could be s

The pro
Edward
when he
itself. I
So you
over for
is as

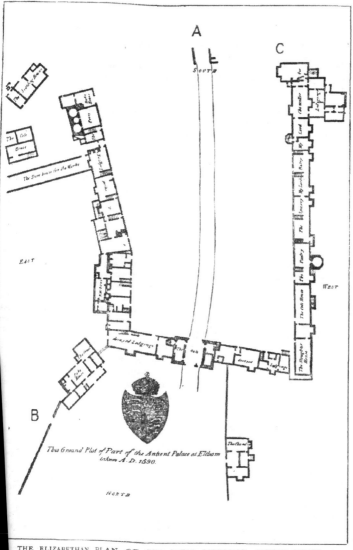

This Ground Plot of Part of the Antient Palace at Eltham taken A.D. 1590.

THE ELIZABETHAN PLAN OF THE OUTER COURTYARD, ELTHAM PALACE.
—The Bridge over the Moat. B.—The Tilt Yard. The break shown in the wall, the Ancient Gate
C.—The road leading to Bridle Lane.
The *Robe House* is the site of the old dwelling (Court Yard House), now occupied by Capt. Holbrooke.
The *Chaundry* site, at that amount, is now occupied by Langerton House, residence of Mrs. Gordon.
The *Chancellor's Lodging*, very much in its original condition, now forms the residence of
Mrs. Milne, Miss Bevan, and Messrs. Brookes. (See photographs.)

memorial to the excellent work of the builders of those days

The old gateway, which stood at the inner extremity of the bridge has gone But, writing in the year 1828, Mr J C. Buckler, who made a close and exhaustive study of the Palace as it was then, says:—

"An inconsiderable fragment of the gateway, joined to the bridge on its eastern side, remains In Buck's Views, published more than a century ago, the entire building is represented Its gradual demolition seems to have been effected as the ruins of the Palace yielded to convenience, and the ground was required for farming operations.

"Till the year 1813 two venerable, but imperfect, stacks of brick chimneys, one on each side of the way, were preserved Since that date one of these relics, with the wall on which it stood, has been entirely removed, and the other so much defaced that it will scarcely be noticed by those who remember how much these fragments of well-wrought brick-work formerly contributed to the picturesque beauty of the view from the bank of the moat "

Commenting further upon the gateway, Mr. Buckler continues:—

"These might have been portions of the work of King Henry the Seventh, who, however, cannot be supposed to have entirely re-built the gate-house, for we are informed that there was a palace here long before the time of Anthony Beke, Bishop of Durham, and that he only repaired, rebuilt, and beautified it, when it came into his hands, and (as Harris has written) 'the *stone work over the outward* gateway looks of that age '

"Another writer (Philpott) says, 'The stone work of the outer gate, being *castle-like*, is a remnant of the work of the age in which that prelate (Beke) lived "

"Of its antiquity, or the predominant material of its walls, I can say nothing," continues Mr Buckler, "but its form and extent may be imagined from the ancient plan of the part of the Palace published by Hasted In Buck's print there is only one archway in front, but the plan shews two, that is, a large arch and a postern, with rooms on the side and two staircase towers "

So, if we walk across the bridge to its inner extremity, remove from our view—in imagination, of course—the cottage on the right, and the house on the left, erect in their places the great archway, with its *castle-like* summit, its "stair-case towers" and rooms, its front gate, and its postern gate, we may almost fancy ourselves standing at the old gateway, seeking permission of the ancient porter to pass into the court beyond, upon the further side of which the "Great Hall" stands out in all its glory.

CHAPTER XXIV.

THE GREAT HALL (1).

Passing beneath the "castle-like" gateway, which, in the days when the Palace was a Royal residence, stood at the inner extremity of the bridge, you would have entered a court surrounded by buildings; and on the opposite side of this court, immediately in front of you, was the doorway of the great hall, which is so familiar a sight to us all to-day The hall was really a part of the central pile of the buildings which made up the Palace itself, but it is the only important part which is left to remind us of its former glory.

The Date.—There is a record that King Edward IV , "to his great cost, repaired his house at Eltham," and there is sufficient evidence to shew that the great hall in front of us formed a portion of the improvements to the Palace carried out by that monarch. As we have already noticed, a Palace existed here centuries before Edward's time, but he seems to have been the first monarch who went to the expense of repairing and adding to it

Edward IV. did much to encourage architecture, and, scattered about the country are many fine buildings, ecclesiastical and domestic, which were erected during his reign Somerset and other counties are specially rich in the architecture of this period, and St George's Chapel at Windsor, King's College Chapel at Cambridge, and the fine ruin at Eltham are monuments to the personal influence of the King in erections of this kind

Although no positive date is given of the building of the great hall, we have no difficulty in assigning it to King Edward IV 's time. The architecture bears the stamp of the

latter half of the fifteenth century, and evidence, even more direct, is found in the badge of a rose en soleil, which is a conspicuous ornament in the "spandrels," or spaces, to the right and left of the archway at the entrance in front of us. This was one of the badges of Edward IV., and it is frequently met with in architecture of that period. There is a beautifully carved example among the ornaments to the lower gateway of Magdalene College, Oxford, another at Queen's College, also at Keynsham Church, near Bristol—Keynsham, whose abbot, by the way, centuries before received the rectorial tithes of Eltham—another at Wells, and so on

A Master Feature.—Mr. J. C. Buckler, the distinguished architect, who in 1828 made a detailed examination of the whole area enclosed by the moat, describes the hall as the master feature of the Palace With a suite of rooms at either extremity, it rose in the centre of the surrounding buildings, as superior in the grandeur of its architecture as in the magnificence of its proportions and the amplitude of its dimensions. He adds, "this fair edifice has survived the shocks which, at different periods, have laid the Palace low Desolation has reached its very walls, and the hand of wanton mischief has dared to injure where it could not destroy; but still the hall of Eltham Palace has not, with the exception of the loover, been entirely deprived of its smallest constituents "

The Quadrangles —It was thought that there were four courts within the enclosed area, two in the north, and two in the south division, and the conjecture arose from the belief that the kitchen and other offices connected with it, and lying east of the great hall, were screened from the north and south quadrangles on the sides of which were ranged the state apartments.

The north side of the hall, that is, the side facing the bridge, and the south side, now facing the lawn, were both open to quadrangles. Their architecture corresponded precisely, excepting that the south parapet was plain,

the elegant simplicity of design, and this specimen of the Palace shews how well the old builders could apply the style to domestic purposes; 'how far removed from gloom were their habitations, where defensive precautions could be dispensed with, and how skilfully they carried out whatever they undertook in architecture.'

The Proportions.—The proportions of Eltham Hall, and the harmony of its design, are evidences of the care and skill of its builders.

BOAR'S HEAD.

while that on the other side, facing the principal gate, was embattled, and the cornice enriched with sculptured corbels. Mr. Buckler adds that, at the time of his writing, "not a portion of either parapet now remains to prove this assertion, though both were nearly perfect twenty-five years ago (1803)." They are represented as here described, in ancient drawings in the King's library, in Buck's print, and in the sixth volume of the Archæologia.

Simple Design.—In this majestic structure the architect scrupulously avoided the frequent use of carvings, which would have destroyed

Other halls may surpass it in extent, but this is perfect in every useful and elegant feature of a banqueting room. It was well lighted, and perhaps required painted glass to subdue the glare admitted by two-and-twenty windows. There are no windows over the high pace (the dais or platform at the end opposite the screen) and none over the screen. This was usual, though, from unavoidable circumstances, Westminster Hall and the Guildhall have windows at the ends. The placing of the hall, too, with its extremities pointing east and west, as in the case of chapels, was in accordance with a general custom.

The Windows.—The windows are arranged in couples, in five spaces on both sides, occupying the length of the building, from the east wall to the angle of the bays Every window is divided by a mullion (an upright bar), without a transom (horizontal bar), and every space by a buttress, which terminates below the cornice, and at the foot of the windows has twice the protection of the upper half

The Buttresses —These supports are slender, and are of the same light and elegant proportion which is a characteristic of the whole building The walls alone are adequate to the weight of the roof, but their strength is increased by the buttresses, which are common to the ancient style of architecture, and were frequently used for ornament when their support was not necessary The buttresses of Eltham are both useful and ornamental, and "as if to determine for which purpose they were mostly required, several of those facing the south are mangled or destroyed "

The Walls.—Since Mr Buckler's time much of the decay has been arrested, and the building partially restored, but writing of the walls, in 1828, he says "The building furnishes a strong proof of the scientific powers of former architects, it shews how accurately they calculated between the support and the weight supported, and though we look with some surprise at the thinness of the walls which have for so many centuries upheld the vast roof of timber, yet we must be satisfied that it was an undertaking of no temerity, since the walls would still have stood as erect as when first built, if the external covering of the roof had not been wholly neglected, or only imperfectly repaired, and so far from exhibiting a fissure through decay, it is difficult in some parts to trace the joints in the masonry, nor is the carved work less perfect."

It will interest many, especially those who are engaged in the building trade, to learn that inaccuracies in measurements exist in the spaces between the buttresses They have not been marked out with the scrupulous accuracy which modern work of the kind demands. "But," as our authority says, " the difference does not exceed three inches, and would defy the closest observer to detect. If the ancients disregarded these minute particulars, which, it must be confessed, were of no consequence to the general effect, they were studious to ensure the firmness of their buildings, and the beauty of their design "

The Bay Windows.—The bay windows at the western end nearly complete the length of the hall, which on the inside is a few inches over one hundred and one feet in length, and thirty-six and a half feet in width The shape of the bays was an "oblong square," and their proportions nearly that of a double cube, having in front two windows, and one towards the east   The opposite ends of both bays were joined to the walls of the house, and, though concealed from view externally, presented internally a uniform appearance The manner in which these appendages are united to the main walls is singular, and, on the outside, where alone the contrivance is observable, certainly inelegant The side windows of the bays are, in fact, recessed in the wall of the hall, with which the basement below, and the parapet above, meet in a right angle On this account nearly half of one compartment of the window is concealed from view, but a moment's inspection of the interior will shew the reason

The architect's aim was to maintain strict regularity of design, and to produce as much lightness as was consistent with stability. These points are now perfectly gained An arch of exquisite delicacy extends over the space between the bays and the hall, in the place of one proportioned to the substance of the main wall, thus securing the lightness of character which was designed

The Doors —The chief door of the hall faces the north, and was nearly opposite the outer gateway by the bridge There is another door on the south side Both opened into a vestibule formed by a screen A rigid economy in the application of ornaments was exercised in the outside of the buildings Both parapets were not embattled, and both doorways on the same account were not ornamented. That on the south side is a plain arch unworthy of the edifice to which it belongs. The other adorns the building and exhibits the workmanship of a hand no less skilful with the chisel than that with the pencil which traced the design.

The doorway facing the bridge, which is familiar to every visitor, consists of a square frame, protected by a cornice, and an arch deeply recessed within its mouldings, resting on pillars. An elegant pattern of tracery, encircling the rose en soleil enriches the spandrels.

This is still the principal entrance, and the shattered screen within still secures the hall from sudden intrusion. Though these doorways have never been sheltered by porches, yet the necessity of something to answer this purpose seems to have been felt. This substitute was probably a cove, or canopy of wood, supported on two stone corbels, which in Mr. Buckler's day were still in existence just above the southern doorway.

HACKNEY COACHES, 1584.

CHAPTER XXV

THE GREAT HALL (2).

Let us now enter the Great Hall, and under the enthusiastic guidance of Mr Buckler examine its chief features

The Interior —"The interior is magnificent," writes Mr. Buckler, "the taste and talent of ages are concentrated in its design, and it is scarcely possible to imagine proportions more just and noble, a plan more perfect, ornaments more appropriate and beautiful, in a word more harmonious than this regal banqueting room." Then follows a graphic description of the hall as it appeared to him in the year 1828

"It requires great strength of imagination to picture this glorious room in its pristine state, the long and lofty walls clothed with rich tapestry, and here and there decorated with the trophies of war, or those of the chase, the canopy of state, hanging over the high pace at the upper end, and all its other enrichments, for on this honoured station are now seen the various instruments of agriculture, and between the two bay windows, whose delicate mullions were enclosed by painted glass, rich in historical groups and heraldic devices, and whose ample breadth shed a profusion of light around the seat of royalty, the sun no longer shines but through the crevices of brick and wood-work, which supplies the place of glass.

"The slender stone tracery, wrought with all the nicety of art, and so carefully preserved, is now clustered with cobwebs, where the stone has been permitted to remain The screen, once sumptuously carved and painted, and furnished with all the instruments known to the age, is now a broken and almost shapeless

frame The floor, once well covered with tables of massy carved oak work, and prepared to administer to thousands (for King Edward the Fourth kept splendid Christmas here, two thousand being feasted at his expense every day), is now an uneven bottom, piled with machines of husbandry and rubbish—these are a few of the changes which three centuries and a half have produced in the hall of Eltham Palace "

It is a satisfaction to know that the hall does not now present such an appearance of neglect Soon after these lines were written, the authorities employed Mr. Smirke to commence the work of restitution

The Roof —"Though now the most perfect, and always the most splendid part of the interior, the roof has suffered its proportion of injury Many of its most delicate enrichments have been removed, but, as its chief ornaments are the constituent members, and not the minute carved work, these remain entire, and compose a design which merits, and continues to receive, as much praise as any existing work of antiquity "

Those who are interested in details of construction will notice that the principal beams of the roof repose on the summit of the walls which are crowned with a broad and boldly projecting cornice of numerous mouldings Every one of the frames thus formed, amounting to seven, includes a wide spreading arch, within and intersected with which are the handsome arches composing the essential features of the design, and the side segments, resting on brackets which terminate on stone corbels most beautifully carved These segments, joined to horizontal beams attached to the side cornice, themselves assume the form, and answer the purpose of brackets, since they sustain the main arches, whose elegance is much increased by the pendant corbels by which they are upheld."

Writing in 1828, Mr. Buckler, with his usual enthusiasm for the beautiful in architecture, declares that "the exquisitely beautiful form and decoration of these appendages surpass description. It may, however, be said that they are octagonal, composed of tracery, surmounted by a capital, and supported by a corbel, both of the same shape, the one broad for a canopy and the other long and tapering to a point."

He adds, "it is less wonderful that the more delicate enrichments of these pendants should be destroyed, than that a single specimen should have remained in its place till the year 1817, to prove the original beauty of the whole. This valuable relic was attached to the wall in the south west corner. Before the next summer it was removed." Mr. Buckler gives an engraving of it in his little book.

"The remaining space between the arches and the apex is occupied by open wrought tracery. The assemblage of features thus disposed on an elegant and well-contrived principle within a triangular frame constitutes the magnificent roof of this room. The precise form of the arches, clustered mouldings, and traceried panels, which please by their variety and the richness of their combination, proclaim the ability of those by whom they were designed and wrought."

"The Loover."—The loover, or chimney, occupied the third division from the upper end. The hexagonal framework, from which it rose above the external roof, rich in pinnacles and tracery, was in existence in 1828, and marked the situation of the hearth below. But the loover itself was destroyed prior to the date of any drawing or engraving then known; and as the hearth was not substituted by a recessed fire-place in the side wall, it is probable that the old method of warming the hall was used, until its destruction, and that afterwards the loover was removed as useless.

"The Wall Spaces."—The blank space below the windows, which is considerable, was once used for the display of tapestry and fresco painting; and on these, and perhaps other accounts, became a distinctive character in the design of the room.

The stone work in the spaces over and between the windows was always uncovered, and on that account is constructed with great care. It is composed of large squares, while the broad space below is of brick, cased, on the outside, towards the south, with masonry of an inferior quality to that above, which resembles the interior, and with which the principal or north side corresponds.

The substantial layer of cement on which the tapestry was fastened was not wholly removed in 1828, and much of a similar composition remains on the walls of Westminster Hall.

The Bay Windows.—The bay windows are of unrivalled grandeur and beauty. In each a rich and elegant pattern of tracery, highly decorated with sculptured knots, the whole wrought in stone of the most delicate workmanship, expands in a uniform pattern over the roof, and reposes its clustered "springers" on the capitals of the slender shafts, which, in the sides and angles of the space, are combined with the mouldings of the windows, and rest on a plinth at their foot.

The great arches leading to the interior are of an obtuse form, but those of the windows excel in beauty of form even the side windows of the hall. Their graceful length admits of a division by a transom, consisting of arches with an embattled cornice, whose upright shafts, united to the pillars of the roof, rest their bases on the sill.

The Inner Doors.—On the inner sides of the bays appear the elegant doorways, by one of which the hall was entered from the withdrawing room. The bays of the halls at Kingston Seymour, Wingfield Manor House, and other places also contained the entrance to the chief apartments; but the arrangement was unusual, and it may be remarked that no other internal doorways appear in the hall of Eltham Palace.

No. 64.

SOUTHEND HALL.

Residence of Mr. A. C. Latter.

No. 65.

ROMAN CATHOLIC SCHOOL.

Formerly the Residence of Mr. Thomas Jackson, Eltham Park.

(From an Engraving).

No. 66.

PARK HOUSE,

Residence of Mr. Hugh Mackintosh.

No. 67.

PARK HOUSE,

Residence of Mr. Hugh Mackintosh.

No. 68.　SEVERNDROOG CASTLE.

(From an old Print).

No. 69.　THE OLD BARN. PARK FARM. (1909).

No. 71.　PIPPEN HALL FARM.

Residence of Mr. J. Grace.

No. 72.　WEST LODGE AND GATE, AVERY HILL.

The Screen.—Mr. Buckler has a great deal to say about the screen, the remains of which still exist at the eastern end of the hall. We may do well to read his comments, that we may be able to compare the screen as it appears now, with what it was in 1828. He says:—

"The prominent position of the screen, which is advanced ten feet six inches into the hall at the lower end, was favourable to the display of handsome decoration, and the ample space was in this instance adorned so as to correspond with the rest of the building. The last fragments of its carved work were destroyed about ten years ago (1818), but it appears that the whole of the perforated tracery was gone when a drawing of this screen was published by the Society of Antiquaries in 1782.

"The main pillars and beams are all that now remain. Of the five spaces into which the front of the screen was separated, the two broadest contained doorways, the capitals and springers of whose arches till lately remained; and, if the rude drawing before mentioned can be relied on, were superbly carved."

It is generally thought that a minstrel gallery existed in the hall, but Mr. Buckler does not seem to share the popular belief. He says, "The screen now supports a rude frame work of wood, which may be mistaken for the remains of a gallery, a feature which frequently belonged to rooms of this class, but one which was so often omitted that it cannot fairly be numbered among the constituents of the design; it at least never formed a part of the internal decoration of this palatial hall; and the passage behind the screen was covered by a ceiling. The strongest confirmation of this opinion I can add is, that there is no staircase or doorway by which a gallery could have been entered, either from the common level, or from the floor of the adjoining apartments.

"There can be no doubt that the screen was designed to shut from the view of the hall the different doorways which were necessarily arranged behind it."

Stone Door-cases.—Our notice is also directed to the two stone doorcases in the wall opposite the screen, and once the entrances to the kitchen, and its appropriate offices. These arches are plain, and Mr. Buckler says, "the remains of bolts and hinges prove the care with which they have been secured."

PLAYING AT BUCKLERS.   MAIDS DANCING FOR GARLANDS.

Chapter XXVI

"ONE FAIR CHAPEL," AND OTHER MATTERS.

It is difficult to say with any certainty what were the actual positions of the other buildings that made up the Palace. But we have sufficient documentary evidence to enable us to form some idea of its size and importance.

The beginning of the end of Eltham Palace may be said to have dated from January 30th, 1649, the day on which Charles I. was executed. The Royal Estates were then vested in trustees, to be surveyed and sold to supply the necessities of State.

An Ordinance was passed on July 16th, 1649, and in the following autumn—in October, November and December, the Parliamentary survey of Eltham was made. From this survey we get the following particulars,—

"*The Capital Mansion House*, built with brick, stone, and timber, was called *Eltham House*, and consisted of one fair chapel, one great hall, thirty-six rooms and offices below stairs, with two large cellars, and above stairs, in lodgings called the King's side, 17, the Queen's side, 12, and the Prince's side, nine, in all, 38 lodging rooms, with other necessary small rooms and closets.

None were garnished, except the chapel and hall, both garnished with wainscot, all covered with lead and tiles, with one green outward court, containing one acre encompassed with out-houses on three sides, consisting of about 35 bays of building, containing in two stories about 78 rooms, formerly used as offices to the said manor, mansion or court house, with one inward court, containing half-an-acre, and one garden called the arbor, lying south of the mansion; also the orchard, encompassed with a brick wall, adjoining the highway leading from the manor house to a piece of ground called the High Lawn, N, upon the said lawn E, upon the Great Park, S, and the manor house, W, containing 3ac 1r 35p.

The said manor, or mansion house, with the scite thereof, is bounded with the said arbor, containing 2ac 2r 10p, SE, the Little Park, SW, and with the highway leading to the said town, N, contains, with the moat, 7ac 2r, and, with all ways, passages, easements, watercourses, commodities, and appurtenances to the said mansion house and scite belonging, worth a year £14 3s. 35d.

The whole being out of repair and untenantable, the materials were valued at £2,753, exclusive of the charge of taking down.

The scite of the above, when cleared, was worth £11 a year.

The out-houses encompassing the outer court, if divided into habitations, worth £25 a year."

The survey also contains many interesting particulars as to the parks, and, although in this chapter we are dealing mainly with the buildings, it will perhaps be as well to make some extracts here, since they throw a good deal of light upon other buildings connected with the Palace, and as it will help readers who may be interested in trying to define the limits of the old parks upon a modern map of the parish.

"*The Great Park*, with a piece called the Parish Lawn, the mansion house, and two closes of pasture, part of the demesne lands called the two ten acres abutting on the N, a lane leading from South End to Cray, and on the E a road leading from Chislehurst to London, containing the whole 596ac 3r 11p, worth £328 4s 10d. a year.

The Great or Manor Lodge, on the N E of the Great Park, with orchard and garden, contained 1ac 2r, worth £6 13s 4d a year

The Keeper's House, or Old Lodge, in the middle of the Great Park, contained 25 perches, worth £2 a year.

The Deer were all destroyed, and the Park disparked by the soldiery and common people since the midsummer before.

The Trees in this Park, besides such as were marked out for use of the navy, were 1062, being old 'dottrels' and decayed, worth £424 16s

Patrick Maule, groom of the late King's bedchamber, was Chief Ranger, by letters patent, dated 12 June, 4, Charles I , at 6d a day for life

The trees, before mentioned, marked for the navy were 1,200."

"*The Little or Middle Park*, between the Great Park on the E , the hamlet of Mottingham, S , and the highway from Mottingham to London, N , contained 333ac 3r 3p , worth £217 15s. 0½d a year

The Keeper's Lodge, a three-storied house in the middle of the Park, with orchard and garden, 2ac 2r , 7p., worth £6 13s 4d a year The *deer* and park were destroyed like the former

The Trees marked for the navy 1,000, the rest old and fit for fire were 334, worth £162 "

"*The Horne*, alias *Lee Park* with the meads and paddocks impaled, in Eltham and Lee, the highway from Mottingham to London abutting E , the hamlet of Mottingham, S , the lane from Lee to Bromley, W., and the highway from Eltham to London, N., contained 336ac 1r , worth £151 6s. 3d. a year

The Lodge, near the middle of the Park, three roods, worth £4 a year

Deer destroyed *Trees*, marked for the navy about 1,700, the rest, old and decayed, 2,620, worth £917

The Chief Ranger and Master of the game was Sir Theodore Mayerne "

.   .   .   .

There are other details in this interesting survey, but those given seem sufficient to indicate the extent of the Palace grounds in the year 1649, when its doom was sealed Reverting to the subject of the "one fair chapel," noticed in the survey, although we cannot locate its exact position, we may pretty safely assume that it formed a part of the extensive pile of building adjoining the Great Hall

It was very likely included in that part of the Palace built by King Edward the Fourth, whose fourth daughter, Bridget, was born here in the 20th year of his reign, and was the next day baptised in the chapel by the Bishop of Chichester

Mr Buckler, whom we have quoted already at considerable length, was of opinion that the chapel was situated on the upper or principal floor, and, with the surrounding apartments, had, below stairs, the thirty-six rooms and offices, and the two large cellars, referred to in the survey He says, "one common characteristic of domestic architecture of the period is the height of the windows from the ground, that is, their appearance on the upper floor, where all the principal apartments were most invariably placed Whether or not this arrangement was originally designed, and afterwards persisted in for the sake of security, it answered that purpose. While in some instances it added strength to an already fortified mansion, in others it formed, excepting the moat, the only protection from sudden intrusion "

We find that in 1810 the ground on the sides of the hall within the enclosure presented nothing but shrubs and heaps of loose masonry "The vault," says Mr Buckler, "in the southwest corner lay open and unoccupied, and the foundation of a wall parallel to the west side, about thirty feet from it, and sixty feet long, was exposed to view."

THE SUBTERRANEAN PASSAGES

Much interest is always taken in the subterranean passages and vaults, and several theories have been put forward as to their origin and purpose These chambers were more accessible at the time Mr Buckler made his investigations, and as he gave them considerable attention, we will reproduce what he has said about them

' "There are no fragments of walls," he writes, "to determine the extent of the south front from the west angle, but the vaults which still remain underground, if not capacious drains, were used for cellars, *and have had buildings over them.*" This observation is important, as it suggests the position of the buildings on the south side. "But these subterranean rooms," he continues, "are not now so easy of access as they were formerly One has been partly, and the other entirely closed up Two on the west side still remain open, and one towards the south, originally sixty feet long, is now a convenient receptacle for garden implements

"All these vaults, except the last, are about three feet wide, and six feet high to the crown of the arch. The principal one, facing the west, extends fifty feet underground, but the one adjoining, and that towards the south merit description.

"The former extends 25 feet from the entrance, and consists of three members, altogether resembling the Roman I The middle space measures 10ft 4in by 4ft The outer division contains the staircase, which formerly communicated with the apartments above, and the inner, a deeply recessed arch, between which and the vault is an aperture in the roof of 24in by 20in., framed with stone, and doubtless once concealed by a trap door.

"The door of the latter, or south vault, appears between the two towers before noticed. Its course is singularly irregular, varying in width from four to six feet, four feet three inches, and four feet nine inches. In the left or west wall is an arched recess, five feet wide, and four deep, and further on a small recess or niche

"But a square aperture in the roof near the outer doorway is the object of primary interest It is neatly formed, and large enough to admit the passage of an individual, and seems to justify the vulgar tales of adventures by means of secret passages, which attach to this and many other celebrated old houses

"It will not, I presume, be rejected as idle or improbable, that formerly there might have been occasions which would render a secret retreat useful. The water approached nearly to the level of the passage floor, and a few moments would suffice to convey the retreating party to the opposite bank

"Whatever might have been their original design, it is evident that these vaults were constructed for long duration The ancient builders, to the other good qualities of their work, added that of strength The cement which unites the stones is no less durable than the material itself."

The underground buildings have survived the noble mansion more than two centuries, without shewing any symptoms of decay, and will probably last for many more generations

THE COURT YARD

If we again take our stand upon the bridge, with our back to the Palace, and our face to the avenue of limes, looking north, we have before us the scene of the old "court yard," the name which it still retains This, of course, was an outer court, and must not be confused with the inner courts of quadrangles which existed within the moat.

In the year 1590, when Elizabeth was queen, a detailed plan was made of this outer court yard, and this plan may be seen at the Record Office The roadway runs now, as it did then, along the middle of the court yard. Still facing north, with the Palace behind us, on the left and right were two rows of buildings The ancient wooden houses on the left of us are the remains of the buildings set out on the plan, and those nearest the moat are called "My Lord Chancellor his Lodgings" Then follow "The Buttery," "The Spicery," "The Pastry," "The Cole-house," and "The Slaughter-house" On the opposite side of the court yard was a corresponding row of buildings, but these have now disappeared They are marked on the plan as "Bake-house," and "Decayed Lodgings." Behind these other buildings are indicated, "The Scalding House," "The Cole Houses," "The Store House for works"

The two rows of buildings form two sides of a slightly irregular rectangle. Immediately in front of us, at the other end of the road from the bridge, and a hundred yards from where we now stand, was the "gate-way" to the court yard, and from the right and left of the gateway ran out rows of buildings marked as "Decayed Lodgings" on the plan, but meeting the two lines of buildings already alluded to, and forming with them the small end of the irregular rectangle. Beyond the "gate," to the left of the road which ran into the village, was "The Chaundry," while "The Great Bake-house" occupied a position also outside the "gate," at the right-hand corner of the rect-angle.

Here we must conclude our brief survey of the ruins and other relics of the Palace, much of which we can still look upon. In our next chapter we propose to begin the story of some of the great events and distinguished personages that have been associated with Royal Eltham.

CROSS-BOWMAN.

HENRY III. (from his tomb in Westminster Abbey).

CHAPTER XXVII.

"BISHOP BEK THE BEAUTIFIER."

According to Matthew Paris, the chronicler of the thirteenth century, King Henry III. visited Eltham for the Christmas festivities of 1270. No record has yet been found of any earlier king taking up his residence here, although the house must have been of considerable importance and notability, seeing that it was the home of the great Baron John de Vesci, and that it possessed sufficient accommodation for the entertainment of the King in state.

Henry III. died two years after his state visit to Eltham, in 1272, and was succeeded by Edward I. (1272—1307). This latter monarch signed several charters at Eltham, but his reign is an important period of Eltham history, because it was then that Antony Bek came into temporary possession of the Palace, and wrought the improvements which have been associated with his name.

It is recorded in the Dictionary of National Biography, that Anthony Bek, the Bishop of Durham, "built the castle at Eltham, and gave it to the queen." Other authorities say that he beautified and improved the building. Whichever statement is correct we may regard it as an undisputed fact that Bishop Bek carried out great building operations, and if he was merely the "beautifier" of the palace, the inference is that there was a palace of some sort before he took the work in hand. This inference would seem to be quite reasonable when we recollect the antiquity of Eltham, even at the Bishop's time, and the fact that for centuries it had been a royal desmesne.

But you may ask, who was Bishop Bek? How

did he become associated with Eltham? Let us try and answer these questions, and let us deal with the latter first—the Bishop's connection with Eltham

If you turn to that part of Hasted's History of Kent which deals with the "Blackheath Hundred" you will find the query answered in a few words Hasted writes:—

"On the disgrace of the Bishop of Bayeux (see chapter six) about four years after, all his estates were confiscated to the Crown This palace afterwards belonged partly to the king and partly to the Mandevils, from whom it came to be called "Eltham Mandevil"

King Edward I gave his part of Eltham, with lands in Northumberland, and other places, in the ninth year of his reign, to John, son of William de Vesci, a potent baron of the north, who had the year before married Isabel de Beaumont, Queen Eleanor's kinswoman In the twelfth year of that reign he procured a charter for a weekly market here on a Tuesday, and a fair yearly on the eve of the Holy Trinity and the two following days

In the fourteenth year of it, having obtained the King's consent, John de Vesci gave the sixth part of the Manor of Luton, in Bedfordshire, in exchange to Walter de Mandevil for his part of Eltham, and died without issue in the seventeenth year of the same reign, holding the Manor of Eltham of the King, by knight's service, and leaving William his brother his heir, and Isabel his wife surviving

William de Vesci—"the succeeding Lord of the Manor"—was summoned to Parliament in the twenty-third year of that reign (Edward I), and having married Isabel, daughter of Adam de Periton, widow of Robert de Welles, had by her an only son, John, who died without issue in his life-time, upon which, "*having no lawful issue surviving, in the twenty-fourth year of that reign he enfeofed that great prelate, Anthony Beke, Bishop of Durham and Patriarch of Jerusalem, in several of his estates, among which was the inheritance of Eltham, then held by Isabel, widow of John de Vesci, afterwards wife of Adam de Welles, for her life, upon the special trust, that he should*

retain them for the use of William de Vesci," *his natural son*

John de Vesci died the year after he had made these provisions, and thus it was that Bishop Bek came into possession

Hasted tells us that this William de Vesci, for whom the Bishop had agreed to hold the Eltham estate, was killed a good many years afterwards at the Battle of Bannockburn His mother was Dergavile, daughter of Dunwald, a petty prince in Ireland

So much for the connection of Bishop Bek with Eltham, where he died on March 3rd, 1310 or 1311, and whence his body was conveyed to Durham and interred in the Cathedral there

Now, let us see what we can glean of the history of this great prelate, who was not only a most powerful prince of the Church, but was a man of exceedingly interesting and picturesque personality, and often a familiar figure in the picturesque village of Eltham

He was the son of a Lincolnshire baron, Walter of Eresby, and as a young man he attracted the notice of Edward I., by whom he was nominated Bishop of Durham in 1283. We are told that "he was already well provided with ecclesiastical preferments, for he held five benefices in the province of Canterbury, and was Archdeacon of Durham"

On the occasion of his consecration there occurred an incident which shewed, to some extent, the kind of man the new Bishop was

The monks of Durham were at variance with the Archbishop of York about his rights of visitation They knew that the Archbishop would not accept any one unless he were supported by the king, so they elected Antony Bek to be their Bishop, who was a nominee of the king

Immediately after his consecration, the Archbishop, John Romanus, ordered the new Bishop to excommunicate the rebellious monks

"Yesterday I was consecrated their Bishop," replied Bek, "shall I excommunicate them to day?"

* * *

"Antony Bek was a prelate of the secular and political type He was one of the magnificent lords of England, and out-did his peers in profuse expenditure His ordinary retinue consisted of a hundred and forty knights, and he treated barons and earls with haughty superiority."

When the Bishop came to Eltham, we may well imagine that his procession through the pretty Kentish lanes was a brilliant pageant upon which the simple villagers would gaze with an admiration that was intermixed with awe

Then he was immensely rich "Besides the revenues of his bishopric he had a large private fortune; and though he spent money profusely he died rich. He delighted in displaying his wealth On one occasion in London he paid forty shillings for forty herrings, because he heard that no one else would buy them At another time, hearing that a piece of cloth was spoken of as 'too dear even for the Bishop of Durham,' he bought it and had it cut up for horsecloths."

In our day we should regard this sort of thing as a weakness in his character, but there was a redeeming feature We learn that "he was an extremely temperate man, and was famed for his chastity"

He was a man of restless activity, who needed little sleep He used to say that he could not understand how a man could turn in his bed, or seek a second slumber In this respect he rather resembled the Duke of Wellington, who is said to have remarked that his first turn in bed was to "turn out" Bek spent his time in riding with a splendid retinue, from manor to manor, and was "a mighty hunter, delighting in horses, hawks, and hounds"

But he was also a great statesman, and exercised much influence at the Court of Edward I He was the chief adviser throughout the troubles connected with Scotland He was the ambassador to Adolf of Nassau to arrange an alliance with Germany against France

And he was a soldier In the expedition against Scotland in 1296, he led one thousand foot and five hundred horse, and before him was carried the sacred banner of St Cuthbert Subsequently, in the battle of Falkirk, Bishop Bek commanded the second division of the English forces An incident of this battle is recorded

When he approached the foe he ordered his cavalry to await re-inforcements before charging

"To thy mass, Bishop," cried a rough knight, "and teach not such as us how to fight the foe"

This remark seems to have fired the Bishop, for we are told that he spurred on, was followed by the rest, and routed the enemy

* * *

After his return from the Scottish campaign Bek seems to have got out of favour with the king Moreover, he was involved in troubles with the monks of Durham, and in ecclesiastical disputes which lasted to the end of his life

The monks at Durham were dissatisfied with their Prior, in 1300, so the Bishop proposed to hold a visitation there Prior Richard de Hoton refused to admit the Bishop as visitor unless he came unattended He knew that if the Bishop brought in his attendants he would be able to enforce his orders

So the Bishop suspended the Prior, and as the latter disregarded this and refused to obey the Bishop, deposition and ex-communication followed This led to breaches of the peace, and the king had to interpose as a mediator

The king decided that the Prior should continue in office, and that the Bishop was to visit the convent accompanied by a few chaplains only The king further declared that he would take action against that party which opposed his decision.

It was a triumph for Prior Richard. The haughty Bishop would not give way He would not withdraw his deposition of the Prior, and called upon the monks to elect another in his place. The monks were in a dilemma They demurred. So the Bishop appointed Henry de Luceby, of Lindisfarne, to the office, and in order to set up his nominee, he called upon the men of Tynedale, and Weardale, to besiege the abbey. This they did, and the abbey was reduced by hunger, and the defiant Prior Richard was seized and put into prison.

But he managed to escape, and hastened to Lincoln, where Parliament was assembled, and there the deposed Prior laid before the King his grievances.

Bishop Bek had few sympathisers, and many were the complaints, from other quarters, brought to the King, of the arrogance of the Bishop Parliament decided in favour of Prior Richard, who was thereupon sent to the Pope with letters from Edward I supporting him against the Bishop The Pope—Boniface VIII. —reinstated the Prior, and ordered Bishop Bek to Rome to answer for his doings

Bek took no heed of the summons, upon which the Pope threatened the Bishop with deprivation Then Bek set out for Rome, but committed a breach of decorum by departing without the permission of the King. This brought more troubles The King made this lapse of etiquette an excuse for seizing the temporalities of the see of Durham, and administering them through his own officers

* * *

But in Rome Bishop Bek carried everything before him There he displayed all that magnificence by which he dazzled the people at home. The Romans were amazed

" Who is this? " asked a citizen as he saw the Bishop's retinue pass by

"A foe to money," was the answer.

We are told that " Bek won over the cardinals by his splendid presents One of them admired his horses, whereupon Bek sent him two of the best, that he might choose which he preferred "

The cardinal kept both

" He has not failed to choose the best," said Bek.

Bek shewed that he was no respecter of persons. "He gave the benediction when a cardinal was present He amused himself by playing with his falcons, even during his interview with the Pope. Boniface VIII admired a temper so like his own, and dismissed the Prior's complaint against Bek." Although, this decision was favourable to the Bishop, it did not settle the question, for Prior Richard was still the recognised head of the monastery

Bek returned from Rome, but in passing through one of the cities in Northern Italy there seems to have been a disturbance between his servants and the people. The mob stormed his house, and even got access to the room where the Bishop was

" Yield, yield ! " was their cry

" You don't say to whom I am to yield," said the Bishop, " certainly to none of you "

His dauntless bearing quelled the tumult

* * *

On his return he made submission to the King, Edward I , and thus got possession of his see But the recognition of Richard as the Prior was a continual offence to his pride, and he renewed again and again his appeal to the Pope for his deposition. At length Clement V. agreed to the dismissal of the Prior, and as a special mark of favour to Bek, he made him Patriarch of Jerusalem, in 1305

Prior Richard did not quietly accept this judgment He hastened to Rome, to appeal against it, and actually got a reversal of the sentence. But he died before he could return to England

The Bishop's troubles, however, were not over. Edward I had taken a great dislike to him, and found a sufficient excuse to deprive him of several of his estates

But on the accession of Edward II he was restored to royal favour, and honours were conferred upon him. Then the Bishop proceeded to punish the monks of Durham who had taken the side of Prior Richard He suspended them for ten years.

Whatever we may think of his actions in these quarrels, we cannot excuse him for one very dishonourable act which, indirectly, was a matter of interest to Eltham We have noticed that William de Vesci, the lord of Eltham Manor, left his property in the Bishop's trust, to his natural son, William de Vesci The estates included others besides Eltham, and among them that of the barony of Alnwick in Northumberland

The young de Vesci seems to have used disrespectful or insulting language to the Bishop, and the latter's pride was so wounded by the incident that to spite the offender, he actually sold the barony of Alnwick to Henry Percy, a circumstance which added greatly to the powerful house of Percy.

The Bishop spent great sums upon buildings in various parts of the country. Among these works was that of the erection or the beautification of the Palace of Eltham, which, it is said, he presented to the Queen.

He died at Eltham, as we have already noticed, and his body was conveyed, we may imagine with great ceremony and pomp, through the length of England to Durham, where it was buried in his cathedral church.

This, then, briefly told, is the story of the proud and powerful prelate, Antony Bek, whose name is so closely associated with the story of Eltham, since it was he who provided it with that stately palace which for centuries after his death was the regular abode of English Kings.

JOHN OF ELTHAM.
(from Tomb in Westminster Abbey).

EFFIGY OF EDWARD II.
(Gloucester Cathedral).

CHAPTER XXVIII.

QUEEN ISABELLA AND THE PRINCE JOHN.

That weak and unhappy prince, who, on the death of his father, Edward I., ascended the throne as Edward II., often resided at Eltham, and it was to the Palace here that he first brought his beautiful, but faithless, Queen, "Isabella the Fair," prior to their state entry into London just before their coronation.

Isabella was daughter of the King of France. At the time of her marriage she was only sixteen years old, and was famed throughout Europe for her extraordinary beauty. Her life was one of troubles and tragedies, partly in consequence of the neglect and weakness of her lord, the king, partly the result of her own perfidy and wickedness.

She enters largely into the Story of Eltham, for she was often here, and the Palace recently enlarged and beautified by Anthony Bek, came into her possession. For a full history of this remarkable woman you may turn to Miss Strickland's "Lives of the Queens of England."

Her marriage with Edward took place at Boulogne, on January 25th, 1308, and her first experience of England was obtained in her progress through Kent, in winter time, to the Palace at Eltham, where the Royal procession was arrested for a time to prepare for the State entry.

The beauty of the Princess was proclaimed on all sides, and when the pageant passed along the lanes that led to the Palace it is easy to imagine the good wives of Eltham, the youths and the maidens, and villagers of all classes, pressing forward, as close as propriety allowed, to get a glimpse of the beautiful girl, who, alas! was destined to play so sad a part in our national history.

Her first child was born at Windsor, some four years later, in November, 1312 He was named Edward, after his father, and afterwards ascended the throne, to which he added strength and lustre, as Edward III. In the following January (1313) the Queen removed from Windsor to Westminster, where she remained a few days

There were great rejoicings in London on the occasion of this visit, and when, after her short sojourn at Westminster, the Queen and the baby Prince proceeded on their journey to Eltham, we are told that the Fishmongers Company organised a great pageant in her honour, and escorted her all the way to Eltham Palace, where she took up her abode

In 1316, some three years later, we find Queen Isabella again in residence here, and on this occasion occurred the birth of her second son, John of Eltham, of whom we shall have more to say presently

We need not follow the history of Queen Isabella, so full of painful and terrible experiences These things you may read for yourself in the pages of your history book Had her husband been a strong man, as his father was, instead of weak and worthless, and the tool of his favourites, it is quite likely that his Queen, who was received in England with so much acclaim, would not have had so dishonourable a reputation

To Eltham people, who are so justly proud of the old Palace in their midst, it is a matter of considerable interest that in 1332, that is, when the Queen was in her fortieth year, after the deposition and death of her husband, and when her son, Edward III , was King, "she received permission to dwell at Eltham whenever her health required a change of air " Eltham air, in those days, even as now, was no doubt noted for its invigorating and health-giving properties

Queen Isabella "the Fair" died in 1358, at the age of 66, at her castle in Hertfordshire, and was buried at the Franciscan Church at Newgate, in London. There is a statue to her memory among the figures which adorn the tomb of her son, John of Eltham, at Westminster.

"JOHN OF ELTHAM"

In the prologue of Miss Bidder's novel, "In the Shadow of a Crown," the writer tells of a weird and uncanny circumstance at Eltham Palace, full of gloomy predictions by the "Witch of Eltham," on the occasion of the birth and christening of the young Prince John of Eltham, July, 1316

The "Witch of Eltham" is, of course, a creature of the novelist's imagination, but as in most properly conducted stories the prognostications of witches often come true, it is not at all surprising to find that John of Eltham died young, almost before he had reached the age of manhood.

In connection with the interesting ceremony of the baptism of Prince John, we find, in the wardrobe accounts of Edward and Isabella, that "a piece of Turkey carpet, and one cloth of gold, were delivered to John de Founteney for decorating the font in the Chapel of Eltham, in which the Lord John was baptized, and to Stephen Faloyse, the Queen's tailor, five pieces of white velvet for making a robe against the churching of the Queen "

Although we like to regard Prince John as one of our most distinguished of Eltham heroes, and probably through its association with his name the Palace has been erroneously called "King" John's Palace, he does not figure greatly in English history. Most writers of history ignore his existence, so that it is quite a common thing for people to ask the question, "Who was Prince John?"

If you are disposed to look into old records you may, however, find a good deal about this young Prince scattered about the pages of that large and cumbersome book, Rymer's "Foedera," which is to be seen at the British Museum, and at the Rolls Office

When he was born, his father was engaged in war with Scotland, and we find that in March, 1319, some provision was made for the little three-year-old Prince, by the grant to him of the forfeited lands of all Scots south of the Trent.

During the period of his early boyhood, his father, Edward II , was engaged in those struggles with the barons and people which occupied so much of his reign, and ended in his downfall. We find, in October, 1326, the Londoners were in revolt against the King They seized the Tower, which at that period was a palace as well as a prison, removed the royal officers, and appointed others, in the name of John of Eltham, whom they styled "Warden of the City and Tower of London " John at this time was only a lad of ten years of age

In the following year his father, King Edward II , was taken prisoner, and confined in Berkeley Castle, where he was soon after mysteriously murdered

Prince John's elder brother, Edward, was then proclaimed King, and we find the Prince created Earl of Cornwall the year after (1328)

Soon after his accession, Edward III. paid his visit to France to do homage for Aquitaine, and during his absence, May, 1329, Prince John acted as Regent.

The Prince himself paid a visit to Aquitaine the following year, 1330, and on two other occasions, namely, in 1331, when the King was in France again, and in 1332, when he was in Scotland, John was responsible for the Regency

In his seventeenth year, we learn that John of Eltham was following the honourable profession of arms The English were warring against the Scots, and the young Prince had command of the first division of the English Army at the battle of Halidon Hill, in July, 1333, while in January, 1335, he defeated the Scots when they made a raid into Redesdale

In February, 1335, he was made Warden of the Marches of Northumberland, and a Commissioner to receive the submission of the Scots

In April, 1336, he received a grant of the coinage of tin in Cornwall, in return for his expenses in Scotland In the same year he was one of the Commissioners to hold a Parliament at Northampton He afterwards proceeded to Scotland in the company of the King, his brother. On Edward's return, John of Eltham was left in complete command of the English forces in Scotland

But it was only for a few weeks that he held this important position. He contracted a fever at Perth, and died in the month of October, 1336

As soon as the fatal news reached the ears of the King, he returned to Scotland with all haste, for the purpose of escorting the body of his brother to London

The sad procession reached London at the beginning of the following year, and with much ceremonial and pomp the mortal remains of John of Eltham were interred in the Abbey of Westminster on January 15th, 1337

You may see the tomb there now, in St. Stephen's Chapel, on the south side of the choir. Some Eltham readers, when next they visit Westminster, may be disposed to examine this interesting tomb, which has been most graphically described by Mr. Hare Let us read his description

"The effigy is of great antiquarian interest, from the details of its plate armour The prince wears a surcoat, gorget and helmet, the last open in front to shew the features, and surrounded by a coronet of large and small trefoil leaves alternated, being the earliest known representation of the ducal form of coronet

"Two angels sit by the pillow, and around the tomb are mutilated figures of the royal relations of the dead

"The statuettes of the French relations are towards the chapel, and have been cruelly mutilated, but the English relations, facing St Edward's Chapel, have been protected by the strong oak screen, and are of the most intense interest

"Edward II., who was buried in Gloucester Cathedral, is represented here Here, on the left hand of the husband, whose cruel murder she caused, is the only known portrait of the wicked Isabella the Fair, daughter of Philip le Bel, who died at Castle Rising, in 1358, she wears a crown at the top of her widow's head, and holds a sceptre in her right hand.

"Here, also, alone can we become acquainted with the characteristics of her aunt, the stainless Marguerite of France, the grand-daughter of St. Louis, who, at the age of twenty, became the wife of Edward I., and, dying at Marlborough Castle, in 1317, was buried in the Grey Friar's Church, in London, she wears a crown of fleur-de-lis over her widow's veil

"This tomb of Prince John was once shaded by a canopy of exquisite beauty, supported by eight stone pillars—a forest of Gothic spires, intermingled with statues; it was destroyed in a rush of spectators at the funeral of the Duchess of Northumberland, in 1776. Fuller mentions John of Eltham as the last son of a King of England, who died a plain Earl; the title of duke afterwards came into fashion."

EDWARD III. (from Tomb in Westminster Abbey).

CHAPTER XXIX

IN DAYS OF CHIVALRY.

Edward III. (1327-1377), one of the most gallant and chivalrous princes of Christendom, was closely associated with Eltham in his boyhood and manhood, and it was during his reign, perhaps, that the royal village witnessed the most brilliant spectacles of pageantry and chivalry in all its history.

It was at Eltham that the young prince received much of his education. It was here, when a king, that he gathered his councillors round him, and held several parliaments. It was at the gates of Eltham Palace that, with pomp and splendour, and surrounded by the flower of his knighthood, he received that voluntary exile and chivalrous monarch, John, the King of France.

These are undisputed facts. But there are other circumstances which, although we cannot point to them with certainty as Eltham events,

we may regard them as having, in all probability, taken place here. Thomas Rymer, the antiquary and royal historiographer of two centuries ago, in that remarkable work, "Fœdera," which may be seen at the British Museum, tells us that it was from Eltham, in 1329, that Edward III. "issued a commission to Thomas Carey to bring before him John le Rouse and William de Dalby," who were said to have discovered the secret of making silver by means of alchemy.

This may interest our young scientists of to-day who, doubtless, with the knowledge that they now possess, will smile at the credulity of the great king, who sent for the alchemist that professed to be able to convert the baser metals into silver.

And there is a tradition that the order of knighthood, known as the "Order of the Garter," was finally established at Eltham.

There seems to be some doubt as to the actual circumstances that led to the creation of this honourable order, with its motto, "*Honi soit qui mal y pense*," but at least one pretty legend is connected with it which we will speak about presently   There is the same doubt as to the actual time and place of its institution

But Sir Nicholas Harris Nicolas, in his "History of the Orders of Knighthood of the British Empire," expresses his opinion that it very likely happened at Eltham

King Edward and the Black Prince had been fighting in France, and their victorious campaign had included the victory of Cressy and the capture of Calais   Their return to England on the 12th of October, 1347, was attended by jousts and tournaments and other forms of festivities and rejoicings, and Nicolas says, "there are strongs reason for believing that the Order of the Garter was finally established at a tournament at Eltham before the close of 1347 "

The writer bases his belief upon an entry in the "royal wardrobe accounts" at the time, which runs as follows —

"*For making twelve garters of blue, embroidered with gold and silk, each having the motto, 'Honi soit qui mal y pensè,' and for making other equipments for the King's joust at Eltham,*" in the same year (1347)

The association with Eltham of the Knighthood of the Garter gives a specially romantic touch to our story, and in connection with the legend which is said to have given rise to the name of the Order, it may interest the reader if we recount something about the beautiful Countess Salisbury, who was a prominent figure in the same, for it throws some light on the motive of the King in giving the name to the Order.

England and Scotland were at war—as was usual. David, King of Scotland, laid siege to Earl Salisbury's castle at Wark   The Earl was at the time a prisoner in France. The Countess successfully defended the castle against the Scots, and when David heard of the approach of King Edward, he raised the siege and hastily departed

King Edward was "sore displeased" when, on his arrival, he found the King of Scots had fled   Then follows an incident inimitably described by Froissart, the great chronicler of the time —

"As soon as the king was unarmed, he took ten or twelve knights with him, and went to the castle to salute the Countess of Salisbury, and to see the manner of the assaults of the Scots, and the defences which had been made against them

"As soon as the lady knew of the king's coming, she set open the gates, and came out so richly beseen, that every man marvelled of her beauty, and the gracious words and countenance she made   When she came to the king, she kneeled down to the earth, thanking him of his succours, and so led him into the castle to make him cheer and honour, as she that could right do it.

"Every man regarded her marvellously, the king himself could not withold his regarding of her, for he thought that he never saw before so noble and so fair a lady, he was stricken therewith to the heart with a sparkle of fine love that endured long after, he thought no lady in the world so worthy to be loved as she

"Thus they entered into the castle hand in hand, the lady led him first into the hall, and after into the chamber nobly apparelled . . .

"At last he went to the window to rest him, and so fell into a great study.   The lady went about to make cheer to the lords and knights that were there, and commanded to dress the hall for dinner.

When she had all desired and commanded, then she came to the king with a merry cheer, who was in a great study, and she said.

"'Dear sir, who do ye study so for? Your grace is not displeased, it appertaineth not to you so to do, rather ye should make good cheer and be joyful, seeing ye have chased away your enemies, who durst not abide you, let other men study for the remnant!'

"Then the king said,

"'Ah, dear lady, know for truth that since I entered into this castle there is a study come to

No. 72.　　　　THE OLD WORKHOUSE.　High Street, Eltham.

Mr. T. W. Mills (Treasurer of the Eltham Charities), and Mr. W. D. Hughes (a Trustee).

No. 73.　　　　THE PHILIPOT ALMSHOUSES.

No. 74.   THE "KING'S ARMS" INN.

No. 75.   SUNDIAL, BARN HOUSE.

Formerly a balustrade of London Bridge.

No. 76.   SUNDIAL, SOUTHEND HOUSE.

my mind, so that I cannot cheer, but muse; nor I cannot tell what shall fall thereof; put it out of my heart I cannot!'

" 'Ah, sir,' quoth the lady, 'ye ought always to make good cheer, to comfort therewith your people. God hath aided you so in your business, and hath given you so great graces, that ye be the most doubted (feared) and honoured prince in all Christendom; and if the

for God's sake mock nor tempt me not. I cannot believe that is true that ye say, nor that so noble a prince as ye be would think to dishonour me and my lord, my husband, who is so valiant a knight, and hath done your grace so good service, and as yet lieth in prison for your quarrel. Certainly, sir, ye should in this case have but a small praise, and nothing the better thereby.'

QUEEN PHILIPPA (from Tomb in Westminster Abbey).

King of Scots have done you any despite or damage, ye may well amend it, when it shall please you, as ye have done diverse times or (ere) this. Sir, leave your misery, and come into the hall, if it please you; your dinner is all ready.'

" 'Ah, fair lady,' quoth the king, 'other things lieth at my heart, that ye know not of; but surely the sweet behaving, the perfect wisdom, the good grace, nobleness, and excellent beauty that I see in you, hath so surprised my heart, that without your love I am dead.'

"Then the lady said, 'Ah! right noble prince,

Herewith the lady departed from the king, and went into the hall to haste the dinner. Then she returned again to the king and brought some of his knights with her, and said:

" 'Sir, if it please you to come into the hall, your knights abideth for you to wash; ye have been too long fasting.'

"Then the king went into the hall and washed, and sat down among his lords, and the lady also. The king ate but little; he sat still musing, and as he durst he cast his eyes upon the lady. Of his sadness his knights did marvel, for he was not accustomed to be; some thought it was because the Scots had escaped from him.

"All that day the king tarried there, and wot not what to do; sometimes he imagined that honour and truth defended him to let his heart in such a case dishonour such a lady, and so true a knight as her husband was, who had always so well and truly served him; on

he was "at London, making cheer to the Earl of Salisbury, who was now come out of prison."

. . . .

Then Edward gave a great feast in the City of London, and among the guests who were invited was the Countess of Salisbury. She came "sore against her will, for she thought well enough whereof it was; but she durst not

EDWARD III. AND COUNTESS OF SALISBURY.

the other part, love so constrained him that the power thereof surmounted honour and truth.

"Thus the king debated in himself all that day and all that night; in the morning he arose and dislodged all his host, and drew after the Scots to chase them from his realm."

. . . .

Soon after we find the king making the release of the Earl of Salisbury an express clause in the treaty which was drawn up between himself and the French king, and shortly after

discover the matter to her husband; she thought she would deal so as to bring the king from his opinion.

"All ladies and damsels were freshly beseen, according to their degrees, except Alice, Countess of Salisbury, for she went as simply as she ever might, to the intent that the king should not set his regard on her, for she was fully determined to do no manner of thing that should turn to her dishonour nor to her husband's."

Commenting upon this incident, a historian writes "It was this same model of conjugal fidelity of whom the well known anecdote of the Garter is told, that gave rise to the illustrious order of Knights Companions, to which monarchs are, in our own time, proud to belong. '*Honi soit qui mal y pense*' (shamed be he who thinks evil of it), said the king, to rebuke the smiles of his courtiers, when the fair countess accidentally dropped her garter. We can well appreciate his feelings, in determining to make the trivial incident the foundation of a lasting memorial of his admiration for a creature so far above most of her sex for the grace and purity of her soul, as for the exquisite beauty of her form."

The "Order of the Garter" originally consisted of the King, the Prince of Wales, and twenty-four Knights Companions, who had stalls in St George's Chapel, Windsor, where they assembled on the eve of St George's Day (April 23)

We have quoted from the "Royal Wardrobe Accounts" an order for "certain twelve garters" that were required for the great event at Eltham in 1347. It will perhaps assist our imagination in making a mental picture of that brilliant scene, if we enumerate the original insignia of the order. They were a garter, a surcoat, a mantle, and a hood, to which the collar and George, star, and under-habit were afterwards added The garter, which is worn a little below the left knee, is now made of dark blue velvet, and has the motto inscribed on it in gold letters The mantle, surcoat, and hood are all of velvet lined with white taffeta, the colour of the two latter being crimson, and that of the mantle purple The badge, a silver escutcheon, bearing a red cross and surrounded by the garter and motto, is worn on the left shoulder of the mantle The collar contains 26 pieces, roses alternating with knotted cords, and from it hangs the "George" a representation of St George slaying the dragon.

Chapter XXX

WHEN KNIGHTS WERE BOLD.

Our young friends who love to linger round and about the old Palace and ponder upon its past glories would probably like to know the exact spot where the great tournament took place, when Edward III returned from France after his victories in the memorable autumn of 1347

We cannot point to the scene with absolute certainty, for, unfortunately, no record of such a detail seems to have been left to us All that we can be quite sure about is that a great tournament actually took place on that occasion, and indeed, it is likely that records of other similar events at Eltham might be found if we sought diligently for them.

Trending northward from the Bridge, in the direction of the village, when you come to the end of the avenue of limes which grow upon the site of the old Court Yard, the road branches to the right and to the left.

Taking that to the right, you will find the lane to the Court-road leads past a high brick wall, which you have only to examine for a moment to discover that it is of great antiquity In this wall is an ancient arch and gateway. Tradition says that this gateway was the entrance to the old "Tilt Yard," and, if tradition is right, this probably would have been the scene of the tournaments. The field within the wall was certainly large enough for such events, for within its area there are now the six houses from "The Elms" to "The Chestnuts," with their respective gardens. Bounding "The Chestnuts," on the side towards Mottingham, may still be seen a portion of the original wall, corresponding with that fine example of ancient brickwork where the archway is situated.

In all probability this extensive area was at one time quite surrounded by a wall, and it may have been from the fact that tourneys and jousts took place there that it derived its name of "Tilt Yard," by which it is known to-day.

In searching for corroboration of this right of title, one naturally goes to the oldest known plan of the locality, the plan of 1590, already alluded to in a previous chapter But the plan throws little or no light upon the point. There is a portion of the old wall, true enough. There is the archway, existing in the days of Queen Elizabeth, just as it is now. But, while the draughtsman has given in detail the names of the many houses upon the plan—the Great Bakery, the Cole-house, the Butchery, and the like—with a tantalising disregard for the needs of students of Eltham three hundred years after, he makes no mention whatever of the "Tilt Yard"

Now, though tradition is sometimes wrong in such matters, it is just as often right, for, as the old saying has it, "where there is smoke there is fire," so, until evidence is forthcoming to prove that tradition is wrong, we may as well regard the "Tilt-Yard" as the scene of the tournaments and jousts

Let us try and picture in our mind one of these royal tournaments in the Eltham "Tilt Yard," so totally unlike the contests, military and otherwise, that go by the name of tournaments in our days They may quite truly be described as kingly diversions, for Edward III would not allow any tournaments to be held in the land without his special leave.

The preparations for a royal tournament extended over many weeks and even months, for the king sent his heralds through his dominions, and sometimes to foreign courts, to proclaim the coming event, and to invite knights of chivalry and valour to take part in the contests.

Then the flower of knighthood, with the blazonry of shields and surcoat, the waving of plume and penon, foregathered at the royal village, with their squires and attendants, making a brave show, to the rare delight of the yeomen and country folk, who flocked Elthamwards to witness what they might of the spectacle.

maidens and pages, sat the "ladye faire" who, for the occasion, officiated as the "Queen of Beauty and Love."

To the right and left the galleries were filled with eager spectators, and the dresses of the ladies, which for beauty and brilliance had never been surpassed, presented a picture which was the talk of matrons and maids of Eltham many a year afterwards.

For, it must be remembered, this was no ordinary occasion. The king had just returned from France as a conqueror. There was jubilation throughout the length and breadth

TOURNAMENT (from Pluvenal's "Art of Horsemanship.")

The "Lists" were prepared in the great "Tilt Yard," where gorgeous tents and pavilions were erected for the accommodation of those who were taking part in the combats, and about the pavilions were hung the armorial shields to witness that the intending combatants were worthy of the fight in respect of noble birth, military prowess, and unspotted character.

On one side of the lists galleries and grandstands were set up, gay with gorgeous tapestry, and penons flying, and furnished with seats from which the king and his court might witness the events of the day. On the opposite side was another gallery, almost equally gorgeous, where, surrounded by her attendant

of the land. "It seemed," writes an old historian, "as if a new sun had arisen, on account of the abundance of peace, of the plenty and the glory of victories." We are told that "there were no women who had not got garments, furs, feather-beds, and utensils from the spoils of Calais and other foreign cities," and "then began the English maidens to glorify themselves in the dresses of the matrons of Celtic Gaul."

The passion for tournaments as a sort of expression of popular exultation was so great that the king felt compelled to regulate these festivals, as we have already said, allowing none to be held without his special permission, although he himself appointed no less than nineteen such displays within six months.

"It was like one long carnival," writes Warburton, "for at these tournaments, as well as at the 'King's plays,' and indeed, on all public occasions, knights, citizens, men and women, and even the clergy, vied with each other in grotesque absurdity of dress The king himself set the example of foppery and extravagance He appeared once in 'a harness of white buckram, inlaid with silver—namely, a tunic and shield, with the motto,

'Hay, hay, the wythe swan!
By Goddes soul I am thy man——,'

and gave away, among other costumes, 'five hoods of long white cloth, worked with blue men dancing,' 'two white velvet harnesses worked with blue garters, and diapered throughout with wild men !' "

Upon the strip of grass between the lists and the high galleries where sat the nobility, there stood in crowds the yeomen and "bettermost" people from Eltham, Chislehurst, Bexley, and other manors of Kent, while the lower orders—the labourers, serving men, and village folk, found standing room, as best they could, at a respectful distance.

The buzz of conversation and excited talk is suddenly arrested by a flourish of trumpets, when the king's herald, in gorgeous dress, rides forth to proclaim the orders of the day, and the rules of the combats

Then necks were craned and eager ears strained to catch the herald's important utterances. It was a great tournament, and would extend over a week or a fortnight, or even longer, and prizes worthy of the occasion, and of the puissant prince by whose proclamation the festival was ordained, would be awarded to the valorous knights who fairly won them.

The laws of the contests, recited in stentorian voice by the herald, had been elaborately prepared, under the personal supervision of the king, and were designed to secure that the engagements should be carried out consistently with the accepted rules of chivalry and knighthood.

The herald, at the close of his oration, withdrew to the side, and then, from the extremity of the lists, there rode forth, upon a magnificent charger, a knight in full armour, in appearance resembling one of those imposing figures illustrating the period which you may see for yourself to-day in the Tower of London As he rode slowly down the lists there were murmurs expressing admiration of his knightly bearing His lance was pointless, for it was not to be a combat a outrance. Riding straight to a pavilion upon which were suspended the shields of the challengers, he selected one and tapped it with the reverse of his lance, then quietly returned to the end of the lists whence he had come

In a short space of time, the owner of the shield, magnificently mounted, and clad in steel from head to foot, emerged slowly from the pavilion, and, proceeding to the opposite end of the lists, took up his position and faced his adversary

There was suppressed excitement and breathless silence among the onlookers during the few moments preceding the charge Then the king made a sign and the old "Tilt Yard" rang with the loud blaze of the trumpets.

This was the signal for the opposing knights to plunge spurs into the sides of their chargers and to gallop towards each other at a frightful pace They met in the middle of the lists with a crash that might have been heard as far away as the old wooden church, beyond the village cross.

The lighter knight of the two had the worst of the encounter His lance was splintered, while that of his opponent, being planted plump into his visor, his horse was first forced back upon its haunches, and then reeled over with its rider upon the greensward Then there were loud acclamations for the victor, and waving of kerchiefs, the vocal explosions being all the louder after having been pent up

Other contests followed, sometimes in singles, sometimes in doubles, and sometimes with as many as four or five on each side Now and then there was a serious accident, a knight maimed, maybe, for life, and having to be carried ingloriously from the field.

So were spent the days without doors, while within the palace there was feasting and merriment.

. . . . . .

It is pleasant to dwell upon the tournaments as schools for the cultivation of chivalry, and all that was noble and valorous in knighthood, but, alas, the best institutions devised by man are always liable to abuse. From what one can gather, the tournaments were no exceptions to the rule.

When they were first introduced into this country by Edward I., the Church sternly set its face against the tournaments on account of the vice with which they were attended. But as time went on we find that the clergy were less and less particular, till, at the period of which we are writing, they openly took part in these forbidden demonstrations.

But their conduct came in for much condemnation. They let their hair hang down their shoulders curled and powdered, as an old writer says, "thinking scorn of tonsure, which is a mark of the Kingdom of Heaven." They were dressed "more like soldiers than clerics, with an upper jump remarkably short and wide, long-hanging sleeves leaving the elbows uncovered, knives hanging at their sides to look like swords, shoes chequered with red and green exceeding and variously pinked, ornamented cruppers to their saddles, and baubles like horns hanging down from the horses' necks."

This was indeed a striking contrast with the sober garb with which we are used to associate clergymen. Well might there have been an outcry against them.

But a stern old writer of the times also reminds us that " Women, not the best in the kingdom, appeared at these tournaments, in divers wonderful male apparel, with divided tunics, one part of one colour and one of another, with short caps and bands in the manner of cords wound round the head, and with mitres of enormous height, decorated with streaming ribbons . . . . . and carried in pouches across their bodies knives called daggers, and thus they proceeded on chosen coursers or other well groomed horses . . . . . and so expended and devastated their goods and vexed their bodies with scurrilous wantonness, that the murmurs of the people sounded everywhere, and thus they neither feared God nor blushed at the chaste voice of the people."

. . . .

We have mentioned these things because we wanted to get as true a picture as we could of what the great Eltham tournaments were like in the days of Edward III. It is to be feared that notwithstanding all the glories of those notable occasions, they may have had their "seamy side." But let us hope that the Eltham episodes were not quite so objectionable as others in this respect.

MALE COSTUME OF EDWARD III.

Chapter XXXI

THE CAPTIVE KING.

When a prisoner of war in England, John, the King of France, was on several occasions at Eltham Palace, and for near upon six centuries his name has been kept in memory closely associated with that of the royal village. There are people who think even that the Palace is called "King John's Palace," because of his residence here, though it is more than likely that such a name is merely a misnomer for "*Prince* John's Palace."

This chivalrous monarch stands out so prominently in our local history that the story of Eltham would not be complete without a special account of his living here and the memorable events which led up to his captivity.

And, in telling the tale of John of France, we are bound to introduce another great prince of chivalry, who frequently visited Eltham, for his residence was no farther away than Bexley.

This was Edward the Black Prince, a soldier of immortal fame, the son of Edward III., who is described by an old poet as:

"Edward, the flower of chivalry, whilom the the Black Prince hight,
Who prisoner took the French King John, in claim of Grandame's right."

England was at war with France. It is not necessary to explain here the cause of the war. You may read this in your history. But in the great campaign, Edward the Black Prince covered himself with glory.

Crecy had been won. Calais had been captured, and, in 1347, as described in the last chapter, England celebrated the occasion with great rejoicings, in which Eltham had its share

It was nine years after, in 1356, that Poitiers was fought, and the Black Prince added to his fame by winning one of the most remarkable victories recorded in history

With an army that barely exceeded 8,000 men, he put to rout the French forces of about 60,000, containing all the flower of French knighthood—an overwhelming force, splendidly armed, and properly handled, quite capable of swamping the little band of Englishmen.

Although efforts were made by Cardinal Perigord, on the day preceding the fight, to bring about an amicable arrangement between the opposing leaders, and although the Black Prince was prepared to listen to any terms that would save his own and his soldiers' honours, the good Cardinal's efforts proved futile, and Monday, September 19th, 1356, saw the historic fight

When the reconnoitring party of the English brought to their leader the news of the position of the enemy, and their prodigious numbers, the full danger of the position flashed upon the mind of the Prince

"God help us," he said, "all that is left us is to fight as best we can."

The unexpected happened Bad generalship and making too sure, on the part of the French, and brilliant generalship, backed by those famous archers who could shoot so straight, and the "do or die" spirit which pervaded their ranks, on the English side, resulted in the confusion and rout of the French

What a stirring chapter is Froissart's account of this battle! And what a noble figure in the great struggle is that of the French King John.

"King John, on his part," says the chronicler, "proved himself a good knight, and, had a fourth of his people behaved so well, the field would have been his"

There he stood, battle axe in hand, in the thickest of the fight, striking to the right and left, woe to any man who came within the reach of its deadly swing, and, strangest of all

sights, crouching close behind him, with his arm around his father's waist, was his little son, Philip, warning the king of unexpected attacks Keeping his eyes constantly on his father, and neglecting all thoughts of himself, he cried out, as he saw any blow about to be struck at the king

"Father, guard yourself on the right, guard yourself on the left "

King John was twice wounded and once beaten to the ground, but he rose again, replying with fresh blows to every fresh command of surrender

"Then there was a great press to take the king," writes Froissart, "and such as knew him cried

"'Sir, yield you, or else ye are dead'"

'There was a knight called Sir Denis Morbeke, who had served the Englishmen five years before, because in his youth he had forfeited the realm of France for a murder that he did at Saint-Omer's. It happened so well for him that he was next to the king when they were about to take him

He stepped forth into the press, and by strength of his body and arms he came to the French king, and said in good French

"'Sir, yield you!'"

The king beheld the knight and said

"'To whom shall I yield me? Where is my cousin the Prince of Wales? If I might see him, I would speak with him'"

Denis answered and said

"'Sir, he is not here, but yield you to me and I shall bring you to him'"

"'Who be you?'" quoth the king

"'Sir,'" quoth he, "'I am Dennis of Morbeke, a knight of Artois, but I serve the King of England because I was banished the realm of France, and I have forfeited all that I had there.'"

Then the King gave him his right gauntlet, and said

"'I yield me to you'"

There was great press about the king, for every man enforced him to say, 'I have taken him,' so that the king could not go forward with his young son the lord Philip with him, because of the press."

*   *   *   *

"The Prince of Wales (the Black Prince), who was courageous and cruel as a lion, took that day great pleasure to fight and to chase his enemies. The lord John Chandos, who was with him, of all that day, never left him nor never took heed of taking of any prisoner: then at the end of the battle he said to the prince:

'Sir, it were good that you rested here and set your banner a-high in this bush, that your people may draw hither, for they are sore spread abroad, nor I can see no more banners nor pennons of the French party; wherefore, sir, rest and refresh you, for ye be sore chafed.'

"Then the prince's banner was set up a-high on a bush, and trumpets and clarions began to sown. Then the prince took off his bassenet, and the knights for his body and they of his chamber were ready about him, and a red pavilion pight up, and then drink was brought forth to the prince, and for such lords as were about him, the which still increased as they came from the chase; there they tarried and their prisoners with them.

"And when the two marshalls were come to the prince, he demanded of them if they knew any tidings of the French king. They answered and said:

"'Sir, we hear none of certainty, but we think verily he is other (either) dead or taken, for he is not gone out of the battles.'

"Then the prince said to the Earl of Warwick and to Sir Raynold Cobham:

'Sirs, I require you, go forth, and see what ye can know, and at your return ye may show me the truth.'

These two lords took their horses and departed from the prince and rode up a little hill to look about them. Then they perceived a flock of men of arms coming together right wearily; there was the French king afoot in great peril, for Englishmen and Gascoons were his masters; they had taken him from Sir Denis Morbeke perforce, and such as were most of force, said,

'I have taken him.'

'Nay,' quoth another, 'I have taken him.' So they strave which should have him.

Then, the French king, to eschew that peril, said:

'Sirs, strive not; lead me courteously, and my son, to my cousin the prince, and strive not for my taking, for I am so great a lord to make you all rich!'

The king's words somewhat appeased them; howbeitever as they went they made riot and brawled for the taking of the king.

When the two aforesaid lords saw and heard that noise and strife among them, they went to them and said:

'Sirs, what is the matter that you strive for '

'Sirs,' said one of them, 'it is the French king, who is here taken prisoner, and there be more than ten knights and squires that challengeth the taking of him and of his son.'

"Then the two lords entered into the press and caused every man to draw aback, and commanded them in the prince's name on pain of their heads to make no more noise nor to approach the king no nearer without they were commanded. Then every man gave room to the lords, and they alighted and did their reverence to the king, and so brought him and his son in peace and rest to the Prince of Wales."

*   *   *   *

Thus did Froissart record the taking of King John of France by the Black Prince, and the thrilling account is of particular interest to Eltham people. Not only were the royal captive and the royal captor associated with our village, but the chronicler himself was afterwards a visitor at Eltham, so the whole incident, thus described, becomes trebly interesting.

The Black Prince won great glory upon the field of Poitiers. And the glory of the warrior has been enhanced by the knightly courtesy which he shewed the captive king, who was now at his mercy.

Read, again, what Froissart says:

"The same day of the battle at night the prince made a supper in his lodging to the

French king, and to the most part of the great lords that were prisoners. The prince made the king and his son, the lord James of Bourbon, the lord John d'Artois, and other lords, to sit all at one board, and other lords, knights, and squires, at other tables.

"And always the prince served before the king as humbly as he could, and would not sit at the king's board for any desire that the king could make, but he said he was not sufficient to sit at the table with so great a prince as the king was.

"But then he said to the king:

'Sir, for God's sake, make none evil nor heavy cheer, though God this day did not consent to follow your will; for, sir, surely the king, my father, shall bear you as much honour and amity as he may do, and shall accord with you so reasonably that ye shall ever be friends together after. And, sir, methink ye ought to rejoice, though the journey be not as ye could have had it, for this day ye have won the high renown of prowess, and have passed this day in vaillantness all other of your party. Sir, I say not this to mock you, for all that be on our party, that saw every man's deeds, are plainly accorded by true sentence to give you the prize and chaplet.'

Therewith the Frenchmen began to murmur and said among themselves how the prince had nobly spoken, and that by all estimation he should prove a noble man, if God send him life and to persevere in such good fortune."

KNIGHTS JOUSTING (Royal M.S.)

Chapter XXXII

THE CAPTIVE KING AT ELTHAM.

The battle of Poitiers resulted in the rout of the French army with terrible carnage, and the capture of King John the Good, with crowds of his nobles, and some two thousand men at arms

We read that our Black Prince distinguished himself mightily in the field that day, setting an example of personal prowess which was followed by his intrepid knights It may be said of the English at Poitiers as was said of the Scotch at Flodden —

"Groom fought like noble, squire like knight,
As fearlessly and well"

The day after the battle (Tuesday, September 20th, 1356) the English Army, greatly encumbered with spoils and prisoners, marched to the city of Bordeaux, where a treaty of peace to last for two years was concluded with Charles, Duke of Normandy, who, since the capture of his father, was acting as the Regent of France

The Black Prince had determined to detain his royal prisoner, and convey him to England But there was a little account to be settled The question of the claim for the King's capture was still being hotly disputed

"In those days a prisoner taken 'to mercy' in battle became the absolute property and chattel of his captor, but when the prisoner was of exalted rank, and the captor a simple soldier of fortune, the king generally speculated on the ransom of the captive, and secured his custody for his own purposes by paying over what seemed a small sum from the royal exchequer, but was in all probability a large one relatively to the means of the captor" (Warburton)

So the Black Prince paid De Morbecq, who was the real captor of the French King, the sum of 2,000 marks, a mark being worth about 13s 4d It is interesting, however, to note that when, subsequently, the question of the king's ransom had to be settled, it was fixed at three million crowns of gold, a sum equivalent to about £450,000 sterling So the bargain which the Black Prince struck with De Morbecq was, after all, a profitable speculation

The Prince and his royal prisoner set sail for England from the port of Bordeaux, and after a stormy passage, which lasted eleven days, the party landed safely at Sandwich

Let us now read Froissart's account of the journey to London, which, of course, was made on horseback He makes no mention of Eltham in this journey, and it is very probable that the party passed along the Old Dover-road over Shooter's-hill, and did not pass through the village.

"Then they issued out of their ships," writes Froissart, "and lay there (Sandwich) all that night, and tarried there two days to refresh them, and on the third day they rode to Canterbury

"When the King of England knew of their coming, he commanded them of London to prepare them and their city to receive such a man as the French King was Then they of London arrayed themselves by companies and the chief mesters with clothing different each from the other.

"At Saint Thomas of Canterbury, the French King, and the prince made their offerings, and tarried a day, and then rode to Rochester and tarried there that day, and the next day to Dartford and the fourth day to London, where they were honourably received, and so they were in every good town as they passed

The French king rode through London on a white courser, well apparelled, and the prince (the Black Prince) on a little black hobby by him "

The spectacle of the conqueror riding upon a pony by the side of the captive king, who was mounted on a fine charger, has been the subject of much comment by historians, and is set forth as evidence of the modesty and courtesy of the Black Prince But Warburton says, " it is difficult altogether to acquit him of affectation and self-consciousness on the occasion of this ride into the city of London, the account of which reads more like that of a Roman triumph than of an English welcome A thousand citizens in the dress of their respective guilds, and headed by the Lord Mayor, received them at Southwark, and marched back with them in procession to the city Arches were thrown across the streets, trophies of arms and gold and silver plate were exhibited in the windows, and all, as it was said, in honour of the vanquished king."

Presently, they arrived at the Savoy Palace, which was the residence of John of Gaunt, Duke of Lancaster, an elder brother of the Black Prince In this palace the French king and his young son Philip were lodged

"There," writes Froissart, " the French king kept house a long season, and thither came to see him, the king, and queen oftentimes, and made him great feast and cheer."

* * *

It will be noticed that King John the Good was not treated in the way that prisoners of war are usually His word of honour not to escape was accepted, and he enjoyed much liberty, he and "all his household, and went a-hunting and a-hawking at his pleasure, and the lord Philip, his son, with him "

It is most likely that on such occasions as these King John of France paid those visits to Eltham which identified his name so closely with the village.

Apropos of this there is a curious story told by Villani, a foreign historian of the time, relative to the coming of the French king.

He says that while the royal party, the Black Prince, and his prisoners were on their way from Sandwich to London, they fell in with King Edward, who was hunting in a forest through which they had to pass

"Whether in levity or simplicity," writes Warburton, "Edward invited the captive monarch to join him in the chase, and on his declining this ill-timed offer, assured King John that he was quite at liberty to enjoy himself in hunting or 'at the river,' when and where he pleased during his stay in England, then, sounding his horn, he spurred on after his hounds, and was lost in the woods "

The story seems very improbable when one considers the character of Edward III., who, "though far from being a perfect character, was rarely found wanting in the tact and delicacy which became a true knight, or (to translate into modern phrase) in the instincts of a gentleman "

It is quite likely that Villani derived this anecdote from some gossip or other relating to the freedom which the nominal captive enjoyed, and it is equally likely that such gossip may have arisen from some incident that occurred in the forests of this particular neighbourhood

* * *

King John of France was in captivity in England for the space of some four years. Meanwhile things had been going very badly in France. There had been an uprising of the people, known as the outbreak of the "Jacquerie," accompanied by much bloodshed and devastation The two years' peace with England had expired, and Edward was again in France with his fighting men Of all this you must read in your book on history.

At last an agreement was come to by which King John of France was to be ransomed for 3,000,000 crowns of gold Of this 600,000 crowns were to be paid before the captive king was allowed to pass out of the gates of Calais, and the remainder of the debt was to be cleared off by annual payments of 400,000 crowns.

The bill was a heavy one, and there was great difficulty in raising the money, nevertheless, the Black Prince conveyed his prisoner from London to Calais, and there the treaty was duly ratified, "both kings kneeling before the altar, taking into their hands the consecrated Host, and swearing to the faithful observance of their engagement on the 'body of Christ'"

The first instalment of the ransom, 600,000 crowns, was raised in an unexpected way A wealthy Italian nobleman, the head of the powerful house of Vesconti, sought the hand of king John's youngest daughter, in marriage for his son, and offered to pay this part of the ransom when such marriage took place

The offer was accepted King John was given his liberty, and the Duke of Orleans, together with the second and third sons of King John, the Dukes of Berri and Anjou, and other members of the royal family, and forty citizens from the principal cities of France, were retained as hostages for the remainder of the debt

In 1363, a year or two afterwards, the "Lords of the Fleur de Lys"—Orleans, Berri, and Anjou—being rather tired of exile sought permission of King Edward to visit their native France, "giving their word of honour that they would return on the fourth day "

The Duke of Anjou broke his word, and did not return, King Edward then wrote a letter to him, and asked him to return " for that by his treachery he had tarnished the honour of himself and all his lineage "

King John, the father of the Duke, was so deeply affected by this lapse from honour on the part of his son, regarding the action as a reflection upon the honour of himself that he resolved to yield himself up again to captivity

Thus came about his second visit to England, this time as a voluntary exile.

It is not surprising that he was received in this country with every sign of veneration and respect, and that our village of Eltham took a conspicuous share in these expressions

Read again what Froissart has said ·

" News was brought to the King of England, who at that time was with his Queen at Eltham, a very magnificent palace which the king had, seven miles from London, that the King of France had landed at Dover

" He immediately ordered many knights of his household to go and congratulate the king on his arrival, the lord Bartholomew Burgharsh, knight of the garter, Sir Richard Pembridge, Sir Allen Boxhall, both knights of the garter, and several others

" They took leave of King Edward, and rode towards Dover, where they found the King of France, who had remained there since his arrival They attended and conducted him with every mark of respect and honour, as they well knew how to do

" Among other compliments, they told him that the king, their lord, was much rejoiced at his coming, which the King of France readily believed On the morrow morning, the king and his attendants were on horseback early, and rode to Canterbury, where they dined. On entering the Cathedral, the king paid his devotions at the shrine of St Thomas à Becket, and presented to it a rich jewel of great value

" The third day he set out taking the road to London, and rode on until he came to Eltham, where the King of England was with a number of lords, ready to receive him It was on a Sunday, in the afternoon, when he arrived, and there were, therefore, between this time and supper time, many good dances and carols

" The young lord of Coucy was there—a grandson of the first Duke of Swabia—who took pains to shine in his dancing and singing whenever it was his turn. He was a great favourite with both the French and English, for whatever he chose to do, he did well and with grace.

" I can never relate how very honourably and majestically the King and Queen of England received King John On leaving Eltham he went to London, and as he came near, he was met by the citizens dressed out in their proper companies, who greeted and welcomed him with much reverence, and attended him with large bands of minstrels, unto the palace of the Savoy, which had been prepared for him."

It was here that he died soon after. His body was embalmed, and put into a coffin, and conveyed to Paris, where it was interred with great solemnity.

LADIES' HEAD DRESSES (Royal M.S.)

Chapter XXXIII

A FAMOUS CHRONICLER.

We have frequently alluded to Froissart, and in the last few chapters have quoted extensively from his Chronicles Moreover, he knew Eltham so well, and wrote about it so often, that it would be a good thing, perhaps, for the information of our young friends, if we gave some little account of this remarkable man himself

Jean Froissart was a Frenchman born near Valenciennes, about 1337, and his ancestors were of lowly origin We do not know much of his childhood, but we find that he was a great favourite with Philippa, the romantic queen of Edward III , who encouraged him in his literary pursuits

It does not seem clear at what time he became a priest, but it is interesting to learn that when John of France was a captive here, Jean Froissart was his secretary, and it was then that he began to collect all that gossipy information which makes his Chronicles so intensely interesting. It was after this time that he set about his great history in real earnest, journeying from place to place on the Continent, collecting much of his material first hand, and writing down his impressions in that delightful way of his

When King John of France returned to exile, as recorded in our last chapter, Froissart came with him, and then it was that he traversed again our Eltham lanes, and looked once more upon the "beautiful palace which King Edward III. had there "

The reception given to his master seems to have impressed him very much, for he has not only left a graphic record of the occasion in his Chronicles, but he also wrote a charming poem, which it has been our good fortune to discover, for it gives a pretty little glimpse of the form the jubilations took at Eltham

The credit of finding these quaint verses rests with our esteemed Librarian, Mr E A. Baker, who, in the course of some studies in Old French Literature, came across them unexpectedly, and at once drew our attention to them. The curious thing is that no student of local history seems, hitherto, to have known of them; at any rate, we can find no allusion to them anywhere It is with all the greater pleasure, therefore, that we present them to our readers now We give them, in the first place, in the Old French, exactly as Froissart wrote them, with its quaint spelling and old time expressions. Those who know Old French will find pleasure in construing the verses Those who do not, will like them in that form, perhaps, to preserve as a sort of local literary curiosity.

But, in the interests of those who are not familiar with the language at all, with the kind and ready co-operation of Miss May, one of the lecturers at Avery-hill, and Mr E A. Baker, both of whom are well versed in Old French literature, we have been able to write a metrical translation, in which we have endeavoured to preserve, not only the form of the original, but to interpret its spirit

There seems to be some mystery about the lines in the fourth verse, beginning with —

"Et si bien se desigeroit, &c"

It is not at all clear who the person is that disguises himself To satisfy ourselves we proceeded to the British Museum, and hunted up Scheler, who is the greatest French authority upon Froissart It was some sort of satisfac-

ST. MARY'S ORPHANAGE.
(The house of Lord Goschen when a boy).

No. 78.

THE NATIONAL SCHOOLS KEPER STREET.

No. 77.

THE OLD LOCK-UP. (High Street).

No. 80.

MAUSOLEUM OF THE
FAMILY OF MR. THOMAS CHESTER HAWORTH.
(By the way-side at Nottingham).

No. 79.

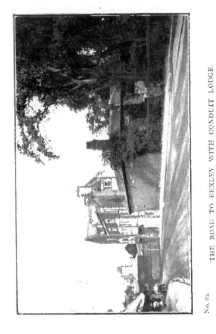

No. 82.   THE ROAD TO BEXLEY WITH CONDUIT LODGE.

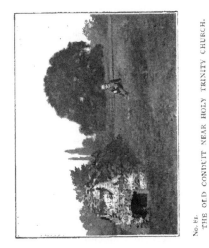

No. 81.   THE OLD CONDUIT NEAR HOLY TRINITY CHURCH.

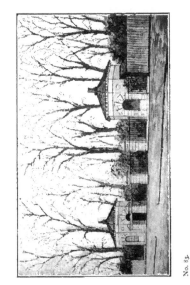

No. 83.

tion to find that Scheler cannot explain the allusion; he is as mystified over it as we were.

For the benefit of our younger readers we might explain that St. Denis, alluded to in the poem, is the Patron Saint of France, and the "Fleur de Lys," literally, "the Flower of the Lily," was formerly the national emblem of the French.

So far as can be discovered, no translation of this poem has ever been before printed in English, but though more than five centuries have elapsed since Froissart wrote the verses, referring, as they do to an Eltham incident, it seems quite consistent, that its first construing into our own tongue, should emanate from Eltham itself.

PASTOURELLE.

Par Jean Froissart.

(Composed on the occasion of the return of the French King John to his nominal captivity in England, at the beginning of 1364, when he was received by Edward III. with great festivities.)

Entre Eltem et Westmoustier,
En une belle preorie,
Cuesci pastoureaus avant heir
La avoit en la compagnie
Mainte faitice pastourelle,
Dont au son d'une canemelle
Cascuns et cascune dansoit,
Dist uns bregiers qui la estoit;
Efforcons nous, pour Saint Denis
Car errant par ci passer doit
　Cils qui porte les flours de lys.'

Adont dist Mares dou Vivier
'Or me dittes, je vous en prie,
Porte il ces flours en un panier,
Ou il les donne, ou il les crie?
Qu'en vent il plain une escuielle?
C'est une flourette moult belle;
De la flour de lys orendroit,
Qui un chapel fait en auroit,
Il en seroit trop plus jolis;
Je croi que bien en fineroit
　Cils qui porte les flours de lys.

Pour ce me vodrai avancier
Et aler ent a chiere lie
Vers lui, et il vodrai prover
Qu'il m'en doinst par sa courtoisie,

Et il aura ma cornuielle,
La mousette et la flahutelle,
Dont mon frere m'esbanioit,'
Dist Raouls qui oï l'avoit:
'Esce or a bon sens que tu dis?
Cuides tu qu'un bregier ce soit
　Cils qui porte les flours de lys?'

'Nennil, point n'est de no mestier,
Ains est rois de noble lignie
Si que pour li mieuls festyer,
It nous couvient a ceste fie
Mettre en ordenance nouvelle.'—
'C'est voirs,' ce respont Peronnelle
Qui moult bien oie l'avoit,
'Et si bien se desgiseroit,
Mes qu'il euist tous ses abis,
Que ja ne la cognisteroit
　Cils qui porte les flours de lys!

Lors prisent a entrechangier
Leurs abis de la bregerie.
Gobins vesti un grant loudier
Et Guois une sousquanie,
Sus se chaindi d'une cordelle;
Et Perrotins sus une aisselle
D'un blanc bastoncel tamburoit,
Et Adins la danse menoit,
Qui souvent disoit par grans ris:
'Diex, pourquoi ores ne nous voit
　Cils qui porte les flours de lys?
Princes, je les vi la endroit,
Ou cascune et cascuns chantoit
A l'usage de leur pays:
'Li tres bien venus ores soit
　Cils qui porte les flours de lys.'

[Translation.]
A PASTORAL.
By J. Froissart.

Betwixt Eltham and Westminster,
Yestreen I saw a meadow fair,
Wherein a band of shepherds were,
In merry guise and debonair.
And, therewith, many a shepherd maid
Went dancing as the pipe was played,
And youth and wench they stepped it
　light;
When cried aloud a merry wight,
"Our cheers for good St. Denis be,
For here shall pass before this night
　The one that bears the fleurs de lys."

Quoth Maurice de Vivier joyously,
"Oh, tell me now, forsooth, I pray,
A pannierful, then, bringeth he,
To sell for pence, or give away?
Right beautiful the fleurs de lys!
A bowlful will he sell to me?
Sure, he that crieth flowers so fair,
Thereof a garland ought to wear,
It were a pleasant sight to see,
He'd soon get rid of them, I swear,
The one that bears the fleurs de lys.

"Good sooth," then answered Peronelle,
That well had heeded Ralph's reply,
"If all his clothes he had but nigh,
A fair disguise I ween 'twould be,
For none would know him passing by,
Not he that bears the fleurs de lys."

And so they gan to interchange
Their shepherd's habits, every one,
And Gobin wore a tunic strange,
Anon did Guy a smock put on,
Which with a cord he straightly tied,

FEMALE DRESS, TIME OF EDWARD III.

And so with thee I fain would go,
To meet him with the fleurs de lys,
And beg he'll some of them bestow
On me, all of his courtesy.
And unto him I'll give my horn,
My flute and pipe, to wake the morn,
Whereon my brother used to play"——
But Ralph, who heard him, answered
      "Nay,
What sense is this thou speak'st so free,
Think'st thou that he's a shepherd, pray,
The one that bears the fleurs de lys?

Nay, he is none of our degree,
He is a King of noble line;
And so, to do him honour, we
The parts we play should now assign,
And in new order bear us well."

And Perrotin, he gaily plied
The drum that 'neath his elbow lay,
And Adam led the morris gay,
And laughed aloud in merry glee,
"Lord! might he see us here to-day
   The one that bears the fleurs de lys!"
   Princes, in truth, I saw them there,
They sang it to a native air——
Those youths and maidens bright of
   blee——
" Welcome to him that cometh here,
   The one that bears the fleur de lys'"

            * * *

From this it will be seen that they had a
merry time of it on the occasion of King John's
last visit to Eltham. Yes, last. Ere many weeks
the "King of noble line" who bore "the fleurs
de lys," was sick unto death.

Two years later (1366) Froissart left England, but returned again after an absence of forty years. He was an old man when he visited Eltham on that last occasion, and brought with him his book about "Love," for the edification of the unhappy Richard II. Great changes had taken place within those 40 years. Of this we will speak in another chapter. It is interesting to note that with his last visit to England his work as a chronicler seems to have ended. The closing pages of his book describe the death of Richard. After this the fate of the historian himself becomes obscure. It is sad to learn how tradition asserts that he died in utter poverty at Chimay ten years after his return to France. He was buried in the church of Monegunda.

RICHARD II. (In Jerusalem Chamber).

CHAPTER XXXIV.

RICHARD II. AND ELTHAM (1).

Richard of Bordeaux, born 1366, was the son of Edward the Black Prince, and Joan, known as the "Fair Maid of Kent." The Black Prince died when Richard was ten years old. In the same year, 1376, Edward III. was lying sick at Eltham, and here it was that the king summoned a parliament; and the young prince Richard was, on that occasion, created Prince of Wales.

It should be noted that parliaments were not always held at one place, as they are now at Westminster. The king could summon his councillors to any meeting-place that seemed to him convenient. So there are records of parliaments meeting at London, Gloucester, York, and other places, including Eltham.

The very next year, Edward III., after a reign of 50 years, died, and the young Prince of Wales became the "Boy King," his age, when he succeeded to the throne, being only 11 years. Rarely has a monarch entered upon his kingly responsibilities with brighter prospects of a happy reign. But, alas! clouds soon arose, and history records few things more pathetic than the tragedy of this young king's life.

It began in sunshine and splendour. An old historian writes: "There are enthusiastic rejoicings to welcome the beautiful boy as he is brought from the Tower to Westminster to be crowned. There are around him a devoted multitude of nobles, knights, and esquires, that dazzle his eye with their costly adornments. The streets they pass through on their gorgeously-caparisoned coursers are hung with floating draperies, the windows are full of gazers The air resounds with rapturous shouts 'God bless the royal boy! Long live King Richard!'

"In Cheapside golden angels bend to him from the towers of mimic castles, presenting crowns, and at other places he is met by beautiful virgins of his own age and stature, robed in white, who blow leaves and flowers of gold in his face, and, as he approaches nearer, they fill gold cups from the conduits flowing with wine, and hand to him High and low delight to honour him for his father's sake. His plastic imagination is, of course, most highly wrought upon by the magnificent pageants, and by the unbounded adulation that he witnesses on all sides. They bewilder his reason, and make him fancy that he is a god, long before he is a man."

Froissart, writing of him, says "There was none so great in England that dared speak against anything that the king did He had a council suitable to his fancies, who exhorted him to do what he list, he kept in his wages ten thousand archers, who watched over him day and night "

What wonder is it that he became a slave to selfish luxury? The effect of all this adulation and worship was disastrous upon a character that, unlike that of his father and grandfather, was decidedly weak. When, at the age of 23, he took over the responsibilities of government, he was incapable of dealing adequately with the difficult questions which the conditions of the times forced upon him.

Richard II. frequently visited Eltham. He held several parliaments here, and much important business of state was transacted at Eltham Palace during this reign

In the year 1381, four years after his accession, when, as yet, the king was only a boy of sixteen, there took place the insurrection of the peasantry, in which Kent played so prominent a part. Its immediate cause was the imposition of the poll-tax, but its real cause lay in the general discontent of the working classes with the manorial system. Although the social condition of the peasantry had undergone some

change for the better during the preceding century, the system of villeinage was still recognised, families were still bought and sold with the estates, and terrible abuses were practised

The culminating point was the poll-tax, which resulted in the resistance of Wat Tyler, at Dartford, followed by the rising of the peasants of Kent, the looting and destruction of manors, and the killing of many officials and landed gentry

All around Eltham the district was affected, and from every direction the countrymen marched in bands towards Blackheath, which was the rallying point prior to the great descent upon London. The old road over Shooter's-hill must have presented a very striking appearance in those troublous days, and the cottages of Eltham, whatever part they may have played in the revolt, must have experienced considerable excitement when they witnessed the bands of lawless men, who had left their ploughs and oxen in the Kentish fields, thronging, in their thousands, towards the Heath.

Did the Eltham men take any part in the rebellion? This was the problem that interested us It was impossible that the Eltham villagers should not have been under its influence at all, seeing how near at hand some of the great scenes of the drama were played It was from Dartford that Wat the Tyler set forth upon his lawless and tragic career It was at Blackheath that the priest, John Ball, delivered one of his most characteristic speeches But, after diligent search, we can discover no record of Eltham men being mixed up with the rebellion. There are old writings to shew the scope and work of the Commission which sat, soon after the event, for the trial and punishment of the ringleaders in the movement. One can discover names of people from Deptford, Blackheath, Dartford, and other places, but we can find no Eltham names

Nor does it seem that any attempt was made to destroy the Palace. In other Kentish villages the manor houses were the special object of attack They were looted and burned, and in cases where escape was delayed, their occupants were cruelly murdered. But Eltham Palace escaped the fury of the mob.

We hardly need wonder at this. Eltham was a Royal Manor, and the labourers would have been the less likely to join in an insurrection of the kind. Then, the wrath of the insurgents was not directed against the king so much as against the nobility. They even professed that they were desirous of getting the king upon their side. Certain it is that the purpose of the rising was to induce the king to grant them concessions. Under these circumstances it would be more likely than not, that Eltham, being a royal demesne, was designedly left alone.

The circumstance of the king's mother seems to suggest that their attitude towards the king was not one of particular enmity. She chanced to fall into their hands at Blackheath, but, although they were flushed with success and their hands were yet red with the blood of the Kentish gentry, they allowed her to proceed upon her way.

"The same day," writes Froissart, "that these unhappy people were coming to London, there returned from Canterbury the king's mother, Princess of Wales, coming from her pilgrimage. She was in great jeopardy to have been lost, for these people came to her chare and dealt rudely with her, whereof the good lady was in great doubt lest they would have done some villainy to her and to her damsels. Howbeit, God kept her, and she came in one day from Canterbury to London, for she never durst tarry by the way."

*   *   *   *

The old historian Holinshed makes Eltham Palace the scene of the leave-taking of Henry Bolingbroke, Duke of Hereford, when on his way to banishment. The story of the quarrel between Hereford and Norfolk, the tournament at Coventry, and the unexpected interference of the king, who stopped the fight, and banished Norfolk for life and Hereford for ten years, is no doubt familiar to our young readers of history.

But the incident was one that really arose out of the weak government of Richard, who, as the age of manhood approached, shewed more and more how incapable he was of managing the affairs of the country. Though the banishment of these two powerful nobles, one of whom, Bolingbroke, was his cousin, removed from the country two men that the king feared greatly, it was fraught with terrible consequences for Richard himself. Norfolk never returned, but the day arrived when the courtly Bolingbroke came back with armed men to claim his rights, and ultimately to mount the throne from which the weak and effeminate Richard was deposed.

The story is set forth in one of the finest of Shakespeare's plays. The Eltham incident, however, finds no place in the drama. Shakespeare makes the final dismissal to take place at Coventry, and Bolingbroke does not return until he comes in force. But the playwright is allowed licence to ignore, and, sometimes, even to distort historical facts when necessary for his play. Shakespeare never neglected to use this privilege whenever he thought fit.

The following, however, is what Holinshed, the Chronicler, has to say about it:

"When these judgements were once read, the king called before him both parties (Hereford and Norfolk), and made them to swear that the one should never come in place where the other was willinglie; nor keep any companie togither in any foreign region; which oth they both received humblie.

"The Duke of Norfolk departed sorrowfullie out of the relme into Almanie, and at the last came to Venice, where he, for thought and melancholie, deceased; for he was in hope (as writers record) that he should have been home, which, when it fell out otherwise, grieved him not a little.

"*The Duke of Hereford took his leave of the king at Eltham, who there released foure years of his punishment; so he took his journie over into Colis, and from thence into Fronce, where he remained.*

"A wonder it was to see what number of people ran after him in every town and street where he came, before he took the sea, lamenting and bewailing his departure, as who would saie, that when he departed, the onelie shield, defence, and comfort of the common wealth was faded and gone."

Thus did Bolingbroke, Duke of Hereford, take leave of his royal master at the Palace of Eltham. The next time we read of him at Eltham he was King Henry **IV.**

FEMALE COSTUME, TIME OF RICHARD II.

Chapter XXXV

RICHARD II. AND ELTHAM (2).

The three successive Christmases from 1384 to 1386 were kept by King Richard II and Queen Anne, at Eltham We find it hard to realise, even in these days, the splendour of the English Court at this time Holinshed tells us that "Richard II kept greater state than any English king before or after him Ten thousand people had meat and drink allowed them daily at his Court, he had three hundred servants, and as many female servants, his yeomen and grooms were clad in silk, and all were sumptuously apparelled Extravagance affected all classes, to the great hindrance and decay of the Commonwealth "

We cannot suppose that such vast numbers as those given above could find accommodation at Eltham, but we may very well believe that the Courts held at the royal village during the residence of this king were no less splendid and extravagant than those of the other palaces

* * * *

In the year 1385, Eltham was honoured by the visit of Leo, King of Armenia The circumstances of the visit are interesting.

King Leo had had the misfortune to be driven out of his kingdom by the Turks. So he went to the King of France, and entreated him to give him means to help him to regain his kingdom The King of France was not only sympathetic, but disposed to give material aid, for to fight the infidel Turk was accounted a worthy thing in those days.

Now it happened that the King of France was not on good terms with the King of England, and war between them was likely. King Leo of Armenia was anxious to avert war between the two countries, because such

an event would probably deprive him of any chance of getting money from France or England, to enable him to go and fight the unspeakable Turk

So it came to pass that Leo offered the King of France to visit the King of England as a sort of intermediary or peace maker

"On his arrival at Dover," writes Froissart, "he was well received, and conducted by some knights to the king's uncles, who entertained him handsomely, and, at proper opportunity, asked him what were his reasons for visiting England

To this he answered that he had come to wait upon the King of England and his council, in the hopes of doing good, and to see if by any means he could negotiate a peace between them and the King of France

The English lords then asked him if the King of France had sent him

"No," replied the King of Armenia, "no one has sent me I am come of my own accord, and solely with a view to do good "

Then they asked where the King of France was

"I believe he is at Sluys," replied the king, "and I have sent to him messengers, entreating him not to put to sea until I return I, therefore, beg of you to give me an interview with your king "

Thomas, Earl of Buckingham, answered, "King of Armenia, we are here solely to guard and defend the frontiers, and we do not concern ourselves in any way with the government of this realm. Some motives of good, or the appearance of them, have brought you hither—

you are welcome, but you must not expect from us any definite answer to what you ask, though we will have you conducted to London, without danger or expense "

The King of Armenia thanked them, and as soon as he was able, set out for London "

* * * *

So Leo, the King, went to London, and thence to Eltham, and in the presence of the King of England delivered himself of his mission After four days of consideration the following reply, prepared by the Archbishop of Canterbury, was given to him

"King of Armenia, it is not usual, nor has it ever been admitted, that in such weighty matters as these now in dispute between France and England, the King of England should have requests made him, while an army is ready to invade his country Our opinion is that you return to the French army and prevail on them to retire, and when ye shall be fully assured that they have done so, do you return hither, and we will pay attention to any treaty that you shall propose."

The King of Armenia, the day after he had received this answer, set out for Dover, making two days' journey of it From Dover he sailed to Calais, and thence made his way to Sluys.

He related to the King of France and his uncles the journey he had made to England, and what answer he had met with, but the king and his lords paid no attention to it, and resolved to set sail the first wind for England.

So the mission of Leo, the King of Armenia, as peacemaker, was a failure. But in another way it was a success He had had the delightful experience of Eltham hospitality Yea, more. Though pleading for peace, he did not forget to relate to King Richard his grievance against the usurping Turks The heart of Richard was touched, and Leo departed from Eltham consoled by a grant from the English Exchequer of one thousand pounds a year for life

* * * *

There is a record in the *Issue Rolls* (Devon, 226), dated 14 November, 1394, of £2 5s. for

expense on the secret arrival of the King (Richard II), at Westminster from his manor at Eltham, to dine, and inspect his jewels.

* * * *

In the same rolls (Devon, 261) we read that King Richard's "second crown" was brought from London to Eltham, and that on the date of 29 July, 1394, the sum of 6s 8d was paid to John Burgh, Clerk, for the safe conduct of the crown, and for the hire of horses and men

* * * *

History tells us of the troubles which fell to King Richard in his dealings with the nobles, and also with his parliament On several occasions of stress of mind we find him coming to the Palace of Eltham in what apears to have been "the sulks" In 1386, the year after the visit of the King of Armenia, he made the bold announcement to his parliament at Westminster that he was resolved to punish the French for their threatened invasion of England, by passing over at the head of a suitable army, and carrying war into France. So he asked for supplies But neither the Lords nor the Commons were in a humour to grant supplies, and met his demand by a joint petition to dismiss his ministers and council, especially the Chancellor

This enraged the King, who even contemplated doing what proved so fatal to Charles I long after, namely, seizing the leaders of the opposition But, finding that he was not likely to get support from the people, he came to Eltham, where, in the palace, surrounded by the parks and woodlands, he allowed his ill humours to exhaust themselves

When the seclusion of Eltham and its refreshing air had effected this change of temper, he changed his mind, drove back to town, and dismissed the obnoxious minister as the parliament had requested.

* * * *

On another occasion, some years afterwards, Richard had retired to Eltham, and neglected to attend to his kingly duties But times were changed. The people were getting tired of his conduct They no longer regarded him with that favour which in his early days had caused them to look upon him almost as a demi-god. So, one fine day, a messenger rode up to the draw-bridge, and thence into the inner courts of the Palace, bearing the rather unpleasant news that if the King continued to absent himself the Parliament intended to depose him.

* * * *

Again, in August, 1397, Richard was at Eltham with his Court, when he received the startling news that his uncle the Duke of

"How old do you think I am?"

"Your highness," replied Gloucester, "is in your twenty-second year."

"Then," said the King. "I must surely be old enough to manage my own concerns. I have been longer under the control of my guardians than any ward in my dominions. I thank ye, my lords, for your past services, but I require them no longer."

* * * *

SHIPS OF TIME OF RICHARD II. (Harl. M.S. 1319).

Gloucester was at the head of a conspiracy, the object of which was to seize him, together with the Dukes of York and Lancaster. The results of this intrigue were of a tragic character.

The Duke of Gloucester was a man of determined character, and of great power and influence in the land. He was one of the guardians of the king during his minority, and in that capacity his power was very great indeed. It was with Gloucester that Richard had the dialogue, in 1389, eight years before, when he shook off the control of his guardians. Suddenly, addressing his uncle, Gloucester, he said,

After the death of Queen Anne, wife of the King, the Duke of Gloucester was anxious that Richard should marry his daughter. The King, however, declined, making near relationship the excuse for his refusal. Gloucester was offended, became "sullen, morose, and destitute of all courtesy, returning the attentions of the nobles with abrupt and curt answers, so that they said amongst themselves, if ever Gloucester could stir up a war he would."

When the danger was revealed to him at Eltham, Richard determined to take action, and his method was to meet conspiracy with cunning. The earls of Warwick and Arundel were artfully entrapped and thrown into prison, but the method adopted for the arrest of the Duke of Gloucester was one of the most revolting and insidious in history

Although Richard had made up his mind to have the life of his uncle, he did not hesitate to pay him an apparently friendly visit at his castle at Pleshy in Essex. "Here Gloucester came forth with his wife and daughter to meet him, without any suspicion, and, according to the accounts of the rolls of Parliament, with a dutiful procession The king caused him to be seized by the Earl Marshall, and conveyed to Calais.

It is said by contemporary chronicles that while this was doing, Richard was conversing in a friendly guise with the duchess

Froissart says that Richard was kindly entertained, and requested Gloucester to accompany him to London, but this does not appear probable, if the Parliamentary rolls are correct. But in any case the manner of the thing was treacherous and unworthy of a great monarch "

Gloucester never returned to England.

On September 24th of the same year, 1397, a mandate was issued to the Earl Marshall to bring his prisoner, the Duke of Gloucester, from Calais, to the bar of the House The mandate was a blind.

Three days after, the Earl Marshall returned an answer, that "he could not produce the said Duke before the King and his Council in that Parliament, for that, being in his custody in the King's prison at Calais, he there died."

The manner of his death is variously recorded There was a talk of apoplexy But there could be but one opinion—murder.

Chapter XXXVI

A BOOK OF AMOURS AND MORALITIES.

The Eltham incidents which we are now about to describe took place some years before the tragic circumstances alluded to in the last chapter, but we take them here because they are in connection with the last visit paid to Eltham by Sir John Froissart

The Chronicler had not been to England for many years, and he had a great desire to see again the land wherein he had spent so many happy days during the glorious reign of King Edward "True it was," he writes, "that I, Sir John Froissart, as at that time treasurer and canon of Chimay in the earldom of Hainault, in the diocese of Liege, had great affection to go and see the realm of England, when I had been in Abbeville and saw that a truce was taken between the realms of England and France and other countries to them conjoined and their adherents, to endure four years by land and sea

"Many reasons moved me to make that voyage one was because in my youth I had been brought up in the court of the noble King Edward the third, and of Queen Philipa his wife, and among their children and other barons of England, that as then were alive, in whom I found all nobleness, honour, largess, and courtesy . . . . . And I had engrossed in a fair book well enlumined all the matters of amours and moralities that in four and twenty years before I had made and compiled, which greatly quickened my desire to go into England to see King Richard, who was son of the noble Prince of Wales and of Aquitaine, for I had not seen this King Richard sith he was christened in the cathedral church at Bordeaux, at which time I was there and thought to have

gone with the prince into Galicia in Spain, and when we were at Dax, the prince sent me back into England to the queen, his mother"

*   *   *   *

So, Sir John came to see the king and his uncles "Also I had this fair book," he continues, "well covered with velvet, garnished with clasps of silver and gilt, thereof to make a present to the king at my first coming into his presence I had such desire to go to this voyage, that the pain and travail grieved me nothing."

He found things greatly changed when he landed at Dover. "Young children had become men and women and knew me not, nor I them."

In his inimitable style Froissart describes his journey through Kent, the visit to Canterbury where King Richard was expected next day on pilgrimage to the shrine of Saint Thomas à Becket, how he felt "abashed" when, among the king's retinue, he could discover nobody that he knew, the ride to Leeds Castle in Kent, and thence to Eltham

At Leeds Castle he found Lord Edmund, Duke of York "Then I went to him and delivered my letters from the Earl of Hainault, his cousin, and from the Earl of Ostrevant. The duke knew me well and made me good cheer, and said 'Sir John, hold you always near to us and we shall shew you love and courtesy, we are bound thereto for the love of time past, and for the love of my lady the old queen, my mother, in whose court ye were, we have good remembrance thereof!'"

During the ride from Leeds Castle to the Manor of Eltham, Froissart learned that important business was to be transacted when they arrived at the latter place.

"The king was sore busied there in council for two great and mighty matters: first was in determining to send sufficient messengers, as the Earl of Rutland, his cousin-german, and the earl marshall, Thomas Mowbray, afterwards Duke of Norfolk, now Archbishop of Dublin, the Bishop of Ely, the lord Louis Clifford, the lord Henry Beaumont, the lord Hugh Spencer, and many other, over sea to prelates and lords of England to be at the feast of Maudlin-tide, at a manor of the king's, called Eltham, seven miles from London."

* * * *

The king and all his brilliant company rode into Eltham on a Tuesday, "and on the Wednesday the lords of all coasts began to assemble." There was a great muster of them, and "on the Thursday, about the hour of three, they assembled together in the king's chamber and in the king's presence."

LEEDS CASTLE, KENT.

Charles the French king, to treat with him for a marriage to be had between the king of England and the French king's eldest daughter, named Isabel, of the age of eight years."

The second cause was to consider the "requests and process," that certain French nobles had made to the king, with reference to the lands, seignories, lordships, and baronies in Aquitaine, which the king had given to the Duke of Lancaster, but which they alleged should not be dissevered from the crown of England.

To have counsel "of these two great matters, the king had sent for the most part of the

We may stand by the moat to-day and imagine that we see these great lords, with their squires and attendants, riding through the gateway that led into the courtyard, then by way of the drawbridge into the inner court of the palace.

Of the great council, Froissart writes: "I was not present, nor might not be suffered: there were none but the lords of the Council, who debated the matter more than four hours."

But he was not slow in finding out what had actually taken place within those closed doors.

"After dinner," he goes on, "I fell in

acquaintance with an ancient knight, whom I knew in king Edward's days, and he was, as then, of king Richard's Privy Council, he was called Sir Richard Stury . .   This knight made me good cheer and demanded of me many things, and I answered him as I knew, and as I walked with him in a gallery before the king's chamber, I demanded of him questions of that council and desired him to tell me, if he might, what conclusion was taken "

The knight replied "Sir John, I shall shew you, for it is no matter to be hidden and kept secret, for shortly ye shall hear them published all openly "

So Sir Richard told Sir John all about it, and the arguments are set forth in the chronicles of the latter   They are, however, too lengthy for reproduction here, but the reader may find them pleasantly translated in Lord Berner's edition of Froissart

The Duke of Gloucester, who was "sore dread," was discordant in his utterance, and the Council broke up, and "some murmured one with another "   "When the king saw all the matter, he dissimuled a little, and it was his intention that they should assemble together again in Council after dinner, to see if any other proper way might be taken for the honour of the crown of England."

The question of Acquitaine brought discord, but they seemed to be in agreement as to the marriage of the widower king of England to the eight-year old Princess of France

"Then the king caused the Bishop of Canterbury to speak of that he had given him in charge in the morning to speak of, that was upon the state of his marriage, and to send into France   The lords were of accord and named them that should go, which were the Archbishop of Dublin, the earl marshal, the lord Beaumont, the lord Hugh Spenser, the lord Louis Clifford, and twenty knights and forty squires

"These were sent into France to treat for the marriage of the French King's daughter Isabel, of eight years of age, and yet she was already promised to the Duke of Bretayne's son by a treaty that was made in Tours in Touraine   Now, behold, how this was broken,

for the French king and his uncles had sealed with the Duke of Bretayne

"Yet for all that the English ambassadors had their charge given unto them, and so they departed out of England and arrived at Calais, and there tarried a five days and then departed in great array, and took the way to Amiens, and they sent before March the herald who had brought them safe-conduct going and coming "

*   *   *   *

So occupied was the king with business that it was not till Sunday that an opportunity came for Froissart to present to the king the book with the silver clasps which he had brought with him

"On the Sunday following," he writes, "all such as had been there departed, and all their counsellors, except the Duke of York, who abode still about the king, and Sir Thomas Percy and Sir Richard Stury shewed my business to the king

"Then the king desired to see my book that I had brought for him, so he saw it in his chamber, for I laid it there ready on his bed

"When the king opened it, it pleased him well, for it was fair illumined and written, and covered with crimson velvet, with ten buttons of silver and gilt, and roses of gold in the midst, and two silver clasps gilt, richly wrought

"Then the king demanded of me whereof it treated, and I shewed him how that it treated of matters of love, whereof the king was very glad. And he looked into it, and read it in many places, for he could speak and read French very well

"And he gave it to a knight of his chamber, named Sir Richard Crendon, to bear it into his secret chamber."

*   *   *   *

The English Ambassadors were well received in France, and saw the young lady Isabel They returned to England with a hopeful answer, though many in France were against the marriage

Ultimately, the marriage took place, and it is interesting to read that the girl-wife, then barely ten years of age, took up her abode in Eltham Palace, prior to her state entry into

London. Here she received valuable presents from the king, his uncles, the Dukes of Lancaster and York, and the nobles. Among these presents was one from the Bishop of Chichester, which took the form of a silver image of the Virgin as big as a child of five years old. (*Traison et mort du Roy Richart*, p. 112).

The sad life of this little lady, while Queen of England, is known to readers of English history. After the deposition and death of her lord, the king, she was brought to Eltham, where she remained for some years, until the new king, Henry IV., allowed her to return to France.

MALE COSTUME, RICHARD II.

CHAUCER ON HORSEBACK (from Ellesmere M.S. of Canterbury Tales).
By permission of Dr. Furnivall and Messrs. Macmillan & Co.

Chapter XXXVII.

CHAUCER AND THE HIGHWAYMEN.

Yet another man of letters, and one whose name and work will be associated with English literature for all time, used to visit Eltham in the days of Edward III. and Richard II. This was Geoffrey Chaucer himself, the "Father of English Poetry."

As a young man, he was brilliant and accomplished, and was a familiar figure at the court of Edward III., and, latterly, also at that of King Richard. He was a great friend of John of Gaunt, the brother of King Edward, who encouraged him in his literary pursuits. Indeed, John of Gaunt became the poet's brother-in-law, when the latter married Catherine Swinford, who was a sister of Chaucer's wife.

Chaucer was a Court official. In his youth, he was one of the thirty-seven squires who were valets to Edward III. Later he was sent on a diplomatic mission, on behalf of England, to the Duke of Genoa, and it is supposed that he met the Italian poet, Petrarch, at Padua, on this occasion.

In after years, when Richard II. was king, Chaucer seems to have been in disfavour for a time. He became involved in the civil and religious troubles of the day, and joined the party of John of Northampton, who was a supporter of Wyckliffe, in resisting the measures of the Court. So the poet thought it

No. 85.
BLACK-BOY COTTAGE.

It stood formerly upon the wayside opposite
Southend House.

No. 86.
THE IVY COTTAGE

Which stood where " The Chestnuts," Court Road,
now stands.

The figure in foreground is " Bishop " Sharpe, the old
schoolmaster, sketching.

No. 87.
THE TILT YARD GATE
(Winter-time).

No. 88.
RAM ALLEY. (High Street).

No. 90.

SITE OF THE LONDON AND SOUTH-WESTERN BANK.

(High Street.)

(House formerly the residence of the late Miss Fry, now of Mr. Colson).

No. 92.

THE COURT YARD, SHOWING THE OLD ELM TREE.

No. 89.

THE OLD FORGE,

Formerly stood on the site of the proposed Municipal Buildings, near the Library.

No. 91.

THE OLD TOLL GATE ON THE LEE ROAD.

(Near Cambridge Road).

wise to flee the country, going to Hainault, and afterwards to Holland.

He returned, however, in 1386, and after three years of troubles and "ups and downs," we find him once more in royal favour, for in 1389 he was appointed "Clerk of the Works" to King Richard, in succession to Roger Elmham.

His duties in this new capacity were to manage the various royal palaces, including Westminster, Tower of London, Castle of Berkhamstead, Eltham, Kensington, Shene, and others. It was a rather responsible position, and entailed his riding from one place to the other, at a time when travelling was not so easy nor so safe as it is now.

It was on the occasion of his visit to Eltham in connection with his official duties that Chaucer had the unlucky experience which we are about to relate.

"The Fowle Oak."

In the "Memoranda Roll, 14 Ric. II. Hilary, Brevia, Roll 20," we may find this curious and interesting Eltham record. It is in old French, or a kind of legal French used at the time. But we have transcribed it just as it stands, that our young students of French, in Eltham, may amuse themselves by its translation.

* * *

1391, January 6. Writ discharging Geoffrey Chaucer, Clerk of the King's Works, from the repayment of the £20, of which he had been robbed near to the "Fowle Oak."

* * *

Pur Geffray Chaucer. Richard par la grace de dieu Roye, &c., as Tresorer and Barons de nostre Escheqer, saluz. Suppliez nous ad nostre ame Clere Geffray Chaucer, clere de noz ouereignes, qicome le tierce iour de Septembre darein passez, (1390), le dit Geffrey estoit robbez felonousement pres de le fowle ok de vyngt liures de nostre tresor, and de son chival and autres moebles, par aucune notables larons, come pleinement est confessez par bouche dun des dits arons, en presence de nostre coroner and autres noz officiers a Wesmonster en nostre Gaole illoeqes a ce qest dit, nous plese lui vyngt douer les dites vyngt liures, and lui descharger en son aconte a nostre Escheqer de les vyngt

liures susdites; la quele supplicacion nous auons de nostre grace especiel grantez and ottraiez. Et pur ce vous mandons, que le dit Goffrey facez deschargier en son aconte a nostre dit Escheqer de les vyngt liures susdites, and eut estre quites enuers nous par la cause auantdite. Done souz nostre priue seale a nostre manoir de Eltham le vj iour de Januere lan de nostre regne quatorzisme."

* * *

Translation.

"Richard, by the grace of God, King, &c.,—To the Treasurer and Barons of our Exchequer, greeting. Having received a petition on behalf of our beloved Geoffrey Chaucer, Clerk of our Works, inasmuch as on the third day of last year (1390), the said Geoffrey Chaucer was feloniously robbed near the Fowle Oak of twenty pounds of our treasure, and of his horse and divers goods, by certain notorious thieves, as is fully confessed by the mouth of one of the said thieves, in the presence of our coroner and other of our officers at Westminister, in our prison there; on this account we are pleased to pardon him the said twenty pounds, and discharge him in his account to our Exchequer of the aforesaid twenty pounds; the which petition we have of our special grace granted and allowed, and we therefore instruct you that you cause the said Geoffrey Chaucer to be discharged on his account to our said Exchequer of the aforesaid twenty pounds, and that he be acquitted towards us for the aforesaid reason. Given under our privy seal at our Manor of Eltham, the 6th day of January, the fourteenth year of our reign."

* * *

The story of the robbery of Chaucer is rather interesting, and as it closely concerns Eltham we will tell it. Mr. Furnival discovered the account of the incident by research among the "Controlment Rolls" of the 14th year of Richard II., which give the records of the trial of the robbers, and it was thereupon printed in the transactions of the Chaucer Society, some thirty years ago.

It seems that about this time (1390) the neighbourhood of London was infested by robbers, who laid wait for travellers, and

carried on their nefarious calling in defiance of
the attempts made by the authorities to catch
them. There turned out to be some seventeen
of these desperadoes, and impudent robberies
were perpetrated on the various highways leading from the Metropolis.

Chaucer had occasion to come from Westminster to Eltham with some ten pounds in his
pocket to pay accounts, in pursuance of his
duties as Clerk of the Works. When he
reached Hatcham, which, of course, was out in
the country in those days, at a spot known as
the "Fowle Oak," he was set upon and robbed
of his money, horse, and all his belongings.

So there was nought to be done but to go back
on foot to Westminster, to get some more
money. Curiously enough, on his return he
was robbed again. The affair, no doubt, caused
considerable stir in Court circles, for it was a
most impudent thing to rob on the king's highway an officer of the king's household, and
Chaucer was put to a great deal of incon-
venience, as the above document shews.

At length, however, some of the miscreants
were captured, and one of them, Richard
Brerelay, became approver; that is to say, he
betrayed the others in order to save himself.

In the quaint wording of the old record we
find that:—

"Richard Brerelay came before Edmund
Brudenell, the King's Coroner, and acknowledged that he was a felon of our lord the
King, for that he, on Tuesday next before the
feast of the nativity of the Blessed Virgin
Mary, in the fourteenth year of the reign of
King Richard the Second, feloniously despoiled
Geoffrey Chaucer of ten pounds in ready money,
at Westminster, and that he is a common and
notorious thief, and he appeals Thomas Talbot,
of Ireland, otherwise called Brode; Gilbert,
clerk of the same Thomas, and William Hunt-
yngfield, for that they, together with the said
approver, at Haochesham (Hatcham) in the
county of Surrey, on Tuesday next before the
feast of the nativity of the Blessed Virgin
Mary, in the year aforesaid, feloniously
despoiled the aforesaid Geoffrey Chaucer of
nine pounds and forty-four pence, whereof each

of them had for his share, four marks, five
shillings, and ten pence."

* * *

It was not at all unusual in cases of this
kind for one of a gang to turn "approver,"
as Richard Brerelay did on this occasion. But
the consequences were sometimes curious, and
illustrate the crudeness of the methods practised by our forefathers in dealing out what
they called justice.

According to the system of "approvement,"
the person accused, unless he had reasonable
and legal exceptions to make to the person of
the "approver," was compelled to put himself
upon his trial, either by battle or by his country. If he fought and was vanquished he was
regarded as guilty, and had to suffer the judgment of the law, while the "approver" was
pardoned.

On the other hand, if the "approver" got the
worst of it in the fight, he (the "approver")
was deemed guilty, and was hanged, upon the
confession of his own guilt, for the condition of
pardon failed, namely, the convicting of some
other person.

* * *

Now, the Chaucer robbery was not the only
confession made by Richard Brerelay.

There was an affair at Berkweywey, in which
Brerelay declared that one, Adam Clerk, took
a part. This led to Brerelay's undoing. Clerk
pleaded "not guilty," and declared that he
was ready to defend himself by his body
against the approver, Richard Brerelay. There
was no escape. Brerelay had to fight.

The duel came off at Tot-hill, on 3rd of May,
1391. Brerelay got the worst of the encounter.
So he was forthwith taken off to the gallows,
and hanged.

Clerk got off, but he did not long enjoy freedom. He was up again next term for house-
breaking, found guilty, and hanged.

* * *

But you will notice that one, William Hunt-
yngfield, was accused by Brerelay as one of the
culprits in the Chaucer robberies. The fate of
this "gentleman" cannot be so certainly
traced. The Rolls shew that he was convicted
of the numerous felonies for which he was

tried, including the Westminster and Hatcham robberies, but the result of these convictions does not appear.

Being, apparently, "in holy orders," he was able to put forward the plea of "benefit of the clergy," by way of arresting judgment. After this plea, we find that he was committed to the custody of the Marshall of the King's Bench, until the Court should have determined whether he might be allowed to clear himself in this manner.

The rest is veiled in mystery. We do not know whether he got off. Let us hope that he was hanged, for he deserved it if the others did.

∗ ∗ ∗

This is about all we know of the robbery of Geoffrey Chaucer when on his way to Eltham Manor, on the third day of September, 1390. Although the King was graciously pleased to forgive him the loss of those twenty pounds, his position at Court was not improved by the incident. Chaucer had many enemies there, and it is not surprising to find that a few years later he was living in retirement at Woodstock, in Oxfordshire.

After all, that retirement was better for us than if he had remained in office to the end of his days, for it was then, when the poet was close on sixty years of age that he wrote, at his leisure, that immortal work, "The Canterbury Tales."

SHOOTING AT BUTTS (from Royal M.S. 19. c. viii.)

HENRY IV. (Tomb at Canterbury).

CHAPTER XXXVIII.

HENRY IV. AND ELTHAM.

In an earlier chapter we referred to that last meeting at Eltham between Richard II. and Bolingbroke, after the affair at Coventry. It was then that the proud noble bade farewell to his king, and the latter reduced his term of exile from ten years to six.

The next time Bolingbroke came to Eltham he was himself a king, and the weak and foolish Richard had been deposed, and was living in captivity.

Stirring and notable events had taken place during the interval between the two visits. Within a few months after Bolingbroke had gone from the country, his aged father, the great John of Gaunt, Duke of Lancaster, died, and the exile himself succeeded to the dukedom.

At this juncture King Richard did one of the meanest actions of his life. He declared that Bolingbroke, being an exile, must therefore be accounted an outlaw, and could not succeed to the Dukedom of Lancaster; so he confiscated all the estates to which the exiled nobleman was the rightful heir, and put them to his own use. This act of dishonesty and tyranny led to the king's downfall, and ultimately to his death.

Richard proceeded to Ireland to complete the work of conquest there, leaving the government at home in the hands of the Duke of York, whom he had appointed regent.

Taking advantage of the king's absence, Henry Bolingbroke returned from his exile in France, landing on the coast of Yorkshire with a handful of men. He declared that his purpose was to claim his rights to the lands and title of the Duke of Lancaster, of which he had been unjustly deprived.

As he proceeded across England, men from all sides flocked to his banner. Even the Duke of York took sides with him, so that when the unfortunate Richard, on his return from

Ireland, landed at Milford Haven, he found that his kingdom was gone. His army fell away from him, leaving him practically friendless.

In this plight, he fled, disguised, to North Wales.

Subsequently he was invited to a conference with the new Duke of Lancaster, at Flint. When he saw the forces of the Duke, he exclaimed·

"I am betrayed. There are pennons and banners in the valley."

It was, however, too late to escape, and he was seized and brought before Lancaster.

"I am come before my time," said the Duke, "but I will shew you the reason. Your people, my lord, complain that for the space of twenty years, you have ruled them harshly. However, if it pleases God, I will help you to rule them better."

"Fair cousin," replied the king, "since it pleases you, it pleases me well."

The events that followed are well-known. Richard was deposed, and the Duke of Lancaster mounted the throne as Henry IV, in the year 1399. But he had no real right to the crown, and he very soon found that his kingly position was not a pleasant one.

Popular he had been when simply Henry Bolingbroke, the Earl of Hereford, indeed, he was in many respects almost an idol of the people, but as soon as he assumed the regal sway, his popularity rapidly waned. There were rebellions against him. His friends abandoned him. Plots were formed against him, and barbarously punished. Altogether his reign was not a happy one for himself or for his people.

It was into the mouth of Henry IV that Shakespeare put those fine lines upon "sleep," which reveal so vividly the mind of the man wearied by the cares of State, and anxious for the safety of a crown that was not rightly his.

"How many thousands of my poorest subjects
Are at this hour asleep? O, gentle sleep,
Nature's soft nurse, how have I frightened thee,
That thou no more wilt weigh my eye-lids down,
And steep my senses in forgetfulness?

"Canst thou, O partial sleep, give thy repose
To the wet sea-boy in an hour so rude,
And, in the calmest and the stillest night,
With all appliances and means to boot,
Deny it to a king? Then, happy, lowly clown,
Uneasy lies the head that wears a crown."

Henry IV spent a great deal of his time at Eltham. He kept his Christmas here on at least five occasions, namely, in 1400, 1404, 1406, 1409, and 1412.

It was on the occasion of his Christmas festivities at Eltham in the year 1400 that he entertained at the Palace Manuel Palæologos, the Emperor of Constantinople, in a most magnificent style for two months. This monarch had come to England to get assistance against the Saracens, and so greatly did his words impress the King of England, that the latter vowed that he would make a pilgrimage to Jerusalem before he died. One of the events of the festival was a grand tournament, at which the king's eldest daughter, Blanche, a nine-year-old princess, presided as the "Queen of Beauty."

When the tidings of the deposition of King Richard reached the ears of the King of France he was anxious to know the fate of his daughter, Isabella, the girl-queen of Richard. So he sent two ambassadors to England to make the necessary inquiries. It was at Eltham Palace, where Henry IV was holding his council in 1400, that he received the messengers of the French king, and entertained them royally.

From the "Acts of the Privy Council" (Nicolas i., 115) we learn that it was at Eltham that the council was held on 15th March, 1400, from which the king wrote, respecting the restoration of his friend, Thomas Arundel, Archbishop of Canterbury, the well-known persecutor of the Lollards, who had been deprived of his see, and banished by Richard II in 1397, at the same time as a similar punishment was inflicted upon the Duke of Gloucester and the Earl of Warwick by the late king.

Arundel had been a fellow exile with Henry himself, but had returned to Scotland, for, after residing in France for a time, the Pope appointed him to the see of St. Andrew's, "a step taken at the request of Richard himself, who thus flattered himself that he had rendered a troublesome adversary harmless."

The decisions of the Eltham Council marked the new attitude taken up by Henry towards Lollardism. It resulted in the Statute of Heretics, with all its formidable provisions.

"By the provisions of this infamous Act," writes John Richard Green, "bishops were not only permitted to arrest and imprison, so long

to spread the new Lollardism, became its first victim. A layman, John Balbie, was committed to the flames in the presence of the Prince of Wales, for a denial of transubstantiation. The groans of the sufferer were taken for a recantation, and the Prince ordered the fire to be plucked away; but the offer of life and of a pension failed to break the spirit of the Lollard, and he was again hurled back to his doom."

QUEEN JOAN OF NAVARRE, SECOND WIFE OF HENRY IV.
(Married by proxy to Henry IV., at Eltham Palace.)

as their heresy should last, all preachers of heresy, all school masters infected with heretical teaching, all owners and writers of heretical books, but a refusal to abjure, or a relapse after abjuration, enabled them to hand over the heretic to the civil officers, and by these—so ran the first legal enactment of religious bloodshed which defiled our Statute Book—he was to be burnt on a high place before the people.

"The statute was hardly passed before William Sawtre, who had quitted a Norfolk rectory

These were some results of the Statute which emanated from that council at Eltham, in the year 1400. Surely it was a bad day's work. "It was probably the fierce resentment of the Reformers" to this intolerant Act "which gave life to the incessant revolts which threatened the throne of Henry IV."

An interesting, but somewhat curious, ceremony took place at Eltham Palace on the 3rd April, 1402, for on that date King Henry was married in the Royal Chapel there, by proxy, to the Princess Joan, daughter of Charles II., the King of Navarre, and widow of John de Montfort, Duke of Brittany. In the absence of the princess, one of her esquires, a certain Antoine Reizi, acted as her representative, and it was upon his finger that King Henry placed the ring, and with him exchanged the usual marriage vows

There is another local record of considerable interest, though of quite a different character There was an ancient custom by which the men of the Royal Manors could travel throughout the kingdom, "toll-free" The privilege had been conceded to the men of Eltham Mandeville, and West Horne, as far back as the reign of Edward III. It is recorded of Henry IV. that he enacted that "the same custom should apply to the men of Eltham, Modyngham, and Woolwich, which manors were of old of the ancient demesne of the Crown of England "

It would seem that King Henry IV ran in danger of being murdered at Eltham Palace on the occasion of his keeping Christmas here in 1404 The king was ignorant of the peril he was in, until the plot was revealed to him by a lady during the following year The incident is set forth by Holinshed, and we will transcribe the old chronicler's words —

"In the sixth year, the fridaie after saint Valentine's dav, the earle of March his sons earlie in the morning were taken foith of Windsor Castle, and conveyed away, it was not known whither at the first, but such search and enquiry was made for them that shortlie after they were heard of and brought back again.

"The smith that counterfeited the keies by the which they had conveyed them thence into the chamber where they were lodged, had first his hands cut off, and after, his head stricken from his shoulders

"The ladie Spenser, sister to the duke of York, and widow to the lord Thomas Spenser, executed at Bristow, being apprehended and committed to close prison, accused hir brother the duke of York, as chéefe author in stealing awaie the said earl of March his sonnes.

"And further, that the said duke ment to have broken into the manor of Eltham the last Christmasse by scaling the wals in the night season, the king being there the same time, to the intent to have murthered him.

"For the proof of hir accusation she offered that if there were anie knight or esquier that would take upon him to fight in her quarrel, if he were overcome, she would be content to burn for it

"One of his esquiers, named William of Maidstone, hearing what answer his ladie and mistress propounded, cast down his hood, and proffered in hir cause the combat The duke likewise cast down his hood readie by battel to clear his innecence

"But yet the king's sonne lord Thomas of Lancastei arrested him and put him under safe guard in the Tower, till it were further known what older should be taken with him, and in the meantime were all his goods confiscate.

"At the same time was Thomas Mowbraie, earl Marshall accused, as privie to the purpose of the duke of Yoik, touching the withdrawal of the earl of March his sonnes, who confessed indeed that he knew of the dukes purpose, but yet in no wise gave his consent there-unto, and therefore besought the king to be good and gracious lord unto him for concealing the mattei, and so he obtained pardon for that offence "

Henry the Fourth's last Christmas at Eltham was a sad one He had been attacked by a fulsome, leprous disease, which had terribly disfigured his face The sickness came on shortly after the execution of the Aichbishop of York, and the people saw in it a judgment from heaven for so sacrilegious an act

It was the last Christmas of his life that he passed, in 1412, at his favourite palace at Eltham "So complete was his seclusion, owing both to his illness and the awful disfigurement of his person, that he scarcely saw anyone but the queen, lying frequently for hours without any sign of life After Candlemas, he was so much better as to be able to keep his birthday, so he was carried from Eltham to his palace at Westminster, where he had summoned the Parliament "

The old historian, Kennet, commenting upon this incident, writ s

"The design of this season seems to have been no other but to furnish him with money for his voyage to the Holy Land, which he intended to begin at the rise of the spring, all things being ready for it.

"But God prevented his design by a relapse into his former distemper! For, being worshipping at St. Edward's Shrine, to take his leave, in order, to his journey, he was so violently seized with another fit of apoplexy that all the standers-by thought he would have died presently; but being removed into a chamber belonging to the Abbot of Westminster, and laid in a pallet before the fire, by the warmth of that and by the application of proper remedies, he at length recovered his senses and speech again.

"After he had lain some time, he enquired where he was, because he perceived himself to be in a strange place, and was told that he was in the chamber of the Abbot of Westminster.

"He then asked them whether the chamber had any particular name, and they said 'It was called Jerusalem,' whereupon he said, 'That then he should die there, because he was long since told that he would die in Jerusalem,' and accordingly he made suitable preparations for his death."

RICHARD II. AND BOLINGBROKE ARRIVED AT LONDON.

A PARLIAMENT OF THE TIME OF HENRY V. (Harleian M S.)

CHAPTER XXXIX.

HENRY V. AND ELTHAM.

Several notable incidents in the life of Henry V., associated with Eltham, are recorded. His father, the late king, kept his last Christmas here, under the sad circumstances we have already alluded to, in the year 1412.

Henry V. kept his first Christmas, as king, at Eltham, in 1413, and, on that occasion, a circumstance came to light which made it necessary for the king to cut his Eltham visit short, and hasten away to the palace at Westminster, and thence to Windsor.

It was while the hall of the old palace was resounding with the mirth and jollity characteristic of the Christmas festivities of the time that the ill news was conveyed to the king of a plot for his destruction, said to have been hatched by the Lollards, in which the friend and associate of his youth, Lord Cobham, was involved, together with Sir Roger Acton.

The tidings so alarmed the king that he hurried from Eltham, as we have said, and the Christmas merriment of 1413 came to an unexpected and sudden termination.

The incident was the beginning of events that culminated in a great tragedy, and, as their relation throws some light upon both Eltham and national history of the time, we will tell, as briefly as possible, the story in which the king and the famous Kentish noble, Lord Cobham, are the prominent characters.

You will have read in your history books of the youthful escapades of Henry V., that on one occasion caused him to be brought before the judge, who had the courage to send him to prison.

One of his boon companions at this time was Sir John Oldcastle, more generally known as Lord Cobham, who associated with the young prince in his gay and frivolous habits of life.

The old king, Henry IV., looked gravely upon his son's reckless living, for he was anxious lest he might develop into a king as worthless and vicious as Richard II. had been.

When, however, at his father's death, the prince, inherited the responsibilities of kingship, he discarded his old habits and his evil companions, lived a life that was consistent with his position, and won the respect and love of his people.

Lord Cobham, too, who had been so prominent as one of those who humoured the prince in his whims, that he was known at the time as the "ruffian knight," turned over a new leaf and began to take life seriously.

In the last chapter we alluded to the Lollards, and the new law, devised at a Council at Eltham, for the purpose of putting Lollardism down, of the persecution under the law, and the prominent part played in that persecution by the Archbishop Arundel.

Now, Lord Cobham became a very thoughtful and able man, and as a nobleman possessed much influence and power. To the surprise of everyone, he embraced the principles of the Lollards, a circumstance which alarmed the Church, and caused the Archbishop to carry on the work of persecution with all the greater vigour.

The archbishop regarded Cobham as the head and great encourager of the new sect, so he applied to King Henry for permission to indict him under the hateful statute De heretico comburendo, already alluded to. Although, for political reasons, seeing that Henry was desirous of securing the full sympathy and support of the Church, he was not entirely averse to the application of rigorous measures to heretics, he could not readily bring his mind to the persecution of his old companion, Lord Cobham.

The archbishop pressed the matter, under the plea that the public execution of the Kentish nobleman would strike terror into the Lollards, and perhaps stamp out the new movement. But the king preferred to see Cobham himself, and to try and influence him by persuasion, declaring that such gentle means were best calculated to convert him. The interview took place, and Henry argued with his friend with such knowledge of divinity that he had acquired at Oxford. But it was of little avail, and it would seem that some severity arose between the disputants, for Cobham

is said to have suddenly left the king, and withdrew to his own house at Cowling in Kent.

The king now took up another attitude. Tenderness towards his friend seems to have left him. Determined to prevail where he had failed to convince, he acceded to the request of Archbishop Arundel.

Then it was that proclamations were sent forth, directing the magistrates to apprehend all itinerant preachers, and action was at once taken against Lord Cobham for heresy.

Upon hearing of these strong measures, Cobham hastened to the king, before whom he laid his confession of faith, a document which is still in existence, and "on looking it over," writes an historian, "one is at a loss, in these days, to discover in it what any true Catholic could object to."

But Henry would not even look at this "Confession of Faith," declaring that such matters were for the bishops to decide upon.

Cobham then offered, according to the spirit of the times, to purge himself from the charge of heresy, by doing battle with any adversary, Christian or infidel, who dared to take up his challenge. But when the king asked him if he was prepared to submit to the decision of the bishops, he refused, at the same time, like a good Catholic, declaring himself willing to appeal to the Pope.

This proposal the king declined to accept, and Cobham was accordingly handed over to the tender mercies of Archbishop Arundel, together with the Bishops of London, Winchester, and St. David's, before whom he was promptly tried and condemned to be burnt alive.

The king, however, did not agree with these desperate measures, and gave the prisoner fifty days' respite, apparently to give him further time for consideration, but more probably, as some writers assert, to give him an opportunity of escape. At any rate, Cobham did manage to escape before the fifty days had expired.

Once at liberty he was very soon in communication with his friends and confederates, and realising that the Church was determined upon, not so much the conversion as the destruction of the reformers, it is said that the Lollards themselves resolved to take desperate measures in self-defence, and to take up arms in an attempt to repel force by force.

It is even recorded of them, although there are many who still doubt the truth of the accusation, that they conceived the design of not only killing the bishops, but also the king and all his kin. There seems to be some mystery about the proceedings, and many refuse to believe that Lord Cobham could have lent himself to such a purpose.

It was, however, the news of this plot which

body was spared the indignity of being burned, so he was buried under the gallows.

The following entry in the "Issue Rolls," I. Henry V., throws some light, perhaps, upon the incident :—

"To Henry Botolf. In money paid to his own hands for four pair of fetters, to pair of manacles, and six pair of 'cleralls,' with locks for the same, purchased by the said Henry for the King's use, and sent to Thomas Erpyngham, steward of the King's household, for certain traitors lately taken at Eltham and elsewhere, to be imprisoned. By

HELMET, SHIELD AND SADDLE OF HENRY V.

was brought to the king at Eltham during the Christmas festivities of 1413, and caused him to get away from the palace as quickly as he could.

*   *   *   *

A great rising of the Lollards appears to have been organised, and some 25,000 men were expected to gather at an appointed spot in St. Giles' Fields, their password being "Sir John Oldcastle." The authorities, however, were sufficiently acquainted beforehand of the danger to enable them to take measures of suppression. The result was a dismal failure on the part of the reformers. Cobham managed to escape, but about four score of his followers were captured, forty of whom were drawn and hanged as traitors, and then burned. Amongst the prisoners was Sir Roger Acton, a friend of Cobham's, who was hanged, but his

direction of the Treasurer and Chamberlain of the Exchequer. 16/8."

Lord Cobham escaped into Wales, where he remained in concealment for some years, and the burning of Lollards was continued with increasing severity.

In the year 1417, Henry was campaigning in Normandy. The Scots, therefore, thought the occasion was favourable for an attack upon England in the north. Cobham seems to have been acting in concert with them, for at the moment when the Scottish inroads began, the nobleman issued from his place of concealment. But whatever hopes the Lollards may have had of relief by the assistance of the Scots, those hopes were doomed to disappointment. Earl Douglas was defeated in the north and made a hasty retreat across the Cheviots.

When Cobham heard the news of the Scottish rout, he had approached as near to London as St. Alban's. There was no alternative but to hasten again towards Wales, in the hope of finding there a place of hiding. But he was intercepted and taken prisoner by the retainers of the Earl of Powis.

"Cobham was brought before the House of Peers, his former indictment was read, and he was asked by the Duke of Bedford what he had to say in his defence. He had begun a bold and able speech in reply, but was stopped and desired to give a direct answer."

He refused to plead, and astounded the court by declaring that it had no authority, so long as Richard II. was alive in Scotland; for, like many others, he was of opinion, that the person who was still paraded in Scotland as the dethroned king, was genuine.

His doom was sealed. Sir John Oldcastle, Lord Cobham, was condemned, and was hanged as a traitor in St. Giles' Fields, and burnt as a heretic, December, 1417, exactly four years after the tidings of the Lollard Plot were brought to the king at Eltham Palace.

SIR THOMAS ERPYNGHAM, STEWARD OF ELTHAM MANOR (from an old Print).

CHAPTER XL.

AFTER AGINCOURT.

In the last chapter the name of Sir Thomas Erpyngham was mentioned. He was the steward of the King's household, and was the person to whom the fetters and manacles were sent for securing certain traitors captured at Eltham.

Sir Thomas was a notable figure at the time, and we may very well give a brief account of him. He was quite an old man when Henry V. ascended the throne, and had served with distinction under previous sovereigns.

When Henry Bolingbroke—afterwards Henry IV.,—was sent into exile, Sir Thomas Erpyngham accompanied him. He was probably present at Eltham upon that memorable day when Bolingbroke bade adieu to Richard II., and had the consolation of obtaining a reduction by four years of his period of exile.

On the return of Bolingbroke as Duke of Lancaster, Erpyngham was still in his train,

for he was always a faithful adherent of the House of Lancaster.

It was he who made Richard II. prisoner, and when the fateful day arrived that Richard laid aside his crown, Sir Thomas Erpyngham was one of the seven who were commissioned to announce to the King his deposition.

He served Henry IV. faithfully, and seems to have always been ready to do his bidding. Although there are records that go to prove that he was brave and fearless as a soldier, there are others which depict him as being exceedingly callous.

In the old chronicle, "La traison et mort du Roy Richart," we are told that Henry IV. put him in charge of the execution of Sir Thomas Blount, and that Erpyngham actually used taunting words to his unhappy victim, while "sitting disembowelled before the fire in which his entrails were being burned."

It is hard to conceive anything more horrible than callousness such as this, even in an age when human life and human suffering were regarded as trifling matters in the policy of government.

It was Erpyngham, too, who executed Lord de Spencer—the husband of the lady, whose name has already been alluded to in connection with an Eltham incident.

His close association with royalty is further seen from the fact that he was one of the witnesses of the will of Henry IV. He is said to

Old man though he was, it was Sir Thomas Erpyngham who threw his baton into the air as the signal for the English advance at Agincourt, and was afterwards in the thick of the fight.

He was near the king at that dramatic moment, just before the battle, when Sire de Helly and two other French knights held a parley with King Henry for the purpose of gaining time.

De Helly had once been a prisoner in England, but was accused of breaking his

BANNERS USED AT AGINCOURT.

have built the Church of Black Friars, at Norwich, and to have been buried in the cathedral of that city.

But Sir Thomas Erpyngham has won a lasting name as one of the heroes of Agincourt. "At Agincourt," writes old John Lydgate, "Sire Thomas Erpyngham, that never did faille," brought a following of two knights, seventeen men-at-arms, and sixty archers, by an agreement with the King, some of whose jewels he took as security for pay.

It is interesting to learn from Hunter's "Historical Tracts" that John Geney, one of his men-at-arms, married Lucy, daughter of Robert Cheseman, of East Greenwich and Eltham.

parole, and now offered to meet in single combat any man who dared to reflect upon his honour.

The King, who saw the trick, replied:

"Sir Knight, this is no time for single combats. Go, tell your countrymen to prepare for battle, and doubt not that for the violation of your word you shall a second time forfeit your liberty, if not your life."

"Sir," replied De Helly, insolently, with the view of prolonging the parley, "I will receive no orders from you. Charles is our sovereign. Him we will obey, and for him we will fight against you whenever we think proper."

"Away, then," said the King, "and take care that we are not there before you."

Then, stepping to the front, he cried "Banners advance!"

At this moment, old Sir Thomas Erpyngham, who had been standing near, watching the interview, flung his baton into the air, and cried aloud "Now strike."

What followed, how the English struck and won, is a matter of history; but it is interesting to us to find that the old knight who was the steward of Eltham Palace took so prominent a part in the great struggle.

There were many notable prisoners taken in this famous battle Among them was the Duke of Orleans, who was found by Richard Waller, of Groombridge, Kent, nearly dead, under a heap of slain His brother, the Duke of Bourbon, was also captured, as well as many knights of high degree

The two princes mentioned had the pleasure of spending a part of their time as prisoners in England, at Eltham, where they were lodged

The return of Henry V, and his victorious army was an occasion of great rejoicing.

"To Caunterbury full fair he past,
    And offred at Seynt Thomas shryne,
Fro thens sone he rod in hast,
    To Eltham he cam in good tyme."

Thus sang John Lydgate to commemorate the joyful day At Eltham, the King and his great company, including his prisoners, remained for the night, to prepare for the triumphant entry into London

The event was one of the historical days in the village story. Eltham youth doubtless looked on and wondered Their grandfathers had told them many a time of the glorious days of Edward III , of the great tournament after the victory of Crecy, of the reception of the captive King But here was a victory greater than Crecy Some of their own kinsfolk had been in the fight Here, too, were royal prisoners from France, brought along in the train of their great and noble King In sooth, it was a day to be remembered.

On the morrow, November 23rd, St. Clement's Day, the procession moved on at an early hour,

for they were due at Blackheath at ten o'clock. Thus the old poet continued.

"To ye Blakheth thanne rod he,
    And spredde ye way on evry side,
(Twenty thousand) men myght wel se
    Oure comely Kinge for to abyde

The kyng from Eltham sone he nam,
    Hyse presoners with hym dede brynge.
And to ye Blake Heth ful sone he cam,
    He saw London with oughte lesynge,
Heil Ryall London, seyde our King "

The progress of victorious Henry from Eltham to London is one of the great events of London history, and it is proposed to represent the scene in the forthcoming "London Pageant" Those who would like to read a really graphic account of the event may find it described in the "Chronicle" of Stow, who tells us how the "Maior of London with the Aldermen and crafts to the number of 4 hundred riding in red, with hoodes red and white, met with the King on Black-heath coming from Eltham, and so brought him through London to Westminster, with all his prisoners of France.

"The gates and streets of the Citie were garnished and apparelled with precious clothes and Arras, containing the victories, triumphs and princely Acts of the Kings of England his progenitors, which was done to the end that the King might understand, what remembrance his people would send down to their posterity of these his great victories and triumphes

"The Conduits through the Citie ranne none other but good sweet wines, and that abundantly.

"There were also made in the streetes many Towers and stages adorned richly, and upon the height of them sate small children, apparielled in semblance of Angels, with sweete tuned voices singing prayses and laudes unto God, for the victorious King would not suffer any ditties to be made and sung of his victories, for that he would wholly have the praise given to God "

In his "History of Great Britaine" (1651), John Speed tells us that on the occasion of Henry's triumphal entry into London, after

Agincourt, "foureteene Mitred Bishops attended his approach unto St. Pauls, where, out of the Cencers the sweet Odours filled the Church, and the Quier chanted Anthems cunningly set by note; in all which the honour was ascribed onely unto God, the King so commanding it."

Yet another account is provided by an old Latin manuscript, in the Cottonian collection (Julius E. IV.), which is translated by Sir

In the "Issue Rolls" (Devon) dated 4 Henry V., August 11th, we get the following entry relating to Eltham:—

"To Sir John Rothende, knight, keeper of the King's Wardrobe. In money paid to him, arising from the fifteenths and tenths, namely, by the hands of John Feriby, receiving the money from a certain attorney of the Lord de Talbot, dwelling in Gray's Inn, at the house of the Treasurer of England, for the expenses of

ENTRY OF HENRY V. INTO LONDON (from an old Print).

Nicholas Harris Nicholas, 1827, from which we make one extract:—

"And when the wished for Saturday dawned, the citizens went forth to meet the King, as far as the heights of Blackheath; namely, the Mayor and 24 Aldermen in scarlet and the rest of the inferior citizens in red suits, with party-coloured hoods, red and white, on about twenty thousand horses, all of whom, according to their crafts, had certain finely contrived devices, which notably distinguished each craft from the other."

The manuscript gives a detailed and graphic description of the whole of the day's proceedings.

the household of the Emperor while at Eltham. By writ, £200."

This great personage, Sigismund, was King of the Romans, and Emperor Elect of Germany. His visit to Henry was in 1416. Its object was to secure the aid of Henry in a great scheme for putting an end to the divisions in the Church of Rome. There were, at the time, no less than three Popes all declaring to have been lawfully elected.

Henry decided to give Sigismund a right royal reception, so "he summoned all the knights and esquires of the realm to attend him in London. A fleet of 300 sail waited at Calais to bring over this unusual guest with all his

No. 94.   THE OLD "RISING SUN."

(Stood where the Public Library now stands).

No. 96.   THE OLD "CASTLE" HOTEL.

No. 93.   THE "GREYHOUND" AND OTHER BUILDINGS.

(From an old Photograph).

No. 95.   THE OLD "MAN OF KENT" INN.

No. 97.　　　SHOOTER'S HILL ROAD.

No. 98.　　THE IRON GATEWAY.　(Todman's Nursery).

POUND PLACE.

Public Library in the distance.

No. 100.

No. 99.　　　KING'S OENE.

Formerly Residence of Dr. D. King.　(High Street).

retinue, amounting to 1000 horsemen; and officers were appointed to escort him from Dover to the capital, discharging all the expenses by the way."

Although Henry prepared to receive his visitor with every show of friendliness and hospitality, he was very cautious not to endanger his national rights.

So, just as the 300 ships of Sigismund approached the shore at Dover, the Emperor was somewhat surprised to see the Duke of Gloucester and several noblemen ride into the water, with drawn swords, and asking whether, in coming in such state, he designed to exercise or claim any authority in England.

The Emperor replied " No," and was at once received with honour and courtesy.

He had, however, a second object in coming to England, and that was to try and bring about peace between England and France.

He seems to have had a good time in England, for he stayed from the time of spring till the month of September, when he returned to Calais, accompanied by Henry himself. During his visit he concluded an alliance with England, and was honoured by being made a Knight of the Garter.

The Emperor Sigismund, King of Rome, and Emperor Elect of Germany, was one of the most distinguished of foreign potentates who made Eltham Palace their residence.

HENRY VI. IN HIS YOUTH.

CHAPTER XLI

HENRY VI. AND ELTHAM.

The reign of the hero of Agincourt was a short one. While campaigning in France he was stricken down by sickness, and died at the castle at Vincennes on the last day of August, 1422. His body was brought to London, and was buried in the Abbey Church at Westminster.

In the first scene of the first act of Shakespeare's play of "Henry VI., Part I." you may read of the sad funeral day at the Abbey, and from the touching words which the poet puts into the mouths of the mourners we may, to some extent, realise the depth of the national grief occasioned by the early and unexpected death of this heroic king.

"Hung be the heavens with black, yield day
    to night!
Comets, importing change of times and states,
Brandish your crystal tresses in the sky,
And with them scourge the bad revolting stars
That have consented unto Henry's death!
Henry the Fifth, too famous to live long!
England ne'er lost a king of so much worth."

"The King is dead. Long live the King," and the king that lived was a baby boy of nine months old, who at the time when the body of his father was being buried with all the pomp and state of a warrior, was at Eltham Palace, oblivious of the greatness to which he had succeeded, and lovingly tended by his mother.

If you follow the scene in the play, you will see how the obsequies were interrupted by messengers from France bringing the evil tidings of the defeat of the English forces there.

Then did the great nobles, alarmed by the news, hurry away to their several vocations.

Said Exeter, a great uncle of the young king :—

"Remember, lords, your oaths to Henry sworn,
Either to quell the Dauphin utterly,
Or bring him in obedience to your yoke."

To which Bedford replied :—

"I do remember't; and here take my leave,
To go about my preparation." (Exit.)

Gloucester declares :—

" I'll to the Tower, with all the haste I can,
To view the artillery and munition,
And then I will proclaim young Henry king "
(Exit)

Exeter then says —

" To Eltham will I, where the young king is,
Being ordained his special governor,
And for his safety there I'll best devise."
(Exit)

Henry Beaufort, the Bishop of Winchester, another great uncle of the baby-king, is then made to use these words of sinister import —
" Each hath his place and function to attend,
I am left out, for me no thing remains,
But long I will not be Jack out of office,
The king from Eltham I intend to steal,
And sit at chiefest stern of public weal "

During the infancy and early childhood of Henry VI he was kept very much at Eltham Palace, and when one remembers the troubles and tribulations which this king endured in after years, we can easily believe that his Eltham associations were among the happiest of his eventful life

If you turn again to your Shakespeare, " Henry VI , Part I , Act I , scene iii ," you will see how the dramatist depicts a stirring incident which really took place just outside the Tower of London This scene has a direct bearing upon the young king's residence here, and it was just by chance that the fight did not occur at Eltham instead of London

Although they were closely related there was a bitter rivalry between Humphrey, Duke of Gloucester, and Henry Beaufort, the Bishop of Winchester The Bishop was very ambitious, and often acted unwisely.

Gloucester was self-willed and headstrong, and harboured a violent dislike of his kinsman They were both rivals in their efforts to exercise an influence over the young king. So one was always trying to check-mate the other.

When Gloucester had gone abroad, on an expedition to Hainault, the Bishop seized the opportunity to garrison the Tower of London with soldiers, and then committed the authority to Richard Woodville with the signifi-cant injunction that he was not " to admit any one more powerful than himself "

The object was, of course, to keep Gloucester out when he should have returned from abroad, which event in due time took place

He was highly incensed at the refusal to admit him to the Tower, for, be it remembered, the Tower was a Royal Palace as well as a fortress, and he attributed, rightly, the insult ' to the secret orders of his uncle the Bishop. The Duke, in a rage, told the Lord Mayor of London to close the City gates, and at once to provide him with five hundred men in order that he might march to Eltham and " pay his respects " to his nephew, the King

But the Bishop was too wide awake for the Duke He posted men at the foot of London Bridge, barricaded the street, placed archers at all the windows on both sides. The Duke of Gloucester was thus prevented from coming out, and his visit with five hundred armed men to the Palace of Eltham did not take place

There does not seem to be any record of much in the form of pageantry at Eltham during the reign of Henry VI We find that he kept Christmas here in 1425, and also in 1427 On the latter occasion, when the little king was only about six years of age, we learn from the records of " Proceedings of the Privy Council " that certain minstrels and travelling players were brought in for the entertainment of his youthful majesty

In his tenth year he was taken from Eltham to Paris to be crowned the king of France Returning from Paris he came to Eltham, and on February 20th, 1432, immediately after the visit to France, he proceeded on horseback, duly attended, to Blackheath, where he was met by the Lord Mayor of London, clothed in red velvet, the Sheriffs and Aldermen, in scarlet cloaks furred, and a large company of loyal citizens. Thence he rode to Deptford, where he was greeted by the London clergy in their robes, and the whole company proceeded to London

" When the king was come to London Bridge," it is recorded in Fabian's Chronicle, " there was devised a mighty giant, standing with a drawn sword, and having a poetical speech inscribed by his side. When the king had passed the first gate, and was arrived at the draw-bridge, he found a goodly tower hung with silk and cloth of arras, out of which suddenly appeared three ladies, clad in gold and silk, with coronets upon their heads, of which the first was dame Nature, the second dame Grace, and the third dame Fortune. They each addressed the king in verse. On each side

accounts we find that this market was in existence in 1602. It has long since gone out of practice.

From the "Proceedings of the Privy Council" we find that in 1445 the young king was putting his house in order at Eltham, in anticipation of the arrival of his bride, Margaret of Anjou. The Clerk of the Works was one William Cleve, who also was chaplain. This gentleman was responsible for the construction of a new hall and scullery,

SHIPS OF FIFTEENTH CENTURY (Har. M.S.)

of them were ranged seven virgins; the first seven presented the king with the seven gifts of the Holy Ghost; the others with the seven gifts of Grace. At the conduit, near the gate of St. Paul's, was a celestial throne, wherein was placed a personification of the Trinity, with a multitude of angels playing and singing upon all instruments of music."

In our day we should rightly regard such a demonstration as this as very profane.

· · · · · ·

In the year 1438, when the king was in his seventeenth year, we learn that he renewed the old charter which permitted a market to be held at Eltham. From the churchwardens'

and the provision of suitable lodgings for the young princess. The latter arrived in due course and abode in Eltham Palace as bride prior to her state entry into London for her coronation.

· · · · · ·

The following entry appears in the "Rolls of Parliament," volume v., page 175. "To prevent exactions from his subjects, part of the Royal farm rents were reserved, 28. Henry VI., 1450, for the support of the King's household. Eltham was assessed at £8 a year."

· · · · · ·

One more association of Henry VI. with Eltham seems to have been recorded, and the circumstance is a pathetic one.

As the years went on the position of Henry, as king, became less and less secure. He was weak as a ruler and incompetent to cope with the difficulties that beset him on all sides. The losses in France roused the people of England against the wretched government to whose weakness the disasters were attributed. The question of the Lancastrian rights to the throne began to be discussed, and, as the story of national history reveals, the great House of York was disputing the title by force of arms. The wars of the Roses had begun.

King Henry was taken prisoner in 1460 at the Battle of Northampton, and it was while a prisoner in the hands of the Yorkists that his last visit to Eltham is recorded of him

In the "Privy Council" records we read that the unhappy king was allowed to come out to Eltham and amuse himself by hunting in the royal woods His reflections must have been sad ones when he thought of the troubled times he had passed through since those happy days, forty years before, when he played in these familiar fields, and since that other time, fifteen years before, when he brought his bride to the Palace at Eltham, full of hope for a happy and prosperous reign.

Now Margaret, his queen, is a fugitive in Scotland, and he allowed, on the sufferance of his enemies, to visit the home of his youth Henry VI. must have realised to the full the truth of those words attributed to his grandfather

"Uneasy lies the head that wears a crown"

EDWARD IV.

CHAPTER XLII

EDWARD IV. AND ELTHAM.

Edward IV. found Eltham a congenial place of residence, and spent much of his time here with his Court. Here, in the year 1469 he held a great tournament, at which his champion was Sir John Paston.

He held his Christmas festivities at Eltham in 1482, and some idea of the accommodation of the Palace as it then existed, as well as of the magnitude of the entertainment, may be gathered from the recorded fact that two thousand persons were feasted daily at his tables.

And Edward left his mark upon the Palace, for what is to be seen of it to-day was erected by him. Not since the days when Bishop Bek beautified the Manor House, some two hundred years before, and made it into a Palace fitted for a king, do any important structural alterations seem to have been carried out.

Edward was a voluptuous monarch and fond of regal display and pomp. It is probable that the accommodation of the Palace as he found it was not sufficient for his purposes, and that the magnificent hall which now remains to us was erected by him to supply the deficiency.

We have already dealt with the building, in considerable detail, in an earlier chapter, but we would again call attention to the badges of Edward IV., the rose en soleil, carved in the spandrels of the hall door facing the bridge. In the ceiling, too, of the south bay—the one leading towards the lawn, as it is to-day—may be observed the falcon and fetterlock, another of his badges.

Another memorial of Edward's handiwork is, of course, the fine old stone bridge across the moat. The bridge that had done duty before was of wood, for it was a draw-bridge. But the necessity for draw-bridges was passing away in Edward's time. They were constructed for purposes of protection. If the enemy, or any other undesirable visitors, wanted to get within the palace, they would have found it a rather troublesome undertaking when the draw-bridge was up. But other weapons of offence had now become superior to the draw-bridge, so the old form was discarded, and the more convenient and substantial bridge of stone was erected in its place.

Edward did not confine his building operations to Eltham only. Windsor and other palaces underwent enlargements or improvements by the order of this king.

It is interesting to learn that, notwithstanding his love of pleasure, and depravity of living, Edward IV. possessed a small library, and it is particularly interesting to Eltham to know that when he came here he brought his books with him, presumably to read. Let us hope he found time to do so.

From the "Wardrobe Accounts" we find certain payments were made which bear out this statement:—

QUEEN ELIZABETH WOODVILLE.

Indeed, building operation was so sufficiently distinguishing a feature of his domestic policy that it found notice in a poem written on his death by John Skelton, who afterwards became a somewhat notable poet of early Tudor times.

The poem alluded to was the first published by Skelton, and was written when the poet was 23 years of age. It contains the following verse which is of local interest. Writing of the dead king, he says:—

"I made Nottingham a Palace Royal,
Windsor, Eltham, and many others mo;
Yet at last I went from them all,
Et nunc in pulvere dormio."

"To Robert Boillet, for black paper and nails for closing and fastening of divers coffyns of fir, wherein the king's books were conveied and carried from the King's Great wardrobe in London unto Eltham, 8d."

"To Richard Carter, for carriage of divers parcels appertaining unto the office of Beds from London unto Eltham, 15d., and to the King's Carman for a reward awaiting upon certain of the King's book put into the King's Car. 8d."

King Edward's library was not a very large one. It contained such books as the Bible,

"Josephus," "Titus Livius," "La Fortresse de Foy," and "Froissart." Nor could reading have been so easy and pleasurable an exercise to the king of those days as it is to the poorest child now-a-days. For these books were in manuscript.

But it is a fact to be borne in mind that at this very time William Caxton was thinking out his plans for making a printing press, and the period of King Edward's reign is distinguished by the fact that Caxton actually brought his machine into operation then.

This was not an Eltham incident, true, but William Caxton was a man of Kent, and there can be no doubt that the wonderful story of his invention was talked about widely enough, and even among the gossips of Eltham village.

. . . . .

A ROYAL CHRISTENING

A rather notable event in connection with the Royal Chapel at Eltham Palace was the christening ceremony of Princess Bridget, the seventh daughter of Edward IV.

In volume numbered 6,113 of "Additional Manuscripts" at the British Museum Library, is a detailed account of this interesting ceremony. We will give a transcription of it, with its quaint expression and spelling, as near as possible, as it stands.

"In the yere of our lorde 1480 And the xxth yere of the Reigne of Kinge Edwarde the iiijth on Sainte Martyns even, was Borne the ladye Brigette, And Cristened on the morne on Sainte Martyns daye In the Chappell of Eltham, by the Busshoppe of Chichester in order As ensuethe.

Furste C (100) Torches borne by Knightes, Esquiers and other honneste Paisonnes

The Lorde Matreuers, Beringe the Basen, Having A Towell aboute his necke

Therle (The earl) of Northumberlande bearing A Taper not light.

Therle of Lincolne the Salte

The Canapee borne by iiij Knightes and A Baron

My lady Matrauers did bere A Ryche Crysom Pinned Ouer her lefte breste

The Countesse of Rychemond did bere the Princesse

My lorde Marques Dorsette Assisted her

My lady the Kinges Mother, and my lady Elizabethe, were godmothers at the Fonte

The Busshoppe of Winchester Godfather.

And in the Tyme of the christeninge, the officers of Armes caste on their cotes

And then were light all the fore sayde Torches.

Presente, theise noble men enseuenge

The Duke of Yorke

The Lorde Hastings, the Kinges chamberlayn

The lorde Stanley, steward of the Kinges house

The lorde Dacres, the quenes chamberlein, and many other astates

And when the sayde Princesse was christened A Squier helde the Basens to the gossyppes, and even by the Font my lady Matravers was godmother to the conformacion.

And from thens she was borne before the high aulter, And that Solempnitee doon she was Borne eftesongs into her Parclosse, accompenyed with the Astates Aforesayde

And the lorde of Sainte Joanes brought thither a spice plate.

And at the sayde Parclose the godfather and the godmother gaue greate gyftes to the sayde princesse.

Whiche gyftes were borne by Knightes and esquiers before the sayde Princesse, turning to the quenes chamber Againe, well Accompanyed As yt Apperteynethe, and after the custume of this Realme   Deo gr'as"

It will be noticed that the spelling in this description is very free, and independent of all rules and regulations. In those days men spelled as they thought they would, and probably they did so phonetically or according to their pronunciation of the word.

The "crysom" which my lady Maltravers wore was a white cloth which had been anointed with "chrism," and chrism was the oil consecrated by the bishop, and used in the Roman and Greek Churches in the administration of baptism, confirmation, and extreme unction. The "crysom" thus anointed was put upon the child by the priest at the time of baptism, and it was preserved as a memorial or emblem of innocence.

The "gossyppes" to whom the squire held the basin were the sponsors, or godfathers and godmothers.

"They had mothers as we had; and those mothers had *gossyps* (if their children were christened) as we are." *Ben Jonson: Staple of News.*

and became a nun at the Priory of Dartford, where she "spent her life in holy contemplation till the day of her death." She is said to have died in the year 1517, when she would have been 37 years of age, and she was buried within the Priory.

Princess Katherine, the sixth daughter of

BEDROOM. TEMP. EDWARD IV. (Cotton M.S.)

The "Parclosse" into which the royal infant was carried was probably a kind of anteroom.

The lady Elizabeth who acted as a sponsor was the eldest sister of the baby, and subsequently married Henry of Richmond, who had become Henry VII., by which act the families of York and Lancaster (the white and red rose) were united.

The little Princess Bridget does not seem to have been physically strong, and at an early age she was dedicated to a religious life,

Edward IV., was also baptised in the Chapel of Eltham Palace in the year 1480. This royal lady had a rather chequered career. She was first intended for marriage to a Spanish Prince, then, afterwards, for a son of the King of Scotland, but ultimately married, at the age of 17, the Earl of Devon. After a life of much trouble and sorrow she died in 1527, and was buried at Tiverton in Devon. In her will she styled herself "Daughter, Suster, and Aunte of Kings."

We have said that in all probability the clerks who wrote the above extracts spelled the words according to their pronunciation. You will observe in the account of the royal christening that the word "bishop" is written "busshoppe." You will also notice that the lawyer who wrote out the will of Princess Katherine spelled the word "sister" as "suster." Now, although a prelate of to-day might, perhaps, feel somewhat shocked if you addressed him as "my lord Busshoppe," it would seem that that was the courtly way of addressing a bishop in the days of Edward IV.

According to the examples we have quoted, the syllables "bis" and "sis" were written as if they were pronounced "bus" and "sus." The words "blister" and "twister," in all probability, were sounded almost as "bluster" and "twuster." It is interesting to note that many such words are pronounced by west countrymen to-day pretty much as they were pronounced in Edward IV's. time.

CHAPTER XLIII

HENRY VII. AND ELTHAM.

There does not seem to be any record of Edward V. or Richard III being directly associated with Eltham during their short reigns. Edward knew Eltham as the pleasant resort in Kent where he spent so much of his early childhood with his brothers and sisters, and Richard, when Duke of Gloucester, no doubt often visited the Palace when his brother, Edward IV , held his splendid Courts there. But during the two years, or thereabouts, which included the reigns of both these kings, there does not seem to have been any royal visit.

After the Battle of Bosworth, when Richard was slain, Henry of Richmond was made king, and shortly afterwards he married Elizabeth, daughter of Edward IV., a princess well-known to Eltham, and the claims of the rival families of York and Lancaster to the throne of England were satisfied

Henry VII and his Queen spent much of their time at the Palace of Eltham. It is recorded that the king commonly dined in the great hall, and his officers kept their tables in it. He seems also to have continued the building improvements that Edward IV had begun, not many years before, for Lambarde, writing a short time afterwards, says, "It is not yet out of memorie that the king set up the fair front over the moat here"

The following details concerning Henry VII.'s building operations, at Eltham, which are to be found in the Egerton manuscripts, 2,358, folio 50, are interesting —

"Expended at Eltham for shifting the oratory of the King, repairs of the bultyng-house, storehouse, bakery, lodges, lower court, near the east part of the bridge, and making a

certain new bridge, *pons haurıabılıs*, and repairing a room within the Manor, from March to November, 15 and 16 Henry VII., 1500, 33 weeks and a day.

"John Brown for four loads of sand used in repairing the foundations of the said bridge there new made, price at Wellowe, 4s 4d

"William Blake and John Brown for 8,000 plain tyles for repairing the roofs of the lodges in the lower court near the bridge on the east and north parts, price per thousand at Eltham 5s , and for half a hundred roof tyles for repairing 100fs, 2s 6d

"John Tanner for half a hundred burnt lime, price 2s. 6d at Greenwich

"John Brown for four load of sand, used on gravelling the house in which the King distributed his alms, price at 4d , 16d

"Barnard Flower, plumber, for repairing the windows in the King and Queen's lodging, for 70 feet of glass called Normandy glass, at 3d a foot, 10 feet of glass, called Renish glass, at 2½d a foot, 1 foot of Normandy glass, painted with hawthorns, 6d , 1 round disc of glass, painted with red rose, and a similar disc, painted with a portcullis, price 12d., used in repairing the windows in the lodgings of the King, Queen, and Prince

"John Norton for making a certain bridge called a 'fawce bridge,' &c., &c

"Total expended in 33 weeks, £44 6s. 6d."

Just one or two comments upon this account The buildings mentioned at the beginning of the entry, with the exception of the oratory, would apparently have stood on the left hand side of the court yard, as you approach the bridge.

The Bultynghouse. This was probably the storehouse for meal or corn for the horses.

The *pons hauriabilis*. The name seems to suggest a bridge leading to some place for the drawing of water. In all probability it existed on the south side, where the modern footbridge across the moat has been erected by Mr. Bloxam. The foundations of an older bridge are plainly discernible here.

The making of "tyles" was apparently an

ments referred to by Lambarde, Mr. Buckler, writing in 1828, says, "Henry the Seventh, who resided much in Eltham, and, as appears by a record in the Office of Arms, most commonly dined in the great hall, re-built the front of the Palace next the moat, that is, the west, or principal front, which extended full three hundred and eighty feet.

"Eltham Palace," he continues, "exhibited

GENERAL COSTUME IN TIME OF HENRY VII.

Eltham industry in the year 1500, and William Blake and John Brown were the proprietors.

The "red rose" painted on the glass was, of course, the "Red Rose" of Lancaster, to which family the King belonged.

The "portcullis" was the badge of John of Gaunt, the founder of the House of Lancaster.

The "fawce" bridge alluded to was probably the pons hauriabilis mentioned above.

The four load of sand which John Brown supplied seems to have been for sanding the floor of the house, an old custom, which is still practised in remote districts, where carpets or floor-cloths are not used.

Commenting upon the structural improve-

the same partial, thought not inconsiderable, re-edification which very few mansions of remote antiquity escaped. The spirit of improvement often, and not infrequently the love of variety, influenced these changes, and the taste with which they were sometimes made, may, without presumption, be questioned, especially where we observe the mutilation of an elegant feature for the accommodation of one destitute of merit as a specimen of architecture, and of propriety, on the score of convenience.

"How far Eltham Palace warranted these observations must remain doubtful; but, referring to the alterations which in former times were made in ancient buildings, I may remark that the hall more commonly retained its original character than any other part of the mansion. This might have been on account of its dimensions, which were always ample, and where no improvement in convenience could be made, none was desired, if attainable, in the architecture Certainly, no improvement in this respect would have followed an alteration of the hall at Eltham

"Henry the Seventh could not have produced in its stead a building with excellencies of so high an order as were commanded by Edward the Fourth If talent had not greatly diminished, the style of architecture on which it was exercised claimed merit, rather for the profusion and delicacy of its ornaments, than for the boldness and beauty of its proportions

"In the order and space of the other rooms, the later ages are entitled to the palm of superiority. Henry the Seventh improved Eltham Palace . . retaining, however, the original great banqueting hall.

"Walls of brick were often, in the period of which we are now speaking, substituted for those of stone The same material forms the walls of Eltham hall, under a case of stone But brick alone was commonly used, and ingrafted on masonry, as in this example. Its peculiar ornaments, in addition to carved work, were distinguished by black bricks, arranged in various patterns over every blank surface, and specimens of these decorations remain on the west and south walls of Eltham Palace (1828) King Henry the Seventh's building, which the record calls "handsome," doubtless partook of the character which distinguished the best designs of that and the succeeding reign, so celebrated for their generous encouragement of architecture The same spirit which guided Edward the Fourth in the building of the Palace seems to have descended without diminution to his royal successor."

Thus wrote Mr. Buckler, in 1828, and it is disappointing that none of the "handsome" work of Henry VII. can now be seen. That of King Edward IV had out-lived it If you want to see it in imagination you might take up your position in the "Bridge-lane," and view the

ruins from that point You will easily see that the hall, as it now stands, was only a portion of a great pile of buildings, "the fair front of which," as mentioned by Lambarde, would have been facing the direction in which you stand.

One of the most notable events in Eltham history occurred in the reign of Henry VII This was the visit paid to the Palace in the year 1500, by Erasmus, the great scholar This famous man was a native of Rotterdam, and became one of the most distinguished scholars of his day The trials and troubles of his parents are set forth in that wonderful story, "The Cloister and the Hearth," by Charles Reade Erasmus made the acquaintance, and ultimately became the close friend of Sir Thomas More, a great and scholarly Englishman, of whom we shall have more to say later on, in the course of Eltham history

In one of his letters, Erasmus tells how when he was staying at Greenwich, with Lord Mountjoy, that More took him for a walk from Greenwich to Eltham, to see the house which the King had there It would be interesting to know which road these two wonderful men took when they made this journey In all probability it was by way of Kidbrook-lane.

When they reached the Palace, they found that the royal children were there, and among them the little prince, Henry, who was to become king in after years, as Henry VIII He seems to have been a very beautiful and also intelligent child, and to have impressed the mind of the distinguished visitor Erasmus, in the letter alluded to, writes —

"When we came to the great hall, there were assembled together, not only those of the Royal Household, but Mountjoy's train also. In the midst stood Henry, then only nine years old, but of right royal bearing, foreshewing a nobility of mind, in addition to a person of singular beauty

"On his right hand was the Lady Margaret, then about eleven years old, afterwards married to James, King of the Scots, the Lady Mary, four years old, was playing at his left, and near at hand was the little Edmund, in the nurse's arms. More, with his companion, Arnold, saluted the youthful Henry, and proffered him something written, I know not what.

"I, not expecting anything of the kind, had nothing ready at the time to present to the Prince, but promised that I would take some other opportunity of shewing my respect to him. Meanwhile, I was a good deal vexed with More, for not having forewarned me, and the

In the year 1485 we find that King Henry VII. entertained the Scottish Ambassadors at the Palace, and in order that they might take full advantage of the opportunity which the Eltham woods afforded for the pleasures of the chase, we are told that by royal command these visitors from the north were supplied with bows and arrows.

SUIT OF DEMI. LANCERS ARMOUR. (Temp. Henry VII).

more so, as the stripling, during dinner, sent me a short epistle as a kind of challenge to write something to him."

It is a satisfaction to learn that Erasmus carried out his promise, for when he reached home, he says, "I invoked the muses from whom I had long been divorced, and composed an elegant ode in Hexameters and Iambics, in praise of England, of Henry VII., and of the Princes Arthur and Henry."

It was to Henry that he dedicated his ode.

We may hope that they had a good time, for, according to the accounts, the amount credited to Sir Richard Gyldeford for the bread and wine they consumed was £6 4s. 7d.

A rather tragic circumstance occurred in 1508, the year before King Henry died. Giles, the famous Lord Daubeny, was riding after the King from Eltham to Greenwich. As they were passing Blackheath, he was taken ill, and died within a few days, May, 1508. It was on this spot that, eleven years before, in 1497, Lord

Daubeney won his famous victory over the Cornish insurgents. The coincidence caused, no doubt, much talk, and the wagging of wise heads.

There is one other matter which closely associates the name of Henry VII. with Eltham. As history records, this king was very exacting in the matter of taxation. It is possible that he found the payment of the "fifteenths" bore very heavily upon the Eltham folk, for we find that in 1492, "King Henry VII. gave thirty-eight acres of land at Eltham (the fifteen-penny lands) to the poor inhabitants of Eltham towards the payment of their fifteenths, in consideration of so great a portion of the land in the parish belonging to the Crown, and not being assessed to the subsidies."

SUIT OF V. LONG BREASTED ARMOUR. (Henry VII.)

HENRY VIII. (Holbein Trin. Coll., Camb).

CHAPTER XLIV.

IN THE DAYS OF "KING HAL."

As we have said already, Henry VIII. spent much of his childhood at Eltham Palace, and when King he came frequently to reside here in the early part of his reign.

In the year 1514 there occurred an interesting incident at the Palace recalling the famous battle of " Flodden Field," which took place the year before, when the king was in France, with a large army, campaigning. The King of Scotland, taking advantage of this absence, marched into England at the head of a great army, and encountered the English at " Flodden" with such disastrous results that the Scots lost 10,000 men, including King James and the flower of his nobility.

An English knight who distinguished himself in that great fight was Sir Edward Stanley. He had command of the English archers which did such dire damage to the Scottish hosts on that fatal day.

Following the banner of Stanley, which bore the device of *an eagle*, his followers drove the Scots over the hill, or *mount*, and so it was that, at Eltham, in the year 1514, King Henry commemorated the event, and did honour to Edward Stanley, by making him Baron *Mont-eagle*.

The Christmas spent at Eltham in 1515 seems to have been in some respects a memorable one. It was on Christmas Eve, in the Palace Chapel, that Cardinal Wolsey, who had risen to great eminence, took the oaths of Lord Chancellor, and was created to that office, in succession to Archbishop Warham, who delivered the Great Seal on the 22nd of December, only two days before.

Wolsey now figures in Eltham history, for he

No. 101.

THE OLD DWELLINGS IN THE COURT YARD.
(Christmas 1908).

No. 102.

THE "GREYHOUND" INN, AND OTHER DWELLINGS
(1909).

No. 103.

THE "WHITE HART," HIGH STREET.

(19)

No. 104.

LAST OF THE OLD BARN AT HORNE PARK,
(August, 1909)

No. 105.

NATIONAL SCHOOL GIRLS IN OLD ENGLISH COSTUME PRACTISING THE MAYPOLE DANCE.
In the field beyond the last travelling Theatre. (1909).

No. 106.

THE "PORCUPINE" INN, MOTTINGHAM
Remains of old Inn, on the left.

frequently attended here at the Court, and the quaint old wooden buildings which you see still in existence on your right hand as you approach the bridge are still known as the "Chancellor's Lodgings," as they were called in the old plan of the Court Yard, drawn up in 1590, and preserved at the Record Office.

On the twelfth night after the "solemn Christmas" kept on this occasion the King and courtiers seem to have had a right jovial time in the enjoyment of a grand masque and banquet in the great hall. There was, in the first place, a performance by the choir boys of the Royal Chapel of the comedy of "Troilus and Pandarus," which has been tersely described by the late Mr. Alexander Milne, from "Letters and Papers, Foreign and Domestic."

"Troilus was richly apparelled," writes Mr. Milne, "and Cressida appeared as a widow, in black sarcenet, while Diomed and the Greeks swaggered as men of war. The barber's charge for cutting the hair and washing the heads of these young persons previous to the performance—there were fifteen of them—was 4d., which does not seem extravagant.

"Afterwards ensued a mask, enacted by the ladies and lords of the Court. A goodly castle had been erected in the hall, in which were ladies and knights, gorgeously apparelled. The castle was vigorously assailed by the other knights, but the attackers were beaten back, many a good stripe having been given, and then the knights and ladies came forth from the castle, and a stately dance ensued, the climax of all being a banquet of 200 dishes, with great plenty for everyone."

A chapter of the Garter was held at Eltham Palace in 1516, to supply the vacancy caused by the death of Julian de Medici, surnamed "The Magnificent," brother of Pope Leo X., and "Lieutenant-General of the Armies of the Church," who had died in the preceding month of March, before installation.

A FAMOUS MAY-DAY FESTIVAL.

"In his sports, pageants, and general habits of life, there was a magnificence not unmingled with a sense of the poetical and the picturesque, which helped to endear the young King Henry to the people of England. We can well understand," writes the historian, Knight, "with what pleasure the tales must have been told and listened to of Henry's coming into London in the habit of a yeoman of the guard, to behold the festivities of Midsummer Eve, or of his excursions into the country on May-day morning."

One of the most picturesque of chroniclers, Hall, thus describes an incident of this kind, which stands in strange and refreshing contrast to the scenes in the later years of the same king's reign:—

"The king and queen, accompanied with many lords and ladies, rode to the high ground of Shooter's Hill to take the open air, and as they passed by the way they espied a company of tall yeomen, clothed in green, with green hoods, and bows and arrows, to the number of two hundred.

"Then one of them, which called himself Robin Hood, came to the King, desiring him to see his men shoot, and the King was content.

"Then he whistled, and all the two hundred archers shot and loosed at once; and then he whistled again, and they likewise shot again; their arrows whistled by the craft of the head, so that the noise was strange and great, and much pleased the king, the queen, and all the company.

"All these archers were of the king's guard, and had thus apparelled themselves to make solace to the King.

"Then Robin Hood desired the King and Queen to come into the green-wood, and to see how the outlaws live.

"The King demanded of the Queen and her ladies if they durst adventure to go into the woods with so many outlaws. Then the Queen said, if it please him, she was content.

"Then the horns blew till they came to the wood under Shooter's Hill, and there was an arbour made with boughs, with a hall, and a great chamber, and an inner chamber, very well made, and covered with flowers and sweet herbs, which the King much praised.

"Then said Robin Hood: 'Sir, outlaws'

14

breakfast is venison, and therefore you must be content with such fare as we use.'

"Then the King departed and his company, and Robin Hood and his men them conducted.

"And as they were returning there met with them two ladies in a rich chariot, drawn with five horses, and every horse had his name on his head, and on every horse sat a lady, with her name written.

"On the first courser, called Camde, sat Humiditie, or Humide; on the second courser,

epidemic raging in London. This was henceforth called the "still Christmas."

It would seem, also, from an entry in an account book of the Clerk of the Works, at Eltham, 27 Henry VIII., that subsequent visits were made by the King and Queen.

The accounts refer to certain repairs made in "The Dewke of Norfioke's chamber, the lorde of Wyltesher's chamber, and Mr. Norris's chamber." They run thus:—

"New furnishing of workehouses for ye Mrs.

HENRY VIII. MAYING AT SHOOTERS HILL.

called Maneon, rode Lady Vert; on the third, called Pheaton, sate Lady Vegetave; on the fourth, called Rimphom, sate Lady Pleasance; on the fifth, called Lamfran, sate Sweet Odour, and in the chair sat the Lady May, accompanied with Lady Flora, richly apparelled; and they saluted the King with divers goodly songs, and so brought him to Greenwich."

Greenwich Palace had by this time become the favourite residence of the King, but from time to time he visited Eltham. We find that he kept Christmas very quietly here in 1525, with a small company, on account of an

Cooke of the Hall-place to caste ther Jelly's and fretts as gengbred and leshe &c."

"New makyng of tabulls Tressells for the Kyngs and for the quenes view—gyffyghts to stand upon and in framyng of a Raylle made by the Kyng's com'andment for to stand rounde a bout the hall and all so in the bordyng of the doures and skrenes and in the gyilftyng and bordyng of a low skaffolde upon the tabull for men to stan upon to see the Bankyt upon xiith daye at nyght."

From "Letters and Papers, Foreign and Domestic," we learn that Henry was at Eltham in 1532, and that he also visited the palace with his Queen, Anne Boleyn, in 1534. On this occasion they came to see their daughter, Princess Elizabeth, who was then a baby of one year's growth, but who was, at the time, declared to be "as goodly a child as hath ever been seen," and that the King thought much of her.

The King and Queen continued to pay visits to Eltham of an intermittent character, but by this time they had discarded the Palace as a permanent abode, and stayed chiefly at Greenwich.

COINS.

HENRY VIII. AND HIS COUNCIL (Hall's Chronicle 1548).

CHAPTER XLV.

"THE STATUTES OF ELTHAM."

In the year 1525, not long after the "Still Christmas" alluded to in the last chapter, Cardinal Wolsey, the King's Chancellor, being then in residence here, drew up the "Statutes of Eltham." The title of this document is rather high sounding, and suggests some matter of national importance. In this respect it is misleading, for it was nothing more than a code of rules designed to bring about a better management of the royal household.

Nevertheless, it is both interesting and instructive. Looked at from the point of view of the twentieth century, we may regard some of its clauses as curious and even amusing. But the twentieth century, we may regard some of value, for they reveal the home life of the monarch, and, it is said, even contain some precedents which are recognised at the present day in the royal household. Moreover, they give us an idea of the habits of life of the time. Reading between the lines, we can certainly form a pretty accurate mental picture of palace life at Eltham in the days of Henry VIII.

The necessity of including in the "Statutes" such orders as the following is rather suggestive.

"His Highness's attendants are not to steal any locks or keys, tables, forms, cupboards, or other furniture, out of the noblemen's or gentlemen's houses where he goes to visit."

Here is another:

"No herald, minstrel, falconer, or other, shall bring to the Court any boy or rascal."

It must have been a sad state of affairs which made the following necessary:

"Master cooks shall employ such scullions as

shall not go about naked, nor lie all night upon the ground before the kitchen fire."

Artificial light was not so much in vogue in those days as it is now. So they made the most of the daylight.

"Dinner to be at ten, supper at four."

"The proper officers are, between six and seven o'clock every morning, to make the fire in, and straw his Majesty's Privy Chamber."

Then as to food.

"Rhenish and Malmsey wines are directed and none other."

"Injunction to the brewer not to put any hops or brimstone into the ale."

There does not seem to have been any stint in the matter of food

"A Duke was allowed in the morning one chett loaf, one manchet, and one gallon of ale, in the afternoon, one manchet, and one gallon of ale, and after supper, one chett loaf, one manchet, one gallon of ale, and one pitcher of wine."

"The Queen's maids of honour were allowed a chett loaf, a manchet, a gallon of ale, and a chine of beef for breakfast."

By way of explanation, we may refer to Holinshed, the historian who lived in the days of Queen Elizabeth, for a description of a "manchet." He writes

"Of bread made of wheat we have sundrie sorts dailie brought to the table, whereof the first and most excellent is the *manchet*, which we commonlie call white bread."

It would seem that manchet bread was not unlike a modern bun in shape, while a manchet loaf something resembled a French roll, rising in the middle. The chett-loaf was probably the latter, and the person who sold manchets was often honoured by being nick-named "Johnnie Manchet."

We will now give some extracts from the "Statutes of Eltham," dealing with the "Kinge's Privye Chamber," reproducing the quaint wording and spelling of the original document

THE NEED SET FORTH.

"In soe muche as in the pure and cleane keepinge of the Kinge's Privye Chamber, with the goode order thereof, consisteth a greate parte of the Kinge's quyett, reste, comfort, and preservation of his healthe, the same above all other thinges is principallye and moste heighlie to bee regarded And consideringe that righte meane persones, as well for theire more commodity, doe retyre and withdrawe themselves aparte, as for the wholesomenesse of their Chambers, doe forbeare to have any greate or frequent resorte into the same

"Muche more it is convenyent, that the Kinge's Highnesse have his Privye Chamber and inwarde lodgeinges preserved secrete, to the pleasure of his Grace, without repayre of any great multitude unto it

THE OFFICERS

"It is therefore ordayned that no person of what state, degree, or conditione soever he be, from henceforthe attempte, or be in anywise suffered or admitted to come or repayre into the Kinge's Privye Chamber, other than such as his Grace shall from tyme to tyme call for or commande, except onlye the minysters now deputed, or in the lieu of them hereafter to be deputed for attendaunce in the same, viz · Marques of Exeter, the Kinge's kinseman, and sixe gentlemen, two gentlemen ushers, four groomes, the Kinge's barbor, and one page, beinge in all fifteen persones, whome the Kinge's Grace, for theire goode behavioure and qualities hath elected for that purpose, and whose names hereafter doe follow, viz Sir Wyllyam Tyler, Sir Thomas Cheyney, Sir Anthonie Browne, Sir Jo Russell, Mr Norrye, and Mr Carye, to be the saide six gentlemen wayters; Roger Radcliffe, and Anthonie Knevett, Gentlemen Ushers, Wyllyam Breereton, Walter Walshe, John Carye, Hizean Breereton, to be the groomes, Permye to be the barbor, and younge Weston to be the Kinge's Page."

Then follows an interesting clause setting forth clearly how these gentlemen were to deport themselves·

"The Kinge's mynde is, the saide six

gentlemen with the ushers and groomes, harbor and page, shall diligentlye attend upon his person in the saide Privye Chamber, in doing humble, reverend, seecrett, and comelye service, about all such things as his pleasure shall be to depute and put them to doe, not pressing his Grace nor advawncinge themselves, either in further service then his Grace wyll or shall assigne them unto, or intermeddle with suites, causes, or matters, whatsoever they be. Of which number of sixe Gents, divers be well languaged, expert in outward partes, and meet and able to be sent on famyliar messages to outwarde Princes when the cause shall requier "

The grocms had to be up between six and seven in the morning, and with their own hands —no deputing the duties to others being allowed—sweep up and clean the King's room

"   . purgeinge and makinge clean the same of all manner of filthinesse, in such manner and wyse as the Kinge's Heighnesse at his uprisinge and cominge thereunto, shall find the saide Chamber pure, cleane, holesome, and neate, withoute anye displeasant ayre or thinge, as the health, commoditye and pleasure of his moste noble person doth requier."

DRESSING THE KING

It appears from the following clause that the dressing of the King was a most important function and needed the services of the fifteen gentlemen that have been enumerated

"It is alsoe ordained, that the six Gent Wayters by seaven of the clock or sooner, as the K. the nighte before determine to arise in the morninge, shall be in the sayde Chamber there diligentlye attendinge uppon his Heigh   Coming forthe, beinge readye and prompte to apparell his H puttinge on such garments, in reverende, discreete, and sober manner, as shall be his H pleasure to weare, and that none of the sayde groomes or ushers doe approache or presume, unlesse they bee otherwise by his H commanded or admitted to laye hande uppon his royall person, or intermeddle with apparrylinge or dressing the same, but onlye the said 6 Gent Ushers, unlesse it be to warme cloathes, or bringe to

the sayde Gents such things as shall appertayne to the apparrellinge and dressinge of the Kinge's sayed person

"It is also ordered   That the Kinge's doublet, hose, shoes, or anye other garments, whiche his pleasure shall be to weare from daye to daye (the gowne onlye excepted) shall be honestlye and cleanlye broughte by the yeomen of the wardrobe of the robes, or in his absence by some other of the same office, to the Kinge's Privye Chamber dore, withoute enteringe into the same, where one of the Groomes shall receive the sayede garments and apparrell, bringinge and deliveringe the same to one of the sayed 6 gentlemen, to be ministered to the Kinge's person, as shall stand with his pleasure "

It was ordained that these fifteen favoured people should be lovinge together, and of good unity and accord, "keepinge seacreate all such things as shall bee doen or sayed in the Kinge's Chamber " If the King should be absent, it was not to be a matter of "when the cat is away the mice may play " But

"   . . they shall not onlye give theire contynuall and diligente attendaunce in the sayde Chamber, but alsoe leave hearkeninge or enquiringe where the K. is, or goeth, be it earlye or late, without grudginge, mumblinge, or talkinge of the Kinge's pastyme, late or earlye goinge to bedde, or any thing doen by his H. as they will avoyde his displeasure.

"And it is also ordered, that in case they of the Privye Chamber shall heare anye of his fellowes, or other person of what estate or degree soever, bespeake or use any unfyttinge language of the K. he shall with diligence disclose and shewe the same with the specyalties thereof unto his H. or unto some of his Privye Counsell, such as he thinks yt meet to shewe and declare unto his H."

There are strict injunctions as to the conduct of the six gentlemen ushers in the presence of the King "keeping a vigilante and a reverende respecte and eye to his majestie, soe that by his looke or countenance they maye knowe what he lackethe or is his pleasure to be hadd or doen "

Then there was not to be any immoderate

card playing and the like in the King's absence, further injunctions against "makinge of suites," and "intermeddling with cases and matters whatsoever they bee."

" . . . . alwayes regardinge and remembering the more nigher his Grace has called them to his person, the more to be humble, reverent, sober, discreet, and serviceable in all their doinges, behaviour, and conversations to th'entent that not onlye therebye they may deserve the increase of the K.'s favoure and good reporte, and brute may arise thereby to the good examples of others, but alsoe greate honor and wisdome may be ascribed to the K.'s Highnesse, that his Gr. hath so circumspectlye chosen such well qualified, mannered, and elect persons to be nighe, about, and attendant uppon his person."

CONCERNING THE BARBER.

After detailed instructions as to the bringing in of food to the King, and, when the day was over, collecting and conveying to the "Chaundrye," such unused things as "morter, torches, quarriers, pricketts, and sises, wholelye and entirelye, without embezzleinge or purloynnynge any part thereof," there follows some definite instructions for the Barber:

"It is also ordeyned that the K.'s barbor shalbee dailie by the K.'s uprysinge readye and attendaunt in the Privey Chamber, there havinge in readinesse his water, clothes, bason, knyves, combes, scissars, and such other stuffe as to his room doth appertayne, for trymminge and dressinge of the K.'s heade and bearde. And that the saiede Barbor doe take an especyall regarde to the pure and cleane keepinge of his own person and apparell, usinge himselfe always honestlye in his conversacion, without resorting to the companye of vyle persons, in avoydinge such danger and annoyance as by that meanes he might doe to the K.'s most royall person, nor faylinge this to doe uppon payne of losing his rome, and further punishment at the K.'s pleasure."

These extracts are sufficient, perhaps, to illustrate the general purport of the "Statutes of Eltham." Those who would like to examine the whole of these quaint rules may find a copy of the original in "Collection of Rules and Regulations for the Government of the Royal Household." It is published by the Society of Antiquaries.

WOLSEY AND HIS SUITE.

MARY.

Chapter XLVI

IN THE DAYS OF QUEEN MARY.

Although Edward VI. was no doubt a good deal at Eltham as a child, there does not seem to be any record of his coming here while King.

When King Henry VIII. deserted the Palace of Eltham, and adopted that of Greenwich as a royal residence, the Manor of Eltham was committed to the custody of Sir John Peche—20th March, 1512—for a term of 20 years, at a rental of £34 6s. 8d.

Ten years later (1522) it was in the hands of Sir Henry Guldeford, who was succeeded in 1534 by Richard Long, by whom it was transferred to Sir Thomas Speke, for it is recorded that in July, 1547, Edward VI., in recognition of services rendered to his father, Henry VIII., granted Sir Thomas "under the Great Seal, the office of keeper of the park at Eltham, of the houses in the manor of Eltham, and of the new park of 'Horne'—sometimes called the Little Park—also the office of Master of the drift of the wild animals in both the parks of Eltham and East Greenwich."

Sir Thomas Speke was succeeded by Sir John Gates, who was one of the four principal knights of the Privy Chamber, and vice-chamberlain of the King's Household.

The circumstances of Sir John Gates' acquisition of the stewardship and keepership of Eltham Manor are rather remarkable, and, as they were associated with certain important and tragic events in national history, we will briefly relate them.

The young king, Edward VI., was lying at Greenwich, sick unto death. While yet his life was rapidly ebbing, it would seem that the Letters and Privy Seal, conveying to Sir John Gates the responsibilities of Eltham, were hastily drawn up at Greenwich, July 5th, 1553.

The boy king died the next day, July 6th, and

on the very day of his death, was issued, "at Westminster under the Privy seal a grant in detail embodying all the clauses of the former grants to Long and Speke of keepership and leases to farm, with the additional benefits of the keeper's house near the capital mansion of Eltham, and a certain mansion called the chantry priest's house within the exterior part of the manor, &c., &c."

It was an ill-fated enterprise, as your history books will tell you. Lady Jane was a queen for nine days only. Despite the deep laid schemes of Northumberland, that nobleman was seized, as also was Sir John Gates, the steward of Eltham, and nine others of the ringleaders.

On August 22nd Northumberland, Gates, and Palmer were executed on Tower-hill. When the Duke of Northumberland and Gates met on

EDWARD VI.

The king's death was kept a profound secret for two days, during which time the conspiracy for putting Lady Jane upon the throne was in active operation. It is a significant fact that at this juncture the grants of the lands and offices of Eltham should have been made to Sir John Gates. Within a few days, we find that officer setting out with the Duke of Northumberland, who had been mainly responsible for thrusting Lady Jane Grey to the fore, to seize the Princess Mary, the elder sister of the young king, before she should have been proclaimed as his successor.

the scaffold, they each accused the other of being the author of the treason. They protested, however, that they entirely forgave each other. When the turn of Sir John came for execution, he addressed the people, admitted his offences, and said that he "had drawn poison from the same flower as the bee extracts sweets." He then submitted himself to the executioner, refused to have his eyes bandaged, and at three blows his neck was severed.

Sir John, by questionable means, came by the stewardship of Eltham, and suffered death before he actually came into possession.

The next steward was Queen Mary's vice-chamberlain, Henry Jernyngham. The Queen was much indebted to Sir Henry for faithful service, and it is not surprising that Eltham should have been put under his care

When Northumberland, accompanied by Sir John Gates, went forth to arrest the princess, she fled into Suffolk, and in order to prevent her escape by sea, the duke had stationed ships along the coast Sir Henry Jernyngham, however, managed not only to capture the ships, but to secure the allegiance of the crews to Mary, and so helped to turn the tide against the Duke of Northumberland So, when she became queen, Mary made Jernyngham Captain of her Guards, as well as steward of the Manor of Eltham

In 1554 we read that the youthful Sir Thomas Wyatt headed a rebellion against the queen, because of her proposed marriage with the King of Spain. Wyatt's headquarters were at Rochester, so we find Sir Henry Jernyngham, the steward of Eltham, marching, with the Duke of Norfolk, at the head of the Queen's Guards, against Wyatt, at Rochester.

It was not a glorious expedition, for, before the gates of Rochester, the royal forces went over to the other side, and the Duke and Sir Henry had to hasten back to the Metropolis as fast as their horses would take them But after Wyatt's attempt upon London, which ended so disastrously to himself, it was entrusted to Sir Henry Jernyngham to convey him, together with Lord Cobham, and Knyvet, as prisoners, to the Tower.

In the churchwardens' accounts, 1556, we get the following entry "Received for the burial of Sir . . . ., Chaplene to Sir Henry Gernygame, knight, who was buried in the Church, vjs. vujd "

In 1556 Queen Mary honoured Eltham by a visit, extending over a fortnight In the diary of Machyn we read —

"The Queen removed from St. James's-in-the-Fields unto Eltham, passing through the Park and Whitehall, and took her barge, crossing over to Lambeth unto my Lord Cardinal's Palace, and here she took her chariot, and so

rid through St. George's Fields unto Newington, there over the fields towards Eltham at five of the clock afternoon She was attended on horseback by the Cardinal, the Earl of Pembroke, Lord Montagu, and divers other lords and knights, ladies and gentlewomen, and a conflux of people to see her Grace, above 10,000 "

IN THE DAYS OF QUEEN BESS

The Parish Records, which date from the first year of Mary's reign, give many details that throw light upon Eltham life during the later Tudor period We have in earlier chapters dealt with "The May-pole," "The Beacon," and many other matters referring to Elizabeth's time We shall now make a few more extracts for further illustration of that period

Queen Elizabeth, like her sister, spent much of her childhood at Eltham Palace, but after she became queen her visits to the "old home" were only occasional, and of short duration

There are several entries in the churchwardens' accounts recording payments to the ringers, on the occasion of the queen's visit. These we have already alluded to, and commenting upon the occasion, a distinguished Fellow of the Society of Antiquaries writes "It was well for the Churchwardens of Eltham that they paid her Majesty that mark of respect, for the Churchwardens of Saint Olave's,, Southwark, were sued in the Star Chamber and heavily fined for not ringing their bells when the same termagent Queen passed down the river in her barge to Greenwich."

There is an interesting record in the churchwarden's account, relating to these times which we have not yet noticed

"Paid for carrying 1j. lodes of timber from Whets elme to the Churche, xijd "

The name "Whett's elm" or "Wyatt's elm" is frequently met with in the parish records.

Of this particular entry, Mr G R. Corner, Fellow of the Society of Antiquaries, an old-time resident of Eltham, in a paper contributed to the reports of the above-named society, wrote in 1850, "It (Whet's or Wyatt's elm) was South End on the road from Eltham town to Foots-cray, and probably at the angle formed by the road leading to Chiselhurst, called Green Lane; but the corner of the road from Eltham to Bexley was called White's or Wyatt's Cross, and I have been informed that there was formerly an ancient elm growing there. Recently (1850) the skeleton of a man upwards of six feet in length has been discovered there. It

recorded reply to Mr. Corner's query, though nearly sixty years have elapsed. It would seem that he has confused the name of Wyatt, who wrote amorous poetry in Henry VIII.'s time, with Sir Thomas Wyatt, who, a mere youth, headed the rebellion against Mary, and suffered for his offence at the block.

A churchwarden's entry in 1572 runs thus:—

ELIZABETH.

was probably the body of a felo-de-se buried at the cross road, according to ancient, but now happily exploded custom, from whom the place may have derived its name of White's or Wyatt's Cross."

Then Mr. Corner puts the following interesting question: "Can Wyatt's Elm or Wyatt's Cross have any connection with Sir Thomas Wyatt or his family? His son, George Wyatt, the poet, is said to have lived at Bexley."

There does not appear to have been any

"Paid at the eating of the buck which Mr. Hatton gave to the Parish, xxxvijs. viijd."

This was Sir Christopher Hatton, who lived at Eltham as the keeper of the parks. He was a distinguished man in his day, for an old rhyme describes him as one

"Whose high-crowned hat and satin doublet
Moved the stout heart of England's Queen,
Though Pope and Spaniard could not trouble
it."

He was appointed keeper of Eltham and

Horne Parks on the 27th July, 1568, for his life, and he appears to have enjoyed the office until his death in 1591, for one of his letters is dated from Eltham, 15th July, 1590. The

Sir Christopher's residence at Eltham. There was the eating of the buck provided by the knight, while the churchwardens provided the necessary drink, in exemplification of the old

QUEEN ELIZABETH "PICNICING" (from Turburville "Book of Hunting," 1575).
By permission of Messrs. MACMILLAN & Co.

Queen doubtless visited him here. She was twice through the town in 1568, once in 1569, and she dined at Eltham in 1576, as appears from the churchwardens' accounts.

They seemed to have very festive times during

saying that "good eating requires good drinking."

And a pleasing notice of Hatton's mode of living here, shewing his taste and liberality, occurs in the intercepted letters of Monsieur de

Champenaye, Ambassador in England from the Low Countries He says —

"I was one day by Sir Christopher Hatten, Captain of the Queen's Guard, invited to Eltham, a house of the Queen's, whereof he was the guardian At which time I heard and saw three things that, in all my travels in France, Italy, and Spain, I never heard or saw the like The first was a concert of music, so excellent and sweet as cannot be expressed, the second, a course at a buck, with the best and most beautiful greyhounds that ever I did behold; and the third, a man at arms, excellently mounted, richly armed, and indeed the most accomplished cavalier I had ever seen. This knight was called Sir Harry Lea, who that day (accompanied with other gentlemen at arms), merely to do me honour, vouchsafed at my return to Greenwich to break certain lances, which action was performed with great dexterity and commendation "

In 1574 there appears this grim notice —

"Itm, paid to John Allee and Richard Feltone for the charges of the mearsement touching the hew and cry for Brown that murthered Mr Sanders at Shutter's Hill, xxxvjs viijd."

This alludes to a horrible murder committed at Shooter's-hill in 1573, by George Brown, who being enamoured of the wife of Master Sanders, a merchant, of London, waylaid and murdered Sanders (with the connivance of his wife), on Shooter's-hill, where he was on his road into Kent in pursuit of his business

Mr Sanders' man servant, who was left for dead by the roadside, fortunately recovered sufficiently before his death to give an account of the murder, and accused Brown, who was apprehended at Rochester, tried, and executed on the spot where the murder was committed, and Mrs Sanders, with two confederates, Mrs. Dewry, and a man called Trusty Roger, were afterwards tried, convicted, and executed at Smithfield.

This horrible tragedy gained for the place, for a time, the name of "The Hill of Blood," and a play was produced on the subject, shewing how great was the public interest in the episode

"1581 Paid at Sir Thomas Walsingham's at the deliverance of Richard a Price to ye gaile, iijs "

Sir Thomas Walsingham, of Scadbury, in Chislehurst, was Sheriff of Kent to 5th Elizabeth. His grandson, of the same name had the honour of Eltham given him, which was the Earl of Dorset's, and the middle park, which was Mr White's. "He has cut down £5,000 worth of timber, and hath scarcely left a tree to make a gibbet " (*Mysteries of the Good Old Cause, 1660, quoted by Lysons*)

The following item shews that they used to have their little disagreements in those days, and were given to litigation, even as people often are now—

"1596 Memorand Whereas there was a controversie between Mrs. Anne Twist, her Mates laundres, and Mr. Wyllm Ellot, about a pewe in the churche; It was ordered by the Lord Bishopp of Rochester that the said Mrs Twist should have the place where the pewe stood, and the said Mr Elyott to have the pewe, and she to builde another of her owne cest, which is already done, this xxvjth of August, 1569 "

"1596.   Paid to the Weyver for degyng of turfe for the bute in Estfeld, carryinge and makinge, ijs "

By Act of Parliament of Henry VIII , every parish was required to provide butts for the practice of archery This item shews us that the parish butts of Eltham were in Eastfield, which was at the back of the houses on the north side of High-street

CHAPTER XLVII

CONCERNING "OLD STUBBES."

In the Churchwardens' Accounts for the year 1556 we get the following entry —

"Itm r'd for torches for old Stubbes, xiijd"

The torches were, of course, for the funeral of old Stubbes, being used, according to the custom of the day, at each corner of the hearse They were provided by the churchwardens, and paid for by the relatives, their cost being in this case thirteenpence

Now this same "old Stubbes" would seem to have been the progenitor of a long line of Stubbeses, who not only figured pretty prominently in Eltham history during the ensuing hundred years, but eventually became a well-known Kentish family, some of its members having attained distinction for scholarship and occupied prominent positions in the Church.

The register shews that no less than thirty members of this family were baptised at Eltham between the years 1584 and 1656. Eleven members were married at Eltham during the same period, and twenty-two were buried in Eltham Church or Churchyard. A perusal of the early history of this family is very interesting, for it throws much light upon the village life of those remote days.

The "old Stubbes" whose burial cost his bereaved relatives the sum of thirteen pence for torches would seem to have been John Stubbes, whose will was proved on September 22nd, 1556

Let us read this document, and note how vividly it brings before our minds many conditions of local life of the time.

"In the name of god Amen. I John Stobbes of Eltham yeoman hole of mynde &c —my body to be buried in the Churchyarde of Eltham—to the highe Aulter of Eltham iijs iiijd —to the mother Church of Rochester xijd   Item two dussen of brede and a kilderkyn of Ale to the pore people of Eltham—to my godchildren both boyes and gerles my blessinge and grotes apece —to Margaret my wif the newe howse &c, as long as she is a wedowe—unto my Sonnes Henry, Philip, Richard, Robert and John Stobbes my ij howses on Chestlest heth in the p'ryshe of Chestle-hur-st—to Alice my youngest Doughter ij. of my best Bease   It'm I bequeyth to Elizabeth Borne my dowghter one of my best bease—to Alice my wife's Dowghter a yonge Bullock—to John Liksgrome one of my best Bullocks—to John and Philip Stobbes the sonnes of Harry Stobbes betwene them one bullocke—unto my wif vj bease and all Rest of quick Cattell aboute the house and all the Rest of my goods to be deuided to my wif and my children in equall porc'ons—Margaret my wif and Richard my sonn exors, John Rolte and John Alce Overseers. Witnesses John Rolte John Alce and Edward Eliott (No date), Proved 22 Sept, 1556"

.   .   .   .

The *Close Rolls* reveal a number of business transactions in connection with the conveyance of land and property of which the descendants of "John Stubbes" were owners

As an example, we make a copy of one or two, since the quaint wording and the local allusions are of direct interest.—

"Recognisance dated 14 March 1586   *John Stubbs* Citizen and Fishmonger *London* to Robert Withers Citizen and Vintner of London in the sum of £1000   Whereas the above bounden John Stubbs by Indenture of Bargain and Sale dated 2 Dec last past and made between him of the one part and the above named Robert Withers of the other part, granted, sold &c., to the latter ' All that newe brick messuage or tenement with the appurten'nces late in the tenure or occupac'on of the sayd John Stubbs set and being in the parrishe of *Eltham* in the Countye Kente' and other property (lands, &c.) there, purchased by him said John. He said *John Stubbs and Mary* his wife if they claim any right title &c , to the said property shall do all such reasonable acts, deeds &c , as shall be necessary or required "

The following "Indenture" shews pretty clearly the position held by the Stubbs family in Eltham in the time of James I

"1611 Indenture dated 5 May 9 James I between *Tobye Stubbs* of *Eltham* co Kent Yeoman son and heir of *John Stubbes* late of the City of London Fishmonger deceased, *Henry Stubbes* of Eltham Tailor sons of *Philip Stubbes* late of London Brewer deceased brother of the said John Stubbes of the one part, and Richard Slyne of Eltham aforesaid Yeoman of the other part, for the sale in consideration of £70 to said Richard of ' All that messuage or ten'te,' &c , 'and garden plott or small orchard' in Eltham aforesaid now or late in the occupation of John Smythe Labourer, also of 'all that messuage or ten'te' now or late in the occupation of Roger Allen Labourer with three roods of Land more or less 'lying at Easte fielde in the p'ishe of Eltham aforessid.' "

. . . .

It will be remembered that East Field was alluded to in the Churchwardens' Accounts as the place where the butts had been set up for the practice of archery, according to the law of Henry VIII The exact situation of these fields does not seem to be quite certain It may be observed that the *West* Fielde are at the west end of the parish, just beyond Well Hall station, where the Eltham football teams used to play their matches It may therefore be assumed that the East Field may have been higher up the hill, as Mr. Corner has noticed in Archæologia, "north of the houses in the High-street."

We will give one more extract from a Stubbs will, because of its great local interest, and the vivid little picture it affords us of the times It is from the will of "Katharine Haighte, of Eltham, widowe " This lady had been the widow of Henry Stubbs, and had taken a second husband named Haighte.

"January 1590 . . . . I give to my sonne John Stubbs that which he did owe me, that I paid for him unto Robert Sonne fishmonger, and to Thomas Harince grocer, both citizens of London

"My best hat to Alice the wife of my son Philipp Stubbs To Katherine, the daughter of John Borne deceased, a sawoer and porringer To Jone Hodgekins daur of Elizth Barker, the wife of John Barker citizen, a joyned chaire To Richard Browne, blacksmith, of Eltham, a mattriss with flocke bolster, and a plaine bedstead To the poor of Eltham, bread and Kilderkin of beare, &c . . ''

Witnesses Thomas Swifte, Philipp Stubbs, the older, James Swifte, Philipp Stubbs, the younger, X, the marke of Katherine Haighte

In a codicil dated "the iiij day of March, 1590," Mistress Katherine Haighte makes the following additional interesting bequests· "I give to my son Phillipp Stubbs the corn wheat and oats with a parcell of ground and five paire of geese. To John and his wife, Eliz Stubbs a pair of Geese To James Swifte vicar of Eltham a paire of Sheets I give to Margaret Shawe two gownes a petticoate and kirtle "

In the year 1568 we find that Robert Stubbes was one of the churchwardens, for, from the accounts of the "Fifteen Penny Lands," it is recorded that John Rolt and Edward Ellyate, Wardens of the Fifteen Penny Lands, in the year mentioned, "paid to Robert Stubbes and John Petley, Churchwardens, for the repairing of the church steaple xxxviijs vijd."

. . . .

It is quite an interesting exercise to trace the progress and development of this Eltham family, occupying, as many of them did, distinguished positions in the City of London, and conjure up mental pictures of the village life through an examination of the many wills that have been collected together in connection with the Stubbses. But it would occupy too much space to deal with the matter in greater detail.

There is, however, one scion of the family to whom we may well devote some space, for he was a scholarly divine, and his life is of additional interest, locally, from the fact that he was at one time Vicar of Woolwich, and also

"1665, Oct. 2. I was born within the Parish of St. Andrew, Undershaft, London, in which Parish 14 died of the plague that week; in the City 68,596 that year; Lord! what respect hadst thou to me and my Father's House? That many should fall in that great sickness on the right hand and on the left, but no evil happen'd unto me, nor did the Plague approach our dwelling. Let me thro' ye whole course of my

MUSKETEER (1603).

one of the first Chaplains appointed to the Royal Hospital for Seamen at Greenwich.

This was Archdeacon Philip Stubbs, the son of Philip Stubbs, Master of the Vintners' Company from 1660 to 1665, and grandson of Richard Stubbs, who had been attached to the Household of Queen Henrietta Maria (wife of Charles I.), as "Clerk of the Cheque."

In a private diary which he kept, the future Archdeacon relates some of the incidents of his youth:—

Life make Thee my refuge even the most High, my Habitation."

Writing in his diary of his early education, he says:—

"1677, Apr. 28. After I had laid a Foundation for ye Latin Tongue at Mr. Speed's Free-School in St. Mary Axe, and for ye Greek at Mr. Snell's Boarding Schole in Hillingdon Midsx., where in a literal sense I became wiser yn my teacher (an honest, good man, but no Clerk), I was transplanted to Merchant Taylors'

No. 107.
PARK FARM PLACE. The Seat of Lady James (From an old Engraving).
(About 1785).

No. 108.
ELTHAM HIGH STREET. (1909).

No. 117.   "ONE ACRE ALLOTMENTS."
(1898.)

No. 116.   THE OLD WOOLWICH ROAD.
(1896.)

No. 115.

POLE CAT END.

(1900.)

* 114.

POUND PLACE.

(1900.)

No. 117.

ENTRANCE TO GRAVEL PIT LANE.

(1908.)

No. 116.

A BIT OF BEXLEY ROAD.

Showing the field opposite the Barn House. (1909.)

No. 119. ELTHAM GREEN FROM THE ELTHAM END.

(1909).

No. 118. THE WAY TO ELTHAM FROM ELTHAM GREEN.

(1909).

for further improvement in Learning, as well as advancement in ye University by a Fellowship of St. Johns, for wch this Schole was designed as a Seminary by the Founder of ym both, Sr Thomas White Lord Mayor of London in Q Mary's Reign, &c."

He became a Scholar of Wadham College, Oxford, and had a distinguished University career. After a curacy in London and a Chaplaincy to the Bishop of Chichester, Mr. Stubbs was collated to the Rectory of Woolwich in 1694 by the Bishop of Rochester. He held this living over five years, and then proceeded to that of St. Alphege, London Wall.

It is interesting to note that he was active in the development of the Christian Knowledge Society in 1698—1704, and of the Society for the Propagation of the Gospel in Foreign Parts. He was elected a member of the S.P.G. on September 15th, 1702, and he wrote its first report, on the last page of which (issued in 1704) was printed the following resolution:—

"At a Court held at St. Martin's Library, Feb. 4, 1704. Resolved that the thanks of this Society be given to the Rev. Mr. Stubbs for the great pains and care he hath taken in preparing the New Account of the Proceedings of the Society. Resolved that this **Order** be printed at the foot of the said Account."

In number 147 of *The Spectator*, August 18th, 1711, an article will be found, from the pen of Steele, on the subject of "Reading the Church Service," which directly refers to Mr. Stubbs and is an interesting testimony to his great credit.

In 1715 he was made Archdeacon of St. Alban's. He died on September 13th, 1738, and was buried at Greenwich.

The tombstone over his grave is still preserved in the mausoleum at Greenwich, and is inscribed:—

"Here lyes till the last day
What was mortal
Of the Revd. Mr. Philip Stubbs, B.D.,
Archdeacon of St. Albans,
Chaplain to Greenwich Hospital,
and
Rector of Launton, Oxfordshire,
What he truly was, that day will discover."

This was one of the distinguished members of a family that originated in Eltham, and for many years, dating from the reign of Queen Mary, played a prominent part in the village life and history.

JAMES I. (Vandyke).

CHAPTER XLVIII.

IN THE DAYS OF JAMES I.

Sir Christopher Hatton, as we have already noticed, held the stewardship of Eltham Manor till he died in November, 1591. In the following July (1592) he was succeeded by William Brooke, Lord Cobham, K.G., who was also the Lord Warden of the Cinque Ports. He held the office for five years, until his death in 1597, when, it seems, the duties were divided between Sir William Brooke, who was made the keeper of the Great Park, and Hugh Miller, who was given the charge of the Little Park.

The reversion of these two offices fell to Lord North in 1599. He died the following year, when he was succeeded by Sir Thomas Walsingham to the keepership of the Great Park, and by John Leigh to that of Horne Park.

James the First came to the throne on the death of Queen Elizabeth in 1603, and soon after his accession a commission was appointed to make a survey of the lands and tenements of the Manor of Eltham.

The survey was held " at his Majesty's Manor of Eltham, by virtue of a Commission under the Seal of his Highness' Court of Exchequer, directed to the Right Hon. the Lord Stanhope, High Steward there, dated June 3, 1605. The Commissioners were Sir Thomas Walsingham, Sir Percival Hart, Sir Olif Leigh, John Doddridge, Esq., Solicitor-General, Sir Francis Bacon, Matthew Hadds, and Ralf Ewens Esquires, Henry Heyman, Esq., his Majesty's Surveyor of Kent. Among the Commissioners fined ten shillings each for not appearing on the jury were William Boughton of Plumpstead, gent., Samuel Abell, of Erith, gent., and Thomas Wildgose, of Lewisham."

In reference to this commission it is interesting to note that one of its members was

Sir Francis Bacon We may well be proud of the association of this eminent man with our village, for he was indeed a great man, one whose writings, as well as whose character, belong to the world He had already attained to distinction under Queen Elizabeth He was learned in the law, had been a Member of Parliament, and had already attracted much notice by his writings The future author of *Novum Organum*, had only just been knighted when he was placed by King James upon the commission of Eltham Manor, but he was, subsequently, to become Baron Verulam, and Viscount St. Alban, and to have his name inscribed upon the roll of immortal Englishmen.

The records of this commission are still preserved They are lengthy, and so full of detail that we can hardly reproduce them here in their entirety We may, however, make a few extracts

Those interested in local field names will, perhaps, like to read the names that were in existence in the time of Henry VIII, as shewn by the report of the Solicitor-General to this Commission of King James

> Brodemead, 4 acres, Littlemersh, near Footbridge, ½ acre, Long Lane, Westfield, Estfield, Estbosommnefield, Clerk's lese, Farnefox, Frethes, Ryddon, Southditch; Horsecroft, Brodeplotte, Great Marsh field, Stockwood, Cannonfield

The following particulars as to the conditions at the time of the Commission are also interesting

"The Demesne Lands sworn to by the jurors, tenants, and Ralf Treswell, sen, the measurer, viz. —

The scite of the Manor house of our Lord Sovereign the King in Eltham with the moate aboute the same Courte, Garden, Orchard, and building within the great gate there, 4 acres, 3 roods, 13 poles

The storehouse with the timber yard without the gate, 3 roods.

The Great Bakehouse without the gate

The Great Parke, the circumference whereof is by the pale and brickwall of the orchard 1,437 perches, which is four miles one quarter and 77 perches, and conteyneth within 612 acres, 1 rood, 10 poles

17 September, 1605 *Item*, upon the view of the Deare in the said Parke there was found about the number of five hundred and Ten Deare, of the which there was about seven score and ten Deare of Antlar, and 50 tymber trees of oake

The Olde Parke *al's* Middle Parke, within the pale, and without the moate and buildngs there, doth conteine about 948 perches, which is two myles ¾ 68 perches, and conteyneth 308 acres 3 roods

Item, upon the viewe of the Deare there was found 240 Deare, of which there was 17 of Antlar, and 250 Tymber Trees of Oake

The New Parke *al's* Horne Parke conteyneth about by the pale 988 perches, which is three myles 28 perches, and conteyneth 345 perches 3 roods

Item, upon the viewe of the Deare there was found 240 Deare, of the which there was 60 Deare of Antlar, and 2,740 trees of Oake, and there is decayed in the same Parke 50 rod of pale on the south side thereof adjoining to the land of Robert Skyffe and Arnold Kinge "

The King's tenants at this time were —

Sir William Roper, holding 35a 2 roods, 4 poles Rent 16s 5d

Sir William Wythens, 2 acres 0 roods, 22½ poles Rent 1s 10d

Hugh Miller, gent, 27 ac. 0 rds 27 pls Rent 41s 2d

Anne Twist, widow (*circ*), 81 acres Rent (*circ*) 25s

William Elliot (*circ*), 130 acres Rent (*circ*) 57s 4d.

Philip Stubbs (*circ*), 53 ac. Rent 33s 8d (*circ*), &c, &c

King James does not seem to have resided at Eltham, but there are records of his coming here on hunting expeditions According to the churchwardens' accounts payments were made to the ringers for the ringing of peals on these occasions

In "*Processions and Progresses of James I.*" by John Nichols, we are told of a visit made to Eltham by the King along with his brother-in-law, King Christian of Denmark, and his son, Henry Prince of Wales. A contemporary writer says of this visit :—

"These gracious Kings, accompanied with our Royal Prince and many honourable persons, mounted on steeds of great price, and furniture faire, hunted in the Park of Greenwich, and killed two bucks. Afternoon, their High Estates went to Eltham, a house of His

and was, apparently, a thing of more than ordinary ingenuity, for its fame reached the Metropolis and people used to come out and witness it.

Ben Jonson in his play, "The Silent Woman," makes one of his characters allude to it.

Morose, a gentleman that loves quietude, has been very much distracted by the noise about him; so he is made to say to his friend *Truewit* and others :—

"You do not know what misery I have

JAMES I. AND ATTENDANTS, HAWKING (from an old Print).

Majesty's, some two miles distant from the Court, and killed three bucks, with great pleasure on horseback."

It seems that the royal personages were followed by "many companies of people, which in their love came to see them," running after them and cheering as Kentish countrymen know well how to cheer.

In the early part of King James' reign Eltham found a sort of special notoriety on account of the "Motion" which was to be seen there.

The Eltham "Motion," was an invention of one Cornelius Drebbel, a native of Alkmaar,

been exercised this day, what a torrent of evil! My very house turns round with the tumult! I dwell in a windmill; the perpetual motion is here, and not at Eltham."

On another occasion, Ben Jonson alludes to the "motion" as the "Eltham thing."

An account of the "motion" is given in the appendix to this book.

In 1616, King James made Sir Theodore de Mayerne the Keeper and Ranger of the New Park of Horne. Sir Theodore was chief physician to the King, and the keepership was in consideration of his services in this capacity, for which he also received 4d. a day.

Sir Theodore was a distinguished Frenchman who had occupied the position of Physician in Ordinary to Henry IV. of France. After the assassination of the French King, he was invited to England, and given a similar post at the English Court. The English physicians did not approve of his treatment of Prince Henry, but the King and Council accorded him satisfactory certificates, and the College of Physicians elected him a Fellow in 1616.

AN ELTHAM HUNT.

(A Ballad of James I.)

James, King of Merrie England,
  A notable Prince was he,
And wide his name was known to fame
  For his philosophie.
But though he was a goodly king,
  And a godly man also,
Great was his shout, whenever gout
  Did take him by the toe.

ANNE OF DENMARK, QUEEN OF JAMES I.

In this same year he was appointed to the stewardship at Eltham. It was while the Court physician was occupying this post here, that the King visited Eltham, 1612, to hunt the buck, and, according to "Carleton's Letters," to bathe his bare feet and legs in the warm blood of the beast, as a remedy for the gout.

In these days, one may well wonder whether this curious prescription was that of the Court physician himself. The following verses upon this interesting incident appeared in the columns of the *Eltham Times* a few years ago :—

For kings, you see, they are but men,
  And queens but women, too;
Though gold their crown, and silk their gown,
  Their blood a hue so blue.
And tics and rheums will rack the limbs
  Of earl and churl likewise;
And sharp be aches for him who takes
  Too little exercise.

The King he groaned a kingly groan,
  And flung the pillows wide;
And grim his speech to the royal leech
  Who stood at his bed-side.

"O King," that Court physician said,
  "Be patient in thy pain,
"And all my skill I'll ply until
  "Thou'rt whole and sound again

"To-morrow, at the break of day,
  "Thou'lt mount thy fleetest nag,
" Whate'er betide, to Eltham ride,
  "To hunt the lordly stag
" To hunt the lordly buck, O King,
  "Till he can run no more
" Then 'twill be meet, thy royal feet,
  " To bathe them in his gore "

The King rode forth from London town,
  With lords and ladies gay,
And towards the shades of Eltham's glades
  They sped upon their way
And Eltham men, from out the tower,
  A merry peal did ring,
Twelve pennies bright they spent that night,
  In drinking to their King

And James, he chased the lordly buck
  From Eltham Court to Lee,
And many a wight declared the sight
  Was goodly for to see
"Yoicks!'" and "Tantivvy!'" echoed wide,
  As through the glades they sped,

Nor rested they, that summer's day,
  Till the lordly buck was dead

Then good King James, upon a log,
  He straightway took a seat,
And hose and shoon were pulled off soon
  From his royal legs and feet
And there, before his courtiers all,
  He bathed them in the gore,
For thus the leech did him beseech,
  As hath been writ before.

In days to come, ere yet the moon
  Had passed from full to wane,
O wondrous thing, for James the King,
  Was quite himself again.
Some said it was the gory bath
  That health to him had brought,
And some, as wise, said exercise
  A wondrous cure had wrought

But be it this, or be it that,
  Or Eltham's healthy clime,
Without a doubt the bout of gout
  Did quit him for the time
So let us sing "Long live the King!"
  Right merrie may he be
When next, in luck, he kills a buck,
  May I be there to see

CHAPTER XLIX.

WHEN CHARLES I. WAS KING.

In "Letters and Papers, Foreign and Domestic," there is a record that Charles I visited Eltham in November, 1629 It was only a short visit, probably for a day, and this seems to be the last recorded instance of a reigning monarch visiting the Palace The glories of Eltham were now become things of the past, to be written about by the historian or to be the subject of the poet's song

But there are one or two names of Eltham residents, at this time, who have played a part in our national story, and to whom we must now give some attention

SIR ANTONY VANDYCK

At the beginning of the reign of King Charles, during the summer months, this great artist used to reside at Eltham, Carpenter says, in apartments allowed him within the Palace, and some of his earlier pictures were painted here

Among the better qualities of Charles I was his love of art. It was this love which prompted him to the generous encouragement of men of genius, and to the spending of large sums of money upon the formation of collections of those works of art which helped to enrich the country so much

When Rubens, the famous painter, was sent to England as an ambassador to bring about a treaty of peace between Phillip IV and Charles I., the English King took the opportunity to commission the painter ambassador to paint two pictures, the "Apotheosis of King James" and a "St George"

In carrying out this work, Rubens gave to the saint the features of Charles I., and to Cleodelinda those of the queen.

Rubens became the fashion and several of the English nobles ordered pictures Thus it was that pupils of Rubens were attracted to England, and amongst them the illustrious artist, Antony Vandyck, who took up his abode at Eltham Palace

Ernest Chesneau, in his book on "The English School of Painting," writes: "Attracted by the accounts of Charles I's liberality, he (Vandyck) came for the first time in 1637, but did not succeed in getting presented to the King He then returned to Antwerp, where for six years he painted a host of masterpieces

"His reputation now reached the ears of the King, who had hitherto ignored him, but who now at once recalled him. The painter, who needed no second invitation, arrived in London in 1632 His success was rapid He received a pension, and in July of the same year was knighted and elected painter to the King in 1633 He was then thirty-four years old

"Vandyck passed the remainder of his short life in England, where he married the daughter of Lord Ruthven. His most valuable works are at Windsor Castle in the hall named after him—portraits of the King, Queen Henrietta, and Vandyck himself, the splendid group of the children of Charles I, a sketch of which is in the Louvre, where, also, may be seen one of his English masterpieces, a full length portrait of the King."

There are pictures by this artist at Hampton Court, the National Gallery, and in the private galleries of the nobility, scattered about the country

So when we contemplate the association of this artist with ur ld-world village we may well remember one or two things. When we are disposed to be over-critical of the actions of the unhappy Charles I. we can set down to his credit that he did much to encourage art in this country. "Elizabeth was at once greedy and pompous; James I. prodigal and mean," writes the author already mentioned; but "the splendid liberality of Charles I." towards art was the means of enriching the country more than one can estimate.

And though the old Palace, as a place of residence, was now forsaken by its royal

Eltham House in 1645 and died there in September, 1646. He was a disappointed man, who had been forced to resign his position of commander-in-chief by the passing of the "Self-denying Ordinance."

Parliament was getting dissatisfied with the progress of the struggle with the Royal Forces, "and Cromwell had become the principal mouthpiece of the dissatisfaction." "Without a more speedy, vigorous, and effective prosecution of the war," he said to the House of Commons, "casting off all lingering proceedings,

DRAGOON (1645).

owners, we may remember with some pride that this prince of painters worked upon his canvases in the discarded rooms, in some degree adding a new glory to their history. For, though the names of most of those who, in the older times, had thronged the courtly train, are lost in the oblivion of the past, the name of this artist, and his work still live, and will continue to live among the heroes of our national story.

ROBERT DEVEREUX, EARL OF ESSEX.

The stern and dogged Parliamentary General, who had had command of the forces against the King through the great Civil War, came to

like those soldiers of fortune beyond the sea, to spin out a war, we shall make the kingdom weary of us, and hate the name of a Parliament."

Cromwell charged the leaders of the Parliamentary Army, of whom Essex was the Chief, with being "afraid to conquer."

"If the King be beaten," said Manchester, "he will still be king; if he beat us he will hang us all for traitors."

To this the reply of Cromwell was, "If I met the King in battle I would fire my pistol at the King as at another."

So Cromwell urged upon Parliament the re-organisation of the Army, and out of this new policy came the "Self-denying Ordinance"

The chief officers who controlled the Army were Members of one or the other of the Houses of Parliament The "Self-denying Ordinance," proposed to the Commons by Cromwell, declared that no Member of either House should hold a command in the Army or a civil office

There was a long and bitter resistance to this measure, for it debarred from office many distinguished officers of the Parliamentary Army. It eventually passed the Commons, but it was thrown out by the Upper House, where it was uncompromisingly opposed by Essex, Manchester, and other lords, whose positions were directly affected by it

But the Commons went on with the re-organisation Essex was superseded in the command by Sir Thomas Fairfax, and thus it was that the former general, soured and disappointed, retired to the quietude of Eltham, where he lived out the few remaining months of his life He died in September, 1646, the chronicler Heath says, "not without suspicion of poison" He was buried in a magnificent manner in Westminster Abbey in the month of October

Charles I had granted to his Queen, Henrietta, for a term of 99 years, the manor and lordship of Eltham, under the trusteeship of the Earl of Holland and the Earl of Dorset The former, by virtue of his office as Chancellor to the Queen, was entitled to a fee buck and doe annually out of the forests, and there is a record of a warrant from her Majesty's Council Chamber, dated 19 June, 1640, to kill a fat buck in the little park called Horne Park

We find that the Earl of Dorset held the manor in 1641, by demise The Earl was one of the loyal adherents to the King, and "on the defection of the Earl of Essex, succeeded to the office of Lord Chamberlain He signed the Capitulation of Oxford in 1646 He had the benefit of Sir Thomas Fairfax's articles. In compounding for his estates, he delivered a list of the tenants of the manor at rents amounting in the gross to £199 0s 3d The names of twenty tenants are given The largest rents were paid by Sir John Cotton, Henry Brabant, Thomas Preston, Thomas Johnson, and Hugh Byen."

These were troublous times, especially for those who supported the royalist cause Among other Eltham gentlemen who found themselves in trouble was John White, a member of Parliament, and a delinquent, who fled to Oxford He had held, from the Queen, the lease of the Little Park and Lodge, and the office of keeper, at three pence a day wages, by letters patent, dated 17 October, 1641, and the value, before the political troubles overwhelmed them, of £50 yearly

Others were in a similar predicament, but in all probability the fate of the Palace and Park was sealed, through the "Royalist rising in Kent, in 1648"

ENGLISH LADY OF QUALITY.   GENTLEWOMAN.   MERCHANT'S WIFE OF LONDON.
(Hollar 1640).   (Hollar 1640).   (Hollar 1640).

CHAPTER L.

THE ROYALIST RISING IN KENT.

Towards the end of the month of May, 1648, there was, one day, much commotion in and about the usually quiet and secluded village of Eltham. Troops of stern and grim-looking soldiers belonging to the Parliamentary Army rode into the place. Some quartered themselves for the night upon the cottagers and other householders; many bivouacked in the open fields.

There were no less than four regiments of horse, three of foot and several companies of Colonel Ingoldsby's famous regiment, and they were all under the command of General Fairfax himself. We may be sure that the villagers regarded the advent of these determined looking men with a good deal of anxiety. They had heard of the battles fought and won by them against the King, and Fairfax was no doubt the object of particular curiosity, for was he not the general who had superseded the Earl of Essex, who had died under rather

peculiar circumstances at Eltham House only a year or so before?

It is more than probable that these military heroes were not very welcome visitors, for it should be remembered that Kent was loyal to King Charles, and we may well surmise that Eltham, with all its traditions of royal associations, would have been one of the most loyal places in Kent.

There was trouble in the air, and for the succeeding week or two Kent was the scene of strife.

Charles was only a king in name. He had fled to the Isle of Wight, where he abode, but very little more than a prisoner. The "Long Parliament," which had been sitting since 1640, and continued to sit till 1660, ruled the country, through local committees, which were appointed for all the counties and cities.

"In every county a certain number of

deputy-lieutenants known to be warm partisans of the Parliament reigned supreme. In Kent, it appears that at last none but the most determined adherents of the Parliament remained to do business. And their business appears to have been to do entirely what they pleased, provided the interests of the Parliament were furthered at all hazards." Such are the words of a commentator upon the doings of this period.

But a contemporary document, entitled "*A Declaration of many thousands of the City of Canterbury and County of Kent, 1643,*" gives us a vivid presentment of the abuses that accompanied this system of local government. It runs thus:—

"The two Houses have sat seven years to hatch cockatrices and vipers. They have filled the kingdom with serpents, bloodthirsty soldiers, extortionary committees, sequestrators, excise men; all the rogues and scum of the kingdom have been set on to torment and vex the people, to rob them, and to eat the bread out of their mouths . . . . They have suppressed the Protestant religion, suffered all kinds of heresies and errors in the kingdom, have imprisoned, or at least silenced, all the orthodox clergy, taken away the livelihood of many thousand families, and robbed the fatherless and the widow."

It is interesting to note that one of the members of the "Committee of Kent" in 1643 was Sir Thomas Walsingham, who was the Lord High Steward of the Manor of Eltham at the time.

Now, although the "Declaration" from which we have quoted is the expression of men who were doubtless strongly partisan in favour of the King, it reveals the spirit that existed amongst Kentish men at the time, who resented then, as they always had done, any attempts to encroach upon their liberties.

The "committees" appointed by the Parliament to carry out their instructions would seem to have been unnecessarily intolerant and aggressive; at any rate, as regarded from the standpoint of the twentieth century. The following narration will illustrate this.

It should be observed that the observance of Christmas, which to Englishmen had always been one of the most joyous of the Christian seasons, was now "Contrary to the ordinances of Parliament, for all superstitious festivals had been by it abolished."

Writing in "Archæologia Cantiana," Colonel George Colomb, F.S.A., says:—

"About Christmas, 1647, no doubt the people of Kent, like their fellows elsewhere, began to think sadly and bitterly of former and freer times. Their apprehensions for the future were probably at this date increased by the behaviour of the Houses towards the King, who was now confined in the Isle of Wight, though not yet closely imprisoned.

"The 'Committee and Mayor,' on Christmas Day, 1647, opposed an attempted divine service at Canterbury, and tried to make the people open their shops.

"The result was a riot, which ended in the seizure of the defences of the City by an anti-Parliament mob, the cry being raised, 'For God, King Charles, and Kent.'

"Some gentlemen at last succeeded in pacifying the incensed people, and, according to Matthew Carter, agreed, with the Mayor and Committee of Kent that no revenge should be taken.

"But within a week, fortified by the commands of Parliament, the 'Committee of Kent' entered Canterbury in state, with an immense force to back them, pulled off the gates, made what they called 'a convenient breach in the walls'—about fifty yards in width—and after a searching inquiry, which lasted about a fortnight, sent the gentlemen who had quieted the people to Leeds Castle, at that time used as a prison for 'malignants,' as the loyal party were termed.

"They also made a long report of their proceedings, in which they recommended that the gentlemen before mentioned, as well as a good many other inferior persons, should be brought to 'condign punishment.' The committee at the same time hinted that, as the people of Kent were in general 'malignant,' a court of war would be the most satisfactory tribunal to refer the business to."

These things happened at Christmas, 1647, and the beginning of the following year.

On May 11th, 1648, a special Assize was held at the Castle of Canterbury, for the purpose of trying the offenders.

"At the impannelling of the jury," says a Royalist pamphlet, "Judge Wild gave them a charge so abominable and bloodthirsty that the people were ready to destroy him"

The grand jury ignored the bill, and when pressed again, brought in a second "ignoramus" Not content with this, they turned the tables on the "Commission" by drawing up that historic document, "The Petition of Kent, 1648," which was

"The Humble Petition of the Knights, Gentry, Clergy and Commonalty of the County of Kent, subscribed by the Grand Jury, on Thursday, 11 May, 1648, at a Sessions of the Judges upon a Special Commission of *Oyer and Terminer*, held at the Castle of Canterbury, in the said county,

"Sheweth, &c, &c."

We have not space to give the whole text of this interesting petition, but the chief features of its prayer were for peace between King and Parliament, disbandment of the Army of Fairfax, government according to the established laws of the kingdom, and protection of property according to the "Petition of Right" from illegal taxation.

We are told that "the effect of the document was electric It started with the signatures of 200 gentlemen of Kent. In a few days 20,000 names were affixed to it The petitioners were to assemble at Rochester on the Prince of Wales's birthday, the 29th of May, and proceed thence to Blackheath

"The Parliament pronounced the petition 'feigned,' 'scandalous, and 'seditious' The 'Committee of Kent' condemned it by proclamation, and at once mustered forces to suppress it" Extreme measures were taken to prevent people signing it.

"The men of Kent, thus provoked, determined to march to Westminster with the petition in one hand and the sword in the other The fleet in the Downs caught the in-fection—put Vice-Admiral Rainsborough and most of the officers ashore, and declared for King Charles and Kent."

The disaffection spread so rapidly throughout the county that Parliament became alarmed, and decided that "they do leave the whole business to the General" The general was, of course, Fairfax, who proceeded at once to take military operations.

Nearly 10,000 men of Kent, with such arms as they could procure, rose up in defence of their "Petition," which they declared to be constitutional, and prepared to carry it to the doors of the Houses of Parliament.

Some of them hastened this way in advance of the rest, and, passing through Eltham, reached Blackheath on the 29th of May, where they found the Lord General Fairfax at the head of 7,000 horse and foot

Here they were unable to obtain a pass from the General to allow ten of their number to present the petition while the main body meantime lay at a distance

"The Kentish men," says the *Bloody News from Kent*, "forced back from Deptford, Greenwich and Blackheath, went to Rochester, and crossed the bridge. The whole resolved not to fight, but to hold the passes."

Hence the exciting day in Eltham village, when, on the evening of May 29th, the soldiers of Fairfax marched in and took up their quarters for the night

Next day, three hundred cavalry sprang to their saddles, and "having taken up 100 foot behind them," set out in pursuit of the retreating "petitioners," under the command of Major Husbands.

At Northfleet they found 600 "petitioners," under Major Childs, who had barricaded the bridge. Husbands, without hesitation, dashed up the river, and the Royalists fled, spreading such dismay that the pursuers found not a man in Gravesend.

Fairfax marched from Eltham to Maidstone, where one thousand Royalist horse and foot who occupied the town had been reinforced by another force of a thousand, under Sir William Brockman.

The general attacked the town on Friday, June 2nd, and a desperate fight ensued. "Fairfax met with such resolute opposition that he was forced to gain each street inch by inch, and the engagement lasted for nearly five hours, almost until midnight. Retreating, step by step, the Royalists reached the churchyard, whence they were at last driven into the church itself, where, after a long fight, they were obliged to make the best terms they could."

The defeat at Maidstone was a crushing blow to the "Petitioners," who never recovered from its effects, and in course of time the "Royalist rising in Kent" was crushed.

．　．　．　．　．　．

Before the year was out the King was captured by the Army, was tried in January of 1649, and on the 30th of that month was executed.

Then the royal demesne of Eltham passed into the hands of the Parliament, and the fate of the Palace was sealed.

CUIRASSIER 1645 (Spec. at Goodrich Court).

CHAPTER LI

THE FATE OF THE ROYAL PALACE.

As we have already noticed, the Kentish rising of 1648 was easily quelled by General Fairfax, and a result of the failure of the "Petitioners" to advance the cause of the King was a severe blow to the royal prestige in the neighbourhood of Eltham

For a while there was a period of lawlessness in the village The "soldiers and common people" tore down the fences that enclosed the royal parks—the Great Park, Horne Park and Middle Park—killed 'the deer, laid waste the gardens and pleasure ground, and ransacked the Palace.

At this period Colonel Rich was a conspicuous figure in the Parliamentary Army. He had helped Fairfax in his operations against the "Petitioners" of Kent, and distinguished himself in the relief of Dover, and in the recovery of the castles along the Kentish coast which had been captured by the Royalists.

On January 30th, 1649, King Charles was executed, and the Manor of Eltham, in common with the other Royal estates, was taken possession of by the Parliament, and vested in trustees, with the view to their being surveyed and sold to supply the necessities of the State.

In consequence of the lawlessness that was going on at Eltham, we find, in July, 1649, Colonel Rich, by order of Parliament, marching into Eltham at the head of a detachment of cavalry, to protect the Palace and parks from plunder But the mischief by this time had been done.

The Parliamentary survey was taken in the months of October, November and December of this same year, a summary of which has

already been given in an earlier chapter of this history

At the time of the survey, the chief ranger of the Great Park was Patrick Maule, who had been groom of the bedchamber to Charles I. Sir Theodore Mayerne, who had been chief physician to James I , was the ranger and keeper of Horne Park. We have already noticed this distinguished man in the chapter dealing with James I. The high steward of the manor was Sir Thomas Walsingham, whom we have already alluded to as one of the Kentish "Committee" appointed by Parliament to administer the local affairs of the county

It will be seen from the survey that the parks were rich in timber. The surveyors carefully marked the fine oaks for utilitarian purposes. No less than 4,000 of these giants were destined for the woodman's axe, and were subsequently felled to provide timber for the national shipbuilding yards at Deptford.

So, although we may feel sorry that the beautiful Eltham parks should have been denuded of these stately trees, it is some consolation to know that they went to the building of those "wooden walls of old England" which served so useful a purpose in national defence during the years that followed

More than 4,000 trees were marked as old "dottrells," and were sold for firewood or any other useful purpose, the proceeds being devoted to purposes of the State.

The following extracts from "Domestic State Papers" throw some light upon the fate of our Eltham trees From these references it appears that the work of tree-felling was already begun by the Government before the survey had been taken —

"7 May, 1649 80 tons of timber, felled by Mr. Bentley in Eltham for wharfing, were sent to Deptford for the navy, and 80 tons more of inferior timber were ordered to be felled there instead. Orders were issued in March for felling 730 more oak, elm and ash trees in Eltham.

"The Act, passed 17 July, 1649, for the sale of the Crown lands, provided that all timber growing within 15 miles of a navigable river, fit for the Navy, should be cut down and carried away before 10 July, 1657 "

NATHANIEL RICH

In 1649, Colonel Rich came to Eltham in his official capacity to protect the Manor from plunderers Two years later, in 1651, we find him to have been a purchaser of a large portion of the estate.

In the "Close Roll," 1653, p 38, Inroll 3 Jan ," we find the following record —

"Ind're 16 August, 1651, between William Steele, Recorder of London, and the trustees, of the one part, and Nathaniel Rich, of Eltham, Esqr., of the other part, for £16,615 13s. 1¼d., part of a gross sum of £34,123 5s. 9¾d , Nath. Rich purchased the Manor of Eltham, with all its privileges and appurts , the manor or court-house, the arbor, Great Park, parish lawn, the Little or Middle Park, yearly value £223 14s. 7¾d , and fees of court, etc., £162, the copyhold, advowson, and navy timber excepted."

Other portions of the Crown estates found purchasers, among whom were Edmund Lisle, of the Isle of Wight, and Azariah Husband, of Chariton, county Southampton, who expended considerable sums.

Colonel Rich, however, played so prominent a part in our Eltham story of these times that we may perhaps say something more about him

According to the "Dictionary of Biography," he was the eldest son of Robert Rich, and was admitted to Gray's Inn, August 13th, 1639. When the Civil War broke out he took sides against the King, and entered the "Life Guards," under the Earl of Essex. He obtained his commission as Captain in 1643 and

raised a troop of horse in the county of Essex. He then joined the army of the Earl of Manchester, and became Lieutenant-Colonel in 1644.

When the dispute arose among the Parliamentary leaders, and Cromwell demanded the passing of the "Self-denying Ordinance," which led to the resignation of Lord Essex, Lord Manchester, and many other leaders, we find Rich on the side of Cromwell, as Colonel in the new model Army.

He fought at Naseby with distinction, and was a Fairfax Commissioner at the surrender of Oxford, while in 1648, when he seems to have first come into the Story of Eltham, his regiment was quartered in London at the mews for the protection of Parliament

We have alluded to the part which he took in that year in putting down the Kentish rising

He seems to have been an able man and a frequent speaker in the House of Commons, where he sat as M.P. for Cirencester, 1649.

Although John Evelyn, in his diary (1656), speaks of him contemptuously as "Rich, the Rebel," and describes him as the destroyer of "the noble woods and park" of Eltham, he is said to have been a man who favoured the widest toleration, which would seem to have been a good trait in his character, when one considers what a rare thing toleration must have been in those years of hot contention.

He had scruples about manhood suffrage, having fears of extreme democracy. Moreover, he is said to have had doubts about the right of the people to execute the King, though he appears to have held it necessary that the king should be tried, and when the time came was quite in accord with the policy of establishing a republic.

Ludlow includes Rich among the "honest republican enthusiasts of the army who were deluded by Cromwell to assist him in the overthrow of the Long Parliament."

In 1655 we find Colonel Rich an open opponent of Cromwell's Government, and deprived of his command in the Army.

In the same year he was summoned before the Protector's Council charged with opposing the levy of taxes and stirring up dissaffection, and was accordingly committed to the custody of the Serjeant-at-Arms There seems to have been trouble, too, in connection with Eltham Manor at this particular time It will have been noticed that among the conditions of purchase of the Eltham estate was one which *excluded* navy timber from the sale.

But in the "State Papers" we get the following record, which points to suspicious practices —

"The Commission certified, 7 April, 1655, to great embezzlement of Timber at Eltham, consequently the Admiralty Committee ordered all trees remaining there to be felled, sold, or exchanged, and the embezzlement to be enquired into, Mr Willoughby to manage the business"

In 1656, we find the Colonel again in confinement

The restoration of the Long Parliament saw Rich, next year, restored to his command

In 1660, Rich perceived that the policy of General Monk would lead to the restoration of the monarchy He therefore tried to induce his regiment to declare against it. For this, Monk deprived him of his command, and appointed Colonel Ingoldsby in his place

In this year the Restoration actually took place, and Rich found himself in prison. He was, however, soon liberated, as he had not been one of the judges of the late King Charles, and was not excluded from the act of indemnity.

Rich was, in religious belief, a "Fifth Monarchy Man," and had been one of the leaders of this short-lived sect. Their belief was of a semi-political character, admitting the idea of "no king but Christ" Some years before (1657), when it was supposed that Cromwell harboured designs of "kingship," the "Fifth Monarchy Men" tried to organise a rising against "The Protector," and Colonel Rich was amongst the leaders.

"They fixed Thursday, April 9th, for the rising They issued a proclamation called 'A Standard set up,' ordered Mile End as the place of rendezvous, and, headed by one Venner, a wine merchant, and other persons of the

City, calculated upon introducing the reign of the Millennium They encouraged each other, says Thurloe, with the exhortation that though they were but worms, yet they should be instrumental to thresh mountains. They spoke, he says, great words of the reign of the saints, and the beautiful kingdom of holies which they were to erect, and talked of taking away all taxes, excise, customs, and tithes. They had banners painted with the device of the lion of the tribe of Judah, and the motto, "Who shall raise him up!'"

But a troop of horse descended upon their meeting at Mile End, frustrated their designs, and Venner, together with Colonel Rich, Admiral Lawson, Major-General Harrison, and other leaders were cast into prison. Cromwell, however, did not mete out any severe punishment

In 1661, soon after the Restoration of the Monarchy, we find that the "Fifth Monarchy Men," led by Master Venner, renewed their attempt to raise their standard. The circumstance gave rise to considerable excitement; suspicion fell upon Colonel Rich, and Charles II ordered his arrest Venner, who was also arrested, was executed, but Rich was, in 1662, transferred to Portsmouth, where he does not seem to have been kept in very strict confinement

In 1663, while still nominally a prisoner, he married Lady Ann Kerr, daughter of the first Earl of Ancram.

This good lady, in a letter to her brother, describes her husband as "a prisoner for no crime, but only because he is thought a man of parts." And so far was he from harbouring any designs against the king, his good wife declares that he was "so resolved upon his duty to his Majesty that I am assured if it were in his power it would never be in his heart ever to set himself against him, directly or indirectly"

Two years after he was released.

When Charles II. "came to his own," the Manor of Eltham reverted to the Crown But the Palace was in ruins. Practically all the buildings had been pulled down and the

No. 123   MIDDLE PARK MEADOWS FROM BRIDLE LANE.
Farm in the distance.

No. 125.   BLACK-BOY COTTAGE, SOUTHEND.
From a Water Colour Drawing by Mr. Sharp, the old Schoolmaster.
(1860).

No. 122   MAKING HAY RICK, LYME FARM.
(1909).

No. 124.   THE NATIONAL INFANTS' SCHOOL.
(1909).

No. 126.

FIRST PAGE OF THE ADMISSION REGISTER OF
ELTHAM NATIONAL SCHOOL.

(1814).

No. 127.

[A PAGE OF "HORTUS ELTHAMENSIS" SHOWING DRAWING
BY DILENNIUS.

From the Copy possessed by Mrs. Dobell.

See the Sherards.

No. 30. OLD FIRE-PLACE IN THE "KING'S ARMS" INN.
(1909.)

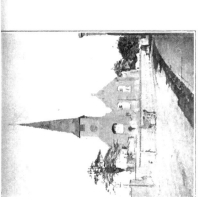

No. 28. THE OLD CHURCH.
(1860.)

No. 31. TOMB OF JOHN OF ELTHAM, WESTMINSTER ABBEY.
(As it appears at present time.)

No. 29. SEVERNDROOG CASTLE.
(1909.)

No. 132.

THE TOMB OF JOHN OF ELTHAM

In Westminster Abbey, as it appeared in 1723, fifty-three years before the destruction
of the Canopy.

From an Engraving in "Westmonasterium" by John Dart.

(Kindly lent for this book by Mr. A. J. Sargent, London Institution).

materials carried away, probably for building purposes. The majestic hall, however, was allowed to stand, seeing that it was so well adapted for use as a barn. Sic transit gloria mundi. We may well be thankful that the vandals of the seventeenth century left us thus much, even though it was to fulfil so lowly a purpose.

"The hall, where oft in feudal pride
  Old England's peers in council came;
When Cressy's field spread far and wide
  Edward of Windsor's warlike fame;
Whose raftered roof and portals long
  Rung, while unnumbered harps awoke;
Now echoes but the thresher's song,
  Or the sad flail's incessant stroke."

PURITAN.

CHAPTER LII.

THE STORY OF WELL HALL.

In conformity with the plan upon which we have been considering the story of our village we now direct our attention to Well Hall, whose history comes next in order of antiquity Newcomers amongst us associate the name of Well Hall with the small town with peculiar street names which has lately sprung up in the valley and upon the lower slopes of Shooter's-hill.

The name so applied is a little misleading, for it diverts the attention from the true Well Hall, which is really the old farm buildings and the quaint looking manor-house which stand between the railway and the corner of Kidbrook-lane

A considerable portion of the old moat is still in existence—a relic of very great interest. Remains of the old mansion itself, now used mainly for agricultural purposes, still exist to tell their tale of Tudor times To the north and south of it are still left some of the picturesque, but rather comfortless, cottages where probaby dwelt the work people who were employed upon the lands of the lord of the manor

In these days of rapid building operations, the present hall must be accounted old, for it was erected by Sir Gregory Page as far back as 1733. It is said that he pulled down a large part of the original mansion in order to carry out the work.

When George the Third was king, the house was occupied by Mr. Arnold, who was watchmaker to his Majesty, and it was he who erected the portions on each side of the main front which are now so characteristic a feature of the building. Mr W. T. Vincent, in his interesting "Records of the Woolwich District," tells us that these added portions were for the

accommodation of Mr Arnold's workmen From the same source we learn that this royal and ingenious watchmaker made "a chronometer so small as to be worn in a ring on his Majesty's finger "

Mr. Vincent, in his comments upon the remains of the old mansion, directs attention to the "double moat, lawn, and garden, overshadowed by cedars—an interesting survival of departed greatness."

Only a few years ago, before the railway which runs close by was constructed, and before the great expanse of slate-roofed houses was even dreamed of, the situation of Well Hall was indeed truly rural The old winding Woolwich road had not then been modernised, and all around were pasture land and cultivated fields

It needs no great effort of imagination to picture the scene anterior to this, when Well Hall Green was the scene of village games, when the woodlands that covered the slopes from Kidbrook and Charlton afforded cover for the game which provided sport for the lords of Well Hall Manor, and Kidbrook-lane was the principal road between Eltham and Greenwich

Modern innovations, the results of modern civilisation, have robbed Well Hall of much of the delightful seclusion and quietude of its earlier days, but even now it has many rustic charms, which are enhanced by the spirit of romance that still pervades it

We read of the Manors of Well Hall and East Horne as far back as in the days of Henry I , 1100, about thirty years after the Conquest, when it was in the possession of one, Joran de Briset, whose name suggests Norman associations.

It was this De Briset who founded a nunnery at Clerkenwell, and, according to Hasted, "gave the nuns ten acres in his lordship of 'Wellyng-hall' in exchange for ten acres in Clerkenwell, on which he founded this Hospital of the Knights Hospitallers of St. John of Jerusalem."

Commenting upon this, Dr. Drake says that "This foundation was the first of the Order in England. The Lord Prior had precedence over all the Barons in Parliament. His service for land in Eltham was 7s. 8d."

In the time of Henry III., in 1253-4, we find that the Lord of the Manor of Horne and Well Hall was one Matthew de Hegham.

In 1346 the estate was held by John de Pulteney, who seems to have been particularly well blessed with landed estates in many parts of Kent. He held Well Hall at the time when Edward III. was king, and when the great tournament organised by that monarch took place at Eltham. We may be pretty sure that the Knight of Well Hall was among those who were present.

When Richard II was conducting his councils at Eltham Palace, or holding those great feasts there for which his Court was noted, the Lord of Well Hall was "Thomas Conduyt, clerk, brother and heir of Nicholas Conduyt, formerly of London," and we find that in 1385 this gentleman granted the manor to Gilbert Purneys, of London.

About ten years later "Philip Burton and his wife, Joan, quit-claimed, for themselves and for the heirs of Joan, a moiety of 3 messuages, 200 acres of land, 30 mead, 40 wood, with appurts, in Eltham, Modyngham, and Kid-broke, to Margaret, once wife of Sir Nicholas Sharnyfield."

Then, in the time of Henry VI. (1426), it seems that a gentleman who rejoiced in the name of John Foxhole, clerk, was in possession, and that he passed the manors of "Wellhawe and Esthorne" on to another who possessed the name of William Basket, a skinner and citizen of London.

Two years later, in 1426, this William Basket conveyed the manors to Robert Myrfyn, "in behalf of John Tattersall, Henry Chicele, Arch-bishop of Canterbury, Thomas Chicele, his nephew, Archdeacon of Canterbury, and others."

The Kentish historian, Hasted, relying upon the statements of Philipott as accurate, states that Wellhawe, Easthorne, and Woolwich were "the possessions of William Chicele, Sheriff of London, brother of Archbishop Chicele, Cham-berlain of London and grocer, one of whose daughters, Agnes, carried them in marriage to her husband, John Tattersall."

But according to the records of an inquisition taken at Deptford, 30th June, 1447, in the twenty-fifth year of the reign of Henry VI., it would appear that both Philipott and Hasted are in error, and that William Chicele, the Sheriff of London, brother of the Archbishop, was not the Lord of Wellhawe Manor.

The King (Henry VI.), by his charter dated at Eltham, 3rd February, 1439, granted the manors to "John Tattersall and the said Henry Chicele (Archbishop), Thomas Chicele (Arch-deacon), John Brykhed, Richard Sturgen, and William Myrfyn, and the heirs and assigns of John Tattersall and Henry (Archbishop), &c."

The Inquisition record then says:—

"The said John Tattersall and Henry died, when Thomas Chicele and others stood seised of the same, worth 20 marcs a year beyond reprises, and is held of the King in socage as of his manor of Eltham by service of 73s. 4d. a year.

"And the jury say that the said John Tatter-sall and Agnes his wife, daughter of John Chicele of London, grocer, were seised in their demesne as of fee, in the day John died, of the manor of Woolwych, with appurts, in the vills of Woolwych, Greenwych, Derteford, and Combe, Kent, as appears by a certain deed dated at Woolwych, 7 August, 14 Henry VI., 1436, made to the said John and Agnes Tatter-sall and their heirs and assigns for ever; and the said John died, and Agnes remained seised of, and now holds, the said manor (worth 10 marcs beyond reprises) of the King in socage as of the manor of Eltham, by service of 36s. per ann."

Agnes, the widow of John Tattersall, subsequently married William Kene, the Sheriff of Kent, 26 Henry VI , who resided at Well Hall

By her first husband, Agnes had a son and two daughters. There does not appear to be any record of what became of the son, but one of the daughters, Margery, married John Roper, of Swacliffe, in the county of Kent By this marriage the Manors of Well Hall and East horne came into the possession of the Ropers

This distinguished family was closely associated with Eltham history for some two hundred years, and though the Well Hall estate passed from them when it was sold to Sir Gregory Page in 1733, the name is still preserved by a Roper Charity, and the name of the street which leads to our National School, while their memory is one of the cherished possessions of our village history.

The second John Roper, who was the eldest son of the heiress of John Tattersall, was Sheriff of Kent in the 12th year of Henry VIII , Attorney-General and Prothonotary of the King's Bench

William Roper, his eldest son, was a very distinguished man. He succeeded his father as Prothonotary, and was also Sheriff of the county in the reign of Queen Mary. He married Margaret, the daughter of Sir Thomas More, Lord High Chancellor of England, who was executed by the barbarous order of Henry VIII. Sir William Roper died in 1577, aged 82 years, and was buried in the vault under the chapel joining the chancel in St. Dunstan's Church, Canterbury.

Thomas Roper, the eldest son of Sir William, succeeded to the Well Hall and Easthorne

estates, and also to the office of Prothonotary of the King's Bench

The estates were held in succession by William Roper, Anthony Roper, and Edward Roper.

The latter had one son, who died in infancy, and three daughters, who succeeded jointly to the estates.

On July 11th, 1733, the three co-heiresses "joined in the sale of the manors of Easthorne and Well Hall, with the house recently erected and the presentation of the vicarage, to Sir Gregory Page, of Wricklemarsh in Charlton, Bart , for £19,000, who pulled down the mansion of Well Hall " From Sir Gregory Page it descended to his nephew, Sir Gregory Turner

The famous picture of the More family, painted by Holbein, used to hang in the great hall of the mansion, where it almost covered one of the walls It had hung there ever since it had been painted, but was removed to Soho-square, to the house of Sir Rowland Wynne, the husband of Susanna Roper, one of the three heiresses, in July, 1731, a short time before the estates were sold

The Ropers were conscientious Papists, who suffered for their faith Sir William Roper the husband of Margaret More, was bound to be of good behaviour, and had to appear before the Council when called upon (State Papers Domestic)

Philip Roper, the grandson of Sir William, was under surveillance for harbouring Papists at Eltham and for consorting with priests (State Papers Domestic).

CHAPTER LIII

THE LADY OF WELL HALL (1).

The story of Eltham Palace recalls many a royal lady and many a noble dame who have figured prominently in national history, but few of them have set a worthier example, or deserved a more honourable place upon the roll of noble women than Margaret Roper, the wife of Sir William Roper, who for upwards of forty years was the doughty squire of Well Hall.

We are tempted to linger over the story of this remarkable woman, for by her marriage she not only became a woman of Eltham, but her story also embraces that of a distinguished and godly man, who knew Eltham Palace well, and who probably resided at the Chancellor's Lodging in the court-yard when his duties to the King called him here.

Moreover, much of the information regarding Dame Roper and her father, Sir Thomas More, we get from a book actually written at Well Hall by Sir William Roper himself

So this story of a noble woman, of filial devotion, unexampled, and of direful tragedy, is a matter of threefold interest to all those who take pride in our village history.

The painter, Holbein, has portrayed on canvas the "Family of Sir Thomas More," and from Erasmus onward many a writer has delighted to describe the domestic virtues and homely life of that distinguished household.

The following is a word picture, written some sixty years ago by Mrs. Owen, of the home where the bountiful Lady of Well Hall spent her girlhood:—

"It is at Chelsea, hard by the river, where the extensive and beautiful gardens reach down to the water's edge. Looking across the terrace, where the two favourite peacocks, Juno and Argus, perched upon the balustrades, unfold their burnished glories, is the pavilion in which Erasmus would sit in converse with his learned and illustrious friend. These are the windows of the "Academia," shaded by their cool green curtains Glancing within, we find three or four fair maidens bending over their desks, some writing, some reading, all with an air of pleasant earnestness Then comes the chapel, and there, far above, one may see the observatory, whither royalty itself oftimes ascends to watch the stars, and discourse upon their nature, with the sire of that gentle sisterhood, the master of that happy household.

"Like a series of dissolving views, rises before us scene after scene of that 'eventful history' Yonder, upon the bosom of the 'cleare shining Thames' barges pass and repass, filled with glittering company. Anon, heralded by a flock of swans, which come breasting the water, a wherry lands three persons—Sir Thomas and the 'deare little man' Erasmus, together with a tall stripling, who carries the cloak of the former. To meet them there issues from the house a fair girl, whom we presently know for the favourite child, the 'best beloved Meg,' and she kisses the hands of the elders, and laughs and blushes when the tall lad, an old playmate long absent, no other than Will Roper himself, makes as if he would perform the same ceremony with her soft cheek, only he has no courage, whereat Sir Thomas laughs, and cries, apropos of his two ineffectual attempts, that 'the third time's lucky.'

"Presently, it is in the hay field, we see the

father and his children, where the summer sun is lying in slanting evening rays along the fragrant rows There the laughing girls pursue the liveliest pastimes of youthful innocence They swathe him, not a whit less merry, in ropes made of the hay, but when at length, in sobered mood, he reclines at full length amongst it, it is upon Margaret's knee his head rests, it is to Margaret's ear he addresses, with closed eyes, the expression of his thoughtful dreaming of 'that far-off, future day, Meg, when thou and I shall looke back on this hour, and this hay field, and my head on thy lap.'

"Now, a less bright vision The favourite child struck down by disease, we see the father watching at her bedside, or praying with almost frantic hope, for her restoration to health In his agony words escape which shew how dearer than child ever can be to him again is that slight suffering form If she die, he says with solemnity, for her sake he will abjure the world, its honours, its triumphs, for evermore.

"Pass on The invalid comes forth to breathe the healthful air Colour steals back to her cheek, the lustre to her eye Guests arrive, among them the two maiden aunts, the 'lay nuns', and it is pleasant to see that these, who have parted for ever with the youthful wreath of rose and passion flower, can yet smile with joy to see the garlands turned around the bright heads of their sister's children

"But in a little time another visitor is seen, a large man, with a fair, handsome countenance, and reddish gold hair. He walks with his arm around the neck of the Chancellor, 'for an hour or soe,' the latter addressing him by the title, just then coming into ordinary use for the first time, 'your Majesty '

"Years pass by. Now we have an artist, painting in a cool, sequestered chamber, where all the light is excluded, excepting that which falls downward upon his work It is Hans Holbein At his side sits the same gentle form which has so often greeted us, less sylph-like in its proportions than of old, and with a graver, yet a deeper happiness, lying in the luminous depths of her beautiful eyes

"Sometimes the 'tall stripling'—stripling no longer—is there, too. Then her cheek is brighter still, her accents tenderer, while, ever and anon, flashes of the old playfulness break out, alike in father and daughter, for a fair-haired boy nestles in her arms, who plays with the painter's colours, and climbs his knee to see if the picture is like 'grandfather.'

"But Hans Holbein and his easel fade away, and it seems as if a cloud were hanging between the sun and that once cheery house, for all the children's smiles and merry singing voices that fill it now There is an air of gloom strangely pervading that cool, flower-studded garden. In the pavilion sits Margaret, alone and in tears, trying to decipher a scarcely legible letter, which seems, as indeed it is, written with a clumsy substitute for ink, a morsel of coal—a letter which dates its mission from a prison!"

Such are some of the scenes of the earlier life of the Lady of Well Hall. Margaret More was the eldest daughter of Sir Thomas More, the great lawyer and brilliant scholar, who became the Lord Chancellor of Henry VIII., and subsequently suffered death by the command of the King She had two sisters, Elizabeth and Cecilia, and a brother, John, who does not seem to have been particularly brilliant

Of the trio of sisters, Margaret seems to have possessed at once the superior talents and the most attractive manners "She was," says her biographer, "to Sir Thomas More what Tullia was to Cicero—his delight and comfort."

She became proficient in Latin and Greek at quite an early age, qualifying herself, if not for a sharer in her father's studies, at least, for an intelligent companion She wrote Latin prose and verse with an ease that surprised the scholars of the day, and none more so than Cardinal Pole and Erasmus. It is said that on one occasion she wrote two declamations in English, which her father, by way of exercise, proposed that she should turn into Latin. He made a translation at the same time, and when comparing his own with that of his daughter, it was found to be difficult to determine which was the most elegant version.

The patriarchal simplicity of More's household is vividly described by Erasmus in a letter to a friend.

"More," he writes, "has built, near London, on the banks of the Thames, a commodious house, where he converses affably with his family, consisting of his wife, his son and daughter-in-law, his three daughters and their husbands, and eleven grandchildren. There is no man living so fond of his children, or who

constant associates of his daughters were Erasmus, Colet, Linacre, Latimer, Lily, Pole, Fisher, and other great scholars and divines. But Erasmus seems to have been the most highly valued of them all. In several of his letters to Margaret, we find him praising her as a woman, famous not only for piety and virtue, but for true and solid learning. He was pleased to call her "*Britanniæ Decus*"—

LADY MAYORESS OF
LONDON.
(Hollar's Theatrum Mulierum).

COUNTRY WOMAN WITH
MUFFLERS.
(Speed's map of England).

CITIZEN'S WIFE OF
LONDON.
(Hollar's Ornatus Muliebris 1640).

possesses a more excellent temper. You would call his house the Academy of Plato. But I should rather do it an injury by such a comparison. It is rather a school of Christian goodness, in which piety, virtue, and the liberal sciences are studied by every individual of the family. No wrangling or intemperate language is heard, no one is idle, the discipline of the house is courtesy and benevolence, and everyone performs his duties with cheerfulness and alacrity."

Among the intimate friends of More and the

the Honour of Britain—a compliment which, coming from him, she must have highly valued.

But it is mainly on account of her intense filial devotion that the memory of Margaret Roper is kept so green. And that phase of her character seems to have been inherited. Sir Thomas himself, at the time Lord Chancellor of England, used to stop every morning on his way to Westminster, to enter the King's Bench, where his father was judge, and there kneel and ask the old man's blessing before going to sit in Chancery.

This attribute of strong filial love existed in a marked degree with every member of the More family, but it seems to have shone most brilliantly in the eldest child, Margaret, and was, in fact, the main-spring of her character

She was in her nineteenth year when she fell a victim to the "sweating sickness," a foul disease, which was almost like a plague, and terrified even the King himself Sir William Roper, in the book we have alluded to, "The Mirror of Vertue in worldly Greatness, or the Life of Sir Thomas More, Knight," gives an account of this circumstance, which throws a vivid light upon the household at Chelsea during those dark days of trouble

" At such a time," he writes, " my wife (as many other that year were) was sick of the sweating sickness, who, lying in so great extremity of that disease, as by no invention or devices that physicians in such cases commonly use (of whom she had divers, both expert, wise, and well-learned, then continually attendant upon her) could she be kept from sleep, so that both the physicians and all other there present despaired of her recovery, and gave her over, her father, as he that most entirely attended her, being in no small heaviness for her, by prayer at God's hand sought to get her remedy

Whereupon going up, after his usual manner, into his aforesaid New Building there in his chapel on his knees, with tears, most devoutly besought Almighty God that it would like His goodness, unto whom nothing was impossible, if it were his blessed will, at his mediation, to vouchsafe graciously to hear his humble petition.

Where incontinent came into his mind that a glister should be the only way to help her. Which, when he told the physicians, they by and by confessed that if there were any hope of health that that was the very best help indeed, much marvelling of themselves that they had not remembered it.

Then was it immediately administered to her sleeping, which she could by no means have been brought into waking. And albeit, after she was thereby thoroughly waked, God's marks (an evident, undoubted token of death) plainly appeared upon her, yet she, contrary to all their expectations, was, as it was thought, by her father's most fervent prayers, miraculously recovered, and at length again to perfect health restored, whom, if it pleased God at that time to have taken to His mercy, her father said he would never have meddled with worldly matters more "

CHAPTER LIV.

THE LADY OF WELL HALL (2).

It was shortly after her recovery from the dangerous illness which had caused so much alarm to Sir Thomas More that Margaret was married, in her twentieth year, to the lanky young lawyer, Will Roper, of Well Hall Her two sisters, Elizabeth and Cecilia, married about the same time, as also did Margaret Middleton, the daughter by a former husband of Sir Thomas More's second wife.

A singular and interesting feature of these marriages is that the young people continued to live in the paternal household

"All lived with Sir Thomas, at Chelsea, nor did the new ties they had formed abate an iota of the devotion to him by his entire family Besides these there was a poor relation of the More family, brought up from a child among them, another Margaret—married several years after to their tutor, Dr John Clement "

It was in this way that this united and loving family lived happily together under their patriarchal head

But the peaceful calm which reigned over this Chelsea household was soon to be dispelled Cardinal Wolsey had fallen into disgrace with the fickle King, and Henry VIII now turned to Sir Thomas More, who most reluctantly was persuaded to accept the high office of Lord Chancellor His penetration and foresight, no doubt, revealed to his mind the dangers to himself which the dignity entailed

The honour thus "thrust upon the unwilling shoulders" of her father deprived Margaret in a great measure of the teaching and companionship which were so precious to her Her children, dear as they were, afforded no sub-stitute for the loss of the one who was equally missed by her husband and herself During these trying days, the courageous endurance of this noble-hearted woman was doubtless called into hourly action. The mind of the father was oppressed by business or distracted by the responsibilities of power Margaret Roper, who, more than any other, was his confidant, must have suffered many anxious moments, for it was no difficult matter to foreshadow the end to which the King's policy must ultimately lead The new Queen—Anne Boleyn—had already compassed the downfall of Wolsey, and, unhappily, she was to be the means of bringing about the destruction of More

Sir Thomas was too sincere for a courtier, preferring integrity to place The Chancellor, after expressing his disapproval of the King's conduct in divorcing Queen Catherine, declared his intention of resigning the Chancellorship Henry resisted this action of his Chancellor for a while, but More, urging that he was growing old, and had need of repose, prevailed at last, and retired from Court in the May of the year 1532, "withdrawing to the quiet home he had long sighed for, and to the daughter who was its chief ornament and his purest consolation "

The household now, however, was confronted by financial difficulties. Sir Thomas, who had hitherto been a liberal patron, found that he could no longer support the heavy outlay of his home establishment Living under the same roof, and in the midst of his family, the expenses of which he had hitherto defrayed from his revenue, the ex-Chancellor and devoted father, would not hear of a separation from them

"Calling us all, that were his children, unto him," writes Sir William Roper, "and asking our advice how we might now in this decay of his ability, by the surrender of his office so impaired, that he could not as he was wont, and gladly would, bear out the whole charges of them all himself, from thenceforth be able to live and continue together, as he wished we should, when he saw us silent, and in that case not ready to show our opinions unto him,

"Then will I,' said he, 'shew my poor mind to you. I have been brought up,' quoth he, 'at Oxford, at an Inn of the Chancery, at Lincoln's Inn, and also in the King's Court, and so forth from the lowest degree to the highest, and yet have I in yearly revenues at this present left me little above a hundred pounds by the year So that now we must hereafter, if we like to live together, be content to become contributaries together.

'But by my counsel it shall not be best to fall to the lowest fare first, we will not, therefore, descend to this Oxford fare, nor to the fare of New Inn, but we will begin with Lincoln's Inn diet, where many right-worshipful and of good years do live full well!

'Which, if we find not ourselves the first year able to maintain, then we will the next year go one step down to New Inn fare, wherewith many an honest man is well contented

'If that exceed our ability, too, then will we, the next year after, descend to Oxford fare, where many grave, learned and ancient fathers be continually conversant.

'Which, if our ability stretch not to maintain neither, then may we yet, with bags and wallets, go a-begging together, and hoping that for pity some good folk will give us their charity, at every man's door to sing *Salve Regina*, and so still keep company and be merry together.' "

This was a sad year for the More family. Old Sir John More, the grandfather of Margaret Roper, and one deeply loved by the whole circle of this united family, died Then, after a brief interval, came the warning to Sir

Thomas from some of his friends, that his refusal to take the Oath of Supremacy would lead him into trouble The trouble came quickly

The ex-Chancellor was sent to the Tower as a means of forcing him into the concession the King wanted "When the King saw that he could by no manner of benefit win him to his side then lo, went he about by terror and threats to drive him thereunto"

Writing of the severance from the old home, Mrs Owen says "He was sent to the Tower as a means of forcing him into the required concession We can form a faint idea, from the attachment already depicted between the parties, of the agony of this separation It was in the lovely spring-time, when everything in Nature teemed with promise, that the dark cloud fell upon that house, the bright face, which had been the source of sunshine throughout it, was withdrawn, and the idolised parent dragged away, never to be again restored "

"Twelve weary months Sir Thomas lay in prison—twelve weary months his eldest and best beloved child wore out a burdensome existence of suspense and pain. It will be scarcely supposed that Margaret would relax her efforts to obtain an interview with the prisoner until that object had been accomplished, and, at length, in consequence of incessant importunity, she prevailed Poignant had been her grief, but upon admission to his prison she was shocked yet more deeply by the discovery of the state of destitution to which the royal tyrant had consigned his former favourite "

Let us now read another short selection from the unique little book written at Well Hall by Sir William Roper It reveals to us the sad spectacle of this good man in prison in close communion with his beloved daughter, our Lady of Well Hall

"Now when he had remained in the Tower little more than a month, my wife, longing to see her father, by her earnest suit, at length got leave to go unto him.

"At whose coming, after the seven psalms and litany said —— which whensoever she

came to him, ere he fell in talk of any worldly
matters, he used accustomedly to say with her
——— among other communications he said unto her.'

"'I believe Megg, that they that have put me
here ween that they have done me a high displeasure, but I assure thee on my faith, mine
own good daughter, if it had not been for my
wife and ye that be my children, whom I
account the chief part of my charge, I would
not have failed long ere this to have closed
myself in as straight a room, and straighter,
too.'

"'But since I am come hither without mine
own desert, I trust that God of His goodness
will discharge me of my care, and with His
gracious help supply my lack among you. I
find no cause, I thank God, Megg, to reckon
myself in worse case here than in mine own
house, for methinketh God maketh me a
wanton, and setteth me on His lap and dandleth
me.'

"'Thus, by his gracious demeanour in tribu-
lation, appeared it that all the trouble that
ever chanced unto him, by his patient sufferance thereof, were to him no painful punish-
ments, but of his patience profitable exercises
And at another time, when he had first questioned with my wife a while of the order of
his wife, children, and state of his house in his
absence, he asked her how Queen Anne did.

'In faith, Father,' quoth she, 'never better'

'Never better, Megg!' quoth he, 'Alas!
Megg, alas! It pitieth me to remember into what
misery, poor soul, she will shortly come!'"

Many efforts were made to induce Sir Thomas
to change his mind as to the oath of supremacy,
not only by his friends, but by Margaret herself, who urged him to do as she herself had
done, namely, to take the oath with the reservation, "as far as would stand with the law
of God"

Arguments, entreaties, and even tears failed,
however, to shake the determination and con-
stancy of the prisoner

"I may tell thee, Megg," he said after one
of these encounters, "they that have committed me hither for the refusing of this oath,

not agreeable with the statute, are not by their
own law able to justify mine imprisonment,
and surely, daughter, is great pity that any
Christian prince should by a flexible council
ready to follow his affections, and by a weak
clergy lacking grace constantly to stand to
their learning, with flattery, be so shamefully
abused "

Another incident, recorded by Sir William,
shews upon what flimsy evidence the charge
of high treason was trumped up against this
good man He writes —

"Not long after came to him the Lord Chancellor, the Dukes of Norfolk and Suffolk, with
Master Secretary, and certain other of the
Privy Council, at two several times by all
policies possible procuring him either to confess to the supremacy, or precisely to deny it,
whereunto, as appeareth by his examinations
in the said great book, they could never bring
him.

Shortly thereupon Master Rich, afterwards
Lord Rich, the newly-made the King's solicitor,
Sir Richard Southwell, and one Master Palmer,
servant to the Secretary, were sent to Sir
Thomas More into the Tower to fetch away his
books from him

And while Sir Richard Southwell and Mr
Palmer were busy in the trussing up of his
books, Mr. Rich, pretending friendly talk with
him, among other things of a set course, as
it seemed, said thus unto him

'Forasmuch as it is well known, Master
More, that you are a man both wise and well
learned as well in the laws of the realm as
otherwise, I pray you therefore, Sir, let me
be so bold, as of good will, to put unto you
this case. Admit there were, Sir, an Act of
Parliament that the realm should take me for
king, would not you, Master More, take me for
King?"

'Yes, Sir,' quoth Sir Thomas More, 'that
would I'

'I put the case further,' quoth Master Rich,
'that there were an Act of Parliament that
all the realm should take me for Pope, would
not you then, Master More, take me for Pope?'

'For answer, Sir,' quoth Sir Thomas More,

'to your first case, the Parliament may well, Master Rich, meddle with the state of temporal princes, but to make answer to your other case, I will put you this case: Suppose the Parliament should make a law that God should not be God, would you then, Master Rich, say that God were not God?"

'No, Sir,' quoth he. 'that would I not, sith no Parliament may make any such law.'

'No more,' said Sir Thomas More—as Master Rich reported him—'could the Parliament make the King supreme head of the Church.'

Upon whose only report was Sir Thomas More indicted of high treason on the Statute to deny the King to be supreme head of the Church, into which indictment were put these heinous words, *maliciously, traitorously, diabolically."*

CHANCELLOR'S COSTUME.

CHAPTER LV.

THE LADY OF WELL HALL (3).

The trial of Sir Thomas More took place in due course at the Court at Westminster, where he had been wont himself to preside as judge, and mainly upon the evidence of Master Rich, to whom we alluded in the preceding chapter, he was declared to be guilty of high treason upon an indictment which contained the odious terms, *maliciously, traitorously,* and *diabolically*

Sir William Roper devotes several chapters of his book to this remarkable trial, which was little better than a travesty of justice, and led to an act which is one of the blackest stains upon our national history

The final scene of the trial, and the incident in which our Heroine was so conspicuous a figure, are thus described by the Squire of Well Hall —

Now when Sir Thomas More, for the avoiding of the indictment had taken as many exceptions as he thought meet, and many more reasons than I can now remember alleged, the Lord Chancellor loth to have the burden of the judgment wholly to depend upon himself, there openly asked the advice of Lord Fitzjames, then Lord Chief Justice of the King's Bench, and joined in the Commission with him, whether this indictment were sufficient or not

Who, like a wise man answered,

"My Lords all, by St. Julian" (that was ever his oath), "I must needs confess that if the Act of Parliament be not unlawful, then is the indictment in my conscience not insufficient "

Whereupon the Lord Chancellor said to the rest of the Lords —

"Lo, my Lords, lo! You hear what my Lord Chief Justice saith," and so immediately gave judgment against him

After which ended, the Commissioners yet further courteously offered him, if he had anything else to allege for his defence, to grant him favourable audience

Who answered —

"More have I not to say, my Lords, but that like the blessed Apostle, St Paul, as we read in the Acts of the Apostles, was present, and consented to the death of St Stephen, and kept their clothes that stoned him to death, and yet be they now both twain holy saints in heaven, and shall continue there friends for ever, so I verily trust, and shall therefore right heartily pray, that though your Lordships have now here in earth been judges to my condemnation, we may yet hereafter in heaven merrily all meet together to everlasting salvation "

Thus much touching Sir Thomas More's arraignment, being not there present myself, have I by the creditable report of the Right Worshipful Sir Anthony Saintleger, and partly of Richard Haywood, and John Webb, gentlemen, with others of good credit at the hearing thereof present themselves, as far forth as my poor wit and memory would serve me, here truly rehearsed unto you

Now, after his arraignment, departed he from the bar to the Tower again, led by Sir William Kingston, a tall, strong and comely knight, Constable of the Tower, and his very dear friend.

Who, when he had brought him from Westminster to the Old Swan toward the Tower, there, with a heavy heart, the tears running down his cheeks, bade him farewell

Sir Thomas More seeing him so sorrowful comforted him with as good words as he could, saying —

"Good Master Kingston, trouble not yourself, but be of good cheer, for I will pray for you and for your good lady, your wife, that we may meet in heaven together, where we shall be merry for ever and ever"

Soon after Sir William Kingston, talking with me of Sir Thomas More, said —

"In good faith, Master Roper, I was ashamed of myself that at my departing from your father I found my heart so feeble and his so strong, that he was fain to comfort me that should rather have comforted him"

When Sir Thomas More came from Westminster Tower-ward again, his daughter, my wife, desirous to see her father, whom she thought she would never see in this world after, and also to have his final blessing, gave attendance about the Tower Wharf, when she knew he would pass by, before he could enter into the Tower There tarrying his coming, as soon as she saw him, after his blessing upon her knees reverently received, she hasting towards him, without consideration or care for herself, pressing in amongst the midst of the throng and company of the guard, that with halberds and bills went about him, hastily ran to him, and there openly in sight of them all, embraced him, and took him about the neck and kissed him

Who, well liking her most natural and dear daughterly affection towards him, gave her his fatherly blessing, and many godly words of comfort besides.

From whom after she was departed, she, not satisfied with the former sight of her dear father, and like one that had forgotten herself, being all ravished with the entire love of her dear father, having respect neither of herself, nor to the press of people and multitude that were about him, suddenly turned back again, ran to him as before, took him about the neck, and divers times kissed him most lov-

ingly; and at last, with a full and heavy heart, was fain to depart from him, the beholding whereof was to many of them that were present thereat so lamentable that it made them for very sorrow thereof to weep and mourn

Another writer, commenting upon this sad journey of Sir Thomas More, tells us that "As he moved from the bar, his son rushed through the hall, fell upon his knees, and begged his blessing"

The same writer, giving another version of the touching interview with Margaret says that upon reaching the Tower Wharf, his "dear daughter, Margaret Roper, forced her way through the officers and halberdiers that surrounded him, clasped him round the neck, and sobbed aloud Sir Thomas consoled her, and she collected sufficient power to bid him farewell for ever, but as her father moved on she again rushed through the crowds, and threw herself upon his neck Here the weakness of nature overcame him, and he wept as he repeated his blessing and again uttered his Christian consolation The people wept too, and his guards were so much affected that they could hardly summon up resolution to separate the father and daughter"

There was confined in the Tower at the same time as Sir Thomas More a close and dear friend of the ex-Chancellor, a learned and godly man, who, moreover, is said to have been, on occasion, a visitor at Well Hall, probably in the days of Mr John Roper, the father of Sir William.

This good man was Fisher, the Bishop of Rochester, who was imprisoned for the same offence as Sir Thomas, and had endured imprisonment for about the same length of time.

Bishop Fisher's case, was, in one sense, even more distressing than that of More He was an aged man, between 70 and 80 years old His sufferings were pretty much those of Sir Thomas More's, as we may judge from a letter written by the Bishop, from his prison in the "Bell Tower," to Thomas Cromwell He writes —

"Furthermore, I beseech you to be good master in my necessity; for I have neither shirt nor suit, nor yet other clothes that are necesary for me to wear, but that be ragged and rent too shamefully. Notwithstanding, I might easily suffer that, if they would keep my body warm. But my diet also, God knoweth how slender it is at many times. And now in mine age, my stomach may not away with but a few kinds of meats, which, if I want, I decay forthwith."

Fisher was executed on the 22nd of June, and there is a picture in the National Gallery showing Sir Thomas More and his daughter, Margaret Roper, standing in the gloomy prison cell, looking through the lattice window at the procession of the Bishop to execution.

Among the notable relics of Sir Thomas More are the eloquent and touching letters that passed between himself and his daughter, while he was in the Tower. He was deprived of writing materials, but bits of charcoal and paper were left about by his considerate keepers, and at least two of these letters were written by means of such clumsy materials.

We will conclude this chapter with a transcription of the last of this series of letters, the last, indeed, that Sir Thomas ever wrote, for it was written the day before his execution. It is reproduced exactly as it appears in Sir William Roper's book.

Sir Thomas More was beheaded at the Tower-hill in London, on Tuesday, the sixth day of July, in the year of our Lord, 1535, and in the xxvii. year of the Reign of King Henry VIII. And on the day next before, being Monday, and the fifth day of July, he wrote with a coal a letter to his daughter Mistress Roper, and sent it to her (which was the last thing that ever he wrote), the copy whereof here followeth.

Our Lord bless you, good daughter, and your good husband, and your little boy, and all yours, and all my children, and all my god-children and all our friends. Remember me, when ye may to my good daughter *Cicily*, whom I beseech our Lord to comfort. And I send her my blessing, and to all her children, and pray her to pray for me. I send her an handkerchief; and God comfort my good son her husband. My good daughter *Dance* hath the picture in parchment, that you delivered me from my Lady Coniers, her name is on the backside. Show her that I heartily pray her that you may send it in my name to her again, for a token from me to pray for me. I like special well *Dorothy Coly*, I pray you be good unto her. I would wit whether this be she that you wrote me of. If not, yet I pray you to be good to the other, as you may in her affliction, and to my god-daughter, *Joan Aleyn*, too. Give her, I pray you, some kind answer, for she sued hither to me this day to pray you be good to her. I cumber you, good *Margaret*, much, but I would be sorry if it should be any longer than to-morrow. For it is Saint Thomas' Eve, and the Utas of Saint Peter; and therefore to-morrow long I to go to God; it were a day very meet and convenient for me. I never liked your manner toward me better than when you kissed me last; for I love when daughterly love and dear charity hath no desire to look to worldly courtesy. Farewell, my dear child, and pray for me, and I shall for you and all your friends, that we may merrily meet in heaven. I thank you for your great cost. I send now to my good daughter *Clement* her aglorism stone, and I send her, and my godson, and all her's God's blessing and mine. I pray you, at time convenient, recommend me to my good son *John More*, I liked well his natural fashion. Our Lord bless him and his good wife my loving daughter, to whom I pray him to be good as he hath great cause; and that if the land of mine come to his hand, he break not my will concerning his sister *Dance*. And our Lord bless Thomas and Austen and all that they shall have.

Chapter LVI

THE LADY OF WELL HALL (4).

Not long before the day of execution Margaret Roper visited her father at the Tower. He inquired after the welfare of the Queen, Anne Boleyn, who, indirectly, was the author of his misfortunes. Margaret replied that the Queen had never been better. Nothing was thought of at Court but music and sporting.

"Never better, you say, Meg?" he replied, sadly. "Alas! it pitieth me to think into what misery, poor soul, she will shortly come. These dances of hers will prove such dances as with them she will spurn our heads off like footballs, but it will not be long ere her head will dance the same dance."

A message was brought to him that through the King's "clemency" his sentence was commuted from "hanging, drawing and quartering" to simple decapitation, to which he replied —

"God preserve all my friends from such royal favours"

One request only did he make, and this again had reference to her, the lady of Well Hall, who, ever since the death of her mother, seems to have been for him the most valuable possession, and the dearest consolation the world afforded

"Let Margaret be allowed the liberty of being present," he pleaded. "Permit my child's eyes to see the last of her father."

The last scene in the great tragedy is thus described by Sir William Roper:—

So remained Sir Thomas More in the Tower more than a seven night after his judgment

From whence, the day before he suffered, he sent his shirt of hair, not willing to have it seen, to my wife, his dearly beloved daughter, and a letter written with a coal plainly expressing the fervent desire he had to suffer on the morrow . . . .

And so upon the next morrow, being Tuesday, Saint Thomas his eve, and the Utas of Saint Peter, in the year of our Lord 1535, according as he in his letter the day before had wished, early in the morning came to him Sir Thomas Pope, his singular good friend, on message from the King and his Council, that he should before nine of the clock of the same morning suffer death, and that, therefore, he should forthwith prepare himself thereto.

"Master Pope," quoth Sir Thomas More, "for your good tidings I heartily thank you. I have been always much bounden to the King's highness for the benefits and honours that he had still from time to time most bountifully heaped upon me, and yet more bounden am I to his grace for putting me into this place, where I have had convenient time and space to have remembrance of my end. And so help me God, most of all, Master Pope, am I bounden to his highness that it pleaseth him so shortly to rid me out of the miseries of this wretched world, and therefore will I not fail earnestly to pray for his grace, both here, and in the world to come."

"The King's pleasure is farther," quoth Master Pope, "that at your execution you shall not use many words"

"Master Pope," quoth he, "you do well to

THE FAMILY OF SIR THOMAS MORE.

From the picture by Holbein, which formerly hung in the hall of the Manor House, Well Hall.
Sir Thomas More's father on the left.   Sir Thomas More on his left hand.   Margaret Roper in the front.

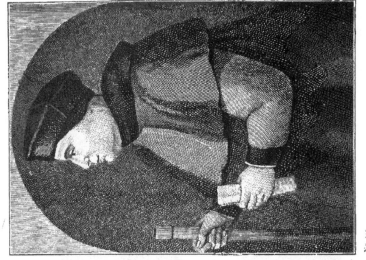

No. 135.

CARDINAL WOLSEY.
(See text).

(By permission of Messrs. Macmillan & Co.)

No. 134.

ARCHBISHOP WARHAM.
(See text).

(By permission of Messrs. Macmillan & Co.)

HENRY VII.

He re-built the West Front of the Palace.

(By permission of Messrs. Macmillan)

No. 137.

FROISSART PRESENTING THE "BOOK OF LOVES" TO
RICHARD II. AT ELTHAM PALACE.

(See text).

No. 138.　　ERASMUS.

A visitor at Eltham Palace

(See text).

No. 139.　　VAN DYKE.

Had rooms at Eltham Palace.

(See text).

give me warning of his grace's pleasure, for otherwise, at that time, had I purposed to have spoken; but of no matter wherewith his grace, or any other, should have had cause to be offended. Nevertheless, whatsoever I intended, I am ready obediently to conform myself to his grace's commandment; and I beseech you, good Master Pope to be a mean to his highness that my daughter Margaret may be at my burial."

"The King is content already," quoth Master Pope, "that your wife, children and other friends shall have liberty to be present thereat."

"Oh, how much beholden then," said Sir Thomas More, "am I unto his grace, that unto my poor burial he vouchsafeth to have so gracious consideration."

Wherewithal, Master Pope, taking his leave of him, could not refrain from weeping; which Sir Thomas More perceiving, comforted him in this wise:—

"Quiet yourself, good Master Pope, and be not discomforted, for I trust that we shall once in heaven see each other full merrily, where we shall be sure to live and love together in joyful bliss eternally."

Upon whose departure, Sir Thomas More, as one who had been invited to some solemn feast, changed himself into his best apparel; which Master Lieutenant espying, advised him to put it off, saying that he that should have it was but a javil.

"What, Master Lieutenant," quoth he, "shall I account him a javil that will do me this day so singular a benefit? Nay, I assure you, were it cloth of gold, I should think it well bestowed on him, as Saint Cyprian did, who gave his executioner thirty pieces of gold."

And, albeit, at length, through Master Lieutenant's importunate persuasion, he altered his apparel, yet, after the example of holy martyr Saint Cyprian, did he, of that little money that was left him, send an angel of gold to his executioner.

And so was he by Master Lieutenant brought out of the Tower, and from thence led to the place of execution; where, going up the scaffold, which was so weak that it was ready to fall, he said merrily to the Lieutenant:—

"I pray you, Master Lieutenant, see me safe up, and for my coming down let me shift for myself."

Then desired he all the people thereabout to pray for him, and to bear witness with him that he should now there suffer death in and for the faith of the Holy Catholic Church.

Which done, he kneeled down, and, after his prayers said, turned he to the executioner with a cheerful countenance, and said unto him:—

"Pluck up thy spirits, man, and be not afraid to do thine office; my neck is very short, take heed, therefore, thou strike not awry, for saving of thine honesty."

So passed Sir Thomas More out of this world to his God, upon the very same day which he most desired. Soon after his death came intelligence thereof to Emperor Charles. Whereupon he sent for Sir Thomas Eliott, our English Ambassador, and said to him:—

"My Lord Ambassador, we understand that the King, your master, hath put his faithful servant, and grave, wise councillor, Sir Thomas More, to death."

Whereupon Sir Thomas Eliott answered that "he understood nothing thereof."

"Well," said the Emperor, "it is too true; and this will we say, of whose doings ourselves have had these many years no small experience, we would rather have lost the best city of our dominions than have lost such a worthy councillor."

Which matter was, by the same Sir Thomas Eliott, to myself, to my wife, to Master Clement and his wife, to Master John Heywood and his wife, and unto divers others his friends accordingly reported.

When the account of More's execution was brought to the King he was "playing at tables" with the Queen, Anne Boleyn. It would appear that even he was somewhat conscience stricken, for, with some signs of discomposure, he said to his wife:

"Thou art the cause of this man's death!"

He then hastily withdrew, and shut himself up in the solitude of his chamber.

Within a year the sequel to the tragedy was enacted, when the beautiful Queen herself was taken by barge from Greenwich to the Tower, from whence she, too, was subsequently led to her awful fate at the block

It was the wish of Sir Thomas More to be buried at the little family church at Chelsea, where an epitaph, written by himself, had already been placed in the chancel

Margaret Roper was determined to see this wish of her father carried out, and by unwearied care and exertion she succeeded in getting his body removed from the Chapel of St Peter's ad Vincula, in the Tower, where it was at first interred, to the church wherein he had so often worshipped, near their old home at Chelsea But there was another enterprise that possessed her mind

Let us read its account from Mrs Owen, who wrote so enthusiastically of Margaret Roper some sixty years ago.

"That beloved head, with its countenance ever uniformly tender towards her, was an object of ardent yearning Immediately after the execution, it had been put upon a pole on London Bridge, where that of Bishop Fisher, his companion and friend, had been fixed The latter's was thrown into the Thames, in order that Sir Thomas More's should replace it

"This circumstance probably suggested to Margaret Roper the only means by which it was possible she could obtain the object she desired Watching and waiting, the time arrived when no guard cared longer about the preservation of 'the head of the traitor' It was lowered from the pole whereon it had been raised, and Margaret tremblingly received the precious relic before it touched the river's edge, and, unobserved, escaped, bearing it with her

"It is not to be supposed, however, that, surrounded by spies, at that time so numerous and so malignant, this pious deed of filial affection remained long a secret

"Margaret Roper was summoned before the Council, and, bold, avowing the truth, and

maintaining her rights as well as sentiments, she was imprisoned by order of the King If they hoped to terrify or subdue her they were, however, mistaken. After suffering with calmness for a period, she was unexpectedly liberated, and permitted, without restriction, to seek her home and family"

The Chelsea home was in unhappy circumstances, for the household was in pecuniary distress, as well as overwhelmed by grief for the loss that had been sustained. They had to thank the King's mercy for the confiscation of Sir Thomas More's property, the widow being *literally* allowed for the proceeds of it an annuity of £20 for the remainder of her life.

There was now a general breaking up of the household Dame Margaret Roper withdrew herself to domestic retirement, devoting herself to the educating of her children, and the doing of good works, as became the lady of Well Hall

She had five children, namely, two sons and three daughters, and herself a lifelong student and distinguished scholar, she was specially qualified to lead them aright along the paths to knowledge

In her Chelsea days she had shewn herself no mean contributor to the stores of literature Many of her Latin epistles, poems and orations had been freely circulated, and met with universal praise. A reply to Quintilian is said to have rivalled in eloquence the production to which it formed an answer Dame Roper also wrote a treatise "Of the four last things," which was characterised by so much thought and reasoning that her father abandoned in its favour a discourse which he had partly composed upon the same subject. Added to these, she made a translation of the Ecclesiastical History of Eusebius from Greek into Latin, and this was afterwards rendered into English, some years after, by Mary, the youngest of her daughters, who followed the literary pursuits of her mother

She died at Well Hall at the age of thirty-five years, and was buried in the Roper tomb at St Dunstan's Church, Canterbury

This, briefly told, is the story of Margaret

Roper, whom we may be proud to call the Lady of Well Hall, and of her father, Sir Thomas More, whose name has been much associated with the history of the royal village of Eltham. We have lingered rather longer than usual over these characters, but we seem justified in doing so by the fact that father and daughter, by their life and works, and the noble examples they have set, stand forth as two of the most beautiful figures in English history.

Chapter LVII

MORE NOTES ON THE ROPERS.

Sir William Roper was the most distinguished of this Well Hall family. We have already read something of him in the short story of Margaret, his wife, and of Sir Thomas More, mainly derived from the facts supplied by the Squire of Well Hall himself, in the book he wrote. Let us now see what more we can gather about the author of the book.

SIR WILLIAM ROPER

William Roper was born in 1496, and died in 1578 He was the eldest son of John Roper, his mother being Jane, the daughter of Sir John Finoux, the chief justice of the King's Bench The father, John Roper, lived at Well Hall, having acquired the ownership of the maner, and he also owned property in the parish of St. Dunstan, Canterbury. He was Sheriff of Kent in 1521, and held for a long time the office of Clerk of the Pleas, or Prothonotary of the Court of King's Bench John Roper was buried in the Roper vault in the Chapel of St. Dunstan's Church, Canterbury, on April 7th, 1524

The will of John Roper was made in January, 1523, and it became somewhat notorious for its provisions, which ignored the Kentish custom of gavel-kind, and were so complicated that it needed a special Act of Parliament, which was passed in 1529, to give effect to them This remarkable will is printed in extenso in Archæologia Cantiana, Vol ii., where it occupies twenty-one pages

We find that the widow of John Roper wrote a letter to Thomas Cromwell, in November, 1539, begging him to bestow the office of Attorney to Anne of Cleves, who was about to become the Queen of England, upon John Pilborough, husband of her second daughter, Elizabeth.

It will be remembered that Cromwell was chiefly instrumental in bringing about the marriage of Henry VIII to Anne of Cleves, and being the Lord Privy Seal, was in a position to obtain favours. The letter craving patronage for her son-in-law, written by Mistress Jane Roper, of Well Hall, is still in existence at the Record Office It is a matter of local interest, so we will make a transcription of it, with all its quaint spelling and phraseology, and we may see in what terms it was the custom to ask such favours in those days

JANE ROPER TO LORD PRIVY SEAL CROMWELL

In my most humble wyse, I have me comended unto your good lordship, and, all though, my goode lorde, I am all ready exceedingly bounden unto you for your manyfolde goodnesses evermore shewyd unto me, and unto my poore freends for my sake, whereof I am not able to recompence any part in dede, but, of bounden dutie, must persever your daily bedewoman to God, for the continuance of your prosperous estate; yet the good behavour of my son PILBOROUGH, your servaunt, towarde me, and my naturall leve to my doughter his wief, compelle me newe to desire most hartely your good lordship to be good lord unto my said son, and preferre hym to be Attourney unto the Quene, wheme, as I here saye, by Goddes grace, the Kynges highnes pleasith shortely moost nobly to mary. And your lordshippes soe deyng shall net be to my said son more pleasure then to me confort, which God rewarde you, you have allwais tendred in me; and, nevertheless, bynde my said son evermore both with dede to his litell power and good wille of his poore hert, to recompence duryng all his lyfe.

And, forasmuch, also, my god lord, that I here saye, it is the Kynges pleasure shortly to come down into this Countrey of Kent, I doo prepaire to receive your lordship moost gladly into my poore house, which is so moche enryched in my remembrance of your ones beyng there, that my special trust is, ye will never hereafter faile to be as bolde thereof as of your owen. And thus, Almyghtie God graunt your lordship prosperously long to lyve in your honourable estate.

Written the xijth day of this present monyth of November, by her which is noo lesse yours then she is bounden,

Jane Rooper

To the Right honourable and my moost syngular good lorde, the lorde Pryve Seale, Geve this.

It will be seen that this singular letter is interesting to us, in that it refers to a visit of the King to Eltham, and alludes to 'a visit which Thomas Cromwell had already made to Well Hall on some previous occasion

The youngest son of John Roper, Christopher, who died at Lynsted Lodge, Kent, was Escheator for the county in 1550. He married Elizabeth, daughter of Christopher Blore, of Teynham, Kent, and was grandfather of Sir John Roper, who was created Baron Teynham on July 9th, 1616. The peerage is still held by a descendant.

The eldest son, William, whose name has been so lastingly associated with Eltham, was educated at one of the Universities, and under his father's will, inherited the larger part of the family properties, including the estates at Eltham and St Dunstan's, Canterbury In 1523, when his father made his will, William held jointly with him the office of Clerk of the Pleas, or Prothonotary of the Court of King's Bench. This post he continued to hold alone, after his father's death, for the rest of his life.

It was his legal duties in this capacity which apparently brought him into contact with Sir Thomas More, and he married Margaret, the

eldest daughter of Sir Thomas, in 1525. As will have been seen already, More was deeply attached to young Roper, and that the affection was reciprocated is evidenced by the charmingly sympathetic life of Sir Thomas More, which his son-in-law wrote at Well Hall after the execution

Sir William Roper was an ardent Roman Catholic to the last, and during the reign of Queen Mary we find that he took a part in public life He was returned to the second and third Parliaments of Mary, as Member for Rochester In this Queen's last two Parliaments he sat for Canterbury He did not, however, re-enter the House of Commons after Queen Mary's death ,

As a Roman Catholic, he fell under the suspicion of Queen Elizabeth's Privy Council, and it is on record that in July, 1568 he was summoned before the Council, charged with having relieved with money certain persons who had fled the country, and had printed books against the Queen's Government

He made his submission, and in November, 1569, entered into a bond to be of good behaviour, and to appear before the Council when summoned.

Along with Sir William Cordell, Master of the Rolls, we find that Sir William Roper was nominated visitor to the new foundation of St. John's College, Oxford, by Sir Thomas Whyte, the founder The validity of the appointment was, however, disputed by Robert Horne, Bishop of Winchester, in 1571

Sir William Roper resigned his office of Prothonotary in 1577, after holding the post for fifty-four years He was succeeded in those duties by his eldest son, Thomas Roper.

Sir William died on January 4th, 1577-8, at the advanced age of 82 years, and was buried in St. Dunstan's Church, Canterbury His wife had died thirty-three years before, at Well Hall. He left two sons, Thomas and Anthony, and three daughters. Thomas succeeded to the Eltham property, and was buried at St. Dunstan's in 1597. The family of William Roper died out in the male line at the end of the seventeenth century, when Elizabeth Roper,

wife of Edward Henshaw, of Hampshire, became the sole heiress of the Eltham and St.
Dunstan Estates

There are frequent references to Sir William
Roper and other members of the family in the
parish records, and the name is also perpetuated by the street leading from the High-street
to the National Schools, which is called
"Roper-street."

A reference to one of the Ropers is that of
John Ford, who was Vicar of Eltham for thirty
years, namely, from 1598 to 1628. This gentleman does not seem to have worked very
amicably with Sir William, who was a Papist,
while Master Ford was apparently Puritan.
The Vicar writes:—

"22 Oct , 1623 Sir William Roper returned
from France, where he had remained a Catholic
for 14 years.

"Memorandum, that Mr William Roper
holdeth a certain parcel of wood amongst his
woods, called the Vicar's spring, containing by
estimate 15 acres, and payed for the same 15s
a year, as a most ungodly lease expresseth more
at large I leave a memorial to all Vicars
succeeding after me, for there are yet so many
years in the lease to come, being granted in the
third of King Edward VI., by one Sir Henry
Underwood, Vicar of Eltham, for four score
and nineteen years by me John Forde, vic , of
Eltham, 44 Elizabeth, A D. 1602 "

"The Vicar's diet at Mr Roper's table was
dew to all Vicars for the aforesaid woed till
Sir William Roper came, but then denied to me
John Forde, Vicar, although justified unto me
by his own mother John Forde "

In an earlier chapter upon the Parish Church
we have already shewn that the advowson of the
Vicarage was at one time in the possession of
the Ropers

Their memory is also kept alive by their
association with the Eltham Charities, but this
is a subject we shall allude to in a later chapter.

CHAPTER LVIII

SHOOTER'S HILL.

We commenced our Story of Eltham with the ancient road which runs over Shooter's-hill, and forms the northern boundary of the parish of Eltham It is a fine, straight road, running from London right away to the sea By the art of the road makers it has been kept up-to-date to meet the changing circumstances of vehicular traffic, but the interesting thing about it is that it runs practically upon the same course as that of the pre-historic trackway which some writers believe to have existed before the Romans came and re-constructed it according to their own methods

So that where to-day the cycles and motors whizz up and down the slopes of the hill, the British basket makers of primitive days may have trudged along conveying their goods to the sea for exportation to the markets of the Continent.

When one thinks of the part which this old road has played in our national story it is easy to see that its complete history would need a book all to itself. And the story of the part of it which forms the Eltham boundary at Shooter's-hill is, to a great extent, that of the road itself, so that it is quite impossible within the limits that we have laid down for our "Story of Eltham" to deal with its historical associations in detail

We have in earlier chapters alluded, in passing, to many of the great episodes it has witnessed, the retreat of the defeated Britons, the march of Cæsar's triumphant hosts, the tragedy of the Roman evacuation, then, farther down in the centuries, the progress of Wat Tyler's disorderly rabble, the woodland festival of Bluff King Hal, the Rogation procession of

priest and people and Parish Clerk from Eltham Church to the cross upon the hill, and, later, that eventful night of the Armada, when the excited villagers beheld the blazing beacon brightening the sky

But this is only a little portion of the tale of Shooter's-hill Before the advent of railways its roadway was the medium of traffic between London and the Continent Many a royal progress has it seen since the days of the early kings down to the time, in the memory of some who are living now, when it was decorated with Venetian masts and flags to celebrate the coming of Prince Albert, the father of King Edward VII. Armies have passed and re-passed, from days anterior to the Crusades down to Waterloo. Along the great highway went the pilgrims, of whom Chaucer has sung, some stopping to rest and pray at the cross upon the hill, on their journey to the shrine of Saint Thomas, at Canterbury And last, but not the least important, that continuous train of traffic borne by pack horses in the early days, and by waggons in later years, of merchandise for the great city.

There seems to be some difference of opinion as to the origin of the name "Shooter's Hill " The popular idea is that it took its rise in the practice of archery, which was so conspicuous a feature of village life before the introduction of firearms. Every village produced its bow-men, who, when the occasion demanded, proved a formidable contingent of the English fighting forces. Many a battle was won for the English through the skill and prowess of the bowmen.

An old " Common Council-book" of the town of Chester throws some light upon the way archery was practised in those days, and shews pretty clearly how the English bowmen were trained from their childhood   Here is an extract.—

"For the avoiding of idleness, all children of six years old and upwards shall on week-days be set to school, or some virtuous labour, whereby they may hereafter get an horest living, and on Sundays and holy days they shall resort to their parish churches and there abide during the time of divine service, and in the afternoon all the said male children shall be exercised in shooting with bows and arrows, for pins and points only, and that their parents furnish them with bows and arrows, pins and points, for that purpose, according to the statute lately made for the maintenance of shooting in long bows and artillery, being the ancient defence of the kingdom "

From this it will be seen that the custom was national, and made necessary by "statute."

We use the term "artillery" now-a-days for the cannon of warfare, but in old days the name was specially applied to bows and arrows. In I. Samuel, xx , 40, we read: "And Jonathan gave his *artillery* (i e , 'bows and arrows') unto his lad."

But an ingenious writer in "The Kentish Note Book," May 14th, 1892, is inclined to dispute the theory that "Shooter's-hill" derives its name from its association with archery He says —

"Every parish, in 1385, had to provide a place where every youth had to practise with the long-bow Where the targets were erected was not called *Shooter's*-hill, green, field, or close, for *Butts* was the term used, the memory of which is often perpetual in local names," such as "Butt-lane," "Butt-close," "Buts-field," "Butts Green," &c.

"I very much question," he continues, "if Butts ever existed at Shooter's-hill, because there was no necessity for them   They were usually in close proximity to the parish church Islington Butts, Lambeth Butts, Newington Butts were so situated In Deptford, Butt Lane led to them and in Greenwich, we learn from old deeds, the 'Butts where the archers

were wont to exercise' were in Stockwell-street, a good bow-shot from the church

"Eltham, in which parish Shooter's-hill is situated, had its Butts in 'Butslow,' west of the main road leading to Southend   Where Woolwich and Plumstead had them I do not know, but, undoubtedly, in conformity with the law, the butts were within the confines of the parish."

With regard to the Eltham Butts, there are frequent references to them in the church-warden's account, and "Eastfields," a position *north* of the main road (not *west*, as the writer in the "Note Book" suggests) was apparently assigned to them.

Being satisfied that the hill was not needed by Eltham, Plumstead, Woolwich, or Greenwich for the purpose of butts, he proceeds to discuss a theory of the origin of the name "Shooter's-hill," which is extremely interesting He proceeds —

"Mr Vincent, on p 634 of *Records of Woolwich*, says that the form 'Shouters-helle,' of the year 1614, is the strangest transformation it has undergone, but 'Shouters-helle' is only a dialectic or phonetic variation of the present name   In the Patent Rolls in 1383 it was written 'Shettereshseld' A 'Shotar's Croft' is mentioned in a Woolwich will, dated 1538; 'Shoters-dich,' and 'Souters-diche' occur in leases of fields adjacent to Shooter's-hill, 1522, all of which seem to contain the word *shaw*, a wood In a deed, dated 1608, relating to Kid-brooke, a wood called 'Shoemakers' is mentioned, which I take to be a corruption of *shaw mycell*, 'the little wood." Shoe-lane was formerly *Shaw* Lane, a path under the trees by the side of the Old Bourne that ran into the Thames at Blackfriars.

" 'Closes' in Eltham called 'Shirte,'' 'Sheterindinge,' and 'Shetterrinding,'' in 1547 and 1608, all seem to point to the place being *Shav-tor*, i e , 'wooded-hill ' This is a more plausible explanation than 'Shooter's,' yet I venture to put forward a more probable one still."

Concerning the many ways of spelling the n im Shooter's hill, the various references in former chapters of our "Story of Eltham," together with the quotations from the old parochial records, afford striking examples.

A second, and perhaps more probable theory is submitted by the writer referred to.

"In former days the meetings of the various 'County Councils' were held in the open air: 'On the summit of a range of hills, on the water-shed from which the fertilising streams descended, at the point where the boundaries

the meetings of the shire-moot. (Gomme's *Primitive Folk Moot*, p. 213.)

"Should this be the case, the name would originally be 'Shire Tor,' and when the usage passed away and the meaning of the second word became obsolete, the modern *hill* would be added as a duplication, as has been the case in various points of Great Britain, as Brindon-hill, Somerset; Pinhow, Lancashire; Penhill, Dumfries; Penlaw, in Dumfries, &c. (Taylor's

PRINCE HENRY.

of two or three communities touched another, was the proper place for the common periodical assemblage of the freemen." (Kemble's *Saxons in England*, vol. i., p. 75.)

"All these qualifications unite in Shooter's-hill; its position is prominent, it is and was a fertile watershed, it is at the junction of several boundaries, and so, probably, was the place where the *moot* was held.

"Many instances occur in which the word 'shire' is connected with some natural place, a river, a brook, hill, ford, &c., in forming a modern place name; and it is not difficult, from the light of other facts, to connect these with

Words and Places, p. 141.) In 1286 a jury was sworn concerning a hunting trespass, and assembled at *Hull Cnole*, now called *Howl Hill*. (Duncombe's *Hereford*, vol. 3, p. 101). The Hill of Howth, near Dublin, is another instance (Joyces *Names of Places*, p. 81), and many more could be adduced did space permit."

These conflicting opinions shew how uncertain we are as to the real derivation of the name "Shooter's-hill." But they are interesting speculations, associated as each one of them is with striking features of the village life in the past, and shewing how illuminating even a place name may sometimes be made in revealing the modes of life of our forefathers.

From an elegantly printed pamphlet by the Rev. T B. Willson, Vicar of Shooter's-hill from 1856 to 1906, we make the following extract, which briefly but eloquently deals with the historical aspect of Shooter's-hill

"If Shooter's-hill, as a parish, is but new, and has little history, yet the hill itself is most closely connected with the history of England Over it, in ancient days, the Romans, after they had added our island to their mighty empire, made one of their great military roads which ran almost as straight as an arrow from Dover to London, and over it the legions passed on their way to extend their conquests further north Then, after the break up of the empire, came the wild days of the Saxon invasion, and when Christianity and civilisation re-asserted themselves in Kent the road became one of the great highways from London to the coast, passing through Rochester and Canterbury

"We can well picture Mellitus, the first Bishop of London, after the revival of Christianity, leaving his brother Justus in Rochester, making his way to London, and pausing when he reached the top of the hill to gaze on the Thames valley and discern in the distance the buildings which clustered round the hill upon which St Paul's now stands Then, as the centuries rolled by, the road as a great highway grew in importance, and the thirteenth and sixteenth centuries saw many parties of pilgrims who passed that way, as 'from every schires end of Engelond to Canterbury they wende' to pay their devotions at the 'Holy blissful Martyr,' St. Thomas of Canterbury, and these parties must often have rejoiced when they safely passed the 'perils of robbers,' which, almost to our own day, alarmed many wayfarers as they climbed the hill

"Thus the years rolled by, and Shooter's-hill witnessed many and noted companies of travellers The days of the mail coaches made it a place of importance as the end of the first stage from London, and the Bull Inn, where they changed horses, saw many famous men and women pass its doors from 1749 (when it was first built) until the iron horse superseded the old method of travelling, and the last coach drove from London to Dover "

Chapter LIX

SHOOTER'S HILL (2).

"THE KNIGHTS OF THE ROAD."

In the old days there were few spots round the Metropolis which had a worse repute than Shooter's-hill for the robberies, outrages and murders committed by highwaymen on its lonely road. Blackheath was infested by robbers of this class, who found cover in the heath that grew so profusely there But the long and narrow road through the Shooter's-hill woods was even better suited for their dark deeds, and to pass the dangerous hill without molestation was a thing to be thankful for.

And it was not for any lack of warning that such ill deeds would bring their punishment that these desperadoes went on with their evil work The gibbet was standing before their eyes, somewhere about the spot where the police-station now is, and it was quite a common thing to see the corpses of miserable wretches dangling from the cross-bars, in chains.

Plenty of examples of the villainous doings of these men can be culled from the newspapers of the eighteenth century, and as the story of Shooter's-hill could not possibly be complete without some mention of them, we will give presently the newspaper accounts of a few of the more notorious cases.

The authorities recognised that the natural characteristics of Shooter's-hill were helpful to the robbers, and from time to time alterations were made in the road with the object of lessening the dangers, as well as improving the roadway.

As far back as the time of Edward II., we find that the highway was enlarged at "Shooter's-hill" — "a place of great dread to travellers, owing to the narrowness of the road over it, and the continual lurking nests of robbers in the woods and coppices" Further alterations were made in the time of Edward III (1327) But it was not till 1739 that the road was re-constructed, a change which deprived the thieves of those natural advantages that enabled them to so easily entrap their victims

Sixty years later the road underwent another change, namely, in 1796, when it was given the form which is familiar to us at the present day. Tradition associates the name of Dick Turpin with Shooter's-hill It is quite possible that this daring highway thief may have committed some of his crimes here, but the story that it was at the old Bull that he perpetrated the brutal crime of putting the landlady upon the tavern fire is questioned by Mr. W. T. Vincent, in his "Records of the Woolwich District" Mr. Vincent, who searched the oldest and most authentic authorities, tells us that the occurrance took place at the Bull at Loughton, in Essex.

THE CAPTAIN'S ADVENTURE

The following circumstances were communicated to the "Kentish Note Book," in December, 1888, the account being copied from a newspaper cutting, dated March, 1792:—

"Captain Dempster, accompanied by a lady, was returning to London from Gravesend, on Friday night, about half-past ten o'clock. At the foot of Shooter's-hill the chaise suddenly stopped, and the captain let down the front glass, and called to the post boy to know why he did not proceed.

"When, after a few groans, he replied that he had been suddenly knocked from off his horse, and that he was at first so stunned by the fall, as to be unable to reply, and that the darkness of the night had prevented his observing anyone coming towards him, but that a man had hold of the horses' heads

"The chaise door on the side the lady sat was in a few moments after opened, and a man appeared at it, at whom the captain discharged a pistol. The fellow fell backwards, but whether from fright or from any wound he might have received, is not ascertained.

The other door was now opened, and the captain fired a second pistol at the fellow who stood at it, but who, from the flash, Mr. D observed kept rather towards the back of the carriage, by which he probably saved his life. The captain had no ammunition left, but refused to deliver his money, and one of the footpads discharged a pistol into the chaise.

In about two minutes after, on his still refusing to deliver, a second pistol was fired through the carriage, and so on, every two minutes, until six pistols were fired. They always keeping rather behind the chaise doors, in order as well to conceal their persons as to protect themselves

"At length, owing to the fright the lady who accompanied Captain Dempster was in, he was induced to comply with their demands. They then ordered him to throw his watch and money out of the window into the road. He threw them one guinea and a half and his watch, which, with the chain and seals affixed to it was valued at one hundred guineas, and by their direction, the chaise drove on."

A GENTLEMAN IN DISTRESS.

The following incident not only reveals the impudence of some of these scoundrels, who went about their business sometimes in broad daylight, and actually committed their robberies in sight of other people, who, possibly through fright, were helpless to render assistance, but there is a touch of humour in the rascal's plea that he was "a gentleman in distress." The account is taken from *The Kentish Gazette* of Saturday, June 24th, 1769.

"Monday evening, about nine o'clock, in the lane between Shooter's-hill and Eltham, in Kent, a post-chaise, with a Lady and Gentleman therein, and some Gentlemen and Ladies on foot, within fifty yards thereof of the same party, who had been regaling on the hill with tea, and reviewing the prospect, in returning home thence, were robbed of their watches and money by a middle-aged, genteel man, who presented an uncommonly large, bright horse pistol, with brass ornaments, and represented himself as a Gentleman in distress."

AN ELTHAM EXCISEMAN ROBBED.

The Birmingham Gazette, or the General Correspondent, of November 16th, 1741, published the following note on a robbery which is Eltham history in more senses than one.—

"On Saturday last, a Riding Officer, belonging to the Excise at Eltham, in Kent, was robb'd by a single Highway man, on Shooter's Hill, of about £20, seventeen whereof he had received of some County Tradesmen to pay in for them for their Duty at the office."

DINERS AT THE BLACK BULL.

The following two cases, among others, are recorded by Mr. Vincent in his "Records of Woolwich".—

"July 22nd,, 1785.—On Thursday evening, exactly at nine o'clock, eight gentlemen, of a respectable character in the City, having been at an annual dinner at the Black Bull, on Shooter's Hill, returning in two coaches to town, were stopped by two highwaymen, well mounted, who thrust their pistols into each coach, and collected upwards of twenty pounds.

"Not being satisfied without their watches, they were opening the door to search, but, a post chaise suddenly coming by, the villains rode after the post-boy, who, not stopping directly they ordered him, one of the robbers discharged his pistol at the lad, and then took a small sum from the passengers, and treated the driver with great inhumanity for what they called his inattention."

POLITE FOOTPADS.

September, 1752.—Last Thursday, in the afternoon, between five and six a young gentleman was robbed in the Woolwich stage-coach by two highwaymen, genteelly mounted, near the Artichoke, at Blackheath. They both came up to the coach door; one of them clapped a pistol to his breast and demanded his money, on which he delivered up all he had, but desired that they would return him one shilling to pay his coach fare, which they refused, but otherwise behaved very complaisantly, shook hands with him and wished him good-night. They demanded money of a woman that was in the coach, but she having only two shillings, they thought that not worth taking. They were both young men, and went off towards Shooter's-hill."

"ON BUSINESS LINES."

As late as the year 1800 we find these "gentlemen of the road" were quite masters of the situation at Shooter's-hill. So impotent were the authorities in the matter that the thieves even went to the extent of organising a system of tolls, issuing tickets or passes, at a certain price, to ensure a safe passage across the hill.

Mr. Vincent tells us that "when Dr. Watson was tutor to Princess Charlotte at Shrewsbury House, in 1800, he was furnished (for a handsome consideration) with a certificate for the knights of the road which carried him safely past their masked videttes upon the hill, and was respected by every bushranger from end to end of the dreaded highway."

A writer in the "Kentish Note Book" tells us, in connection with this circumstance, that the impudent rogues would not allow the Princess herself to pass from Shrewsbury House to and from London until they had been "squared" by Dr Watson, on behalf of Her Royal Highness. Those were, indeed, "the good old times"

CHAPTER LX.

SHOOTER'S HILL (3).

MORE ABOUT THE HIGHWAYMEN.

In our own day, with our highly organised system of police, it is difficult to imagine the conditions of social life which permitted such bare-faced outrages as those which were regularly perpetrated at Shooter's-hill, even as late as a hundred years ago

But the opportunities for these practices were greater then than now. Travelling was slow, there was no telegraphic system in operation, and the officers of justice, who were the precursors of the modern policemen, were more or less impotent individuals, quite incapable of dealing with such an evil

Nevertheless the "gentlemen of the road," notwithstanding their successes, led a precarious life, they were driven to living in hiding, and to be constantly on the alert against surprise and arrest, while the grim-looking gibbet at the cross-roads was a perpetual reminder of the fate that awaited them should they be captured

Mr. Vincent says: "I have met with old inhabitants who remember two ruffians being hanged and gibbeted at the top of the hill, and two others by the cross-roads at Eltham Bottom. These latter were Russell and King, a couple of desperadoes, who resided at Blackheath, and suffered the penalty of their crimes in 1809. Their bones were discovered when the police-station was built"—just above where the Herbert Hospital stands.

Many of our best writers of fiction have made the highwayman an interesting and picturesque figure in the tales they have had to tell, and the rascal has often been made to contribute to a humorous situation, generally at the expense of someone else But occasions have sometimes occurred outside the sphere of fiction in which that gentleman has met his match, and found the tables turned upon him, and the laugh against him. An incident of this kind actually took place at Shooter's-hill We will give the circumstance in the words of the one who was best qualified to recount it:—

"THE TABLES TURNED."

This exquisite story of how a sailor, on his way from Chatham to London, turned the tables on a band of highwaymen, who were in wait about Shooter's-hill, is contained in—

Jackson's Recantation,
or the Life and Death of the notorious High-
wayman now hanging in chains at Hampstead
Delivered To a Friend a Little
before Execution,
Wherein is truly discovered the whole
Mystery of that Wicked and
Fatal Profession of
Padding on the Road
London, Printed for T B in the year 1674

The story is reprinted in the third volume of Messrs Reeves and Turner's *Old-Book Collector's Miscellany*, 1873, where it occupies 52 pages

Mr Jackson and his associates were hovering about Shooter's-hill, expecting paid-off seamen from Chatham on their way to town After easing the pockets of a great many stragglers, but carefully avoiding those who came three, four, or five in a body, they met with a parson coming from London, from whom they took fifteen pounds, generously returning him twenty shillings on receiving his promise that he would inform none what had happened, but he, meeting with a seaman, warned him to turn back, lest he should meet with the same misfortune.

The remainder of the story we will tell in Mr. Jackson's own words:—

"The resolute seaman would not believe the parson, thinking it some idle *chimera* of his own invention, and so went on his way, and the parson on his

"Coming up to the seaman, we told him to stand, who asked us what we meant.

"We told him that we wanted money

"'Alas! gentlemen,' said he, 'It is true I have some, which I received for my pay in his Majesty's Service, and therefore it is pity to take that from me which I am carrying home for the maintenance of my poor wife and children'

If he had persuaded an angel to have been his orator, and pleaded in his behalf, it would have been all one, for no other sound pleased us but his money

"When he saw that there was no remedy, he delivered all he had, which was sixty-five pounds

"'Now, gentlemen,' said he, 'let me beg one request of you, and that is, since I dare not go home to my wife, and at present know not what course of life to steer, admit me into your company, you see I am limbed well enough, and I have courage and strength enough to qualify me for your occupation'

"We asked him whether he was in earnest; he swore a hundred oaths he was in earnest, and was ready to be tried at that instant; insisting farther that he was greatly in love with a trade that could get as much money in six minutes as he could in three years

"I was then the purse-bearer, and, finding that we had done enough for that day, we appointed a place to meet at, and so distributed ourselves for the present; only I had the charge of the seaman, who was wretchedly mounted, and therefore I needed not to fear him; besides as we rode along, I bound him over and over again, by oaths, to stand to what promise he had made us.

"At length, riding in a lane, suspecting nothing in the least, he turned his little hobby on me, and, seizing my bridle before I was aware, claps to my breast a little ugly brass-barrelled pistol, and swore, as if he had been one of the trade for above twenty years, if I would not instantly dismount he would send a bullet through my heart

"I saw by his frightful countenance that there was no dallying, so I dismounted, and gave him my horse, and he in his kindness bid me take his.

"Such a beast I never saw on a common, so poor, so weak, that I was thinking to commit my safety to my own, and not to his legs

"You may imagine what a sweat I was in, being thus dismounted, for having committed so many robberies that day, should I be met by any of the country, they would conclude me one of the robbers, seeing a man so splendidly accoutred, riding on a beast hardly fit to feed crows and ravens.

"The night coming on favoured me, and I got among my associates, and now I shall give you guess whether their laughter or sorrow was greatest? First, that a stout thief (for so I was accounted) should be robbed by a hobby-horse and a pot-gun, and, secondly, so much money lost (above one hundred and eighty pounds, we learn from a previous part of Mr Jackson's narration), money that we thought secure beyond the probability of re-taking

"We heard that the seaman, after he had paid himself, summoned in such brethren as had been robbed by us, and none else, but the parson, and he returned them their money."

SAMUEL PEPYS AND SHOOTER'S HILL

In the quaintly written but most interesting diary of Samuel Pepys, we get several references to Shooter's-hill. One of them bears directly upon that aspect of the history of the place which we are now considering, and gives us a grim and realistic picture of what was a common sight for the wayfarer in the days of Charles II.

Pepys had been paying a visit to Rochester, and in his characteristic style describes the journey from Dartford to Shooter's-hill, in the company of Captain Cuttance and Mrs. Anne. On coming to Shooter's-hill, the diarist says:—

"By-and-bye we came to two little girls keeping cows, and I saw one of them very pretty, so I had a mind to make her ask my blessing, and telling her that I was her godfather, she asked innocently whether I was Ned Wooding, and I said I was.

"So she kneeled down, and very simply called:—

"'Pray, godfather, pray to God to bless me.'

cruelly murdered two men near unto Shooter's-hill, in Kent; the one of them was a wealthy merchant in London, named George Sanders, the other John Beane of Woolwich.

"On Tuesday the said George Brown, receiving recent intelligence by letter from Mistress Ann Drewry that Master Sanders should lodge that night in the house of one Master Barnes, of Woolwich, and from thence go on foot to Saint Mary Cray the next morning, lay in wait for him and John Beane, servant to Master

"Which made us all merry, and I gave her twopence."

Then follows a gruesome picture. "Going on," he writes, "Mrs. Anne and I rode under a man that hangs at Shooter's-hill, and a filthy sight it was, to see how his flesh is shrunk to his bones. So home, and I found all well."

Yet another old writer, John Stow, has left on record a tragic incident of Shooter's-hill, which reveals to us its condition in the days of Queen Elizabeth, and, as Mr. Vincent observes, earned for the locality the name of the "Hill of Blood." The following is Stow's record:—

"On the 25th of March, 1573, being the Wednesday in Easter week, George Brown

Barnes, but John Beane, having ten or eleven wounds, and being left for dead, by God's providence revived again, and, creeping away all four, was found by an old man and his maiden, and taken to Woolwich, where he gave evident marks of the murderer, who was afterwards hanged up in chains near unto the place where he had done the fact."

We often like to talk of the "good old times," and to try and realise the bright, sunny and happy features of "merrie England," sometimes wishing perhaps that we might see those days again. But the story of Shooter's-hill reminds us that there were dark and ugly

No. 140.

THE EARL OF ESSEX,

Parliamentary General, who died at Eltham Palace

(See text).

No. 141.   SIR JOHN SHAW.   (First Baronet, Created 1665).

From the Family Portrait by Sir Peter Lely.   By special permission of the
Rev. Sir Charles Shaw, Bart.

(Copyright for this book only)

blots on the picture, and, notwithstanding the fact that we are far from being perfect, even in the early years of the twentieth century, we may very well congratulate ourselves that the journey from Eltham to Woolwich is not now the dangerous enterprise that it was in the days of Samuel Pepys, or even at the beginning of last century, nor is the fair face of the countryside disfigured by the gruesome spectacle of the gallows tree at the cross-roads.

Chapter LXI

SHOOTER'S HILL (4).

SHOOTER'S HILL IN LITERATURE.

Shooter's-hill is frequently alluded to in English literature Pepys we have already mentioned Charles Dickens makes it the scene in the opening chapter of "The Tale of Two Cities," and those who know their "Pickwick" will remember with pride that when the elder Weller gave up driving his famous coach he retired to an "excellent public-house" at Shooter's-hill Lord Byron gives it some prominence in "Don Juan," and that humble but sincere writer, Robert Bloomfield, the Suffolk poet, has left some interesting verses upon it.

The magnificent prospect to be obtained from the summit of Shooter's-hill has often been described The grand old river, with the mighty city upon its banks, on the one hand, and the fair fields of beautiful Kent on the other, are, indeed, worthy themes for the descriptive writer, whether of prose or poetry

One of such descriptions is to be found in the little-known novel, "Roxana," by De Foe, and as it describes the scene as it appeared in the reign of Charles II , we will make some extracts from it here Roxana, the lady who is the central character of the book, is on a journey from London to Dover, and she is supposed to be the writer —

"At St George's Church, Southwark, we were met by three gentlemen on horseback, who were merchants of my husband's acquaintance, and had come out a-purpose to go half a day's journey with us, and as they kept talking to us at the coach side, we went a good pace, and were very merry together, we stopped at the best house of entertainment on Shooter's-hill.

Here we stopped about an hour, and drank some wine; and my husband, whose chief study was how to please and divert me, caused me to alight out of the coach, which the gentlemen who accompanied us observing, alighted also. The waiter shewed us upstairs into a large room, whose window opened to our view a fine prospect of the river Thames, which here, they say, forms one of the most beautiful meanders

"It was within an hour of high water, and such a number of ships coming in under sail quite astonished as well as delighted me, insomuch that I could not help breaking out into such like expressions 'My dear, what a fine sight this is, I never saw the like before!' 'Pray will they get to London this tide?' At which the good-natured gentleman smiled, and said, 'Yes, my dear, why, there is London, and as the wind is quite fair to them, some of them will come to an anchor in about half-an-hour, and all within an hour.'

"I was so much taken up with looking down the river that till my husband spoke I had not once looked up the river, but when I did, and saw London, the Monument, the Cathedral Church of St Paul, and the steeples belonging to the several parish churches, I was transported into an ecstasy, and could not refrain from saying 'Surely that cannot be the place we have just come from! It must be further off, for that looks to be scarce three miles off, and we have been three hours, by my watch, coming from our lodgings in the Minories! No, no, it is not London, it is some other place!'

"Upon which one of the gentlemen present offered to convince me that the place I saw was

London, if I would go up to the top of the house, and view it from the turret. I accepted the offer, and I, my husband, and the three gentlemen were conducted, by the master of the house, upstairs into the turret If I was delighted before with my prospect, I was now ravished, for I was elevated above the room I was in before, upwards of thirty feet. I seemed a little dizzy, for the turret being a lantern, and giving light all ways, for some time I thought I was suspended in the air; but, sitting down, and eating a mouthful of biscuit, and drinking a glass of sack, I soon recovered, and then the gentleman who had undertaken to convince me that the place I was shewn was really London thus began, after having drawn aside one of the windows —

" ' You see, my lady,' says the gentleman, 'the greatest, the richest, the finest, and the most populous city in the world, at least, in Europe, as I can assure your ladyship, upon my knowledge, it deserves the character I have given it '

"But this, sir, will never convince me that the place you now shew me is London, though I have before heard that London deserves the character you have with so much cordiality bestowed upon it And this I can testify, that London, in every particular you have mentioned, greatly surpasses Paris, which is allowed by all historians and travellers to be the second city in Europe

"Here the gentleman, pulling out his pocket glass, desired me to look through it, which I did, and then he directed me to look full at St Paul's, and to make that the centre of my future observations, and thereupon he promised me conviction

"Whilst I took my observation I sat in a high chair, made for that purpose, with a convenience before you to hold the glass I soon found the cathedral, and then I could not help saying: 'I have been several times up to the stone gallery, but not quite so often up to the iron gallery. Then I brought my eye to the monument, and was obliged to confess I knew it to be such The gentleman then moved his glass, and desired me to look, which doing, I said 'I think I see Whitehall and St James's

Park, and I see also two great buildings, like barns, but I do not know what they are.'

" 'Oh,' says the gentleman, 'they are the Parliament Houses and Westminster Abbey.' 'They may be so,' said I, and, continuing looking, I perceived the very house at Kensington which I had lived in some time. But of that I took no notice, yet I found my colour come, to think what a life of gaiety I had lived The gentleman, perceiving my disorder, said 'I am afraid I have tired your ladyship, I will make but one remove, more easterly, and then I believe you will allow the place we see to be London

"He might have saved himself the trouble, for I was thoroughly convinced of my error, but to give myself time to recover, and to hide my confusion, I seemed not yet to be quite convinced I looked, and the first object that presented itself was Aldgate Church, which, though I confess it to my shame, I seldom saw the inside of it, yet I was well acquainted with the outside . I saw the church, or the steeple of the church, so plain, and I knew it so well, that I could not help saying, with some earnestness, 'My dear, I see our church, the church, I mean, belonging to our neighbourhood, I am sure it is Aldgate Church ' Then I saw the Tower, and all the shipping, and, taking my eye from the glass, I thanked the gentleman for the trouble I had given him, and said to him that I was fully convinced that the place I saw was London, and that it was the very place we came from that morning "

This is the description which the author, De Foe, makes " Roxana " write It is distinguished by the realism, which is characteristic of De Foe's fiction. But, fiction or not, it certainly suggests that the author had visited Shooter's-hill, and surveyed the prospects himself

Now let us turn to the simple verses of Robert Bloomfield (1766-1823), the Suffolk poet, author of the " Farmer's Boy," and many other pieces descriptive of the various phases of country life He seems to have dwelt at Woolwich for a time, and while there to have suffered from ill-health. He used to

climb Shooter's-hill as a "constitutional",
and these excursions gave rise to the lines from
which we now quote

SHOOTER'S HILL.

Health! I seek thee, dost thou love
  The mountain top or quiet vale,
Or deign o'er humbler hills to rove
  On showery June's dark south-west gale?
If so, I'll meet all blasts that blow,
  With silent step, but not forlorn,
Though, goddess, at thy shrine I bow,
  And woo thee each returning morn

I see thee where, with all his might,
  The joyous bird his rapture tells,
Amidst the half-excluded light,
  That gilds the foxglove's pendant bells,
Where, cheerily up this bold hill's side
  The deepening groves triumphant climb,
In groves delight and peace abide,
  And wisdom marks the lapse of time.

O'er eastward uplands, gay or rude,
  Along to Erith's ivied spire,
I start, with strength and hope renew'd,
  And cherish life's rekindling fire.
Now measure vales with straining eyes,
  Now trace the churchyard's humble names,
Or climb brown heaths, abrupt that rise.
  And overlook the winding Thames.

Sweet Health, I seek thee! Hither bring
  Thy balm, that softens human ills,
Come, on the long-drawn clouds that fling
  Their shadows o'er the Surrey hills
Yon green-topped hills, and far away,
  Where late as now I freedom stole
And spent one dear, delicious day
  On thy wild banks, romantic Mole

Aye, there's the scene! beyond the sweep
  Of London's congregated cloud,
The dark brow'd wood, the headlong steep,
  And valley paths without a cloud!
Here, Thames, I watch thy flowing tides,
  Thy thousand sails am proud to see;
But where the Mole all silent glides,
  Dwells peace—and peace is wealth to me.

This far-seen monumental tower
  Records th' achievements of the brave,
And Angria's subjugated power,
  Who plundered on the eastern wave.

I would not that such turrets rise,
  To point out where my bones are laid;
Save that some wandering bard might prize
  The comforts of its broad, cool shade

O, Vanity! since thou'rt decreed
  Companion of our lives to be,
I'll seek the moral songster's meed,
  An earthly immortality,
Most vain!—O let me, from the past,
  Remembering what to man is given,
Lay Virtue's broad foundations fast,
  Whose glorious turrets reach to heaven.

In strong contrast with the homely lines of
this peasant singer, are those of different senti-
ment written by Lord Byron in the eleventh
canto of "Don Juan" This is how he describes
the incident of the highwayman who attacked
Don Juan, who was journeying over Shooter's-
hill, in the direction of London :—

Don Juan got out on Shooter's-hill,
  Sunset the time, the place the same declivity
Which looks along that vale of good and ill,
  Where London streets ferment in full
    activity,
While everything around was calm and still,
  Except the creak of wheels, which on their
    pivot he
Heard—and that bee-like, bubbling, busy hum
Of cities, that boil over with their scum

I say, Don Juan, wrapt in contemplation,
  Walk'd on behind the carriage, o'er the
    summit,
And lost in wonder of so great a nation,
  Gave way to't, since he could not overcome it
"And here," he cried, "is Freedom's chosen
    station,
  Here peals the people's voice, nor can entomb
    it,
Racks, prisons, inquisitions, resurrection
Awaits it, each new meeting or election

"Here are chaste wives, pure lives, here
    people pay
  But what they please; and if that thing be
    dear,
'Tis only that they love to throw away
  Their cash, to shew how much they have a
    year.
Here laws are all inviolate, none lay
  Traps for the traveller, every highway's
    clear;

Here"—he was interrupted by a knife,
With—".......your money or your life!"

These freeborn sounds proceeded from four
    pads,
  In ambush laid, who had perceived him
    loiter
Behind his carriage; and, like handy lads,
  Had seized the lucky hour to reconnoitre;
In which the heedless gentleman who gads
  Upon the road, unless he be a fighter,
May find himself within that isle of riches,
Exposed to lose his life, as well as breeches.

  Though taken by surprise, and knowing no
English, Juan readily understood the purport
of his assailants. The poet writes:—

Juan yet quickly understood their gesture,
  And being somewhat choleric and sudden,
Drew forth a pocket pistol from his vesture,
  And fired it into his assailant's pudding—
Who fell, as rolls an ox o'er in his pasture,
  And roar'd out, as he writhed his native mud
    in,
Unto his nearest follower, or henchman,

Oh, Jack! I'm floored by that 'ere . . . French-
    man!"

But Jack and his accomplices thought fit to
run away, leaving their wounded comrade with
the enemy. By this time the friends of Juan
had gathered round, and preparations were
made to bandage the wound.

But ere they could perform this pious duty,
  The dying man cried, "Hold! I've got my
    gruel,
Oh! for a glass of gin! We've missed our
    booty;
Let me die where I am!" And as the fuel
Of life shrunk in his heart, and thick and
    sooty,
  The drops fell from his death-wound, and he
    drew ill,
His breath—he from his swelling throat untied
A kerchief, crying, "Give Sal that!"—and died.

Lack of further space precludes from giving
more, but this extract enables us perhaps to
form some idea of what sort of reputation
Shooter's-hill had at the time Lord Byron
wrote.

Chapter LXII

SHOOTER'S HILL (5).

THE VICTORY OF SEVERNDROOG

The interesting tower which peeps out from among the trees on Shooter's Hill, making a picturesque feature in the landscape, is such a well-known landmark, and the cause of so much inquiry as to what it is, and why it is there, that we will devote this chapter to the historical event which it helps to commemorate We have already alluded to it briefly in the account of Sir William James, whom we have included amongst the historical dead who sleep in Eltham Churchyard.

In a number of "The Mirror," printed in 1828, we get the following account of the Tower, as it existed then —

"Severn Droog Castle consists of three floors In the lower rooms are several Indian weapons, armour, &c , brought from Severn Droog in 1755, by Commodore James, as trophies of his victory The different stories are neatly fitted up, and on the ceiling of the first, in six compartments, are several views of the fleet and fortress on the day of assault The summit is embattled with turrets at the angles From the windows and roof the visitor is gratified with extensive and beautiful views of a great part of Kent, Surrey, and Essex, with the Metropolis and River Thames

"This tower was erected by Lady James, the wife of Sir William James, who resided at Park Place Farm, Eltham. Over the entrance there is a broad tablet of stone, upon which is cut the following inscription —

This Building
was erected MDCCLXXXIV , by the
Representative of the late
Sir William James, Bart ,
To commemorate that gallant officer's
Achievement in the East Indies,
During his Command of the Company's
Marine Forces in those Seas
And in a particular manner to record the
Conquest of
The Castle of Severn Droog,
On the Coast of Malabar,
Which fell to his superior valour and
able conduct
On the 2nd day of April, MDCCLV

The Story of Severndroog is set forth in Orme's " Hindostan " as follows —

" Conagee Angria was a notorious freebooter, belonging to the Morattoe pirates, who had declared war by sea and land against the Grand Mogul, because he had employed an admiral to protect his Mahometan subjects against their depredations.

By means of his prowess during this war, Conagee Angria had raised himself from a private man, not only to be Commander-in-Chief of the Morattoe fleet, but was entrusted with the government of Severndroog, one of the strongest holds belonging to the Saha Rajah, or King of the Morattoes, and, having seduced others of his fellow-subjects, set up a government against his sovereign along the sea-coast to the extent of one hundred and twenty miles, and an inland country of between twenty and thirty miles towards the mountains

The successors of this fortunate robber took the name of Angria, and so fortified themselves that the rajah consented to let them have peaceable possession upon acknowledging his sovereignty, and paying a small tribute.

In the course of fifty years, this state, by means of piracies exercised indiscriminately upon ships of all nations, had rendered itself so formidable to the European traders to India that the British East India Company alone were compelled to keep up a maritime force, at the annual expense of £50,000, as a check upon Angria, and a protection to their ships and colonies.

Attempts had frequently been made by different nations to overturn this piratical system, but Angria's successes had made him insolent He threw off his allegiance to his sovereign, and slit the noses of his ambassadors who came to demand the tribute Under these conditions the Rajah made proposals to the British to attack this common enemy with their united force.

Commodore James, at that time Commander-in-Chief of the Company's marine force, sailed on the 22nd of March, 1775, in the Protector, of forty-two guns, with a ketch of sixteen guns, and two bomb-vessels, but such was the exaggerated opinion of Angria's strongholds that the Presidency instructed him not to expose the Company's vessels to any risk by attacking them, but only to blockade the harbours whilst the Morattoe army carried on their operations by land

Three days after, the Morattoe fleet, consisting of seven grabs and sixty gallivats, came out of Choul, having on board ten thousand land forces, and the united fleets proceeded to Comara Bay, where they anchored, in order to permit the Morattoes to get their meal on shore, since they are prohibited by their religion from eating or washing at sea.

Departing from hence, they anchored again about fiftten miles to the north of Severndroog, where Rama-gee Punt, with the troops, disembarked, in order to proceed the rest of the way by land

Commodore James, now receiving intelligence that the enemy's fleet lay at anchor in the harbour of Severndroog, represented to the admiral of the Morattoe fleet that by proceeding immediately thither they might come upon them in the night, and so effectually blockade them in the harbour that few or none would be able to escape

The Morattoe seemed highly to approve the proposal, but had not authority enough over his officers to make any of them stir before the morning, when the enemy, discovering them under sail, immediately slipped their cables and put to sea

The Commodore then flung out the signal for a general chase, but as little regard was paid to this as to his former intention, for, although the vessels of the Morattoes had hitherto sailed better than the English, such was their terror of Angria's fleet that they all kept behind, and suffered the protector to proceed alone almost out of their sight.

The enemy, on the other hand, exerted themselves with uncommon industry, flinging overboard all their lumber to lighten their vessels, and not only crowding on all the sails they could bend, but also hanging up their garments and even their turbans to catch any breath of air.

The Protector, however, came within gunshot of some of the sternmost, but, the evening approaching, Commodore James gave over the chase, and returned to Severndroog, which he had passed several miles

Here he found Rama-gee Punt, with the army besieging, as they said, the three forts on the mainland, but they were firing only from one gun, a four-pounder, at the distance of two miles, and even at this distance, the troops did not think themselves safe without digging pits, in which they sheltered themselves, covered up to the chin, from the enemy's fire

The Commodore, judging from these operations that they would never take the forts, determined to exceed the instructions which he had received from the Presidency, rather than expose the English arms to the disgrace they would suffer if an expedition in which they were believed by Angria to have taken so great a share should miscarry.

The next day, the 2nd of April, he began to bombard and cannonade the fort of Severndroog, situated on the island, but, finding that the walls on the western side, which he attacked, were mostly cut out of the solid rock, he changed his station to the north-east, between the island and the mainland, where, whilst one of his broadsides plied the north-eastern bastions of this port, the other fired on Fort Goa, the largest of those upon the mainland

The bastions of Severndroog, however, were so high that the Protector could only point her upper tier to them, but, being anchored within a hundred yards, the musketry in the round tops drove the enemy from their guns, and by noon the parapet of the north-east bastion was in ruins, when a shell from the bomb-vessel set fire to a thatched roof, which the garrison, dreading the Protector's musketry, were afraid to extinguish

The blaze spreading fiercely at this dry season of the year, all the buildings of the fort were soon in flames, and amongst them a magazine of powder blew up On this disaster, the inhabitants, men, women, and children, with the greater part of the garrison, in all near one thousand persons, ran out of the fort, and embarking in seven or eight boats, attempted to make their escape to Fort Goa, but they were prevented by the English ketches, who took them all

The Protector now directed her fire only against Fort Goa, when the enemy, after suffering a severe cannonade, hung out a flag as a signal of surrender; but while the Morattoes

were marching to take possession of it the Governor, perceiving that the Commodore had not yet taken possession of Severndroog, got into a boat, with some of his trusty men, and crossed over to the island, hoping to be able to maintain the fort until he should receive assistance from Dabul, which is in sight of it

Upon this, the Protector renewed her fire upon Severndroog, and the Commodore, finding that the Governor wanted to protract the defence until night, when it was not to be doubted that some boats from Dabul would endeavour to throw succours into the place, he landed half his seamen, under cover of the fire of the ships, who with great intrepidity, ran up to the gate, and, cutting down the sallyport with their axes, forced their way into it, on which the garrison surrendered

The other two forts on the mainland had, by this time, hung out flags of truce, and the Morattoes took possession of them This was all the work of one day, in which the spirited resolution of Commodore James destroyed the timorous prejudices which had for twenty years been entertained of the impracticability of reducing any of Angria's fortified harbours "

It was in recognition of this signal service of Commodore James, that he was honoured by being made a baronet, and it was in memory of the battle that, after Sir William's death, Dame James erected the tower, which is so familiar a feature of the landscape

JOHN LILBURNE (from Print—1649—in British Museum).
By permission of Messrs. MACMILLAN & CO.

CHAPTER LXIII.

"FREE-BORN JOHN."

About the middle of the seventeenth century a familiar figure in the rural lanes of Eltham was the Quaker, John Lilburne. Prematurely old, for he was only forty-three when he died, dressed in the quaint and quiet Quaker's garb, those who knew him not would scarcely have recognised in that peaceful-looking person the turbulent colonel, the restless political agitator who had proved equally troublesome to the Government of Charles and to that of Cromwell, and whose name was a by-word from one end of the kingdom to the other.

What a number of exciting experiences had been crowded into his short life, since the time when, as a boy, John Lilburne used to roam the fields between Greenwich and Eltham!

What sufferings he had undergone! Persecutions he probably regarded them, for John conceived that he was fighting for a righteous cause. The irrepressible pamphleteer and politician had suffered imprisonment, with all the horrors that characterised that form of punishment in those days, the pillory, and exile from his native land. On at least one occasion he narrowly escaped execution, and it was only the force of circumstances which caused him to retire to Eltham, tired and disappointed, where, by the grace of Cromwell, he was allowed to remain in peace, so long as he behaved himself and where, in his new rôle of a Quaker, he lived out his last years.

We can only briefly relate the principal circumstances in the life of this very notorious and rather eccentric citizen of Eltham, for his life would really be the history of the political unrest and agitation of the days of Charles I. and Cromwell But we will relate some of the episodes, as they afford us a pretty vivid glimpse of life in those eventful years

"Free-born John," as posterity has nick-named him, although an Eltham man in the latter years of his life, was of Greenwich by birth, where he first saw the light in 1614

In his youth he read Fox's "Book of Martyrs" and the writings of the Puritan Divines, and by this means became imbued with the Puritanism which a few years later not only effected a tremendous influence upon his own life, but also upon the life of the nation

In 1636, that is when 22 years of age, the impressionable John became acquainted with John Bastwick, who was then a prisoner in the Gatehouse This acquaintance resulted in Lilburne's having a hand in the printing of Bastwick's "Litany," with the further result of his having to fly to Holland to avoid arrest.

He, however, did not long remain abroad, but returned in December, 1637, when he was seized and brought before the Star Chamber, on the charge of printing and circulating unlicensed books, more especially Prynne's "News from Ipswich." For this offence he was fined £500, whipped, pilloried, and imprisoned until he was in a mood to be obedient.

When liberated he soon entered upon the "war-path," for in April we find him again under arrest, and whipped from the Fleet Prison to Palace Yard But repression of this kind only provoked him to greater activity From the pillory he loudly denounced the bishops, scattered a number of Bastwick's tracts amongst the crowd, and when he absolutely refused to be silent, was finally gagged by the officers. He was taken back from the pillory to the prison, where he was treated with great barbarity.

Notwithstanding his confinement, he contrived to write, and to get printed, some of his stirring tracts One of these was an apology for separation from the Church of England, entitled, "Come out of her, my people", another was an account of his own imprisonment, styled, "The Work of the Beast." It must be borne in mind that Lilburne at this time was only a youth of little more than twenty-three years of age

Now comes a petition from Lilburne to the Long Parliament It was presented by Cromwell, and the Commons voted that Lilburne's sentence was "illegal and against the liberties of the subject," and also, "bloody, wicked, cruel, barbarous, and tyrannical"

The same day, Lilburne, who had been released at the beginning of the Parliament, was brought before the House of Lords, charged with speaking against the King, but the witnesses disagreed, and the charge was dismissed

A little while after we find John directing his energies into another channel He went into business as a brewer In our own day it is difficult to associate the puritan agitator with an avocation of this kind. But he did not stick to the business long, for a few years after the Civil War broke out, and John Lilburne was not slow in getting a commission in Lord Brooke's foot regiment. In his new capacity he fought in the battle of Edge-hill, but had the ill-luck to be taken prisoner at the fight at Brentford, November 12th, 1642 John was now put upon his trial at Oxford on the serious charge of high treason and taking up arms against the King. It would have gone hard with him, and Eltham would not have known him in after years, nor would this history of him have been set down, had not the Parliament intervened by a declaration, on December 17th, 1642, threatening immediate reprisals if Lilburne were put to death So he was let off

A few months after he obtained his liberty by exchange, and Lord Essex, the Parliamentary General, gave him £300 by way of recognition of his undaunted conduct at his trial, and he says that "he was offered a place of profit and honour, but preferred to fight, though it was for 8d a day, until he saw the peace and liberty of England restored."

The same year (1643) he took part in the capture of Lincoln, and was made a Major Next year he was transferred to Manchester's "Own Dragoons," with the rank of Lieutenant-Colonel. But he left the Army in 1645, finding that he could not enter the "new model" without taking the oath.

Colonel Lilburne obtained a great reputation for courage, and seems to have been a good officer, but was unlucky in his military career. He spent six months in prison at Oxford He was plundered of all that he had at Rupert's relief at Newark. He was shot through the arm at Walton Hall, and received but little pay for his military services

Moreover, he succeeded in quarrelling, first with Colonel King, and then with the Earl of Manchester, both of whom he regarded as lukewarm, incapable and treacherous. He did his best to get Colonel King cashiered, and was one of the authors of the charge of high-treason against him. The dispute with Manchester was due to Lilburne's capturing Tickhill Castle against Manchester's orders, and subsequently Lilburne was one of Cromwell's witnesses against Lord Manchester.

Now we find our "Free-born John" engaged in a quarrel with two of his quondam fellow sufferers. In 1645 he addressed a letter to his old friend, Prynne, attacking the intolerance of the Presbyterians, and claiming freedom of conscience and freedom of speech for the Independents. Prynne, bitterly incensed, procured a vote of the Commons, summoning Lilburne before the Commons for examination, but when he appeared the committee discharged him with a caution. A few months after, Prynne a second time caused Lilburne, to be brought before the committee, this time on a charge of publishing unlicensed pamphlets, but he was again discharged

Then Prynne vented his malice in two pamphlets against Colonel Lilburne: "A fresh discovery of prodigious wandering stars and fire-brands," and "The Liar Confounded," to which the gallant Colonel replied by means of a pamphlet, "Innocency and truth justified "

Meanwhile Lilburne was ineffectually endeavouring to obtain from the House of Commons compensation for his suffering Cromwell supported him. But his chances of obtaining what he wanted were entirely destroyed by a new indiscretion He was overheard relating in conversation some scandalous charges against Speaker Lenthal His old associates, Colonel King and Bastwick, reported the matter to the Commons, and Lilburne was arrested.

When brought before the committee, he refused to answer the questions put to him, unless the cause of his arrest was specified, saying that their proceeding was contrary to Magna Charta and the privileges of a free-born denizen of England. He was sent to prison, from whence he managed to issue pamphlets, giving an account of his examination and arrest, in which he attacked, not only several members by name, but the authority of the House of Commons itself For this offence he was sent to Newgate, and the Recorder of London was ordered to proceed against him at Quarter Sessions

This, however, did not come off, for the charge against the Speaker having been investigated, and found groundless, no further proceedings were taken against John Lilburne, who was released in October

Soon after he petitioned the Commons for arrears of pay, but as he refused to swear to his accounts, he did not succeed His case against the Star Chamber was pleaded before the House of Lords by Bradshaw, and the Upper House transmitted to the Commons an Ordinance, granting him £2,000 in compensation for his sufferings But the ordinance hung fire in the Commons, and in the meantime Prynne and the committee of accounts alleged that Lilburne owed the State £2,000, and Colonel King claimed £2,000 damages for slander.

In this dilemma, John wrote and printed a letter to Judge Reeve, before whom Colonel King's claim was to be tried, explaining his embarrassments, and asserting the justice of his cause Incidentally he was indiscreet enough to reflect upon the Earl of Manchester, observing that if Cromwell had prosecuted his charge properly, Manchester would have lost his head.

For this Lilburne was at once summoned before the House of Lords, Manchester himself occupying the chair Lilburne refused to answer questions, or acknowledge the jurisdiction of the Lords   So he was committed to Newgate, where he continued to defy the authorities. To avoid obedience to their summons he barricaded himself in his cell, refused to kneel, or take off his hat, and stopped his ears when the charge against him was read

The Lords sentenced him to be fined £4,000, to be imprisoned for seven years in the Tower, and to be declared for ever incapable of holding any office, civil or military.

This sentence was followed by the inevitable appeal to the Commons, as the "only lawful judges as a Commoner of England, or free-born Englishman."

The Commons appointed a committee to consider the case, but it presented so many legal and political difficulties that their report was delayed.

Lilburne now appealed to the people by means of an almost interminable series of pamphlets, and in the course of his campaign he found time to attack abuses in the election of city magistrates, to bitterly assail the monarchy, and to quarrel with his gaolers about the exorbitant fees demanded of prisoners in the Tower Finally, he abused the Commons for delaying his release, and again was called before the committee to answer for his scandalous pamphlets.

Despairing of help from the Commons, he now appealed to Cromwell and the Army. The agitators took up his case, and demanded his release as one of the conditions of settlement between the Army and Parliament.

Lilburne was now allowed to argue his case before the Commons, who ordered that he should have liberty to come abroad from day to day to attend the committee and to instruct his counsel, without a keeper.

Before his release, Lilburne offered, if he could obtain a reasonable proportion of justice to leave the kingdom, and not to return as long as the present troubles lasted

But he had suspicions of Cromwell, whom he very soon regarded as a "treacherous and self-seeking intriguer."   The negotiations of the Army leaders with the King, and the suggestions of royal fellow prisoners in the Tower, led him to credit the story that Cromwell had sold himself to the King Even Cromwell's breach with the King in Nov , 1647, which Lilburne attributed solely to the fear of assassination, did not remove his suspicions, and the simultaneous suppression of the "levelling" party in the Army seemed conclusive proof of Cromwell's tyrannical designs.

Soon afterwards we find the gallant Colonel allying himself with the London "Levellers" and the mutinous part of the Army, and raising the cry of "Down with the House of Lords"

It is impossible within the compass of this article to follow the tumultuous career of this remarkable man through the years that followed. His frequent arraignments, imprisonments, intrigues, and endless pamphleteering campaigns provide enough material for a book. It is curious to note that he refused to agree with the trial of Charles I. Though holding that the King deserved death, he thought he should have been tried by a jury, instead of the High Court of Justice.

This restless man continued his political intrigues and activities after the execution of the King, and when Cromwell held supreme power At length he was banished from England for life. But from his place of retirement in Holland he could not refrain from issuing more and more pamphlets.

News of the expulsion of the Rump Parliament in 1653 excited Lilburne's hopes of returning from exile Counting on the placable disposition of Cromwell, he boldly applied to him for a pass to return to England. It was not granted. So John came back without one. He was duly arrested, and sent to Newgate. Then followed his trial at the Old Bailey.

Popular feeling was on his side. Parliament was petitioned on his behalf. Crowds flocked to see him. Threats were made to rescue him. Tickets were circulated with the legend:

"And what, shall then honest John Lilburne die?

Three score thousand shall know the reason
  why."

Cromwell filled London with troops, but the
soldiers shouted and sounded their trumpets
when they heard that Lilburne was acquitted.

He was transferred to the Tower; thence to
Jersy, where he remained for a time. Finally
he was brought back to England, and became a
Quaker, much to the surprise of Cromwell himself, who, when satisfied that friend John really
intended to live quietly at Eltham, granted him
a pension of forty shillings a week. He died in
Eltham village in 1657, and was buried at
Moorfields.

A critic, writing of Colonel Lilburne, says
"His political importance it is easy to explain.
In a revolution, where others argued about the
respective rights of King and Parliament, he
spoke always of the rights of the people. His
dauntless courage and powers of speech made
him the idol of the mob. He was ready to
assail any abuse, at any cost to himself, but
his passionate egotism made him a dangerous
champion, and he continually sacrificed public
causes to personal resentment.

In his controversies he was credulous, careless about the truth of his charges, and in-
satiably vindictive. He attacked in turn all
constituted authority—Lords, Commons,Council
of State, and Council of Officers—and quarrelled
in succession with every ally.

His epitaph, written in 1657, runs thus —
" Is John departed, and is Lilburne gone!
Farewell to Lilburne, and farewell to John;
But lay John here. Lay Lilburne here about.
For if they ever meet they will fall out "

QUEEN HENRIETTA.

CHAPTER LXIV.

ELTHAM LODGE.

In the brief history of Sir John Shaw, which we gave in an earlier chapter, we referred to the building of Eltham Lodge, the fine old mansion which stands in the park, and now used as the headquarters of the Eltham Golf Club.

Sir John Shaw had supplied funds to Charles II. when that prince was obliged to live abroad during the administration of the Commonwealth. After his return, however, and when he was made King of England, he rewarded his benefactor, Sir John Shaw, by granting him the lease of the Manor of Eltham on easy terms.

In the interesting little book on " Eltham Golf Club House," written by the Rev. T. N. Rowsell, a former Vicar of Holy Trinity Church, and published 14 years ago, but now out of print, we get a description of this lease, which runs as follows : —

"I have before me as I write," says Mr. Rowsell, " in excellent preservation, the original lease of the Manor of Eltham, granted by the trustees of the Queen (Queen Henrietta, the mother of Charles II.), to Sir John Shaw and another. It is splendidly emblazoned in black and gold, with the portrait of her Majesty, her own signature in her own hand-writing, with her full titles, ' by the Grace of God, Queen of England, Scotland, France, and Ireland, Henrietta Marie.' Also the signatures of the Earl of St. Alban's, Lord Chamberlain; Sir Kenelm Digby, Chancellor; Sir Peter Balle, Attorney-General; and others of celebrity. It assigns the Manor and sets out the boundaries distinctly, from Southend, Eltham, to Horne Park, Lee, embracing the old ' ruinated' Palace (Eltham Court), and all rights of fishing, hawking, hunting, &c., for the sum of £9 per annum, with 20s. additional for the old house It is true," continues Mr. Rowsell, "that a fine of £3,700 was appended to this, but even so, at the then rate of money, the payment demanded was nothing like equivalent to the value. In reading 'between the lines' we may see how it helped to clear off some of the score between Charles and his friend."

Having obtained possession of the Manor on a long lease, Sir John Shaw proceeded to the building of the present house, about the year 1663 We may fix this date pretty accurately from an entry in the diary of John Evelyn. On July 14th, 1664, the famous diarist wrote thus —

" I went to take leave of the two Mister Howards, now going for Paris, and brought them to Bromley, thence to Eltham to see Sir John Shaw's new house now building The place is pleasant, if not too wett, but the house is not well contrived, especially the roofe, and rooms, too low pitched, and the kitchen where the cellars should be, the orangerie and aviarie handsome, and a very large plantation about it."

Notwithstanding this somewhat depressing description by Evelyn, there was no doubt that as mansions went in those days, Sir John Shaw's new dwelling was regarded as an imposing structure, and worthy of the loyal knight who took up his residence there

Extending from the house towards Chislehurst was a long avenue, which was known as the Chase This avenue was probably in existence at the time, for it was said that centuries before, King John of France, when in voluntary exile here, used it as an exercising ground

To quote again from the charming little book alluded to we get a vivid glimpse of the times of Sir John Shaw In reference to the sport Mr Rowsell says, "One of the ponds bears the name of the "Pike Pond," though no one of the present generation has ever seen the ghost of a pike on it. The small stream by Mottingham is said to have been full of trout; and there were heronries within easy reach, which would, doubtless, supply plenty

of quarry for the hawks or falcons London —not the huge, smoky, bustling nation which we now call by that name, but the London of Evelyn and Pepys, the London of the Restoration, fair without but foul within, with its glittering veneer of wit, beauty, and gaiety concealing its corruption—was only nine miles away, a right royal 'pleasaunce' must this have been, a charming resort for the jaded courtier, or the faded Court beauty, or for those rarer souls of finer and nobler mould who loathed the filthiness of the age, and would fain get away, at least for a time, into a purer atmosphere Some such friends one would hope, Sir John Shaw must have had, for he was a staid merchant, and held much aloof from the Court "

The environment of the Lodge has greatly changed since the days of Sir John Shaw It is a long step from conditions such as those described in the last paragraph to those associated with the business of a Golf Club House But the old building possesses many distinguishing features which recall the days of two centuries ago, and contains objects of considerable antiquarian interest

The Rev T. N Rowsell deals with many of these matters in his characteristic way, and as his book is now out of print we cannot do better than read what he has to say about them.

An old picture was found in one of the upper rooms which would seem to have been a rather crudely drawn representation of the house as it originally appeared "As a work of art it leaves much to be desired, but, while we marvel at the curious notion of perspective, and admire the simpering ladies and gentlemen, who disport themselves on the canvas, we can scarcely help trying to conjure up a vision of the conditions of life in which the scene was laid "

In comparing this picture with the house as it now presents itself, many changes are apparent Such changes mark the progress of time.

"There are persons still living who recollect the roof being entirely stripped and renovated, in place of the old red tiles and dormer windows, the present clumsey top of slates was substituted, and the chimneys were 'improved' with the present heavy stacks. The two old turrets which are shewn in the picture are gone, if they ever existed, and no trace remains. But the old walls, some 3ft. thick, and the old foundations, strong as adamant, and the bold proportions of the solid Dutch style remain unchanged, defying time and elements, and giving us a house 'four-square to all the winds that blow.'"

was brought to perfection a little later by Grinling Gibbons. And the beams which run athwart the ceilings of the lofty rooms—who ever saw the like! They are enough to make the hair of a 'jerry-builder' turn grey with envy. 'Hearts of oak were our ships, hearts of oak were our men,' and a good deal of the same material went to the making up of our houses, it appears, in the old days."

Mr. Rowsell, who was a frequent visitor at the house during the lifetime of the aged Mrs.

LANDING OF CHARLES II. AT DOVER (Painting by West).

In the room which is now devoted to billiards it will be noticed that the 'oak-leaf,' a symbol so intimately associated with King Charles, is represented in the mouldings, while over the huge fire place "the name of the first owner is carved solidly into the upper cornice of the woodwork."

Our attention is specially directed to the "lordly old staircase." "What a sense of space!" Mr. Rowsell writes enthusiastically. "What a command of timber! What massive balustrades! The carving is not elaborate, but it is fine and bold, of that style which

Wood, the last tenant, prior to its occupancy by the Golf Club, and had ample opportunities of studying the building closely, has much to say about the old tapestry which hangs upon the walls of the billiard room.

There is a supposition that these tapestries were brought from the old Palace after the Parliamentary Survey of 1649. Mr. Rowsell strongly combats this idea, and as his comments are so interesting, and the theories he advances as to their actual origin are so probable, we may be forgiven, perhaps, in quoting his views at length.

No. 142.

ANNE, daughter of Sir Joseph Ashe, Knt. First wife of
Sir John Shaw, Bart.

(From the Family Portrait by Sir Peter Lely. By special permission of
Rev. Sir Charles Shaw, Bart., for this book only).

No. 143.

BRIDGET, daughter of Sir William Drury, and relict of Charles,
Viscount Kilmorey. Second wife of Sir John Shaw, Bart.

(From the Family Portrait by Sir Peter Lely. By special permission of
Rev. Sir Charles Shaw, Bart., for this book only).

No. 145.

BISHOP HORNE.

Buried in Eltham Churchyard.

(See text).

No. 144.

JOHN EVELYN (The Diarist),

Frequent Visitor at Eltham.

(See text).

"The most interesting feature of the Lodge by far is the collection of tapestries which surround the walls of the billiard-room. I find, by the way, in the second lease after the original one, which is still in the possession of the Office of Crown Lands, that this room was even then called the 'billiard-room,' and it is curious that it should have reverted after the lapse of so many years to its original purpose. This room was the only sitting-room of the aged Mrs. Wood during all the closing years of her life, and she loved to call attention to those tapestries round the walls, long, long after she herself had ceased to be able to see them.

When she came with her husband to inspect the house for the first time those walls, she said, were covered with a common pattern of wall-paper. While they were discussing the question of a new and better paper to replace this, the accidental discovery by one of the party of a small hole in the surface led to the stripping of the walls and the disclosure of those fine old tapestries buried beneath. Similar tapestries, it is said, adorned several other of the rooms. I am told by old inhabitants that they recollect seeing in their youth large pieces of similar tapestries used in place of carpet upon the floors of cottages in the neighbourhood, which had been brought there after a sale in the old house.

"Tradition says that these were a gift from Charles II. to Sir John Shaw, at the time of the building of the house, and that he had brought them from his wanderings, and that they were in some way traceable to Spain. There is nothing improbable in this story.

'They are certainly not, what some have supposed, a part of the furniture of the old palace transferred hither, for, in the first place, they are not of sufficient antiquity to be a part of the ancient 'Arras'; and in the next place the Parliamentary Survey of 1649 speaks of the palace being 'out of repair and untenantable,' and makes no mention of any furniture. (Hasted's Kent, p. 182.)

"On the other hand, the work is just of such a kind as was turned out by the looms of the Low Countries, and may well have owned its origin to the teaching of the Spaniards, and been inspired by Spanish motives. As to the story which they are evidently designed to portray, it has always been a puzzle to the curious."

Then follows an interpretation of the pictures, which the writer asks us to accept "for what it is worth."

"There is obviously one common feature running through the series of pictures, and linking them together into consecutive story; and this feature is a piece of fruit, something like an apple. Is it the 'Apple of Discord?' or is it a 'Love apple?' or is it not, I venture to fancy, a 'Pomegranate?' Now the meaning of 'Granada' is pomegranate, and Spain is the land of the pomegranate, and the pomegranate was, and is, the emblem of Granada; and the struggle with the Moors for the possession of Granada was the most memorable thing in Spanish history, and the King and Queen of the time, Ferdinand and Isabella, were the most conspicuous figures in the annals of the country; and everyone knows the close connection between Spain and the Low Countries, and the way in which the Spanish occupation impressed itself upon the arts of the Netherlands.

"Imagine, then, a commission being given to the Flemish looms to weave some tapestries for Henrietta Maria, Queen, or for her son, Charles II. What subject would they be so likely to choose as the history of Granada? And is there not enough in those pictures to recall that history!

"There we seem to have a King (may it not be Ferdinand?) choosing for himself a Queen, Isabella of Castile, and offering her the emblem of the State. Another panel gives the prophetic utterance of a beggar to the King, such as is so common in all old histories. Another panel is the great battle-piece representing the last struggle with the Moors. Another, the safe return in triumph, with the fruits of success. Further, we come to the more peaceful triumphs of the reign—the studious Isabella, with globe and books around her, holding an interview with Columbus, the King and Queen upon their throne granting him his first commission for the discovery of America, and so on. This, at least, appears to me a reasonable interpretation, and we must remember that these tapestries are but fragments, and that if we had the whole before us we might be able to follow out the thread with more conclusive results."

The house ceased to be associated with the Shaw family in 1839 when the lease expired. Mr. Benjamin Wood, the husband of the lady already referred to, came to reside at the Lodge in 1838. The tenants before him were Lord Rivers, Lady Crewe, and Lord Wynford.

CHAPTER LXV.

SHERARD HOUSE.

One of the most interesting of the private residences of Eltham is Sherard House, the quaint Jacobean dwelling next to the Congregational Church, in the High-street. The front of the house has been changed considerably, but the elevation towards the garden is, apparently, as it was built in the year 1634. It is now covered with ivy, and, with the spacious garden, suggests the associations which made it known so well amongst the students of botany close on two centuries ago. There are many quaint and interesting features within doors, notably the handsome mantel-pieces of carved oak, which date back to the time when the house was built. The old oak panelling which surrounded the library is now covered with paper, and the quaint, open fire-place, where the logs once burned across the dog-irons to warm the feet of James Sherard, is now substituted by a modern grate.

But the library contains a priceless work, in the two great volumes, " Hortus Elthamensis," which represent the labours of Sherard in the field of botany, and are a lasting memorial to his long and earnest study. These massive books were published in the year 1732, are printed in Latin, beautifully and copiously illustrated, and strongly bound in leather. They are very rare, and though out of date, so far as botany is concerned, they are regarded with reverence by students of that fascinating science, for at the time of their production they were the greatest works on plant life that had been produced by English botanists.

There is consistency, too, in their being preserved in this room by Mrs Dobell, the present occupier of the house, for in all probability it

was within those four walls, overlooking the beautiful garden, which in his day had attained a world-wide fame, that James Sherard wrote them. And we may easily imagine that earnest student, along with his friend, Dilennius, a botanist of European fame, engaged here upon their work of research and record.

By the kindness of Mrs Dobell, we are able to give some particulars of the early occupiers of this interesting house. The date of its erection—1634—is fixed by the engraving upon the water-pipe, high up upon the wing at the east end, facing the street.

In 1699 it seems to have been occupied by a Mr Uvedal, who kept a school here, and is said to have been interested in botany.

Dr James Sherard bought the house, and came to reside here in 1718-19. Dr William Sherard, a distinguished brother of James, died here in 1728, and is said to have been buried at Eltham. It was he who founded the Botanical Gardens at Oxford.

The Rev. Peter Pinnell, who was Vicar of Eltham from 1749 to 1783, and was the immediate predecessor of the Rev Shaw Brooke, resided here, and also kept a school.

The Dorrington family occupied the house for a long time, and Mr Edgeworth also dwelt there in the first half of last century. He was a relative of the famous writer, Maria Edgeworth, whose books were so highly prized by our grandmothers when they were girls.

The next occupant was Mr. Jeffreys. He was followed, in 1857, by Mr. Henry William Dobell, and Mrs. Dobell, his widow, is still residing there.

THE SHERARDS

Now that botany is becoming so universal a study, our young Eltham students will no doubt like to have a more comprehensive account of these two distinguished Eltham scholars, William and James Sherard So we will give them their history, as it is recounted in the "Gentleman's Magazine" for 1796.

"William Sherard, LL.D, and Fellow of All Souls' College, Oxford This learned naturalist, born at Busby, in Leicestershire, in 1659, was better known by the name of Consul Sherard, in which capacity he resided from 1701 to 1715 at Smyrna, where he had a country house at a place called Sedekia It is not yet forgotten as the residence of Sherard In 1749 Hasselquist visited this retreat, and viewed with all the enthusiasm of a young botanist the spot where the "Regent of the Botanical World," as he styles him, spent his summers, and cultivated his garden

Here Sherard collected specimens of all the plants of Natolia and Greece, and began that famous Herbarium which at length became the most extensive that had ever been seen as the work of one man, since it is said finally to have contained 12,000 species And here he is said to have begun the much celebrated Pinax, to which he continued to make additions throughout his life.

He returned into England in 1718, soon after which time he had the degree of Doctor of Laws conferred upon him by the University of Oxford.

On his returning from a tour on the Continent, in 1721, he brought over with him the celebrated Dillenius, with whom he had before corresponded, and whom he had encouraged to prosecute his inquiries into the cryptogamia class and in publishing his Plantæ Grssenees

Sherard had himself been among the earliest in England to promote attention to this hitherto neglected part of Nature, and in this Dillenius had already excelled all who had written before him Although Dr Sherard had acquired a considerable fortune in Asia, yet he lived in the greatest privacy in London, wholly immersed in the study of Natural History, except when he went to his brother's seat at Eltham.

Dr. Dillenius assisted him in his chief employment, the carrying on his Pinax, or collection of all the names which had been given by botanical writers to each plant Dr Sherard was in a particular manner the patron of Mr. Mark Catesby, and himself affixed the Latin names to the plants of "The Natural History of Carolina" He died August 12th, 1728, at Eltham, and by his will gave £3,000 to provide a salary for a Professor of Botany at Oxford, on condition that Dr. Dillenius should be chosen the first professor He erected the edifice at the entrance to the garden for the use of the professor, and gave to this establishment his Botanical Library, his Herbarium and Pinax

Dr Sherard was among the last of those ornaments in England of that era which Linnæus calls the "golden age of botany" Having from his earliest years a relish for the study of natural history, and in his youth acquired a knowledge of English botany, his repeated tours to the Continent, and his long residence in the East afforded ample scope for his improvement, and the acquisition of affluence, joined to his learning and agreeable qualities, rendered him, after his return home, a liberal and zealous patron of the science and of those who cultivated it. Some manuscripts of Dr Sherard's were presented to the Royal Society by Mr Ellis in the year 1766 "

James Sherard, M D, brother of William Sherard, was apprenticed in 1682 to Charles Watts, an apothecary, who was curator of the Botanical Gardens at Chelsea. Under the guidance of Watts, he devoted himself to botany, but at the same time he worked hard as an apothecary, and by many years' practice in Mark-lane, London, accumulated an ample fortune.

He purchased estates in Lancashire, and came to reside at Eltham in 1718-19, when he bought the house now known as Sherard House It is interesting to note that about this time

Thomas Doggett, the actor, of whom we have already written ,was living at Eltham.

Here James Sherard put into practice his knowledge of botany by laying out a garden, where he pursued the cultivation of rare and valuable plants, until the garden became noted as one of the finest in England It was the catalogue of the plants grown here which was the subject of the two noted books, "Hortus Elthamensis," we have already alluded to

He was a singularly versatile man In addition to his accomplishment as a botanist, he was also an accomplished amateur musician and violinist He is said to have composed "twenty-four sonatas and twelve pieces for the violin, violoncello, and bass, extended for the harpsichord."

The University of Oxford conferred upon him the honorary degree of Doctor of Medicine, and the College of Physicians admitted him to their Fellowship without examination, and without the payment of fees. It is recorded that the University expected a legacy from him, but were disappointed by his dying on February 12th, 1738, without his having left them anything by his will His age at death was 72 years.

He was buried at Evington, in Leicestershire

In *Notes to Illustrations of Literary Anecdotes*, by J. Nicholls—an old book—there are printed a number of letters from William Sherard to Dr Richardson, in which are frequent references to Eltham We will transcribe a few of these :—

"London, July 28th, 1719 . . . My brother's business will not permit him to stay long out of town, so that I am obliged to stay most of my time at Eltham to look after the workmen.'

The following may interest local botanists —
"London, January 20th, 1719-20 —Dear sir,— Though I have often remembered you and drank your good health in an evening after feasting on your kind present, yet I have not had so much time by daylight as to consider and compare your curious collection of mosses as I could wish, having been most of my time

at Eltham I go thither again next week, with my brother, and design one day each week to make an excursion to look after mosses, but cannot expect much success If I meet with anything new you shall have it. There are more of the Polytrichoides kind than I at first imagined, but they rarely bear heads, and without seeing them in that state I cannot distinguish whether they be musci or lichens "

"London, May 10th, 1720 —My brother gives you his service He is busy building his greenhouse and two stoves, one at each end, and has laid out another "

(A building supposed to have been one of Sherard's greenhouses still exists at the lower end of the garden)

"London, March 28th, 1721,—My brother is busy at Eltham, building another stove to answer that at the east end of the greenhouse . . Mr. Rand is now with my brother at Eltham, and rides to town as oft as he pleases, and returns thither at night "

"London, September 7th, 1721 —It is a fortnight this day that my brother and I returned from our excursion to Paris, by way of Holland . . . I have brought over with me Dr Dillenius, who has with him most, if not all, of his fungi painted, and all his lichens and mosses neatly designed . . My brother is at Eltham, busy in looking after his new acquisitions and building new stoves."

"May 12th, 1722 . . . The Doctor (Dillenius) has found some new mosses about Eltham, but he has not had time to rove far . My brother has taken Dr Dillenius this afternoon to spend the holidays "

"November 17th, 1722 Dr. Dillenius gives you his humble service, we are not idle, though now and then I am forced to spare him to paint the aloes and other plants that are not yet figured, which flower at Eltham, and sometimes a day to look after fungi and mosses "

(How much these old letters help us to picture life in Eltham in those remote days! The next shews us Sherard at work The building referred to is probably the one now in exist-ence at the lower end of the garden.)

"London, February 23rd, 1722-3. . . . . . My brother seldom comes to town; of late, indeed, he could not well, his gardener having been in Holland, and returned last week, and now the season of sowing prevents him.   He has built a very convenient house to the south of the large mulberry tree, divided into two rooms, one for raising seed on hot beds, the other for keeping plants in Tanners' bark . . . ."

thoughts of seeing you and Madame Richardson another year."

"Eltham, May 3rd, 1725. . . . . . . I thank you for your invitation . . . . but my old gar-dener having left things in the utmost disorder, and my new one not understanding much of my garden, this pins me down, and obliges me not to stir from home this summer. . . . . ."

"Eltham, August 20th, 1728. . . . . I presume the public papers may have given you an account of my poor brother's death.   We

GATEWAY TO BOTANNICAL GARDENS, OXFORD.

There are many other letters, full of interest in the Eltham Garden, till at last comes the following:—

"London, February 20th, 1724-5. . . . . . My brother's gardener has left him in a huff (which he will have reason to repent), and he has sent to Holland for another . . . ."

We will conclude this chapter with some ex-tracts from letters written by Dr. James Sherard to Dr. Richardson, full of interest as they are to Eltham readers.

"September 10th, 1720. . . . . You are so good as to excuse the poor entertainment you found at Eltham, but I pleas myself with the

buried him last Monday at Eltham; he desired to lie where I thought to be buried my-self. . . . ." (Then follows an account of his brother's bequest to establish a botany pro-fessorship at Oxford, already alluded to.)

In a subsequent letter, after alluding to the legal proceedings on account of his brother's bequest, he says:—

". . . . . . . I had determined to give my garden to Oxford, in case the University would build proper conveniences to keep and preserve them; but if we find that their design is to get the professorship, and neglect the garden, they shall not have one plant, nor the value of one halfpenny from me. . . . . , . . ."

"Eltham, December 5th, 1732. . . . . . Dr. Dillenius has now finished his "Hortus Elthamensis," and I would take the liberty of making you a present of one copy, if I knew how to convey it to you. It is a large book, weighs 16 or 18 pounds."

It would seem that Dillenius was responsible for the beautiful drawings in "Hortus Elthamensis." The literary work was by James Sherard himself.

There is still another letter, November 9th, 1739, giving considerable details of the conveyance of the Eltham plants to Oxford, and other matters of interest, but lack of space prevents our giving more The concluding words are:—

"I hope next year to see things entirely settled, and the garden pretty well furnished, though I cannot possibly send all my plants in less than two or three years Dr. Dillenius went with me to Oxford. I expect he will settle there next spring . . . . . . James Sherard."

CHAPTER LXVI.

TWO NOTED ELTHAM FAMILIES.

THE CÆSAR FAMILY

In the Public Library, Eltham, there hangs a portrait of " Charles Cæsar, Esq , the last Surviving Male Descendant of his very numerous and eminent Family, Born at Eltham in Kent, June 30th, 1697, Died January 19th, 1780, Buried at St Mary le bon "

The portrait has excited a good deal of interest, and many inquiries have been made as to the identity of this interesting gentleman

Charles Cæsar was one of a family of ten Cæsars, most of whom were born at Eltham in the latter part of the seventeenth century Their father was another Charles Cæsar, who was a rather noted politician of his day, being M P for the town of Hertford in 1700, and filling the office of Treasurer of the Navy

The family of Cæsar was of Italian origin, and its ancestors, under the name of Adelmare, were nobility residing near Venice. Cæsar Adelmare, a member of this family, having been educated for the medical profession, in which he had taken his degree of Doctor, in the University of Padua, came to England in the year 1550. Italy had at that time a great name for producing eminent men of that science, and he added to the stock of its general fame. Having practised largely for some time in London, he was appointed a physician to Queen Mary, and in the following reign was at the head of the medical department at the Court Many favours were heaped upon him, and he became very rich. He was the progenitor of the Cæsar family in this country.

His son Julius Cæsar Adelmare dropped the final name, and being knighted, was known as Sir Julius Cæsar. He was born at Tottenham in 1557 He was made Master of the Rolls, and was a very distinguished judge. He was buried in the Chancel of Great St Helen's, Bishopsgate-street, London.

Another member of the family was Sir Thomas Cæsar, who became a baron of the Exchequer Henry Cæsar was Dean of Ely, and buried in Ely Cathedral in 1636

Sir Charles Cæsar, son and heir of Sir Julius, was also Master of the Rolls. (Born 1589, died 1642) Buried at Bennington in Hertfordshire

Eventually, the elder branch of the family died out, and the title seems to have gone with it The Eltham Cæsars belonged to a younger branch

Mr Charles Cæsar, father of the gentleman whose features are familiar to those who frequent the Eltham Public Library, was M P for Hertford, 1700, and also Treasurer of the Navy He resided in Eltham a good number of years, where most of his children were born

His conduct in the House of Commons was bold, if not intemperate, and became, at least on one occasion, the object of a heavy punishment On the nineteenth of December, 1705, to use the exact words of the Journals of the House, the question being put, that the ingrossed Bill from the Lords, intitled an 'Act for the better security of her Majesty's person and government, and of the succession to the Crown of England in the Protestant line,' be now read the second time, the House divided," and the Bill was carried in the affirmative, Mr. Cæsar being one of the Tellers for the Noes

" The Bill, therefore," continue the journals,

" was read a second time and Charles Cæsar, Esq , upon the debate of the said bill, standing up in his place, saying the words following, which were directed by the House to be set down in writing at the table, viz , ' There is a noble Lord, without whose advice the Queen does nothing, who in the late reign was known to keep up a constant correspondence with the Court at St. German's.' And the said Mr Cæsar endeavouring to excuse himself, and being directed to withdraw, and he being withdrawn accordingly,

Resolved, that the said words are highly dishonourable to her Majesty's person and government,

Resolved, that the said Charles Cæsar, Esq , be, for the said offence, committed prisoner to the Tower

Ordered, that Mr. Speaker do issue his warrant to the Sergeant at Arms attending this House, to take into his custody the body of the said Charles Cæsar, Esq , and him to deliver into the hands of the Lieutenant of her Majesty's Tower of London, to be there kept in safe custody during the pleasure of this House, and also to the Lieutenant of the Tower to receive and keep him accordingly "

The nobleman reflected on is elsewhere stated to have been the Lord Treasurer Godolphin, and the truth of the charge on him, and the other leaders of the Whigs in that reign, was subsequently pretty fully established

As Mr Cæsar's liberation is not recorded in the journals, it may certainly be presumed that he remained a prisoner till the conclusion of the session, which was not till the nineteenth of March This set him at liberty. On the first day of the next session, we find him on the Committee for framing the address to the Queen's speech. His party, however, after a long struggle, prevailed, and, on the downfall of the Whig administration in the autumn of 1710, he was appointed to the office of Treasurer of the Navy, in succession to Robert Walpole.

Dean Swift seems to have been a friend of the Cæsars, and to have honoured the family with the " unreserved freedom of a perfect intimacy." Among his works may be found two letters from him to Mrs Cæsar, wife of the gentleman of whom we have been writing, a lady, says the editor of Swift's Works, " remarkable for her good sense, friendship, and politeness, and much esteemed by the nobility and gentry, and all people of taste, genius, and learning "

With the death of Queen Anne, Mr Cæsar's party went out of power, and all hope of further ministerial advancement was lost. It is sad to find that this able and distinguished man, now took to gaming In the end he gambled away the greater part of his estates, and left his family almost destitute

Harris Cæsar, his eldest son, was born at Eltham, September 30th, 1691 Foreseeing the almost total alienation of his inheritance he entered holy orders He obtained the Rectory of Kensington. On the very day of his induction to the living he caught a cold, while officiating at a funeral This was followed by a rapid fever, of which he died, unmarried, in the prime of life

Charles James Cæsar, the second son, whose portrait hangs in the Public Library, was also born at Eltham, on the 30th June, 1697 He is said to have borne a remarkable resemblance, both in person and features, to the supposed son of King James the Second

On one occasion when that unfortunate person was suspected to have been in England, Mr. Cæsar was so far mistaken for him as to have been apprehended, and for a while detained in custody.

He followed no profession, but lived on a small part of the wreck of the fortune of which he became possessed by the death of his eldest brother In the latter part of his life he was deprived of a great part even of that pittance by an intimate, for whose payment of a sum of money he had become a security He died in 1780, and was buried at " St Mary le bon."

Henry and *Julius*, other brothers were born at Eltham, but died minors

THE PHILIPOTS.

The name of Philipot has been preserved in Eltham in connection with the almshouses in the High-street, which were established by the will of the younger of that name Although the elder Philipot was not an Eltham man by birth he was closely associated with the parish, and his wife and eldest daughter were buried in Eltham Church   Moreover, he was a distinguished Kentish gentleman, and we will therefore, give a few notes about him, as well as of his son Thomas, to whom the parish is indebted for the Philipot Charity.

John Philipot was born in 1589, and died in 1645   His parents were Henry Philpot, and his wife was daughter of David Leigh, servant to the Archbishop of Canterbury   His place of birth was Folkestone, where his father possessed considerable property, and had filled the office of Mayor of the borough   The father's name was " Philpot," but the son changed it to " Philipot "

John Philipot married Susan Glover, one of the gentlemen ushers' daily waiters at the Court of James 1.   Robert Glover uncle to Mistress Philipot was Somerset Herald, and probably it was he who introduced John to the College of Arms

John Philipot was " appointed a pursuivant-of arms extraordinary, with the title of Blanch Lion, in October, 1618, and in the following November he was created Rouge Dragon pursuivant-in-ordinary "

It was while occupying this office that he was brought into familiar contact with William Camden, the distinguished antiquary topographer, and herald   Camden frequently nominated Philipot as his deputy in his visitations   In July, 1623, the King appointed him bailiff of Sandwich, and he also held   the position of lieutenant or chief gunner at Tilbury Fort, with the fee of one shilling per day

On another occasion, in 1633, we find that he was sent abroad to confer the Order of Knighthood upon William Bosville, records of which visit may be found in the Harleian MS, 3,917, at the British Museum.

In 1635 he was again sent on a foreign mission, this time to invest Charles Ludovic, Count Palatine of the Rhine and Duke of Bavaria, with the Order of the Garter.

When the Civil War broke out Philipot arrayed himself on the side of

the King   He was present at the seige of Gloucester, and was the bearer of the summons of the King comanding the citizens to surrender. Subsequently, he was taken prisoner by some of the Parliamentary soldiers, in the vicinity of Abingdon, and was sent to London as a prisoner, in, or about, 1644   But he was soon set at liberty   He died a few years after, in London, where he had been living in great obscurity, and was buried within the precincts of the Church of St Benet, St Paul's Wharf   His wife survived him about twenty years.   She was buried in Eltham Church in 1664, where her eldest daughter, Susan, was also interred

John Philipot's principal literary work is, "Villare Cantianum, or Kent surveyed and illustrated   Being an exact description of all the Parishes, Burroughs, Villages, and other respective Mannors included in the County of Kent "   This work was published by and under the name of Thomas Philipot, the author's son, "who thus endeavoured dishonestly, to pass it off as his own work "   Many other works of his were published, mostly of an historical or topographical character, and some manuscripts are still preserved

Thomas Philipot, of Eltham fame, was the son of the former   There seems some doubt as to the exact date of his birth, but we find him as a " fellow-commoner " at Cambridge in 1632-1633, where he graduated as M A in 1635   Wood says of him, " he was, by those who well knew him, esteemed a tolerable poet   when young, and at riper years well versed in matters of divinity, history, and antiquities "   He was buried at Greenwich on September 30th, 1682

" By his will, dated 11th September, 1680, after devising certain premises at Clare Hall, Cambridge, for establishing two Kentish Scholarships, he left his houses in the town of Eltham, and a field, sold in 1866 to the Commissioners of woods and forests for £630, to the Clothworkers Company, to establish six almshouses for four people from Eltham and two from Chislehurst. allowing them £5 each a year

Thomas Philipot has left behind him much literary work of a historical and philosophical character, but the publication, as his own, of " Villare Cantianum," which was the work of his father, brought down much severe criticism upon his head.

PIKEMAN 1635 (Goodrich Court).

INFANTRY ARMOUR 1625.

CHAPTER LXVII.

AN ELTHAM VICAR.

Although nearly seventy years have passed since the Rev J K. Shaw Brooke was laid to rest in the great Shaw vault under Eltham Church, his name is still a household word in the village, for he was a man greatly revered, of strong character, and, holding the office of Vicar for the long period of fifty-seven years, he has left a mark upon parochial history more indelible, perhaps, than that of any preceding Vicar

Of memorials of this village divine, who was so affectionately regarded by all his parishioners, there are several of a material character in existence In the sacristy of the Parish Church there hangs an oil painting of the venorable Vicar, from the brush of Mr J Hayes, which has been described as "an admirable and faithful likeness" Engravings from this picture may be seen in many of the homes of Eltham There is one also in the Public Library His name is also perpetuated by an endowment which he left to the National Schools, while "Jubilee Cottages," the quaint wooden dwellings at the rear of the National Schools, were so named by their owners to commemorate the jubilee of the Rev. J. K Shaw-Brooke, the great parochial event of the year 1833

So impressive were the demonstrations which took place upon this memorable occasion that the children and grandchildren of those who witnessed them find them, to this day, a congenial theme for conversational purposes.

At the back of a small framed engraving, kindly lent to us by Mr. Whitaker Smith, shewing the old Vicarage Field, where this village festival took place, we chanced to find an original ticket to the celebrations Apparently, it had been there for nearly three-quarters of a century We have taken the liberty to copy the words printed upon this ticket, for, to the old people of Eltham they will recall the pleasant memories of a notable occasion, while those who are new residents will get, through them, a glimpse of village life seventy-five years ago.

On one side is printed —

"1833 Eltham Jubilee, in commemoration of the 50th year the Rev J K Shaw Brooke has resided within the parish as Vicar, universally beloved and respected "

On the other side we get.—

"Peter Wakeman You are invited to partake on Thursday, the 5th of September, of a dinner provided by public subscription in token of the respect and regard entertained for the Vicar of this Parish Eltham, 1833

N B —You are requested to wear this card with the other side in front, in a conspicuous manner, to attend on the day named at half-past one o'clock in the Court Yard, and to bring with you a knife and fork "

There can be no doubt that Mr. Wakeman carried out the instructions literally, for around the card are the needle marks to shew that it had been carefully sewn upon some conspicuous part of his attire

Yet another memorial to this highly esteemed and good man lies before us as we write It is a booklet of twenty-two pages, written in the year 1841, by one who worked with him for many years and knew his worth As this little publication, long since out of print, is the record of so interesting a chapter in Eltham history, we will reproduce its title page, and cull largely from its contents—

AN HUMBLE TRIBUTE

OF

REGARD AND RESPECT

TO THE MEMORY

OF THE

REV. J. K. SHAW BROOKE, M.A.,

LATE VICAR OF ELTHAM, KENT

"Cui Pudor, et Justitiæ soror incorrupta Fides,
NadaqueVeritas, quando ullum inveniet parem."

Hor. b. 1 o 24

BY

THE REV. W. T. MYERS, M.A.

CURATE OF ELTHAM

DEDICATED TO THE PARISHIONERS, IN GRATEFUL
ACKNOWLEDGMENT OF THEIR AFFECTIONATE KINDNESS

TO HIM

LONDON

ROAKE AND VARTY, 31, STRAND

1841.

Died, December 16, 1840, at his residence, Eltham, Kent, the Reverend John Kenward Shaw Brooke, M.A., formerly Fellow of All-Souls College, Oxford, Vicar of Eltham, and Rector of Hurst-Pierpoint, in the County of Sussex

"There are certain individuals who, by common consent, are deemed worthy of particular distinction, which renders a more than common notice of them, in the page of Obituary Record, a less invidious duty than otherwise it would be We have, we believe, perfect liberty so to distinguish the venerable and revered Vicar of Eltham, whose decease, much as it will be lamented by all that knew him, we, however, cannot strictly regard as a deplorable event.

"To have attained the far-advanced age of eighty-two, in the enjoyment of almost uninterrupted health, to have been permitted to exercise the ministerial office in one parish for the uncommon period of fifty-seven years, with little or no intermission, till within a few days of his death, and with a power of voice and vigour of mind not exceeded by many of his younger brethren; and, finally, to have sunk into the grave, full of faith, and full of years, like a shock of corn ripe for the harvest, and

free, for the most part, from the sufferings of mortality,—these distinguished marks of favour and mercy, in the dealings of a kind Providence with His faithful and aged servant, can only be viewed by his surviving brethren, whether relations or friends, as a cause of thankfulness and praise, and not of lamentation and mourning It better accords with our sense of duty to relate some of the particulars of so long and favoured a life, and of the sphere of usefulness in which it was spent

"The Reverend John Kenward Shaw Brooke was born in London on the 22nd of December, 1758, but passed the earlier years of his life at Eltham Lodge, the seat of his father, Sir John Shaw, Baronet. He was educated at the public school of Harrow, under that distinguished scholar, Dr Sumner, the headmaster From Harrow, in due time, he migrated to the University of Oxford, and on the 25th July, 1774, was entered a Gentleman Commoner at Trinity College He proceeded, in the regular course, to the degree of B A , April 29th, 1778, and to that of M A., June 14th, 1782 In the year 1783, he was elected a Fellow of All Souls' College, and although few, if any, of his contemporaries survive to bear record, we have abundant sources whence we derive our knowledge of the high esteem in which he was held, for his amiable manners, and strict conformity to the moral and religious discipline of the university

"In this year, also, he entered into Holy Orders, and upon the death of Dr Pinnell, succeeded to the Vicarage of Eltham, and at a later period, was presented to the Rectory of Hurst-Pierpoint, in Sussex, where respect and esteem ever awaited him, and where, although his residence was limited to a few weeks annually, he lost no opportunity of promoting the well-being of his parishioners, by his sanction and liberal support of every means of advancing their temporal and spiritual interests, proposed to him by his greatly esteemed friend and curate, now the Rector of Edburton

"In 1796, by the decease of Mrs Brooke, he succeeded to the property of the late Joseph Brooke, Esq., of West Malling, in Kent, and took his name.

"Upon this accession of property he resigned his Fellowship at All Souls, and took up his constant residence at Eltham This was the vineyard in which he exercised his ministerial labours during the extended period before mentioned And how faithfully and diligently he discharged the various public and private duties of his large parish those alone can duly estimate who have experienced the benefit of his preaching and been witnesses to the practical good which has resulted from his personal intercourse with every class of his beloved parishioners

"Who could hear him read the inspiring services of our National Church, without being deeply impressed by the devout and solemn manner of one evidently so fully impressed himself? Most admirable was his correct and dignified style of reading the Scripture-Lessons and especially those of the prophetical books of the Old Testament, when his voice assumed a variation of tone and power according most happily with the varied character of that portion of Holy Writ Nor will they soon forget, when he ascended the pulpit with what simplicity, and yet with what energy, he preached the saving truths of the Gospel, with what animation, and often eloquence, he appealed to, and pleaded, with his people—' Be ye reconciled to God'—as an ambassador of Christ. In voice, how clear and distinct! In manner, how unaffected, and calm, and temperate! 'In doctrine, shewing uncorruptness, gravity, sincerity' It is as remarkable as it is true, that as this venerable divine advanced in years, his energy was observed to increase, rather than abate and the very last time that he read and preached (on the first Sunday in Advent, November 29th, 1840) from I John ii, 1, only sixteen days before his death, he exhibited a vigour and power of voice, which called forth the particular notice of many who were present"

The selections which we now give from the interesting pamphlet by the Rev. W T. Myers allude to some of the parochial work established or carried on by the Rev J K Shaw Brooke The Jubilee Festival is also described as well as the impressive funeral scenes when the venerable Vicar was laid to rest in the tomb of his fathers These matters from the pen of one who was not only an eye-witness of them but who also took part in the ceremonies will doubtless be read with interest by the old parishioners of Eltham

"But we are desirous of tracing other features in the character of our departed pastor," continues the writer, "other striking particulars in the course of the long and useful life of this benevolent clergyman, by whose death many public, religious, and charitable societies, besides those of his respective parishes, have lost a kind and liberal supporter, but how great a loss his death will be to private individuals the unostentatious character of his benevolence will ever keep a secret And, first, we would notice his attention to the importance of moral and religious education in this parish

"The National Infant and Sunday Schools, which he had the happiness, with the aid of his liberal parishioners, to establish in the village, were the objects of his anxious care, and afforded ample means for the instruction of the children of the poor in the principles of the Christian religion, as taught by the Established Church And although the infirmity of deafness, in his later years, caused him to leave the duty of visiting and examination chiefly to his Curate, his constant attendance as the treasurer at the monthly meetings of the school committee, to which he made all other engagements subservient, will be recollected by its members as a valued record of his desire to promote and advance the efficiency of the schools by every means in his power

"The extensive charities of the parish, of which he was also the treasurer, were a favourite object of his unremitting regard and attention to the very last, and the accuracy and regularity of his accounts, which have ever been the admiration of his co-trustees, as well as the judicious appropriation of the funds, called forth an expression of the highest approbation from the Commissioners appointed by Parliament to inquire into the state of the charities throughout the country.

"In order that these extraordinary claims

upon his time might not be prejudicial to his
other calls of ministerial duty, he, from the
first, gave himself and his parishioners the
advantage and assistance of a resident Curate
This afforded him the opportunity of personally distributing, among his poor brethren,
the benevolence which Providence had influenced the hearts of the rich to bequeath to
them, and gave him a knowledge of the character and circumstances of his people so desir-
able and necessary to the due exercise of
charity

"We need not observe how much this constant practice of domiciliary visiting among the
poor conciliated their respect and affection
But these feelings were not confined to the
poor only, nor indeed to any class of his
parishioners, let public testimony proclaim
that it was universal.

"Let the Eltham Jubilee, held on the 5th
September, 1833, which was celebrated in commemoration of the fiftieth year of his incumbency, speak volumes of the regard and attachment which a grateful people are wont to enter-
tain, and are delighted to express, towards a
faithful minister. And if ever there were an
adequate demonstration of the love and affection that should engage and influence the
hearts of the flock towards their beloved shepherd, it was abundantly displayed on this
happy occasion. No means of expressing their
long-cherished feelings could be so truly
acceptable to their pastor as to associate the
honour and distinction intended him with the
exercise of Christian charity towards the poor

"This was the judicious and Christian
principle which influenced the more opulent
portion of his parishioners and the liberal
tradesmen, to unite with one heart and hand
in the laudable and benevolent purpose of giving a public dinner to the poor inhabitants
of Eltham, as a Jubilee Festival, in commemoration of the blessing of Almighty God
in so graciously preserving the life and health
of their beloved minister, and in acknowledgment of the faithful and unwearied discharge
of his pastoral care during the period of 50
years—at the same time to express their most
fervent wish and prayer that it might please

the Almighty long to preserve him to watch
over them in the enjoyment of health and
happiness

"The scene of this joyous festivity was the
Vicarage field, where the families of the poor,
amounting to nearly 1,400 persons, including
the children of the National Schools, sat down
to a plentiful and substantial repast of true
old English fare, waited upon by the gentry
and tradesmen, and where the venerable and
respected Vicar was received and welcomed, on
his entrance upon the ground, with a burst
of acclamations and blessings from his enthusiastic and happy people which must be remembered with unmixed satisfaction by those
who had the happiness to be present to the last
day of their lives And we must add that the
uninterrupted course of good order and good
conduct which prevailed during the whole day
of festivity forms by no means the least mark
of respect shewn by a grateful flock to the
minister of peace

"To meet this costly feast and other honourable accompaniments the liberal sum of four
hundred pounds was contributed, and, among
the latter we must not omit to mention the
jubilee portrait, an admirable and faithful
likeness of the Vicar of Eltham, so happily
painted by J Hayes, Esq, and placed in the
care of the Rev W T Myers, the Curate, at
the Vicarage House, where it may be seen
by any of his friends and parishioners"

(This picture now hangs in the sacristy of
the Parish Church)

"How rich a source of personal happiness
and comfort, how sacred a cause of thankfulness to God, how strong a claim of gratitude to
his people this public testimony to his character as a faithful and respected minister of
the Gospel was to him could be truly estimated by no one but himself Great, however, as we may suppose his inward satisfaction and sense of obligation to have been, it was
not entirely without alloy, as those who knew
him best could well observe.

"The innate diffidence and retiring modesty
of his character, had he yielded to the natural
bent of his disposition, would have withheld

him from taking a prominent part at any public meeting; and on this occasion he was obliged to occupy the honourable and enviable station to which the voices and hearts of his people and his own exemplary conduct, had called him, with a painfully joyous struggle within, from which no one could have been free, but which must have been trying indeed to one

Whose sober wishes never learn'd to stray,
But "kept the noiseless tenor of their way!"

"When, therefore, his high sense of duty constrained him to attend the occasional calls of public life, in presiding over the meetings of his parish, it has often been lamented by his friends and admirers that these inherent qualities, so amiable and delightful in private society, should have deprived them of the full and unrestricted exercise of a powerful and cultivated mind, and of a remarkably cool and sound judgment. The calm and dignified composure, and the wisdom and discretion with which he quietly regulated the often personally difficult circumstances of the parish, demonstrated an habitual discipline of mind and temper which is rarely to be met with.

"This constant exercise of self-control, springing doubtless from the influence of Christian principles, he carried with him in all the relations of domestic life; and it formed a feature of his private character which, blended with his other mild and amiable virtues, so entirely engaged, and won the hearty esteem of his friends and equals, in his social intercourse with them, that no party nor friendly meeting was considered complete without his animating and ever welcome presence.

"It will not be difficult to imagine how universally, as we before observed, the influence of the same 'ornament of a meek and quiet spirit' gained upon the hearts of the tradesmen and of the poorer classes in his daily association with them.

"The writer, who has the mournful satisfaction of offering this last tribute to the cherished memory of his beloved friend, can truly say, in reference to the benevolent mind,

and cheerful temper of this amiable clergyman, that during the 20 years, and upwards, that he had the happiness of sharing the labours of the Christian vineyard with his aged brother, the Father of the Diocese, no difference ever for a moment disturbed the harmony that subsisted between them; nor did ever unkind word proceed from his mouth to betray the slightest variation from the entire confidence which he reposed in his fellow labourer, whose happiness it was to attend upon him in his last short illness and whose privilege it was to close his eyes in prayer, as 'the spirit returned to God who gave it.'

"Shall we attempt to seek, or can we hope to find, more eloquent, more convincing testimony of unfeigned regard and attachment, than that which both public and private esteem have combined to offer to living virtue? We neither seek nor hope to find any. But to departed worth a tribute may be found, flowing from the same fountain of tenderest sympathy and affection, the grateful heart, which speaks a language still more affecting and sincere; even though it speak in sorrow. That tribute was reserved for the day of the funeral of our lamented friend, Wednesday, December 23rd, 1840.

"On this occasion a scene presented itself in the parish of Eltham which will not soon be forgotten, and which will, perhaps, best portray the character of the deceased in the estimation of his friends and parishioners.

"From the hour of his death every house and shop exhibited mournful evidence of the sad event and of the gloom and distress which it had thrown over the whole village. But on the day of the interment of the venerable patriarch a testimony of respect was given to departed worth which we attempt not to describe. Facts must speak for themselves.

"Every shop was closed, and all business ceased during the whole day, and every house seemed to bespeak a loss in the family. Long before the hour appointed for the melancholy last offices of the Church over her deeply-lamented minister, crowds of the dejected people were seen to assemble, 'like sheep that

No. 147.   ARCHDEACON STUBBS

(See text.)

No. 146.   Mr. CHARLES CÆSAR.

(See text.)

No. 149.

Rev. J. K. SHAW BROOKE.

From the Painting at the Parish Church.

(See text).

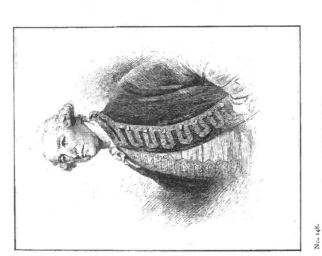

No. 148.

SIR WILLIAM JAMES.

(See text).

No. 151.   Mr. RICHARD MILLS.
(See text.)

No. 152.   Mr. R. J. SAUNDERS.
(See text.)

No. 153.

Mr. THOMAS JACKSON.

(See text).

No. 152.

Mr. THOMAS LEWIN.

(See text).

had lost their shepherd.' But when the hour arrived the solemn procession from the residence of the deceased to the church will best evince the anxiety shewn by the parishioners to pay the last tribute of affection and love to one who had so long and so faithfully watched over them.

"A large body of the neighbouring clergy, six of whom were pall bearers, with the Curate of the parish at their head, preceded and surrounded the coffin of their respected and beloved friend, the Father of the Diocese. The relatives, Sir John Kenward Shaw, Baronet, the Rev. Robert Shaw, and other branches of the Shaw family, with the Rev. J. Scholefield, and the Rev. J. C. F. Tufnell, and the domestics, followed as mourners.

"Next came the churchwardens and sidesmen, and in long succession the gentlemen and tradesmen of the village, closing with a numerous concourse of the poorer people. Nay, the whole parish as one man were assembled to form the solemn and mournful train, which slowly and silently took its way towards the Parish Church. And here, again, the solemnity of the scene was beyond description imposing!

"A dense mass of the parishioners, in deep mourning, filled almost every part of the church, eager to witness the performance of the last sacred rites over the mortal remains of their pastor. The service was read by the Rev. W. T. Myers, who had ministered, with his departed elder brother, for more than 20 years, and who was not disappointed in his hope that grace and strength would be given him to fulfil this trying but privileged duty towards his late beloved fellow-labourer in the vineyard of the Lord.

"We have thus been brought to the closing scenes of this just man's life, for 'the just shall live by faith'; and truly the life which he lived in the flesh was by faith in the Son of God, who loved him and gave himself for him. And being justified by faith he has now peace with God, 'being washed, and justified, and sanctified in the name of the Lord Jesus and by the Spirit of our God,' that Spirit has borne witness with his spirit that he is a child of God; and if child then heir, heir of God, and joint heir with Christ, but as he has suffered with him so may we hope he shall be glorified also together with Him, 'who is the resurrection and the life; and in whom whosoever believeth, though he were dead, yet shall he live; and whosoever liveth and believeth in Him shall never die.' O, 'may we die the death of the righteous, and may our last end be like his,' for 'blessed are the dead that die in the Lord.' Whether we live may we live unto the Lord, or whether we die may we die unto the Lord, for both living and dying we may be the Lord's.'"

Thus wrote the Rev. W. T. Myers in the full-hearted panegyric which was printed and published a few months after the closing scenes were enacted. The writer has long since passed away, most of those Eltham people who witnessed the solemn obsequies have themselves crossed the bourne whence no traveller returns. There may be some of the very oldest who recollect the actual circumstances, and there are many who will have had the incidents of that day described to them by eye-witnesses. To all of these Mr. Myers' words will, no doubt, be read with interest. To the student of local history they are a historical document of considerable value. They reveal to us why the name of "Shaw-Brooke" is still a household word in Eltham. They present to us a learned and dignified personality, who, for nearly 60 years, dominated to a great degree the life of the village. We are shewn in the life a fine specimen of the old-time village parson, one of the "old school" as he is sometimes described. We may learn, too, in a large measure, from this "song of praise," what the conditions of village life were like during the first half of last century. We may almost breathe again the atmosphere of those far off days. Then, when we look around us we realise the change that has come over so many phases of Eltham village life. Whether the change is for the better, or for the worse each will probably decide as his experience and knowledge dictate, but it will be many a long year before the name Shaw-Brooke ceases to hold an honoured place in the memory of Eltham people.

Chapter LXVIII

SOUTHEND HOUSE.

Another Eltham house with a long and extremely interesting history is "Southend," the residence of Mr E Warner, to whose family the property has belonged for more than a hundred years   The beautiful gardens of this old-time abode are screened from the highway by the fine old brick wall which is so notable a feature of the road on the way from Eltham to Pope Street

Like most of the old houses of this class, the front has undergone considerable changes since its first erection, but the back still possesses many distinctive and interesting features of the early Jacobean period.

This residence was formerly the country seat of Sir William Wythens, Kt , Sheriff of London in 1610, died 1631   The estate in his time was much larger than it is to-day   A record of the details of this estate, which is still in existence, is valuable to the local antiquarian, on account of the field and place names which it contains We will, therefore, transcribe it here.

"Sir William Wythens, Kt , Holdeth (June, 1605) his mansion house, with orchard, garden, backside, and other houses, adjoining Sir Wm. Roper's pett howse S , Southend Green, E , Barber's shaw in parte, N., all cont . with the meadow, 4 a. 3r.

He holdeth (as follows) one close, sometimes three closes, the one called Calves garden, the other Bushie close, and the third Alders grove, the way to Craye W. and N , parish land called Princitors, John Stubbes' old howse leys, and Bromley close E , Southende green N., a close of said Wm 's S. and W., 6ac.

A close at the south end of the same the waie at Butt's flowe W , the xv pennie land and a close of the said Sir Wm.'s and John Stubbs' field called Upperfield al's old howse leys S , John Stubbes'meadow called old howse leys and Upperfield in part W , a close and hedgerows called ——— (sic), the xv pennie land E , Hugh Miller's close and wood at Butt's flow S. and W., great Dominick crofte at the S W   end 1a 3r. 7p

One close called great Dominicke crofte, Mrs Baker's Damson crofte S W , ye waie from ye Parke pale to Wiatts Elme, S E , a coppice of the said Sir Wm. E., 5ac 2r.

One grove great Dominick croft S.W , a close of Philip Rott's E , John Stubbes' upper field N , the waie aforesaid S 5ac

One other grove S E side the King's way leading from the Parke to Wiatt's Elme, the waie to Cray S W , Mrs Bakers grove caled old grove E , a close of the said Sir Wm E , 6 ac. 3r.

A close E side the grove before, a close of his W., the waie from the parke pale to Wiatt's Elme, N , a close of his own S E., 3ac.

A close, the close before W., Mrs Barker's Webb field E , two closes of his own S., the waie from the park pale to Wiatt's Elme, N , 5ac. 0r. 35p

Two closes, the other two closes N., Mrs. Baker's pond field and Webb field W., Mrs. Baker's Longlands S W , a close of his own and Mrs Baker's old grove in part W , 18ac

Two other closes thear called old grove, the way to Cray W , and Mrs Baker's grove called old ground W., his own above closes N , Francis Reston's copice called Shalon's S., 12ac. 3r. 12p.

Two closes land and wood called Coleman's heath al's Shallens, the King's land called

Edgburies N W , Francis Raston N E , the King's highway S , 7ao 3r 8p.

One messuage called Coleman's with garden backside, with a close of meadow adjoining sometime divided into two closes, a tenem of Henry Manning's son and his own close called Greatfield N , Southende Green W , Great Brookes and Long croft E , 6ao 1r. 11p.

One field with the marle pitts called great field, Colman's, S , the Kings nether well field, N , a ten'te of Henry Manning's and a mess of Fras Reston, a parcell of the King's ground in the marl pitts W , Philipp Stubbes and the xv pennie lands in East croft E , 10ac.

Long crofte, 5ao 0r 11p

One field called greate Brookes, the way to Wiatt's Elme from Southend greene and little Blackland S , Colman's W., long crofte N W , great Blackland E., 5 ao. 3r 38p

A parcell called Braky springe, a howse in Eltham towne lately purchased of Ric Dyer and others, in tenure of Walter Parry, the Street of Eltham S , Mr Twyst W , Philipp Stubbs E , 22p.

One field near Wiatt's Elme, the parrish land in parte E , the waie from Winchbridge S., 4ao 0r 18p.

In Eastfield 1ac. 2r ——

One howse in the towne of Eltham with a garden backside, and other howsinge lately purchased of Tho. Raston deceased, the Street of Eltham N. a parcell of the Kinge's ground next upper tenn acres S., a tenem. of Fras. Reston W., and a ten'te of the heires of Mannynge E. 12ao

A field with an orchard, sometime iii. fieldes, called Shotlandes, Pittfield N , Southend meade S , the way to Southende E., wherein lyeth a parcell of ye King's land, 7ac.

In Eastfield bought of Mr. Reston 2r.

One close called Laddes hall, Smithfield, W , Sir Wm Roper's parke N , the King's highway, S., the King's land E 4ao."

The family of Sir William Wythens continued in residence at Southend House until the death of Sir Francis Wythens, in the year 1704 This would be about a century.

The members of this family were distinguished in their day, and one of them, Sir Francis, has left behind him a reputation which may be regarded by most people as somewhat unenviable

Sir William's son, Robert Withens, was a Sheriff and Alderman of London, 1610—died 1630, at Southend House

Robert's son, Sir William Withens, Kt , was Sheriff of Kent in the seventh year of King James He was buried at Eltham, December 7th, 1631

A grandson of this gentleman was Sir Francis Withens at one time a judge of the King's Bench, and a friend of the notorious Judge Jeffries.

Sir Francis was Member of Parliament for Westminster in 1679, the thirty-first year of Charles II He was a warm supporter of the Stuarts, even in their most tyrannical acts, and his enthusiasm for their cause got him into trouble with the Parliament

He was knighted by Charles II on April 18th, 1680, after presenting an address, expressing abhorrence for any interference with the King's prerogative in assembling a Parliament. But he was expelled from Parliament the same year, in the month of October He received the Speaker's sentence on his knees at the bar of the House, and the "Journals of the Commons" thus record the Speaker's words· "You being a lawyer, have offended against your own profession, against yourself, your own right, your own liberty as an Englishman, this is not only a crime against the living, but a crime against the unborn, you are dismembered from this body "

Notwithstanding this, he was made Serjeant-at-Law in 1682, and a Judge of the King's Bench in 1683. In the latter capacity he was the judge who presided at the historical trial of Titus Oates, and passed sentence upon the prisoner. Oates was the moving spirit of a small group of mischief mongers, who, in the autumn of 1678, pretended to have discovered a Popish plot, concocted, they declared, for the object of murdering Charles II , and James, and the re-establishment of Roman Catholicism by means of a French Army Oates even accused the Queen of designing to poison the King These frauds produced great excitement in the country, and the nation lost its head. For two years any person who was suspected of adherence to, or even being in sympathy with, the Church of Rome might be accused of plotting by any informer, with a good prospect of obtaining a verdict of guilty from juries and a death sentence from the judge.

In a year the storm had exhausted itself, and Oates returned into private life But on the accession of James II , Oates was tried for perjury, convicted, and sentenced to imprisonment for life, exposure in the pillory, and a flogging.

Sir Francis Withens, of Southend, Eltham, was the judge, and it is recorded that on passing sentence he said that " he never in his life passed sentence but that he had some compassion, but he could find none in his heart for so hardened a villain."

But Oates survived the ordeal He seems to have been liberated by the next king, William III , and to have lived in the enjoyment of a pension from his Majesty, and even went to the extent of concocting another plot, with the aid of one named Fuller

Judge Withens was also one of the judges of the unfortunate Algernon Sidney, the other judge being Jeffries

Sidney was charged with being implicated in the famous Rye House Plot, but there was no evidence to sustain the charge Nevertheless, he was brought to trial, condemned to death on the testimony of a single perjured witness, and beheaded at Tower-hill

Alluding to his trial, John Evelyn has some comments in his diary, not entirely to the credit of Judge Withens

" 1683, 5th December. I was this day invited to a wedding of one Mrs. Castle, to whom I had some obligation, and it was her fifth husband, a Lieutenant-Colonel of the City She

was the daughter of one Burton, a broom-man, by his wife, who sold kitchen-stuff in Kent-street, whom God so blessed that the father became a very rich, and was a very honest man, he was sheriff of Surrey, where I have sat on the bench with him . . . . There was at the wedding the Lord Mayor, the Sheriff, several Aldermen and persons of quality; above all, Sir George Jeffreys, newly-made Lord Chief Justice of England, with Mr. Justice Withings, danced with the bride, and were exceeding merry. These great men spent the rest of the afternoon, till eleven at night, in drinking healths, taking tobacco, and talking much beneath the gravity of judges, who bad but a day or two before condemned Mr Algernon Sydney, who was executed on Tower Hill, on the single witness of that monster of a man, Lord Howard of Escrick . . . . ."

Judge Withens was further associated with Jeffries, whom he accompanied on the occasion of the " Bloody Assize" at Taunton and the West of England.

" After acting the part of a pliant timeserver, he was removed, April 21st, 1687, for denying the King's right to exercise martial law in time of peace without an Act of Parliament He was elected Recorder of Kingston-on-Thames, 1685, from which office William III removed him He was buried at Eltham, May 12th, 1704."

With the death of the judge, the association of the Withens with Southend closed The estate was then occupied in turn by Sir Comport Fytche, and Sir John Barker The latter's son, Sir John Fytche Barker, disposed of it to Robert Nassau, a member of a family descended from Frederick of Nassau, an illegitimate son of Henry Frederick, Prince of Orange, and grandfather of William III

The eldest son of Robert Nassau became fifth Earl of Rochford, and the second son, George Nassau, sold Southend to Joseph Warner, in the latter part of the eighteenth century It has remained in the Warner family ever since.

CHAPTER LXIX

OTHER OLD DWELLINGS.

HENLEYS

There is an ancient record (Originalia, 43 Edward III., M. 10) which runs as follows.

"On the 3rd of May, 1369, Spalding was directed to take possession of all the property of the manor called Henle, in the town and parish of Eltham, which William de Brantingham by charter had conveyed to the King, his heirs and assigns "

This manor possessed a house which was moated round, and its position is said to have been in the Conduit Field, below the Conduit Head, somewhere about the neighbourhood now occupied by Holy Trinity Church

It would seem that prior to the date of the above extract the manor was held by John de Henle of the Earl of Albemarle, and there is another record to the effect that Edward II "commanded John de Henley, keeper of his Manor at Eltham, 1290, to supply fodder from his own farm for the deer in the park, as they were like to perish from the inclemency of the winter "

CORBYE HALL.

In one of the leases of Henry VIII., dated 1 September, 1522, we read of a lease to Sir Henry Guldeford, for 40 years, of the manor and park of Eltham, at £30 1s 8d , rent, *with Corby Hall and 16 acres at 6s 8d.*

Although the name of Corbye Hall is practically unknown to the present generation of Eltham people, it was a place of some account in the early days of the village history. It was apparently in existence at the same time as "Henleys," already alluded to, for we find that, "on the 24 June, 1348, the King (Edward III) granted his manor of Lyndon in Rutland to

Robert de Corby, partly in consideration of good services rendered to his mother, Queen Isabella, and partly in exchange for certain lands and tenements in Eltham Mandeville, which Robert had conveyed to the King in perpetuity "

This seems to suggest that Corbye Hall was the place indicated. In the records of an inquisition by Henry VI we find that "among the possessions seized into the hands of that monarch by act of resumption was Corby Hall, *alias* Corbynhall in Eltham " In later years it was leased to Sir John Shaw

"THE CHANCELLOR'S LODGING."

The quaint wooden buildings lying to the right as you enter upon the Palace Bridge are indicated upon the Elizabethan Plan (1590) as the "Chancellor's Lodging " Although some slight alterations have, from time to time, been made in the construction of these interesting dwellings, they are practically the same now as they were in Tudor times, when More, Wolsey, Nicholas Bacon, and other distinguished men of those days may have in turn resided there. We have already alluded to these houses in the chapters dealing with the Palace

They are now two abodes, one part being occupied by the Misses Bloxam, and the other by Mrs Milne, the widow of the late Mr Alexander Milne, whose family resided therefor many years, and to whose extensive and accurate researches in Eltham history we are greatly indebted for sure guidance in writing much that herein is set forth in relation to the Palace

Adjoining are two other very old and picturesque dwellings, occupied by the Misses

Brookes and Mr Hollis respectively They were originally the "spicery and buttery" of my Lord Chancellor, though in the course of years they have had more alterations than the Chancellor's Lodging itself.

ELTHAM COURT

This is the name of the house adjoining the "Great Hall" The gabled portion on the left hand is the old part of the dwelling, which dates back several centuries Until the year 1859 it was detached from the Great Hall, the intervening space being an entrance to the farmyard on the south side—the portion now a lawn Mr Richard Bloxam wrought great improvements during his tenancy He built the new part of the house connecting it with the Hall, transformed the yard into the garden and lawn, changed the moat on the south into the rosary which is a distinguishing feature of the precincts, and brought about other changes of an improving and reclaiming character Mr. R. J Saunders lived at Eltham Court in the early part of the last century. He was succeeded by Mr Bloxam, after whom the lease was held by Mr Stevenson, who died there some years ago On the death of Mrs Stevenson the remainder of the lease was taken by Mr C. D Wilson, who came into residence during the present year, 1909

THE MOAT HOUSE.

This is another private residence, standing within the area enclosed by the Moat, adjoining the bridge on the left It was originally a cottage, and is shewn in the old prints of the Bridge, but it was converted into a commodious residence by the late Mr. Richard Mills, who lived there through the greater part of last century, was a contemporary of the Rev. J K Shaw Brooke, and took a prominent part in all matters of parochial interest. The next occupier was Mr Crundwell At the present time it is the residence of Mr Dunn.

The gardens belonging to this house, on the other side of the moat, with their stately trees and undulating lawns, are very picturesque

COURT YARD HOUSE.

This old-world dwelling lies to your left as you enter the "avenue" in the direction of the bridge, and it stands near to the site, possibly upon the site, of what is shewn as the "Great Bakehouse" in the Elizabethan plan. Adjoining it is the old gateway leading into the "Tiltyard" The present occupier is Captain Holbrooke. Former residents have been Messrs J. Hawley (after Sir J. Hawley), H Scudamore (father of F J Scudamore), F. Molling, Captain Thacker, and Messrs Delpratt, W Willemott, and T Miskin.

QUEEN'S CROFT

This old house, now the residence of Colonel H. B Tasker, and situated in the High-street. on the side opposite to Sherard-road, just below its junction with the street, dates back some three centuries, the original title deeds being still in existence. The last holder of the lease was Miss Newman.

LANGERTON HOUSE.

This house lies to the right on entering the Court Yard, and is now in the occupation of Mrs Gordon, widow of the late Mr. H M. Gordon, of Abergeldie It stands close to, if not actually upon, the site of "The Chaundry," as shewn in the Elizabethan plan After Mrs. Pott, the occupier was the Rev J K. Shaw Brooke, who died there in 1840, other residents being Miss Hill and Mr L Richardson.

SHERARD HOUSE

The home of the Sherards has already been described in an earlier chapter

MERLEWOOD HOUSE

Now the residence of Mr J. Rosselli. It was formerly occupied by a Mr Alnutt, of Penshurst Mr Richard Lewin purchased the house in 1798, and sold it in 1853 Mr C S Mann occupied it in 1856, subsequently Mr L. Crowley, and then Mr Howard Keeling, who left a benefaction to the National Schools.

CLIEFDEN HOUSE.

The present occupant is Mrs Yeatman. It was formerly held in succession by Colonel Hernes, Mr. T Haughton, Mr. Dick, Mr A G Milne, Mr. Hopkirk, who kept a school there for young gentlemen, and Mr H Alprese

ELTHAM HOUSE

The present occupant is Dr. St John. Former residents were: Mr. Philip Burton, the father-in-law of Bishop Horne, Mrs. Kirby, Alderman

Sir Richard Welch, Mr A Aislabie, Sir Henry Onslow, R A., Mr. J. M Teesdale, Admiral Mackenzie, and Mrs Rivers, the mother of the present Vicar of Eltham.

Students should note that there were two houses bearing the name of "Eltham House" They should not confuse this house with that of Sir John Shaw, now called the "Golf Club House"

IVY HOUSE.

Facing Roper-street, and now the residence of Mrs. Brown Among its former occupants were Dr Wilgress, Reader of the Temple, Mi. W. Willemott, Mr T. Charrington, and Mr G S Pritchard

EAGLE HOUSE.

This is the house which faces Victoria-road and was the residence of the late Mr A J Scrutton

At the end of the eighteenth century it was the residence of the Whomes family It was subsequently occupied by Mr. H Latham, Mr. H Baines, Mrs. Lambert, Mr. G J Goschen (afterwards Lord Goschen, recently deceased), Mrs Walrond, Mr. C. Hampshire, and Mr C. W. Bourne

The father of the late Lord Goschen—Mr. J. Goschen—lived in the house that stands between Ivy House and the Roman Catholic Church Here the future Lord Goschen spent his childhood. It was afterwards the residence of Mr Knightly, who kept there a private school for young gentlemen

CONDUIT HOUSE.

This house stands at the angle formed by the junction of the Southend-road with the Bexley-road It is at present the residence of Mr. W. H. Burman. In the grounds attached is the old Conduit Head, from which the Palace and the Moat were supplied with water. In the old lease there used to be a clause entailing upon the tenant of this house the responsibility of keeping the Conduit in proper repair.

Of former tenants there was the beautiful Lady Rancliffe, the daughter of Sir William James, of Severndroog fame Subsequent tenants were Miss Wollaston, Mr R. Courage and Mr J Griensbields

BARN HOUSE.

Now the residence of Mr. James Jeken, who took up his abode in Eltham as a medical practitioner exactly fifty years ago Former occupiers were the Ravenhill family, Dr. Teggart, of Pall Mall, and Mr. T. Lewin. The latter gentleman was contemporary with Mr R Mills and the Rev J K Shaw Brooke. He took a great interest in parochial matters, and was instrumental in forming the Eltham Friendly Society

PARK FARM PLACE.

The old house which stood on the site of the Roman Catholic School at Eltham Park A picture of this house is given on another page. It was formerly occupied by Mrs Nunn, the widow of Mr Richard Nunn. Their daughter was the first wife of Harry Powlett, the Duke of Bolton. She died, however, before her husband succeeded to the dukedom, and her burial is recorded in the Parish Registers of Eltham, 8th June, 1764. Their daughter, the second wife of John Viscount Hinchinbroke, inherited the property under her grandfather's will. The tenant, after Mrs Nunn's death, was Sir Benjamin Hammett Eventually, it was sold to Mr Thomas Lucas, of Lee, who re-sold it to Sir William James. The latter resided there until December, 1783, when he died suddenly, on the occasion of his daughter's marriage to Lord Rancliffe

Subsequently, the property came into the possession of the Misses Jones, who sold it, with 195 acres of land, to Mr Thomas Jackson, of Eltham Park, the adjoining estate. It now forms a portion of the Corbett Estate

WELL HALL

The present house has already been alluded to in the chapters dealing with the Roper family. It was re-built by Sir Gregory Page, and the workshops were added to it about 1800 by Arnold, the chronometer-maker to George III Among those who subsequently resided there were Mr Lee, banker, of Lombard-street; Mr S. Jeffreyes, the Rev C G. Fryer, and Mr E. Langley. The present occupiers are Mr. Hubert Bland, the distinguished essayist and journalist, and Mrs Bland, who, under the pen-name of "E. Nesbit," is so widely known as a poet and novelist

Chapter LXX

SOME NOTES ON MOTTINGHAM.

In ancient times the hamlet was called Modingham, the name, according to Philipott, being derived from two Saxon words, *modig*, proud, and *ham*, a dwelling. Its story goes back far away into antiquity. It was always a part of the parish of Eltham, until the recent County Council Act severed the connection, placing Mottingham in Kent and Eltham in Woolwich. There is a mention of the name "Modingeham" in the confirmation of Edward the Confessor's gift of the Manor of Lewisham to the Abbey of Ghent; and in the time of Edward I., when Walter de Mandeville disposed of his property in Eltham to John de Vesci, "Modingeham" was recognised as a part of the honor of Gloucester.

We learn also that in the reign of William Rufus the fee of the hamlet of Modingham was in the possession of the King's Chamberlain, Ansgotus, who gave the tithes to the Priory of St. Andrew in Rochester, and in recognition of this gift, Bishop Gundulf made Anfred, the Chaplain of Ansgotus, a monk of St. Andrew's, "to celebrate for the souls of the donor, his family, and the King."

With regard to this tithe, there is an interesting note in the diocesan records which we will transcribe, as it gives, among other matters, the names of the fields as they existed in those remote days, nearly a thousand years ago.

"The lordship of Modyngham (to be tithed) begins at Readhelde; it extends to the wood of the Lord Bishop called Elmestediwood, towards the south, and to the field called Charlesfeld towards the west, and to the woods and lands of the King at Eltham towards the north and east. The names of the fields are: Southfelde, North-felde, Stofelde, Merefeldes, Strode, Trozleys, Benelondys, Westdene, Somerteghe, Wastegh, Bakevellyfielde, Bolysheth, Bryztredyn, Snorehell, Lotredefield, one row of meadow at the end of Breggmede, Kytebrokemede, Bentefelde, Westhynne, Kyngefedde, Bettescoftes, Eastfedde, Balte, Woodcroftys, Great and Little Altaeh, Southolde, Lytlemede, Upple Medegrove, Lamhynescroftys, Chychylyland, Snellegoryscroftys or Cotycroftys, Kyngeswotegh, Knyghtsstegh, Raynoldishaugh, Cortasytagh, Bertelottyshagh, Fullysland, with others."

This rather long list of ancient field names of Mottingham may provide a useful exercise in identification, for the old folks of the village who are familiar with the field names as they have existed in their memory.

The early Rectors and Vicars of Eltham do not seem to have been very well pleased with the Mottingham tithes going to the Priory of Rochester, and as a consequence we find records of disputes arising between these holy fathers. But the Prior seems to have had the best of the argument.

In 1243, fifth year of the pontificate of Richard Wendover, we read: "Richard, Bishop of Rochester, confirmed the sentence of his Official, Roger de Cantuaria, in the cause between the perpetual Vicar of Eltham and the Prior and Convent of Rochester, in favour of the latter."

When Henry VIII. dissolved the monasteries these Mottingham tithes reverted to the King; but it is some satisfaction to learn that the unscrupulous monarch did not long retain them, for we find that in 1540 he caused letters patent to be drawn up, conferring them upon the newly created Dean and Chapter of Rochester.

But after the death of Charles I , January, 1649, the Parliament abolished Deans and Chapters, 30th April, 1649, and their possessions were sold. So "the great and small tithes of Mottingham were surveyed, being then leased to Nicholas Buckeridge, at rent £5, but worth upon improvement £20 a year."

King Charles II. re-established the Church of England, and once more the Dean and Chapter of Rochester came in for the tithes

In further reference to the extent of the bounds of Mottingham, there is a good deal of interest in the following entry, dated 15th day of September, 1701, and extracted from the parochial records of Lee —

"From the bridge or water called Mottingham bridge, or Water, downe Lodge Lane, leading to London, to the Middle Park Watercourse, from thence all along around the new grounds abutting upon the Parish of Eltham, northward to Mottingham Corner, and from thence round High-field all along by the Park Pale to the upper end of Junipers abutting upon the said parish of Eltham east, and from thence from a tree marked with a cross in the highway, cross the road through a mead called the Readhill mead, abutting upon the Parish of Chislehurst, Southerly, and crossing the said mead along by the hedge side of Lambethheath to a wood called Stennetts full South, abutting upon the said Parish of Chislehurst, and from thence upon a field called Tomlins Bushes to an old oak in the said field all along abutting upon the parish of Bromley, cross Empstead Lane to the corner of Great Marvell's wood against the Parish of Lee, and through Mr. Stoddard's grounds and the College of Greenwich lands bounding upon the said parish of Lee, to the parish of Eltham Westerly, and so upon the said Parish of Eltham down to Mottingham Bridge or Water as first aforesaid North-West

"We whose hands are hereunder sett went these bounds the day and year above mentioned . . . . . to be true accompanying the Ar. . . . . . Clement Hobson, Thomas Stoddard, George Wilson, R. of . . . . Natha, Ryley, Tris,

Manis, Michael, the mark of Comp. . . . . Thoma, Dently."

The Cheeseman family were associated with Mottingham in the latter part of the fifteenth century, and continued to hold land there for close on two hundred years. Hasted tells us that the last of the Cheesemans who held estate in Mottingham, according to Philipott, was Thomas Cheeseman, whose heir, Alice, carried it in marriage to Robert Stoddard, and his son, George Stoddard, and Anne, his wife, in 3 Elizabeth 1560, built the mansion house called "Mottingham Place," which, with the lands belonging to it, continued in the family till Nicholas Stoddard, dying in 1765, unmarried and intestate, there appeared many claims to the inheritance. After a long Chancery suit, it was adjudged to William Boureman, of Newport, Isle of Wight.

The Place was afterwards sold to Robert Dynely, who modernised the house for his own occupancy When his property was sold in parcels, after his death in 1805, Mr Auldjo purchased the house, and his family occupied it till 1837, when it was let. Mr H R. Baines bought it in 1851, and Mr. Schroeter in 1855

An interesting lawsuit occurred in the time of King James I , when Sir Nicholas Stoddard held the manor, and as the record throws a light upon the times, we will transcribe it as it was extracted by Dr Drake from the "Exchequer Bills," 7 Charles Trin 94

Sir Nicholas Stoddard, of Mottingham, pleaded in the Exchequer Court that he had long been seised of certain lands in the manors of Lee, Bankworth (sic) and Shraffold, called Lee Park, adjoining the Parks of Eltham and Greenwich, and had stooked it with deer

King James hunted in it, and wished him to enlarge it by emparking 100 acres of the Crown lands called Coblands, Hitchin Grove, Mayeswood, Mussard's heath, Roughchinbrook, and Long Croft, and to encourage him to be at the expense, the King granted a commission to Sir Thomas Smith and Sir John Scott to compound with William and Nicholas King, lessees of Coblands, alias Roughchinbrook, and Mussard's Heath, to whom he paid £303 13s 4d. for their unexpired term

He bought 42 acres, and laid in 60 acres of his own inheritance. He ordered the ridings and lawn as the King directed, and expended £1,500 at least, as he sold lands worth £37 a year, and used the money for the park, in which the King had killed 80 deer, at least.

He had a horse worth, at least, £150, which the King fancied, and took in consideration of a grant to him of the 100 acres in fee-farm.

These, in reply, admitted that they had broken down the park palings to gain an entrance under power of a grant to them of the premises for 41 years by letters patent, dated 23rd July, 1630.

John Saunderson and Thomas Lewin, as fermers of the Crown lands of Roughchinbrook, Coblands, Stockchinbrook, and woodland called Mussard's Heath, in Lee and Lewisham,

CAVALIER 1629.

Delays occurred in obtaining the great seal to the estate bought of William and Nicholas King, whose lease was nearly expired, and to recoup himself this outlay, made to please the King, he felled timber, as he might have done by virtue of the grant under the great seal, but Sir Lionel Cranfield, the Lord Treasurer, restrained him under a warrant, addressed 22nd January, 1622, to the bailiff and constable of the Manor of Lee, and William and Nicholas King's term being determined, Thomas Lewin and John Saunderson laid claim to the estate.

charged Sir Nicholas Stoddard with forcibly entering and cutting down timber in contempt of the King's authority, and with threatening to bring suits against them in the Court of King's Bench, to the disinheriting of the King; they prayed, therefore, that Sir Nicholas might be summoned to appear in the Court of Exchequer.

It would appear, as the result of this action, that a special commission was appointed to inquire into the circumstances. This commission found that Sir Nicholas had cut down timber contrary to the terms of his lease, and Sir Robert Heath, the Attorney General, laid the information. In consequence, Sir John Lewknor, High Sheriff, was directed to amove Sir Nicholas, and to establish Thomas Lewin and John Saunderson, H M lessees, in quiet possession thereof Sir Thomas Walsingham and Sir John Fanshawe, H M. Surveyors, were to assess the damages The jury convened found that 65 acres had been converted "from good woodland to ill pasture" from time to time by Sir Nicholas at his own will and pleasure, but, although the wood was lying on the ground, there was not sufficient evidence to direct their judgment in fixing damages.

Philipott records a strange accident that happened at Mottingham on August 4th, 1585, near Fairy-hill, in a field then belonging to Sir Nicholas Hart, Kt.

Early in the morning the ground began to sink so much that three large elm trees were suddenly swallowed up in the pit, the tops of them falling downwards into the hole, and before ten o'clock they were so overwhelmed that no part of them could be discerned, the concave being suddenly filled with water.

The compass of this hole was about 80 yards, and so deep that a sounding line of 50 fathoms could hardly reach the bottom. At about 10 yards' distance from the above there was another piece of ground which sank in like manner, near the highway, and so near a dwelling-house as greatly to terrify the inhabitants in it

The situation of this extraordinary subsidence is marked to this day by a deep circular depression in the orchard belonging to the house lately occupied by Mr Elliott Many theories have been advanced as to the cause of sinking, but in all probability the mystery will never be solved

CHAPTER LXXI

SOME LAND MARKS—OLD AND NEW.

Let us now make a sort of perambulation of the parish of Eltham, and notice some of the land marks, old and new, which have not yet come under our observation in the "Story of Eltham."

POLE-CAT END.

This is the old name of the vicinity of Southwood House, where the roads to Lamorbey and Pope-street branch left and right The origin of the name seems to have been lost, though it may probably be pretty accurately guessed, when it is remembered that the Crown Woods extended in this direction, that game-keepers are the relentless enemies of pole-cats, and any other cats, and that they sometimes affix the skins of such animals as they had destroyed to a wall or door, as an example to others. The name of "Pole-cat End" may have originated in some such tragedies

In the days of Mr. Vicat, who resided there, Southwood House itself was included with "Pole-cat End" Mr J J. Smith, however, re-named it Southwood House The latter is now the property of the London County Council, who have converted it into a hostel for the use of the students attending the Avery Hill Training College, which is hard by. The change took place this year, 1908.

"THE BLACK BOY."

This was the name of a wayside public-house, said to have stood on the site now occupied by "Forest Lodge," also in the vicinity of Pole-cat End, towards Lamorbey The present house stands upon the parish boundary. Mr Woolley says that when, as a boy, he accompanied the authorities on the expedition of "beating the bounds," he recollects having to pass through this house, where the occupier of the time regaled them with bread and cheese and ale.

WYATT'S, OR WHITE'S CROSS.

One meets with occasional references to "Wyatt's" or "White's Cross" in the records of parochial history There is also mention of "Wyatt's Elme" in several places, e g , in the will of John Collynson, by which he established the "Collynson Charity," April, 1534, making provision for funds for the "repairs of the highway between Wyatt's Elm and the town of Eltham, and between West End Cross and the town", and again in the records of the estate of Sir William Wythens, who lived at Southend House, "Wiatt's Elm or ye waie to Craie," is frequently mentioned It is difficult to find any person in Eltham who can indicate with certainty the position of "Wyatt's Cross," or "Wyatt's Elm " The references seem to suggest the neighbourhood once called "Pole-cat end "

But why Cross? It is within the bounds of possibility that a pilgrim's cross may have existed at the junction of these two roads, but there seems to be more probability in the suggestion that some person named Wyatt was hanged at the spot The gibbet, or "cross-tree," was no unfamiliar feature of the wayside in olden days, and it may be that "Wyatt's Cross," or "White's Cross," derives its name from such a circumstance.

AVERY HILL

The mansion house of "Avery Hill," built by the late Colonel North, stands within its beautiful park, on the left hand side, as you proceed from "Pole-cat end" towards the ·

Bexley-road. Prior to the time of Colonel North, there was a house upon the same site, where dwelt Mr. Hale. Afterwards Mr. Boyd lived there, and during his residence he considerably improved and enlarged the dwelling. A curiosity of the old house was a room which was exactly a cube in internal dimensions. When the new mansion was built this curious room was retained by the architect, and still forms part of the present structure A few years ago the mansion and park were purchased by the London County Council. The house has been transformed into a training college for school-mistresses, and the park has been converted into one of the public parks of London.

In an auction bill advertising the sale of the old house on the 19th May, 1859, it is interesting to note that the house is spelt "Aviary Hill" It is also spelt this way upon a tombstone in the churchyard, Eltham

A ROAD DIVERSION.

The old road from "Lemon Well" to "Pole-cat End" passed along much nearer to the house than the present road does. To divert this highway, Colonel North constructed the handsome piece of road between "Lemon Well" and the Bexley-road, at a great cost The small farm house that stood near the old road was pulled down, and the park and mansion were enclosed completely by the fine brick wall which runs along the north side from one lodge to the other.

THE CROWN WOODS

Mention should be made of the beautiful Crown Woods which lie to the east and north of Mr. Low's farm Here bird and plant flourish joyously, and the leafy lanes in the proximity of the woods are suggestive of secluded country life a hundred miles away, though they are actually within the boundaries of the London area

LEMON WELL

This is a bricked well by the wayside on the road from Avery Hill to Eltham. There are old allusions to this spring. At one time it had a reputation for its medicinal properties, and was resorted to for affections of the eye It is said to be frequently used for the same purpose even at the present day. The well gives the name—Lemon Well—to the house hard by which is the residence of Sir Harry North, son of the late Colonel North It is a comparatively modern house. The occupier before Sir Harry North was Mr. Smithers The spring which supplies the well is in the grounds of Lemon Well House.

THE WARREN.

To the left of Gravel Pit-lane, a road leading northward from the highway is "The Rabbit Warren." This piece of land is now used as the links of the Warren Golf Club. At one time the portion adjoining the lane formed the butts where the Eltham Volunteer Corps used to practise with the rifle in the early years of its existence Owing, however, to the local conditions, a range of 300 yards only could be obtained So when the late Mr Thomas Jackson provided the corps with an extended range upon his estate in the neighbourhood of what is now called "Well-hall," the "Warren" butts were given up. Within the "Warren" there is a spring which, in historic days, supplied the water for the Moat and the Palace, and other houses in Eltham. It was in the first place conducted by means of a pipe to the "Conduit," the remains of which may still be seen in the grounds of Mr. Burman, near Holy Trinity Church Thence it was conveyed to its destination.

BARN-HOUSE CLOCK.

For many years the Barn House clock has been a familiar feature of this part of the village, and though a private instrument, it has fulfilled the purpose of a public clock to the neighbourhood It was placed there by Mr Thomas Lewin, and upon it is engraved the following inscription

Edv Griffin de Dingley
in Agro Northton
otiose fecit et Amico donavit
1786

We may mention that on the lawn of the "Barn House" is a sun-dial, fixed upon a pedestal from one of the balustrades of old London Bridge.

"THE MONUMENT.

One of the most conspicuous of our Eltham land marks is the structure which stands near the Broadway, where the Southend-road joins the Eltham and Bexley-road, and popularly called " The Monument " It is an object of interest to strangers, who often imagine that it is in some way associated with one or other of the many historical events of Eltham.   It was, however, in the first place nothing more than a ventilation shaft to the sewer, and the erection of so imposing a structure for such a purpose is in some measure a " monument" to the originality of Mr. Thomas Chester Haworth, who at the time was the local Surveyor of the Board of Works

It would seem that this gentleman was responsible, too, for the name " The Monument," which is likely to cling to the building as long as it exists, for such words were actually engraved upon it, though afterwards, for some reason or other, they were obliterated by cement

LOVE LANE.

This was the romantic name of a very rural lane that ran along the course of what is now Victoria-road.   At the northern extremity you entered it from the High-street, and the entrance was protected by posts   At the lower end, where Victoria-road now joins the Foots Cray-road, was a stile and steps, known as " Step-stile."

Between Love-lane and Southend-road, on the right hand side of the High-street, about opposite to the Golf Club House there used to be a pond called " Dodson's Pond," which was a prominent landmark of the day

THE POLICE STATION

The present police-station was erected in the year 1864, and opened in the spring of 1865. The head-quarters of the police, which served the purpose of a station, before that time was on the spot where Mence Smith's stores are now—immediately opposite the electrical sub-station

THE CAGE

Prisoners could not be accommodated in the old station, so they had to be taken to the " Cage, or " Lock-up," which is still in existence, at the entrance, on the right, to the wood-yard, near the old Workhouse. The " Cage "

in fact, is in the corner of the garden of Eagle House   The entrance is from the High-street, where the door may be seen, secured by a pad-lock

At least two stories are told of the " Cage "' On one occasion the constable arrested a youth for stealing fruit, and duly consigned him to the " Cage," placing him in the inner cell, but neglecting to lock the inner door   When the constable withdrew, the prisoner ventured to open the inner door, and come into the outer cell   On the constable's return the youth discreetly concealed himself behind the outer door, and when the officer proceeded to the inner chamber the prisoner quietly slipped out, locked the constable in, and effected his escape   The police records do not seem to shew that he was again captured, and the story goes that he joined the Marines

A very old Eltham inhabitant says that when a boy, he recollects a batch of pickpockets, who had come down to the races, a noted Eltham event, were arrested and put into the " Cage "   He was standing by at the time, and noticed that the constable went away, omitting to lock the door, although it was closed   As it happened, the prisoners were unconscious of the oversight, or they might have escaped.   When the officer returned, and the omission was pointed out to him, he was at first greatly alarmed, but, learning that his men were all secure, " he scratched his head, and thanked his lucky stars for his good fortune "

THE FIRE STATION

This useful institution, provided by the London County Council, was opened in the year 1904   It is a necessary attribute to growth of the population during recent years It is one of the signs that mark the transition from the rustic state which characterised Eltham village in the past to the new conditions involved by the absorption of the village by the expansion of London.

ELM-TERRACE

There seems to be some doubt as to the origin of the name of this street, but in all probability it is derived from the two old elm trees which at one time stood at the end of the road remote from the High-street

BLUNT'S-ROAD

This name is derived from "Blunt's Croft," upon which it is situated The Croft consisted of a meadow of 1a. 2r., which is included in the "Fifteen-penny-lands," one of the Eltham charities

THE WORKHOUSE

The old parish workhouse was erected in 1738, upon a portion of Blunt's Croft. "In the book of orders in vestry an entry is made, and signed by the Vicar and several of the parishioners, that, at a vestry held 17th February, 1737, it was agreed that a workhouse should be built at Blunt's Croft at the charge of the said parish; and that the annual rents of the said parish given to the use of the poor should be applied to the payment of the same as the said rents should arise At a vestry, held May 23rd, 1738, the parish contracted for the building of the same for the sum of £313." (*Report to Charity Commissioners, Sept , 1895.*)

PHILIPOT'S ALMSHOUSES

These interesting dwellings, which form so prominent a feature of the Eltham High-street, are also built upon "Blunt's Croft" An account of Thomas Philipot, who provided the means for the erection and maintenance of these almshouses, has been given in an earlier chapter The Charity Commissioner's report of September, 1895, says —

"Thomas Philipot, by his will, bearing date, 11th September, 1680, after devising certain premises to Clare Hall, in Cambridge, for establishing two Kentish fellowships, devised his houses in the town of Eltham, and a field, in the possession of Henry Snow, to the Clothworker's Company, to establish an almshouse in a convenient place in Eltham, allowing six poor people of that parish and Chislehurst £5 per annum each, four to be chosen out of Eltham and two out of Chislehurst."

"The almshouses, comprising six tenements, were built in 1694, at an expense of £302, out of the funds of this charity on part of a field called Blunt's Croft, part of the Fifteen-penny Lands. Each tenement contains a room

below and one above, with a wash-house and small garden. They are kept in good repair at the expense of the trust"

THE PUBLIC HALL.

This building in Elm-terrace was erected in the seventies as a British school, of which the late Mr. Rathbone was the headmaster. On the opening of the Pope-street (Board) Schools the Eltham British School ceased to exist The Public Hall, as its name implies is now used for meetings, concerts, and similar purposes.

THE OLD GASWORKS

The original Eltham gasworks were at the back of what is now the Public Hall The gas company erected their new works on Eltham Green about the year 1860

"GATHERCOLE'S."

In the same neighbourhood, at the rear of the Public Hall, stood "Gathercole's Envelope Factory" The industry employed a considerable amount of local labour

THE OLD CHAPEL,

The building now occupied by Messrs Smith's coachbuilding works, was once the Congregationalist Chapel. More particulars of its history will be given in a subsequent chapter The upper room over the shop is now used for meetings, &c

THE OLD RISING SUN

When the Borough Council acquired the site now occupied by the Public Library, electric lighting station, and the open space extending to the lane, a large piece of genuine "Old Eltham" was obliterated It consisted of the Rising Sun, Sun Yard, the workshops of Messrs. Smith, coachbuilders, a picturesque old smithy, and a number of quaint wooden buildings, including the coffee shop at the corner, all speaking eloquently to us of generations of the ancient village long passed away

The Rising Sun itself was a fair specimen of a village inn, as it has existed for some two hundred years.

SUN YARD.

A row of wooden cottages lying at the rear of the inn, and approached by an archway formed by part of the inn buildings These cottages were condemned by the authorities, and the inhabitants were scattered. At the end of Sun Yard was a wooden building, in which the Congregationalist community in their earliest days used to meet for public worship.

THE OLD SMITHY.

The farrier's shop which stood to the west of Sun Yard nearer to the lane was one of the features of the High-street. It was very old, and just before its destruction was in a dilapidated condition. It was at one time worked by Mr. Foster and his two sons, Richard and William. The last tenant was Mr. Metcalfe.

An interesting adventure of old Mr. Foster is told in connection with this shoeing forge. He had been shoeing a horse which was to be afterwards taken down to the Court. So he got astride the animal and proceeded to take it home himself. On crossing the Moat bridge, however, the horse was frightened by a boy with a hoop, and bearing his rider with him jumped over the parapet. Horse and man alighted upon a stack of bricks, and both of them miraculously escaped injury. Fate, however, was not always so kind to Mr. Foster. Not long after he had escaped the perils of that terrible leap, he chanced to be getting over the stile at the end of the lane near to his smithy, slipped, and broke his leg.

POUND PLACE.

This is the name of the street on the side of the High-stret, opposite the Public Library. It derives its name from the fact that the old "Pound" occupied the spot where Mr. Cook's shop now stands at the corner near the High-street. The latest Pound was at Eltham Green.

WOOLWICH-LANE.

For the benefit of future generations who may read these lines we will describe the lane which runs by the National Schools, because its character will in all probability be completely changed shortly, by its transformation into a forty foot road. It is merely a farm road leading to the fields which are still cultivated. But along its side is a public right-of-way which has been used from time immemorial. The footpath leads to the field at the end of the school premises, which was entered by means of a stile. A branch to the right is an ancient pathway to Shooters Hill, a branch to the left, sometimes called "The Slip," leads to the Parish Church, while the main path follows a direct course to Well Hall, the ancient seat of the Ropers.

A year or two ago the Borough Council, in pursuance of an agreement which had been made with the owners of the land, made an attempt to close two of these paths. Their action caused a good deal of irritation in the parish, and the boards notifying the closing of the paths were forcibly removed. The Council, however, were acting strictly in accordance with the law. Parliament had duly authorised the obliteration of these paths, though none of the inhabitants was aware of the fact. Good feeling was eventually restored, by the owners of the land agreeing to let the paths remain open until such time as it would be necessary to divert them for building purposes.

The "Woolwich-lane" was so called because it led to the old Woolwich-road, now called Well Hall-road.

ONE ACRE ALLOTMENTS.

These allotments lie to the right of the lane. Years ago the field they occupy was known as One Acre. It was a meadow, and was often used to accommodate for the night the herds of cattle or flocks of sheep that were being driven out of Kent into the London market.

ROPER-STREET.

So called because it is situated upon land which, at a very remote period, belonged to the Roper family. Some four acres of this land formed a part of the Roper Charity. The National Schools were erected upon a portion of this field.

RAM ALLEY.

The narrow passage between the houses on the right, immediately west of Roper-street, is popularly known as "Ram Alley." There is a tradition, and only a tradition, that centuries ago an Eltham man, named Stevens, was in the habit of stealing an occasional sheep from the flocks that were driven through the village to London, and concealing it some-

No. 154.   COLONEL J. T. NORTH.
                      (See text.)

No. 155.   AVERY HILL. Residence of Colonel North.

No. 138.   Mr. H. W. DOBELL.
(See text).

No. 137.   Dr. DAVID KING.
(See text).

No. 136.   Mr. W. J. MORTIS
(See text).

where up this passage. The tradition further asserts that he was ultimately hanged for the offence on Shooters Hill   There does not appear to be any record of this case, nor have any old plans or records revealed the name " Ram Alley " So the story is given here for what it is worth

JUBILEE-COTTAGES.

These curious wooden dwellings were known for years as Fry's Buildings, but as they were erected at the time of the jubilee of the Rev. Shaw Brooke, in the year 1833, they were given the name of Jubilee-cottages. They are approached by the opening in the street on the side almost opposite to " The Carpenters' Arms " This was also the entrance to the old brewery

THE OLD BREWERY

The old Eltham Brewery lay to the left of the entrance alluded to   The buildings are now used for stabling and other purposes. There is a curious narrow pathway unknown to many who are only familiar with the High-street, which leads by this old brewery entrance along by Jubilee-cottages to the pathway known as " The Slip," already alluded to

We will continue our walk down the High-street, and note some other points of interest

THE OLD "CARPENTERS' ARMS"

The present inn bearing this name is quite a new building, but it was erected upon the site of a house of the same character, but of considerable antiquity. That it was in exist-ence two hundred and fifty years ago is proved by a trade token bearing that date   The wording of the token runs thus :—

O   RICHARD . GREENE   IN — The Carpenter's Arms.

R   ELTHOM : IN . KENT . 1667 — R   I   G

The trade value was one farthing

For the benefit of those who are not familiar with the technicalities of these token records we may explain

O means "obverse," R. means "reverse."

The sign — refers to the "field" or the centre space of the coin   On the obverse side of this coin the "field" is occupied by the term, "The Carpenters' Arms."

On the reverse side the "field" contains the initials R I G

R is the initial of the landlord's Chris-tian name, Richard

G is the initial of his surname, Green

I. is the initial of his wife's name, which is not given

This combination of the initials of man and wife is the common rule of such tokens

THE OLD CASTLE TAVERN.

The old inn was pulled down a few years ago, and the present modern and somewhat im-posing structure was erected upon the site after the usual "set back" of the foundations   It was an old posting house   The coaches pass-ing this way always stopped at the Castle   Two "tokens" are in existence which prove the antiquity of this tavern   One of these is possessed by Mr Whittaker Smith   The other was in the possession of Dr Jeken, who has placed it in the care of Mr. Taffs   The legend of these tokens runs as follows :—

O   THE   CASTELL   TAVERNE — A Castle

R   IN   ELTHAM   1649 — N T M.

In this case it will be noticed that only the initials of the landlord and landlady are given. The trade value of this token was one farthing.

SOME OTHER TOKENS AND COINS

We are fortunate in having as an Eltham resident the distinguished numismatist, Mr H. W Taffs, who has made Kentish Coins and Tokens a special study   By his assist-ance we are able to give some particulars of other tokens and coins of local interest that have come under his notice

Mr F Nash, some years ago, found a token in his garden bearing the following inscrip-tion :—

O   JOHN   WATSON — A heart pierced with an arrow.

R   IN . GRAVSEND   1653 — I.E W.

The value of this token was one farthing   It is interesting to learn that John Watson was twice Mayor of Gravesend, namely, in 1660, and again in 1670

The following tokens were found under the Old Castle Tavern   The trade value in each case is one farthing :—

(1) O WILLIAM CRICH — Grocers' Arms
R IN DEPTFORD — W S C. 1663

(2) O THE CROWN COMMANDS — Lion and Unicorn with Crown.
R IN . LONG ACRE. 1663 — M M C

(3) O WILL CROUCH . MEALMAN — Arms
R IN CRICK LANE 1663 — W N C.

The following coins were also found beneath the Castle Tavern when the building operations were in progress :—

(1) "The Rose," or Royal Farthing of Charles I
O. CARLOUS. D O MAG. DEI — Crown with two sceptres in saltire
R FRAN ET . HIB . REX. — Rose.
On both sides, a mint mark, Mullet

(2) A "Maltravers" Charles I. Royal Farthing with Double Kings
O CAROLUS D O MAG BRIT — Crown with two sceptres in saltire
R FRAN . ET . HIB REX — A harp crowned
The mint mark on the obverse is a "wool-pack" On the reverse, a "rose "

An Italian plaque was dug up during the digging of the foundations of David Greig's Stores

Upon the same site there were also found—
(1) An old leaden bale-mark with an S
(2) An Irish half-penny, George III , 1781, with the counter-mark INO DUNN

Upon this, Mr Taff remarks, "As the lettering of the countermark is contemporary with the Georgian period, it would be interesting to find out that John Dunn was a local tradesman of the period, and that this circulated as his halfpenny token."

During the construction of the new road from the church to the Well Hall station the following coins were unearthed at the end near the High-street.

(1) A George III Three Shilling Bank of 1811
(2) A second brass coin of Hadrian.

To the uninitiated the following note will perhaps throw considerable light upon the use and object of Trade Tokens

"A token, strictly speaking, is a piece of money current by sufferance, and not coined by authority. In a wider sense the term is applied to coins or substitutes for coins made of inferior metal, or of a quantity of metal of less value than its name would indicate.

"Owing to the scarcity of small change, and the great loss occasioned to the poor for the want of some coin of less value than the silver penny in use down to the time of the Commonwealth, half-penny and farthing tokens were struck in brass, copper, tin, pewter, lead, and even leather, not only by the Government, but by tradespeople tavern-keepers, and others for circulation in their own neighbourhood

"When copper coinage became sufficiently abundant to meet the wants of the population it was made a criminal offence to issue these private tokens, although they continued to circulate in small quantities down to quite recent times."

With regard to the trade tokens found at Eltham, Mr Taffs points out that he has not yet come across any specimen which suggests any direct trading with Woolwich. They all point to trade with London, or with such a place as Gravesend which lies upon the highway into Kent

It is probable that in those days Eltham had but little doings with Woolwich. As will be seen later the only direct communication with Woolwich was along a small lane which followed generally the track now occupied by the fine "Well Hall-road "

OTHER INTERESTING INNS.

The Greyhound and the King's Arms are obviously very old houses The "Crown" and the "Chequers" are new buildings, but each stands upon the site of an older house bearing the same name It is somewhat difficult to trace the history of these inns There is at the British Museum an old and very rare book, published about the middle of the seventeenth century, which gives a list of the principal taverns of the counties round London. But the book gives only one "taverne" for Eltham, and does not record its name, so we are left to decide, as best we can, which "taverne" is referred to. The "Castle Taverne" token which we have just described, and which is about the same date as the book, would indicate that the "Old Castle" was the one tavern mentioned in the book Nevertheless, there can be little doubt that the "Greyhound" and "King's Arms" are very old inns

A characteristic feature of the King's Arms is the quaint fire-place which still exists in the parloui, as well as the ancient clock, the old bacon rack, and the distinct air of antiquity which all the rooms wear, and it is easy to imagine the association of the house with times earlier than the middle of the seventeenth century, the date mentioned in the book on taverns

In the old days it was usual to transact parochial business at the inns, and there are various records in the parish books of visits to the inns for such a puipose, and, apparently, it was the custom to lighten the labours of the day by refreshment. The drink consumed on these occasions was always a considerable item in the parochial expenses At the Easter vestry of 1812 it was reported that the refreshment item for the past year had reached the sum of £39 12s. 10d The details of this account are rather interesting —

1811 Easter Monday Paid at the Castle Inn, £10 10s.

31st May Paid at the Crown on making a rate, £6 9s. 2d.; paid at the Greyhound on taking the population, £4 8s. 4d

2nd November. Paid at the Castle Inn on putting out two apprentices, one to Mr Pattenden and to Mr. Nightingale, £2 1s. Paid at the Greyhound Inn on making a new rate, £6 8s 6d, expenses of different meetings held at inns respecting the Militia, £3 13s

30th December Expenses at the Crown at a meeting to consider what plan to take respecting Groombridge, £16 10s. Paid at the Greyhound Inn at binding two apprentices, one to Mr Rolfe, Eltham, one to Mr Ward, Woolwich, £1 10s. Expenses at the Greyhound on the Militia business, 11s

January, 1812 Paid expenses at the Greyhound, 5s., and at the Castle, 6s. 6d., respecting Groombridge. Paid expenses at the Greyhound Inn, binding Thomas Rolfe, £1 1s. 4d

March Paid at the Greyhound Inn in settling rates, £1 2s Paid at the Castle Inn, 12s

THE COURT YARD

The short street now called the Court-yard is erroneously named It is really the street leading to the Court-yard, which was approached by a handsome gateway, and occupied the area of the open space now forming the approach to the bridge over the Moat, and plainly shewn by the Elizabethan plan of 1590

If you take up a position upon the spot where what we now call the Court-yard meets the High-street, you will be standing at the centre of village activity and trade in the olden times The main street was, as it is now, the highway from Kent to London The bye street led directly to the Palace Hard by was the Parish Church, not far from where you stand was, in all probability, the cross which was a conspicuous object in the pre-Commonwealth days The parish stocks are said to have existed on the left hand side of the way, not many yards from the High-street, and here, for centuries, were held the fairs and markets for which Eltham was at one time noted With these things in one's mind, it is not at all difficult to form mental pictures of the scenes that were enacted here in times now passed away for ever.

MARKETS AND FAIRS

As early as the end of the thirteenth century, 27th September, 1299, we find that the then lord of the manoi, John de Vesci, obtained a charter for a weekly market at Eltham on Tuesdays, and a fair yearly on the eve of Holy Trinity and two following days.

One hundred and forty years after this date, namely, in 1439, we read that Henry VI renewed this charter at a council held at Overton The renewal was "in consideration of the increase of his (the King's) lordship, and the slender means of his tenants, giving liberty for all frequenting the market and fair to come, stay, and go, with immunity from impost, and from attachment by law, excepting for felony or treason "

The witnesses to this document were the Archbishops of Canterbury and York, the Bishops of Bath and Wells and Salisbury, "our dear uncle Humphrey, Duke of Gloucester, our dear cousins, Richard, Duke of York, and John, Duke of Norfolk," &c , &c ,

The market was long since discontinued, but down to 1778 there seem to have been four annual fairs held, on Palm Monday, Easter Monday, Whitsun Monday, and October 10th, for horses, cattle, and toys

PARISH PUMPS

The odd aspect of "Court-yard" was quite different from what it is to-day Where most of the houses now stand were open fields There was a row of trees beside the road, and many still alive can recollect the pond which existed near the point where the Back-lane joins the "Court-yard " The last of the old trees, bent low with age, was blown down a few years ago There were two parish pumps in the Court-yard One of these was on the left-hand side not far from the High-street near the quaint corner building now occupied by Whistler and Worge The water from the well of this pump was so pure and delicious that the common saying was that whoever "took a suck at the pump never left Eltham " The other pump was a little further on, upon the same side of the road   It is said that though these wells are closed down they were never filled in.

There was yet another public pump near the lower gateway, leading to the churchyard, and still another on the Lee-road near the point where the road to Middle Park Farm joins the main road.

COURT ROAD

This road, leading from the "Court Yard" to Eltham station and Mottingham, is quite modern. It is constructed mainly upon the course of an old farm road leading from Eltham to Chapel Farm. The road now leading from the Railway Station to Chapel Farm is a continuation of the old road mentioned.

CHAPEL FARM

There do not seem to be any tangible records which enable one to say authoritatively what was the origin of the name "Chapel Farm " The frequent references to "chapel" and "chantry" which are met with in Eltham history refer to the "chapel" and "chantry" attached to the Palace that actually stood within the area enclosed by the moat, forming part of the Palace buildings.

We are unable to find any evidence that a chapel existed upon the site of the present farm buildings Neither is there anything architecturally about the building that suggests the remains of a chapel What is sometimes pointed out as the remains of a window of an ecclesiastical character will not bear investigation The brickwork about the spot is original There is no break in the layers of bricks, as would have been the case had they been built about a window The faint marks which have suggested the window idea seem to point to a pigeon hutch having been suspended upon the end of the house, at no greatly distant date, thus protecting a portion of the wall from the weather. The removal of the hutch left this part less weather worn than the rest of the wall, suggesting the form of a window There are people now living in Eltham who remember this pigeon hutch This statement seems necessary to dispose of a fallacy which obtained considerable publicity recently.

As to the origin of the name, "Chapel Farm," the following suggestion has been thrown out for those who may be disposed to investigate the matter further

The old road leading from the Court Yard direct to the farm, and nowhere else, seems to suggest that the farm was attached to the Palace.   The establishment of ecclesiastical officials at the Royal Chapel, within the precincts of the Palace, was a large one, consisting of close upon a score, including the singing boys Their residence, too, was permanent, for they performed their religious functions whether or not the Court was in actual residence Considering the large number and the permanent abode of the chapel staff, it is quite possible that they may have been supplied with their dairy and agricultural produce from one particular farm, and the farm in question may have derived its name from this fact There is no direct evidence to substantiate this statement It is merely a suggestion as to the direction in which we may find a solution of the mystery that surrounds the name of Chapel Farm

THE BRIDLE LANE

This interesting lane, one of the favourite walks of Eltham people on summer evenings, leads from Eltham to Mottingham, passing the Palace grounds on the western side It is sometimes called "King John's Lane," possibly from the association of King John, of France, with the Palace, or as a corruption of "Prince John's Lane."

THE PARISH BEADLE

Returning to the High-street, we now pass the Parish Church, and must mention that very historic "land mark," if it may be so called, the office of Parish Beadle

Eltham is one of the very few parishes which still possesses an official of this kind. The office is depleted of most of the important parochial duties which were connected with it in ancient days when the Parish Beadle was an officer of the law and a terror to evil-doers, controlling, as he did, the village stocks The office is now maintained out of the funds of the Parish Church, and the officer, who, in his picturesque garb, is one of the special features of our village, does duty at the Parish Church on Sundays and other important days, in the preservation of order, as his predecessors have done for centuries past

The present holder of this honourable position is Mr J. Haywood, who has performed the duties for nearly fifty years His father was beadle before him, having held the post from the year of the Rev. Shaw Brooke's jubilee, 1833

THE OLD VICARAGE.

This building used to stand upon the site now occupied by the houses adjoining the Eltham Brewery. The grounds in which the present Vicarage stands were the old Vicarage grounds in which the Shaw Brooke Jubilee festivities took place.

THE VICARAGE BARN

The old tithe barn used to stand between the church and the old Vicarage It was destroyed by fire in the year 1868.

SHERARD-ROAD

The name of Sherard-road has been, of recent years, bestowed upon that portion of the old winding road which led from Eltham to Woolwich, which lay between the High-street and Well Hall Station It was formerly known as the Woolwich-road The name of "Sherard" was applied to it in commemoration of that of the distinguished botanists who lived in Eltham in the 18th century

AT "TODMAN'S NURSERY"

Tradition attaches considerable interest to the handsome iron gates which guard the entrance to "Todman's Nursery," the rectangular garden upon the side of the Lee-road, opposite to Lyme Farm These gates are of wrought iron, and from the initials woven into their design, they are thought by some to have been the work of Sir Anthony Van Dyck, who was given rooms in the Palace by Charles I, where he painted some of his great pictures There does not appear, however, to be any documentary evidence to support this interesting theory

It is supposed, also, that the gateway formed at one time an entrance to the Palace, directly from the high road This may have been the case, but, if so, it is curious that Van Dyck should have put his own initials so prominently upon the gates which protected the entrance to a royal residence.

The interesting brick structure in the corner of the garden is undoubtedly old, and may have been a kind of summerhouse This building, together with the general aspect of the grounds, which are walled in, are consistent with the suggestion that what people recollect as "Todman's Nurseries" may have been in more remote times the grounds of some pretentious dwelling that has long since passed away. In any case, there is a mystery about the splendid iron gates and the ancient

"summerhouse" which needs to be explained
This may be an interesting exercise for some
patient antiquarian of the future

MIDDLE PARK FARM

This farm was greatly renowned in the sixties
of the nineteenth century as the breeding
establishment of thorough-bred race horses. Mr.
Blenkiron was the proprietor, and his stud included many of the celebrated horses of the
day Amongst them was "Caractacus," which
was the winner of the Derby in 1862 Among
other of the famous horses of Middle Park
Stud were "Kingston," "Hermit," "Gladia-
teur," and "Blair-Athol" The annual horse
sales were notable events, and brought together
many of the celebrities of the turf

An interesting anecdote of the thorough-bred
"Caractacus" is recorded He was not the
favourite for the Derby of his year, the odds
against him being 40 to 1. But a week before
the race, "Rhyming Richard," a contributor
to "Bell's Life," wrote the folowing doggrel
"tip" concerning the horse:—

"Caractacus, whose shape and make,
    Sets every country clown agape,
    And, if of the outsiders there,
    One horse should pass the winning chair,
    Take the 'tip,' and list to me,
    'Caractacus' that horse will be "

When the race took place, Mr. Snewing, the
owner, instead of employing his usual jockey,
instructed a stable boy, named Parsons, to ride
the horse The result was a surprising victory

THE ELTHAM RACE COURSE

The Eltham Races were also notable local
events of the sixties The course was in the
"Harrow Meadows," which lie between Eltham
Green and Kidbrook-lane. The meet was
usually attended by prominent patrons of
sport, amongst them on one occasion being his
Majesty King Edward, who was then Prince of
Wales

THE TOLL GATE.

The old toll-gate, on the London side of
Eltham, existed at a point a little distance on
the Eltham side of what is now Cambridge-
road, Lee A story is still told of an Eltham
tailor, named Stevens, who jumped the toll-

gate for a wager, and won The next toll-gate
on the Foots Cray-road was a considerable
distance beyond the Eltham boundary It was
in the vicinity of Pound Place, Sidcup

WELL HALL COTTAGES

These cottages, which stand on the left-hand
side, beyond Well Hall, on the way to Woolwich, have of recent years, without the faintest
authority, been called "Nell Gwynne's
Cottages" There is no record of the famous
actress having been in any way associated with
them They are very old and picturesque, and
have always been known as the "Well-
cottages." The fallacy connecting them with
"Nell Gwynne" has apparently arisen through
the enterprise of picture post card publishers

KIDBROOK-LANE

This interesting road from Well Hall to
Kidbrook and Blackheath is of great antiquity
It was the direct route between Eltham and
Greenwich, and when the latter became the
abode of royalty it was along this road that
the Tudor Monarchs probably travelled when
going from one place to the other.

THE OLD CONDUIT

The ancient pile of brickwork which still
exists in the meadow near Holy Trinity Church
is what remains of the old conduit. This
reservoir dates back to a very remote time, for
it was the means of supplying the Palace with
water The water was brought from a spring
in the Warren, originally through wooden
pipes From the conduit it was conveyed to all
the houses of the Crown It was first conducted to "Step-stile" house and gardens,
thence through the Park, supplying on its way
the Mansion, thence, by way of what is now the
"Chestnuts," it went to the Palace By means
of branches it supplied the old houses about
the Court Yard.

The present new conduit, which is to be seen
in the Conduit Meadow, also in the vicinity of
Holy Trinity Church, was constructed in the
year 1838, at which date the old conduit was discarded, and an entirely new main, consisting
of iron, was laid in the place of the old wooden
pipes There is a clause in the ancient lease
of the Conduit House which entailed upon the

Crown the responsibility of keeping the moat supplied with water

POPE-STREET

The somewhat contradictory name of "New Eltham" is quite a modern name for the part of the parish it now refers to. The old name of the locality was "Pope Street" It was probably derived from Dr Pope, who was Chancellor to the Bishop of Rochester at the beginning of the seventeenth century, and who may have been the owner of property in the neighbourhood In the parish records, we find that on December 16th, 1617, expenses were incurred for this Dr Pope, with regard to the disposal of a pew at the Parish Church that belonged to a Mr. Miller, deceased.

THE RAILWAY-STATIONS

With the construction of the two railways through the parish began the disappearance of many of the rural characteristics of Eltham Direct railway accommodation with the City made Eltham a profitable field for the builder, pretty lanes and meadows began to disappear, and new houses were erected in large numbers, the population increasing by leaps and bounds.

Eltham and Mottingham and Pope Street Stations were opened at the same time as Cannon Street, namely, September 1st, 1866 Then followed the development of Mottingham and New Eltham. Well Hall Station was opened on May 1st, 1895, and was succeeded by the extensive building operations in the district now known as Well Hall The Shooter's Hill Station was opened during the present year, 1908

THE ELTHAM DENE-HOLE

In February, 1878, a shaft, 140 feet deep and a little over four feet in diameter, was discovered at Eltham Park, in the grounds of Mr Thomas Jackson, and about 300 feet from his house It was lined to a depth of 75 feet with brickwork nine inches thick at the top and 14 inches below, laid in mortar, the next 40 feet below this were lined with chalk blocks laid in courses from three to eight inches in height and seven inches back, with a second set behind, making 14 inches in all, to correspond with the brickwork The lowest 22 feet were cut through the solid chalk without any holes

or ledges being left The excellence of the work was remarkable throughout; courses of brickwork occurred amongst the chalk blocks and vice versâ The whole lining rested upon a foundation of wood four inches thick, which lay on a chalk ledge. The bottom of the shaft opened into a large chamber, 63 feet by 40 feet and 9½ feet high, excavated in the solid chalk, having bays at the side, and columns left standing in the chalk to support the roof, which is flat, under a course of flint It is computed that at least 1,000 tons of material had been removed

Before reaching the chalk, it was necessary to sink through a considerable depth of ferruginous and quartzose sand and gravel, then clay, green-sand, a pebble bed, and white-sand followed in order

We have no certain knowledge of the antiquity of this shaft, the discovery was made through investigating the cause of a great waste of water that had been laid on, and it was found that the water escaped into a brick culvert leading to the shaft

This remarkable excavation has now been filled in, and houses have been built over it

The origin of dene-holes is still a debated matter with antiquarians. Some are disposed to attribute such works to pre-historic times. If such be the origin of the Eltham dene-hole, it was the most ancient relic that the village possessed

THE BACK-LANE.

This is one of the characteristic landmarks of Eltham village, and no doubt dates back to a very remote period in the village history. It ran from the Court-yard to "Love-lane," or what is now Victoria-road At about the angle where it joins the Court-yard there used to exist a pond, upon the site of which houses have been erected An interesting story in the history of the Back-lane is associated with the wooden cottages which open upon the lane a little way below the Infants' School.

It was proposed to divert the course of the lane by running it in a straight line from the point where it crosses Park-place right away to the extreme end of Pound-place. This diversion would have formed one side of a sort of rectangle, and would have saved the pedestrian the trouble of walking the other three sides But the diversion of public rights-of-way is not easily accomplished if there happens to be opposition to the proposal. This proposal did not meet with universal approval. Nevertheless, the usual legal formalities were proceeded with, and the diversion would have taken place had not a flaw been discovered at the last moment in the legal proceedings.

This necessitated going over the course again, resulting in a considerable delay During the interval the wooden cottages referred to were run up hastily, and as these opened directly upon the old lane their erection effectually blocked the way to further proceedings in the direction of diversion.

THE SCOTTISH STREET NAMES

The Scottish names that have been given to the streets of the Eltham Park Estate are often the subject of comment, and people sometimes wonder why names so entirely foreign to local associations should have been applied, and whence the names have been derived As these names have come to stay, and as they will henceforth play their part in Eltham's story, it will be a matter of interest to explain their origin

The names were given by Mr. and Mrs. Cameron Corbett, and in nearly all the instances have Scottish associations —

GLENESK, CRAIGTON, and GRANDEHILL are the names of Scottish estates

BEECH-HILL, BALCASKIE, EARLSHALL, and GREEN-VALE are estates in the county of Fife

DAIRSIE and DEANSFIELD are estates in the vicinity of Edinburgh.

GREENHOLME is an estate in Dumfriesshire.

BERRY-HILL, a road which is not yet made, is named after an estate in Berwickshire.

ELIBANK This name comes from the estate of a nobleman in Midlothian, whose eldest son is known as "The Master of Elibank."

CROOKSTONE-ROAD is from a small village in Lanarkshire, a few miles out of Glasgow.

DUNBRFK is a suburb of Glasgow.

DUNVEGAN-ROAD, so named from Dunvegan Castle, in the island of Skye, the seat of the MacDonalds.

GLENLEA, GLENLYON, GLENSHIEL and GLENHOUSE are all of them the names of Highland Glens

ELDERSLIE   There is a decided touch of romance about this name, for it is after the birthplace of the illustrious Scottish patriot, William Wallace

WESTMOUNT, is from "Westmount," near Paisley, the home of the late Mrs. Cameron Corbett.

GLENURE This, presumably, is named after the place where "James of the Glens" was assassinated, as set forth by R. L Stevenson in his novel "Kidnapped "

GOUROCK is the name of a fashionable watering place on the Firth of Clyde

SOME ANCIENT ROADS

We will now conclude our chapters on "Land-marks" by giving a list of the few roads that existed in the reign of James the First, together with their situation and the direction in which they ran We are enabled to do this by referring to records of the "Survey" which was made of Eltham by order of King James the First in the year 1605 The Commissioners who carried out this work were Sir Thomas Walsingham, Sir Percival Hart, Sir Olif Leigh, John Doddridge, Esq , Solicitor-General, Sir Francis Bacon (afterwards Lord Bacon), Matthew Hadds and Ralf Ewens, Esquires, Henry Hayman, Esq , Surveyor of Kent Among the Commissioners fined ten shillings each for not appearing on the jury were William Boughton, of Plumstead, gent , Samuel Abell, of Erith, gent , Thomas Wildgoose, of Lewisham

The report of the Commission gives many interesting details of the lands, tenants, woods, rentals, and other matters connected with the royal estates in Eltham and the neighbouring parishes These details are too numerous to be reproduced here, but the survey may be well studied by those who would like to know more of the ancient field names of the parish, with the situation and extent of the fields indicated We transcribe, however, the following extract which deals with "*Presentment of Highways, Commons, and Wastes of the Manor of Eltham*"

1 A highway from Eltham town by the gravel-pit, in our knowledge a common watering-place for the parishioners of Eltham, leading to Wellhaw-green, and thenceforth by Thomas Roper, Esquire.

2. A lane called Horne-lane, leading from Wellhaw-green to Ryfield style, and so to Bexley and Darfort, ditched and hedged on both sides from the lands of Mr Thomas Roper, and Hogs' sties of the parishioners, and free herbage common, and passage for horsemen and carts till exchange was made between Mr. Thomas Roper and the parishioners for a parcel of land called Hungerdynes.

3 A lane leading out of Horne-lane to the Common of Eltham, near Broad Oke, and so to Canterbury, ditched and hedged from the lands of Mr Thomas Roper. The parishioners of Eltham had free herbage till the exchange with Mr. Thomas Roper for four acres in the Common field of Eltham called Eastfield.

4 A lane from Theewing-lane, eastward to Canterbury highway against the beacon called Pickpurse-lane, fenced on one side, and the King's wood called Jakeshill al's Mumbey's spring on the other, exchanged

5 Claypit-lane, leading from Wellhaw-green to the lower side of Eltham Common and to Woolwich.

6 Kakehill-lane, leading from Wellhaw-green to the Manor of Kydbroke, Canterbury highway, and Charlton

7 Kedbroke-lane from Wellhaw-green to Kedbroke-green, and so to Blackheath, hedged and ditched out of the land of Mr Thomas Roper, and free herbage so far as the parish doth go

8 Also called Kedbroke-lane from Pope's Street, fenced on both sides to Stony acre, free pasturage for parish of Eltham. The lane was through Gray-field and into Stone acre, and through Henley to the highway to town.

"The common called Wellhaw-green is parcel of his Majesty's waste belonging to the Manor of Eltham, as by former surveys, and by exchanging between the King and Mr. John Roper, the parishioners and tenants here always had free Common.

9 A Common lying at Shooters Hill, the tenants and parishioners only have had free Common in pasture and estovers, it extends from one side of Heathen-lane by the wood of Sir William Roper, called Shooters Hill, along the same road to Broad Oke and Pickpurse-lane, and along by Gonnewood over London way to Plumstead wood, and to the way leading from Heathen-lane to Woolwich, and from thence to Heathen-lane aforesaid "

By referring to No 5, it will be seen that "Claypitt-lane" was probably somewhere about the course of the road leading to Woolwich.

From 7 and 8 it would appear that "Kedbroke," now Kidbrook-lane, ran from Pope's Street to Kidbrook

No mention is made in the above of the road that now runs from Eltham to Lee But in another part of the Survey there is evidence that the Lee-road was in existence at the time After the enumeration of a number of fields and grounds other than those of the Ropers the "Survey" says —

"All which grounds aforesaid do lie on the north side of *the way from Leye Green to the lane leading to Welhawe-green*, and from that lane end to Welhawe-green, &c."

This settles a disputed point as to the antiquity of the Lee-road

There is also an interesting reference to Bell-rope Acre " It runs as follows —

"First his house (Sir William Roper's), called Welhaw, with grounds adjoining, 6ac. 3r One field called Westfield, in the middle lyeth one acre called 'Bell-rope acre,' which is for the finding of bell-ropes for the said parish of Eltham, 16ac. 3r. 2p."

CHAPTER LXXII.

THE ELTHAM CHARITIES.

The "Story of Eltham" would not be complete without some account of the charities, in which the parish is richer than most villages To deal with these endowments in full is outside the possibilities of the space at our disposal here, as many chapters would be needed for the purpose We therefore propose to give a brief notice, chiefly historical, of the various charities, and would refer those who desire to make themselves acquainted with all their details and the present methods of their administration to the reports issued from time to time by the Charity Commissioners.

Most of the charities have existed for many centuries, and, as the years have gone on, local conditions have changed, and such changes have necessitated variations in administration The latest official order for this purpose was issued by the Charity Commissioners to the Trustees, in July, 1907.

THE PHILIPOTT CHARITY.

Thomas Philipott, by will, dated 11th September, 1680, after devising certain premises to Clare Hall, Cambridge, for establishing two Kentish fellowships, devised his houses in the town of Eltham and a field (sold in 1866 to the Commissioners of Woods and Forests for £650) to the Clothworkers' Company to establish six almshouses for four poor people from Eltham and two from Chislehurst, allowing them £5 each a year.

In consequence of an information filed by the Attorney-General against the Clothworkers' Company, the widow of the testator, and others, the will was confirmed, and the Clothworkers' Company being unwilling to act in the trust, it was decreed that the master,

wardens, &c, should appoint seven trustees from Eltham and four from Chislehurst, they by an indenture dated 9th December, 1685, conveyed the devised estate to Sir Francis Wythens and ten other trustees, inhabitants of Eltham and Chislehurst, appointed by the Court of Chancery.

At a meeting of the Trustees and others of the parishes of Eltham and Chislehurst, held 10th May, 1693, concerning Philipott's legacy, it was agreed that the parishioners of Eltham should raise not over £300 for building, and £20 for the purchase of a site, and to have the exclusive benefit for their poor until reimbursed the money advanced by the proceeds of the rents.

The Almshouses were built the following year (1694) at a cost of £302, on Blunt's Croft, part of the Fifteen-penny lands. Each tenement contained an upper and a lower room, with a washhouse and small garden

In 1871 the Charity Commissioners sanctioned the erection of three additional almshouses, two for Eltham, and one for Chislehurst, near the old houses on a piece of Blunt's Croft, exchanged for land near the High-street.

FIFTEEN-PENNY LANDS.

This name is supposed to have been so given from the ancient tribute of the value of a "fifteenth" of every man's goods paid towards the exigencies of the State. Henry VII in 1492, in consideration of the fact that Eltham was heavily taxed, in consequence of its being a royal demesne, granted to the parish some 38 acres, scattered about the estate, the proceeds of which were intended to discharge the State charge of "fifteenths."

The title was established 8th December, 1674, by decree of a commission of inquiry. On 14th February, 1711, an exchange was effected between the trustees of this charity and Abraham and Peter Foster for a piece of ground near the "White Lion," with four almshouses to be erected by the Fosters in lieu of half an acre and a building then divided into four almshouses

The old building, known as the Workhouse, was built on Blunt's Croft in 1738, out of the charity funds. The Workhouse was a parochial institution, and the erection of the building by means of charity funds was an instance of the kind of thing our ancestors would sometimes do to save the rates. The annual income of this charity is about £361

PASSEY'S CHARITY.

John Passey, by will, dated 5th July, 1509, desired his feoffees, after his wife's death, to convey certain property in Eltham to twelve honest men in trust, to the value of 26s 8d a year, of which 13s 4d. should go to the borseholder of Eltham, for the time being, toward the discharge of the head-silver or common fine payable to the Crown at the Michaelmas and Easter Lawe-days, 6s 8d for an obit in the Church, and 6s. 8d. for church books and ornaments. Passey's gift was afterwards vested in the trustees of the Fifteen-penny Lands (1833) Its annual value at the present time is about £170

An obit was a service for the soul of a person deceased celebrated on the anniversary of his death

Note.—The Berseholder was the functionary who in some counties was called the "tithing-man." He was chosen to preside over the "tithing," which was a tenth part of the "hundred," for one year The office was supposed to have been instituted by King Alfred.

ROPER'S CHARITY.

The earliest deed relating to this charity is an indenture bearing date 20th November, 1616, whereby, reciting that Thomas Roper and William Roper, by their deed of feoffment, bearing date 4th July, 1578, granted to John Smithson and others a parcel of ground in Eltham, containing, by estimation, four acres

in the common field, called East Field, abutting on the lands of the vicar south and west, George Tubbs, and two others, the then survivors, in discharge of the trust in them reposed, granted the said premises to Sir William Wythens and others, and it was agreed that, whenever there should be only four, three, or two survivors, they should convey the premises to twelve other discreet parishioners and inhabitants of Eltham On 25th July, 1833, the lands were united under the same trust as Fifteen-penny Lands.

The annual income of this charity is about £58

QUILTER'S LANDS.

By indenture, 20th May, 1656, Thomas Quilter, and Elizabeth, his wife, in consideration of £120, granted twelve acres in Pope-street, Eltham, to Daniel Shatterden and Nicholas Hailey, and others, who, after levy of a fine, by indenture of lease and release, dated 1st and 2nd June, 1671, in discharge of the trust, conveyed to certain trustees, the vicar, parishioners, and freeholders of Eltham and their heirs, the said 12 acres for the benefit of the poor. The land, measuring about 15½ acres, was united with the Fifteen-penny Trust in 1833

The present income is about £40 a year.

COLLYNSON'S CHARITY

John Collynson, by will, dated April, 1534, gave a house and nine acres of land in Pope Street in trust to John Bricket and three others for the repairs of the roads between Wyatt's Elm, West End Cross, and the Town of Eltham The annual income of this charity is about £57.

KEIGHTLEY'S CHARITY.

Henry Keightley, by his will, dated 20th May, 1620, appointed that twelve honest men of Eltham should take his house and land in Pope Street, by estimation 13 acres 3 roods, for the use of the highway from Pope Street to Church Style, and thence to Mile Oak in Eltham, 12d a year to be paid to the highways in Bromley, and the same sum to twelve poor men in Eltham, a copy of his will in parchment to be hung up in the church at Eltham This charity was united to the Fifteen-penny Trusts in 1833 Its income is about £83 a year.

The Charity Commissioners require that the net yearly income of the Collynson and Keightley Charities be paid by the Trustees to the Local Authority charged with the care of the highways in the Parish of Eltham, provided that the local authority to whom the said payment is made shall make such provision as will give to the parish of Eltham the benefit of such payment by way of reduction in the rates of the parish

SAMPSON'S CHARITY

Thomasin Sampson, by her will, dated 23rd March, 1634, gave to the parish of Eltham the reversion, after the death of her son, of 28 acres in Meopham at Priestwood Green. The rents to be distributed among the poor at the rate of 12d. each a year.

By order of the Commissioners, a moiety of the income of this charity must be applied by the trustees in apprenticing poor children, bona fide resident in the parish of Eltham, to some useful trade or occupation The remaining moiety goes into the General Fund of the Charities. The income of the Sampson Charity is about £10 a year.

PRICHARD'S CHARITY

Dame Sarah Prichard, by will, dated 20th April, 1707, gave £2 17s. 8d, dividends from Consols, to be distributed among ten poor widows and maids in Eltham, being 5s. 9d. each An account of this charity will be found in the parish of Kingsthorpe, county Northampton, from which it will appear that, out of the dividends on £1,228 8s, Consols, £2 17s 8d is payable to the parish of Eltham It is administered by the Vicar and Churchwardens

CLAPHAM'S CHARITY.

Mary Clapham, widow, by her will, dated 15th December, 1733, bequeathed to the Minister and Churchwardens £100 Three Per Cents, to be paid in coals for distribution, in the week before Christmas, among 20 poor housekeepers

SMITH'S CHARITY.

William Smith, by his will, dated 14th October, 1751, bequeathed £200, the yearly dividends to be applied in purchasing copies, neatly bound in calf, of *The Great Importance*

of a Religious Life Considered, the balance, if any, to be laid out in coals for distribution among a limited number of poor housekeepers not receiving alms, at the rate of five bushells to each family in the year.

Dorothy Smith, widow of the above William Smith, by her will, dated 20th September, 1754, gave £100 for the same purposes as her husband's bequest.

The Charity Commissioners have decided that these are " Educational Endowments," and as the book prescribed has been long since out of print, the trustees are directed to expend the money in " Bibles and Prayer Books," as prizes to the children of the National Schools.

WALL'S CHARITY

John Wall, 12th February, 1787, bequeathed £80 Navy Five Per Cents. for the benefit of six poor widows, a chaldron of coals each, and the surplus money divided among them.

DAME ANN JAMES' CHARITY

Lady James, 1798, bequeathed £500, the interest of which to be expended in coal for the poor some day in December, before the 14th of the month

COLFE'S GIFT

By his will, dated 7th September, 1656, Abraham Colfe gave all his lands, tenements, and hereditaments to the Leathersellers' Company. Among other trusts, the testator directed that in certain parishes, of which Eltham was one, upon every Lord's Day at the public church, at the end of divine service in the afternoon, two sweet penny wheaten loaves should be distributed by one of the chief officers of the church to two of the godliest and poorest householders, to be chosen by the minister and parish officers annually at a vestry or church meeting, at the usual time of the choice of officers for church and poor, or within one month from 25th March, the same poor persons not to be chosen two years together unless there were no more people in those parishes, and, if any being in health, refused to come to church for the bread, another should be chosen on the next Lord's Day.

Colfe's Charity came under the Endowed Schools Acts in 1887, but the scheme directs

that payment shall be made out of the endowment of certain yearly sums specified in a
schedule to the scheme, including a yearly sum
of 8s 8d to Eltham for bread.

SLINN'S CHARITY

Richard Slynn, by will, date unknown, gave
12s a year, issuing out of a house and land on
the north side of High-street, Eltham, to be
laid out in bread for the poor, and 8s for a
sermon on the 5th of November. The sermon
has been discontinued for many years

HEWETT'S CHARITY

William Hewett, by will, 13th March, 1779,
gave 30s a year for the repair of Robert
Street's tombstone, the surplus for bread for
the poor

KEELING'S CHARITY

William Henstridge Keeling, by will, dated
15th December, 1820, left the interest of £150,
part of his Five Per Cent. Bank Annuities, in
trust of the churchwardens, to purchase bread
for the poor, and for keeping in repair his own
gravestone, and those of John Henstridge and
Pricilla Smith.

LEGATT'S CHARITY

Mrs. Elizabeth Legatt, by will, dated 12th
May, 1714, devised a messuage called
Hargraves at Little Heath in the forest of
Waltham, Barking, Essex, and two pieces of
land in Hainault Forest and Barking, with £70
Three Per Cents., the surplus rents (over £10
a year to a school at North Weald, Essex) to be
applied for teaching poor children of Eltham
"to read, write, and cast accounts," and "to
be carefully and diligently instructed in the
catechism, liturgy, and doctrine of the Church
of England." The premises consisted of a
small farmhouse and 42 acres of land

A National School was established at Eltham
in 1814, and £20 a year was paid to the master
for teaching twenty boys on Mrs. Legatt's
foundation

Subsequently, £32 a year was paid out of this
charity towards the salary of the schoolmaster
Prior to the abolition of school fees a sum of
about £25 a year was applied in payment of
the fees of the children attending the schools,
and a further sum was devoted to prizes for

the most regular children in attendance
Special grants towards the maintenance of the
schools were also made from time to time

In 1904 the Hargraves property was sold to
the West Ham Corporation for the sum of
£10,600 This amount was at once invested in
the purchase of £11,960 two and a half per
cent Consols.

BELL ROPE ACRE

In the survey of 1605, among the particulars
of the lands of Sir William Roper, mention is
made of "One field called Westfield, in the
middle lyeth one acre called 'Bell Rope Acre,'
which is for the finding of bell ropes for the
said parish of Eltham, 16a 3r 2p "

An entry in the parish register, made by
John Forde, vicar (1598-1628), states that "Bell
Rope Acre is worth 20 shillings a year for grass,
beyond the feed "

For many years an annual payment of 15s
has been received by the churchwardens, from
the owner, in respect of the land in question
The money is paid into the general account of
the church, out of which bell-ropes are purchased

OTHER CHARITIES

The Rev J K Shaw Brook, 12th June, 1799,
gave a sum of money to redeem the land tax
on Mrs. Elizabeth Legatt's land

One of the Ropers (date doubtful) "gave a
piece of land, of which the annual produce was
6s 8d , for the use and benefit of the Clerk of
the parish of Eltham "

RIGHTS OF COMMON

From Hasted's "History of Kent," we get
the following interesting reference:—

A committee, appointed by a vestry, to inquire into parish right to Eltham Common,
near Shooter's Hill, found by the parish
records that the parish had exercised the
rights of ownership for nearly 300 years, at one
time 40 oak trees were cut on the common for
the repair of the church, at another 20 oaks
were felled for the repair of the school-house.
In 1636 the parish sold all the trees growing on
the common for £200, and afterwards leased
the land. The earliest mention of right was
in 1556. In 1572 an action for trespass was
sustained against William Harnett for cutting

wood on the common. In 1811 the Commissioners of Woods and Forest sold to the Board of Ordnance all the manorial rights of the Crown in Eltham Common, 42a. 1r. 3p., and in Kidbrook, 11a. 1r. In 1815 the encroachments of the Board of Ordnance were brought under the notice of a vestry, and on representing the case the Board desisted. The Rev. J.K. Shaw Brook obtained permission from the Ordnance Board for the poor of the parish to dig clay on the common by payment of 20s. rent per acre. It was afterwards thought the payment of rent would prejudice the parish rights, and the case remained in statu quo. In 1785 the parish vestry recognised the right of the lord of the manor in the soil, whatever the right of the parish in the produce.

In August, 1785, 3a. 17p. of common land were granted to Lady James, on the top of Shooter's Hill, for a lease of 21 years, at the rate of £1 1s. per annum, half to be paid to the lord of the manor and half to the overseers of the poor of the parish. In 1791 another piece of land (1a. 3r. 27p.) was leased to Lady James for 19 years, at a rent of £2 2s. per annum. Subsequently "they further consented that Lady James should have leave to make a carriage road over Eltham Common from the high turnpike road to the Castle on top of Shooter's Hill, without paying more money or consideration.

SOLDIER OF TRAINED BAND 1638.

CHAPTER LXXIII.

THE CHURCHES OF ELTHAM.

For many centuries the Parish Church was sufficient to provide for the spiritual needs of the people, but when the railways were brought into the district, and the population began to rapidly increase, additional church accommodation had to be provided. Where one church only existed at the beginning of the nineteenth century six new edifices have arisen for the ministration of religion according to the principles of the Church of England, in addition to a Roman Catholic Church, and the Chapels of various denominations.

We have already dealt with the history of the Parish Church in considerable detail, extending as it does far back into the mists of antiquity. In the case of the offsprings which have all come into existence within the memory of man there is very little history to record.

HOLY TRINITY CHURCH

Erected in Southend-road, in the year 1869, and consecrated on the 30th August of that year. The first incumbent was the Rev. R. N. Rowsell, who held the post until 1903. He was followed by the Rev. F. C. Bainbridge Bell, who was Vicar till 1907, when he was succeeded by the Rev. H. A. Hall. During the time of Mr. Bainbridge Bell, the Parish Hall was erected, and since the present Vicar has had the church considerable structural improvements and additions to the sacred edifice have been carried out. The style of Holy Trinity Church is early English. The architect was Mr. G. L. Street.

ST PETER'S CHURCH.

St Peter's was erected in the year 1871 to accommodate the inhabitants of the new houses that had sprung up in the vicinity of the Lee-road. The architects were Newman and Billing.

ST ANDREW'S, MOTTINGHAM

The Church of St Andrew's is built in a pointed style, of red brick, with stone dressings, and consists of nave, north-west transept, and a temporary chancel. It was consecrated on March 12th, 1880. The transept alluded to was added in 1897. The Rector, the Rev. G. B. P. Viner, has held the living since the parish was formed. An interesting historical fact in connection with the living is that of the tithes, which, as we noticed in an earlier chapter, were the property of the Diocese of Rochester, having been presented to Gundulf, a famous Bishop of Rochester, by Ansgotus, who was the Chamberlain of William II (Rufus).

At the dissolution of the monasteries the tithes of Mottingham passed over to King Henry VIII., who, ultimately, in 1540-1, settled them by letters patent on his newly erected Dean and Chapter of Rochester.

But after the execution of Charles I the Parliament passed, on 30th April, 1649, an ordinance, for abolishing Deans and Chapters, and selling their possessions. So the great and small tithes of Mottingham were surveyed, being then under lease, dated 20th November, 15, Charles I, 1639, term twenty years, to Nicholas Buckeridge, at rent £5, but worth upon improvement £20 a year.

On the restoration of Charles II, and the re-establishment of the Church of England, this portion of the tithes returned to the Dean and Chapter, by whom they were in turn leased to a Mr Henry Towert, a Robert Dynely, Mrs.

304

THE STORY OF ROYAL ELTHAM.

Anne Burdus, Mr. Nathaniel Clayton, of New-castle, and it was for the Rev. G. B. P. Viner to eventually redeem them at a cost of nearly £500.

The Rectory was built in 1886, the land upon which the Church and Rectory are erected, was presented by Queen Victoria, and the estimated value was £900.

CHRIST CHURCH.

"Christ Church," Shooters Hill, was erected in 1864.

ALL SAINTS.

"All Saints," Pope Street, was first opened as a Mission Hall in 1884. Fourteen years later (1898) the present church was opened.

ST. LUKE'S.

The following historical notes are from the St. Luke's Magazine for May, 1909:—

"In 1903 the Church people in the fast growing town on the Corbett Estate, having made their wishes very explicitly known for a place of worship of their own, at the instance of the Church Extension Association, the Bishop of Rochester issued a commission of inquiry into the subject. Amongst those present were the Bishop of Woolwich, Sir George Vyvyan, and the Vicar of Eltham, and, a site having been purchased in 1904 (February), it was unanimously agreed that a separate district should be formed, and a new mission started, to which the Bishop appointed Mr. Rowley, and on the 20th March, a public meeting was addressed by the Bishop, the Vicar presiding, when Mr. Rowley was introduced as missioner. Previous to this, the Vicar of Eltham and his church-wardens had raised about £250 towards a mission hall, which amount, on the formation of a new committee, was handed to them, to-gether with the plans and estimates of the present hall, which, for the sake of convenience, were adopted by the committee.

On September the 22nd the Hall was opened by the Bishop, about 320 people being present.

In April, the Building Account was closed, and the amount of £232 placed to the credit of a Building Fund for the erection of a Church, which, on July 10th, at a public meeting, it was decided to build, and the Building Committee was strengthened by additional members.

In October, Mr. Temple Moore was selected as architect, and in June, 1906, the tender of Messrs. Goddard, of £4,315, was accepted.

On July 14th, the stone of the new church was laid by Mr. Talbot, the brother of the Bishop, and on July 6th, 1907, the Church of St. Luke's was opened, and dedicated by the Bishop of Southwark, the church being packed with a crowded congregation.

Owing to a difficulty as to the ultimate patron-age, consecration had to be deferred, the patron being in China; but on May 22nd, 1908, Mr. Poll-hill Turner met the Bishops of Southwark and Woolwich and Sir George Vyvyan at Bishop's House, and gave up all claim to the patronage, in favour of the Bishop of the Diocese, and all difficulties being thus happily removed, the church was formally consecrated on July 4th of that year. Laus Deus."

The incumbent of St. Luke's is the Rev. W. P. Rowley, and the churchwardens are Mr. F. W. Clark and Mr. J. Hall.

THE ROMAN CATHOLIC CHURCH OF ST. MARY.

There is much of historical interest in the association of the Roman Catholics with Eltham. Prior to the Reformation, Eltham, like every other English village was, in point of religious observance, a Roman Catholic com-munity, where the Pope was recognised as the spiritual head of the Church, and the ministra-tions of the parish priest were according to the forms of the Roman Catholic ritual and custom.

Then in 1534 came the great *coup d'état* of Henry VIII., when the King declared himself as the head of the Church. The unexpected stroke of policy on behalf of Henry threw the administration of ecclesiastical matters into considerable confusion for a long time; but we must not imagine that it made the people Protestant all at once. It was not easy for people even at the command of a king to ignore religious associations, which had come down to them through many centuries. The spirit of Protestantism was of a comparatively slow growth at first, and in every parish were those who persistently clung to the teaching of their childhood.

In Eltham a powerful Roman Catholic influ-

No. 159.

LORD RIVERS AND HIS GREYHOUNDS IN
ELTHAM PARK

(A former Resident at Eltham Lodge.)

No. 160.

HERMIT," born and bred at Mr. Blenkiron' Stables at Middle Park
Purchased by Mr. Henry Chaplin.
Winner of the Derby in a snow storm. 1867

Amusements
TO TAKE PLACE AT THE ELTHAM
JUBILEE
5th. SEPTEMBER, 1833.

GINGLING MATCH,
All Persons to be properly attired. No. 2.

Scrambling for Penny Pieces
Candidates not allowed to fall down. No. 3.

Flogging the Ball out of the Hole,
No unfair whipping, and not to cut his neighbour too close.

EATING ROLLS & TREACLE
Boys to come with clean faces. No. 5.

DIPPING FOR MARBLES,
No candidate to wear Hair Powder. No. 6.

Dipping for Oranges,
No Boys to wear Night Caps, and their Mouths not to exceed Six Inches. No. 7.

Climbing the Pole,
No candidate to come with Bird Lime, no objection to Chalk.

JUMPING in SACKS
No Person will be admitted with a Wooden Leg. No. 9.

HURDLE STAKES
Short Sighted Persons need not apply. No. 10.

Carter's best Mather Wout, and best Crack of the Whip.
No Domb Person to offer himself candidate.

UNDER THE MANAGEMENT OF
The Sub-committee, Mess™ SMITH, LEKEUX, & ROBERT.
THE WHOLE TO CONCLUDE WITH

A Grand Display of Fire Works.

No. 161.

NOTICE OF THE SHAW BROOKE JUBILEE, 1833.

(From a photograph taken by the late Mr. Geo. Rathbone).

ence existed, long after the Reformation, in the Roper family at Well Hall, who, notwithstanding the pressure brought to bear upon them, which, in these days, we might almost regard as persecution, continued in the Roman Catholic Faith in Eltham for about two hundred years.

In this connection the following notes, written at our request, by the Rev. Father McGregor, upon the present Catholic community in Eltham, will be read with great interest. Father MacGregor writes:—

"Catholisism lingered on at Eltham long after the old faith had been proscribed. The Roper family, of Well Hall, though harassed by the penal laws, continued true to the ancient religion, and here, doubtless, as in many other parts of the country, the family chapel became the religious centre for Catholics scattered over a considerbale area. Sir William Roper had as chaplain a Fr. Colleton, a man who attained considerable distinction in certain questions relating to the status of the Catholic clergy which arose in the reigns of Elizabeth and James I. This priest lived here to an advanced age. His body was buried in the churchyard, and a tablet was erected to his memory in the old Parish Church. The last male heir of the Ropers of Well Hall died in Spain about the middle of the eighteenth century. His property was divided between his two sisters. They married, and Well Hall was sold. Thus ended an old Catholic family, and the closing of the domestic chapel meant the discontinuance of Catholic worship, and the dispersal of the congregation.

"The beginnings of the new Catholic mission were small. In 1870 the Rev. Fr. Cotter, of Woolwich, bought two properties adjoining each other in the High-street, Torrington Lodge and Meadow View. The Sisters of Mercy opened an industrial school for girls at Torrington Lodge, and a poor school in Meadow View. Two rooms in Torrington Lodge served as a chapel for the institution and the district. For some few years the mission was served from Woolwich. In 1875 a resident priest was appointed, the Rev. Francis M. English, who remained here some three years, living in a house in the village. The Rev. Father John Arundel took over charge of the mission in 1878, and was here a year more or less, being succeeded by the Rev. J. B. Harth, whose stay extended to about four years. The Rev. Thomas Malpass, who followed Fr. Harth in the incumbency in 1883, died (probably here) in 1886, and his place was taken by the Rev. Joseph J. Kavanagh. Under these priests the congregation had increased considerably, and numbered about one hundred souls; and its status advised a forward move, the lines of which attendant circumstances made very definite. In 1887 the industrial school for girls was removed to larger premises at Croydon. The two houses in the High-street were the personal property of the Rev. Jeremiah Cotter, who was now aged and mentally impaired; moreover, one was empty and unfurnished, the other in urgent need of extensive repairs. Father Cotter's trustees decided to sell them, and to save the mission the Bishop of Southwark (Right Rev. John Butt) bought them. In 1888 when this much had been accomplished Fr. Kavanagh was succeeded by Fr. Martin, who is still so well remembered. He took up his abode in a couple of rooms in Torrington Lodge to begin with, and superintended the beginnings of the poor law school for boys which Bishop Butt started for the custody of Catholic boys from the Workhouses, and in a few months this work necessitated the return of the Sisters of Mercy to Eltham. Father Martin moved out of Torrington Lodge, and as soon as Meadow View was ready for his occupation, he took possession of it as his Presbytery. A long room of this house (extending over the ground now occupied by the premises of the London and Provincial Bank) was adapted as a chapel. This chapel opened upon the street, and was far more convenient for parochial purposes than the former chapel in St. Mary's. It was never intended though to be anything but temporary, and in less than a year the building of the present church was begun. The late Mrs. Allpress was the prime mover in this project, and a generous contributor; Bishop Butt also gave large assistance, and other benefactors were not wanting. So that by the autumn of 1890 the present modest but elegant little church was completed It was opened on November 4th, 1890. Bishop Butt attended, and assisted at High Mass, which was celebrated by Fr Sheehan, of Blackheath The choir came from Bermondsey, and Canon Murnane, of Camberwell, preached.

"Not long after the opening of the church the Poor Law School had to be enlarged, and was at length certified under Poor Law regulations for the reception of 100 boys.

"A word should be said of the other Catholic institutions in the place Mottingham House was acquired by Father von Orsbach in the later eighties, and he there for some years conducted a preparatory school for Army officers Later on this house was taken over by the Diocesan authorities, who established therein a school for boys (other than Poor Law children) for whose custody primary education, owing to peculiar and varying circumstances, the Bishop makes himself responsible This work was, however, transferred to Eltham Park House some five years ago At the same time the Poor Law School, St Mary's, was moved to the Mottingham Institution, which was placed under the management of the Sisters of Charity of St Vincent de Paul, and St. Mary's Convent (the old Torrington Lodge) while remaining under the care of the Sisters of Mercy, was converted to the purposes of a Hospital Orphanage, under the Poor Law, for Catholic Children of the Home Counties who are suffering from certain specified illnesses These children have a gallery to themselves in the church with its separate entrance The institution is fully equipped with the most modern apparatus and appointments for its purpose

"Fr Martin was succeeded in 1901 by the Rev James Lonergan, who was here for five years In 1906, on the invitation of Bishop Amigo, of Southwark, the ancient order of the Canons Regular of Lateran undertook the care of the united missions of Eltham and Mottingham, and the Rev. Fathers Augustin White, George MacGregor, and Francis Jeffrey came into residence here, and are here still A few months ago Fr White was raised by his Superiors to the dignity of a mitred Abbot.

"So at the present time the Catholic status may be summed up A church at Eltham (St. Mary's), with a convent and orphanage adjoining, a chapel at Mottingham (St. Vincent's), with a convent and orphanage attached, a boys' school under Diocesan control, a congregation of some hundreds (exclusively of the institutions), all cared for by a Right Rev. Abbot and two other priests

"In Catholic circles one hears of a projected new church and other things, but as prophecy is not history we close this paper "

THE CONGREGATIONAL CHURCH

For the following brief history of the Congregational Church we are indebted to a pamphlet, kindly lent to us by its author, the Rev E. J. Penford, the present pastor of the church It was written by him on the occasion of the Jubilee of the formation of the Eltham Congregational Church, and publicly read by him on October 27th, 1896

Speaking of the Eltham community, Mr Penford writes —

"The church came to be in the month of October, 1846 We must, however, go back another 50 years for the beginning of the movement, out of which it sprang. The closing years of last century (the 18th) were marked, as all will remember, by a considerable quickening of the vitality and zeal of the Churches. A wave of revival swept the land Its force was witnessed to by the founding of the Baptist Missionary Society in 1792, the London Missionary Society in 1795, and the Church Missionary Society in 1799 Among the Home Missionary agencies that came into existence at the time was the 'London Itinerant Society,' whose principal design was 'to spread the knowledge of Christ and of His salvation in the villages which are destitute of the Gospel, within about ten miles of London, by opening Sunday schools and prayer meetings, and by preaching the Gospel of Christ in and out of doors, as occasion may offer '

"Local associations," continues Mr Penford, "having similar aims, became established here and there One of these was formed at Greenwich, and it was not long before Eltham became one of the spheres of its operations

"Preaching was begun in a cottage In a little while so many were found eager to hear 'the good tidings,' that it became necessary to erect a chapel, which was accordingly done in 1799. The pulpit was supplied from Green-wich, Deptford, Woolwich, and elsewhere Then, for some years, it was occupied by the Rev Mr. Wightman, who subsequently became a Baptist minister at Exeter A time of diffi-culty and depression followed. The congrega-tions became smaller and smaller, and at last the work seems to have come to an end. The chapel was closed and converted into three cottages The building stood at the bottom of what was known locally as 'Sun Yard.' It seems to have been felt at the time that the situation was not all that could be desired, and that to that circumstance was partly due the want of success"

It was not till some thirty years after that Congregationalism was able to get anything like a permanent footing in Eltham

Mr. Penford proceeds.—

"The Greenwich District Association of Con-gregationalist ministers now turned their at-tention to Eltham, and under their auspices a new chapel was erected in the High Street."

(This, of course, was the building now occu-pied by the coachbuilding works of Messrs Smith).

"It costs, together with the freehold, £1,200, and was the property, not of the congregation, but of Mr. William Joynson, of St. Mary Cray, who, in response to an appeal, had found the necessary funds The new chapel was opened on October 22nd, 1839, the Rev Dr Bennett, of Falcon Square, preaching in the morning, and the Rev J. Blackburn, of Claremont, in the evening."

But the workers were imported from Wool-wich, Deptford, Bromley, Lewisham, and other places. It was not till 1845 that Mr. Henry W Dobell came to reside in the village. He proved a tower of strength to local Congregationalism, and was the principal means of establishing it firmly as one of our religious communities.

This is how Mr. Penford describes the advent of Mr. Henry William Dobell —

"In spite of having many friends and helpers, the cause did not make the progress that was hoped. It continued to be the day of small things Such was the case when, on a certain Sunday morning in the summer of 1845, a gentleman put in an appearance for the first time, who was destined to exert an in-fluence in the congregation and upon the neigh-bourhood of which at the time he can have little dreamed. That day the supply was late —very late After sitting there in silence for some time, the stranger offered to begin the service, and his offer was accepted A *long* hymn, a *long* lesson, and a *long* prayer followed, and at last the preacher came The stranger then left the pulpit, whereupon the preacher begged him to return to it, and preach the sermon, which he did . The preacher must remain anonymous, the stranger was Mr. Henry William Dobell, than whom no Church ever had a warmer and more generous and de-voted friend than he proved himself to be to the struggling cause to which he was intro-duced that day Mr Dobell had come from the large and flourishing Church worshipping at Trevor Chapel, Brompton, under the pastorate of the Rev Dr Morrison, where, as Sunday school superintendent, he had rendered con-spicuous service

"Dr Morrison was reluctant to lose so efficient a worker 'What can you be thinking of,' he wrote, 'to bury yourself in such a place?'"

Not a very complimentary way of speaking of this ancient abode of English sovereigns! But we will forgive Dr Morrison because of the im-plied testimony to the work of one to whom we owe so much To the doctor's question the characteristic reply was:—

"If I have learnt anything from your preaching, it is that the worse the disease the greater the need of the remedy'" . .

"Mr Dobell brought to Eltham the ability and energy which he had displayed elsewhere, and very soon the leadership of the little com-munity to which he had come fell into his hands   Some of the old members of the congregation, whose views were narrower than those which now seemed likely to find favour, fell away, but others took their place, and the little cause began to make progress.

"Up to this time the chapel had been a preaching station, not the home of a Church. To Mr. Dobell's initiative was due the formation of the Church proper"

This was done at a meeting held in October, 1846

"It was a small beginning, for only eight members were enrolled—Mr H. W Dobell, Miss Mary Dobell, Mrs Blanchett, Miss Blanchett, Mr Richard Taylor, Mr Cooper, Mr Copper, Mrs Hannah Smith   Not for 3½ years had the Church a settled pastor, but the services were maintained, and the membership increased   The Sunday preachers at this time were the students of Hackney College   Mr Dobell himself was practically lay pastor during this period, as, indeed, he was at other times   Again and again he conducted both the Sunday and week-day services, and was a frequent and welcome visitor in the homes of the sick   But at length it was felt that the time had come for the appointment of a minister, and the choice of the Church fell upon the Rev W. R. Noble"

This gentleman held the pastorate for a few months only, for he removed to Bexley in the autumn of the same year, 1851

"After the removal of Mr. Noble, there was an interregnum of nearly three years, during which time the pulpit was again supplied by students of Hackney College, and other friends, Professor Ransom coming, as a rule, on the first Sunday in the month."

The second   pastor was the Rev William Jackson, who fulfilled the duties till the year 1856   Mr Penford has much to tell us about the careers and   characters of the successive ministers.   We regret that the limits of our space prevent   us from transcribing these matters   We must, however, give an anecdote of the Rev William Jackson.

"Early in his ministry," writes Mr Penford, "he appeared one Sunday in a gown, and

thinking the circumstance called for remark, he said 'Some of you may be surprised to see me in a new garb. I wear it for convenience It is convenient to preach in a loose robe   But I would as soon preach in the smock frock of the ploughman as in this gown, and,' he went on, 'I do not mind whether I preach in a barn or in a pulpit, so long as souls are saved as the result of my preaching'"

The Rev. Thomas Kennerley was the next minister   He was called to the pastorate on May 1st, 1857.

During   the first year of his ministry the Church became possessed of the building in which it worshipped in the High-street.   It had been the property of Mr. Joynson, who had found the money for its erection   "He now generously offered to relinquish his claim to it, and to the ground on which it stood, and other ground at its rear, on part of which   his envelope factory had stood, on payment of the sum of £500—a much smaller sum than the property was worth   His offer was gladly accepted, and thus the Church became its own landlord

"In 1865 a successor to Mr Kennerley was found in the Rev Jabez Marshall, of Hallaton, Leicester, a man of cultivated mind,   gentle spirit, and devout heart"

It was during the pastorate of Mr Marshall that the present chapel was erected   The accommodation in the High Street had become too limited   A larger building was now necessary, but great difficulties were experienced in getting a suitable site   The Crown Commissioners for a time refused to sell or lease a suitable piece of land, and there was a great outcry on account of the obstacles that seemed to be put in the way. The action of the Commissioners was actually brought before the notice of Parliament   But they persisted in their refusal, except that they offered to sell the site of the National School at the corner of Pound Place   This site was, however, regarded by the Congregationalists as unsuitable

"At last," writes Mr. Penford, "when every door seemed closed, Mr. Dobell, with the full concurrence of his devoted wife, resolved to find a site for the new church on his own premises He, therefore, pulled down his stables and coach-house, and gave for the purpose the ground on which they stood, together with the stable-yard and part of the garden "

The foundation stone of the new church was laid by Mr Samuel Morley, on July 23rd, 1867. The Rev Joseph Beazley, of Blackheath, offered the dedication prayer, and the Rev. J. Kennedy, M A , of Stepney, delivered an address Already nearly £2,000 had been contributed to the Building Fund. The church was ready and opened for divine service about a year later, viz , on July 15th, 1868, the Rev Samuel Martin preaching in the morning, and the Rev Dr. Raleigh in the evening It was reported that the whole amount required was forthcoming—about £4,500—and that the building was free of debt Mr Dobell himself contributed generously—how generously only he himself knew Mr Samuel Morley gave £500, Mr W Joynson also gave £500, and Mr Thomas Jackson, of Eltham Park, £200 "

In 1871 the Rev Benjamin Price began his ministry in succession to the Rev J. Marshall, who had removed to Godalming.

The Rev. E J. Penford, the present pastor, succeeded Mr. Price in 1879. "In 1882, the church and schoolroom were renovated, and the organ re-built and enlarged at a cost of about £500, and a schoolroom was added to the mission chapel at New Eltham—which had been erected during the ministry of Mr Price —at a further cost of £400

In 1894 the church and schoolroom were again renovated at the cost of about £500. On this occasion the old church windows were replaced by windows of coloured glass.

"In 1895, Mr. Dobell, of whom so much has had to be said, passed into the Unseen He died on the 2nd March, in the 82nd year of his age, and was buried on March 8th, the Rev Morlais Jones, a valued friend for many years, conducting the service in the church, and the pastor that at the grave in the parish churchyard."

THE BIBLE CHRISTIANS

The first chapel of the Bible Christians was built in what is now Elizabeth-terrace The chapel is now used as a workshop by Mr.

Brand (builder, &c.). In the year 1880 the little community migrated to Park-place, where a more commodious building had been erected

A year or two ago the Bible Christians allied themselves with the Free Methodists and New Connection Methodists, and the community thus formed was called The United Methodist Church It is under this designation that its religious work is now carried on The pastor is the Rev. F L. Buxton.

ELTHAM PARK BAPTIST CHURCH

We are indebted to the Rev. A C. Chambers (pastor) for the following note upon the history of the newly-formed Eltham Park Baptist Church —

"The Baptist settlers on the new estate became desirous of a place of worship for their own teaching and practice They formed a small committee in 1903 The London Baptist Association came to their aid by purchasing an excellent site in Westmount-road, and upon this was erected a school chapel, affording accommodation for some 300 persons. This building was dedicated and opened for public worship on Good Friday, April 10th, 1903, a special sermon being preached by the Rev. R. O. Johns, of Dalston Junction. In the following year the Rev Arthur C. Chambers, of Belvedere, was unanimously chosen as the first pastor, and he commenced his ministry on Easter Sunday, 1904 The present membership of the church is 140, with a congregation that completely fills the present building, and that, together with an excellent Sunday school of 150 scholars, warrants the hope of a permanent and commodious church being erected at no distant date "

THE BAPTIST CHURCH (SALCASKIE-ROAD)

Mr. Alfred Smith has kindly provided us with the following brief history of the Baptists in Eltham :—

" The Eltham Baptist Church, of Balcaskie-road, was formed as far back as the year 1883. A few friends had been in the habit of walking either to Woolwich or to Lee to attend chapel, and at the invitation of Mr. A Smith they met together to consider the possibility

22A

of forming a Baptist Church for Eltham, there having been no Baptist Church, prior to this, in the village.

"The result of the meeting was that steps were taken to provide a suitable building, which proved to be a difficult undertaking Ultimately, however, the premises, afterwards known as the Eltham Baptist Meeting Room, were secured The room was really a part of the old brewery, at the entrance to Jubilee-cottages It was made quite comfortable, and seated, at an expense of about £75

"On Tuesday, May 29th, 1883, this room was opened for public worship and Mr John Box of Soho Baptist Chapel, London, preached at 3.15 p m , and in the evening at 6 30 a public meeting was held Through the kindness of the Strict Baptist Association and many friends the whole of the money was collected, and the church was started free of debt For 21 years the Church met in this room, and although during that time they tried to get a more suitable building, or ground to erect a building upon, and had formed a fund for this purpose, it was not until the estate known as the Corbett Estate was opened that their efforts were successful

"At this time they had as their pastor Mr S Banks, and through his strenuous efforts, also his wife's and other members of the Church, a big effort was made to secure a suitable site and erect a building Entirely through the great kindness of Mrs Kennard, of St. Margaret's, Foots Cray-road, New Eltham, they were presented with the freehold of their present ground, which cost, apart from law expenses, the sum of £245. This handsome gift without a farthing cost to the Church was made over to trustees, and is now the property of the Church This is only part of the gift of this generous lady, as many more tokens of her kindness were received during the building and the opening of the present chapel, to which a memorial stone in the front testifies Many other friends gave substantial help, and many more gave of their penury, while others gave themselves to the enormous work entailed It

is recorded that over a hundred pounds was spent in postage appeals and receipts

"On Whit Monday in June, 1904, the building known as Eltham Baptist Church, Balcaskie-road, was opened for public worship, and it does great credit to the architect, Mr Charles Chapman, and also to the builder, Mr Lowe, of Chislehurst "

THE WESLEYAN CHURCH

The following notes upon the history of the Wesleyan Church in Eltham are written for us by Mr G W E. Dowsett:—

"The development of the Wesleyan Methodist Church in Eltham is very interesting. When the Eltham Park Estate had been partly built upon, and a fair proportion of the houses occupied, there were naturally a few Methodists amongst the inhabitants Their presence set in motion projects for the erection of a church of their own denomination.

"Eventually, a site was acquired at the junction of Earlshall and Westmount-roads, measuring 250ft. by 120ft , and costing £860 Upon this site a temporary iron building was erected at a cost of £280, and opened on September 25th, 1902.

"It was in this building that the late Dr Walford Green, a greatly beloved minister of the Wesleyan denomination, and then chairman of the Third London District, preached his last sermon on Sunday evening, February 1st, 1903, and administered the sacrament of the Lord's Supper

"The pulpit in this temporary church was supplied during the first year by local preachers from neighbouring Circuits, and in the second year by a resident lay agent, Mr Norman Martyn

"It was not long, however, before it became evident that this structure was far too small to accommodate the ever increasing population, and a movement was made in the direction of erecting a permanent building. Plans were passed, and as the whole scheme from its beginning had been so closely associated with Dr Walford Green, it was decided to designate the church about to be erected 'The Walford Green Memorial Church.'"

"The stone laying ceremony in connection with the church was held on July 11th, 1905, and the building, which seats 650, and cost £5,500, was opened for public worship on Wednesday, April 25th, 1906, and attached to the Blackheath Circuit in September of the same year.

"When the permanent church was about to be erected it was deemed advisable to appoint a resident minister, and the Rev. John J. Johnston rendered admirable service for two years covering the difficult period of transition from the iron building to the present structure.

"At the close of his second year, according to Methodist custom, he being ordained, was entitled to a married man's privileges, but as this young Church was not called upon, and, indeed, not in a position to provide these, Mr. Johnston removed to another Circuit, and the Rev. W. J. Hartley was appointed. At the end of one year, he also was ordained, and the position with regard to him was precisely the same as that which applied to Mr. Johnston, and he also removed. He was followed by the present minister, the Rev. E. Harold Chappel, who is just entering upon the second year of his ministry."

A "CASTLE" TOKEN, 1649.

CHAPTER LXXIV.

THE SCHOOLS OF ELTHAM.

The earliest record of a village schoolmaster at Eltham is in the Parish Registers, in the year 1592.

"Paid to Goodman Bourne and William the schoolmaster for keeping the clock that quarter that he rang the bell from St. Christmas to the Lady Day, 2s."

In the year 1605 there is another entry which refers to schoolmasters, in the plural, and also alludes to a school house. It runs thus —

"Paid to goodman Wyborne for charges at the cominge of the Kinges maiestie into the towne and for ringinge one the byrthe daie of the younge prinse and for charges of Scholmasters the xviij of June 1605 latteses for the skole wyndowes, vjs"

There does not seem to be any indication of the situation of the school in these remote times, but the general belief is that the scene of William, the schoolmaster's, pedagogic labours was in the room over the church porch. In later years the school, in all probability, was near the Vicar's barn, which stood a little way to the west of the church

THE NATIONAL SCHOOLS

The oldest of our existing educational institutions is the National School, which dates back close upon a century, for it was established in connection with the National Society, by the Rev. J K Shaw Brooke, in the year 1814

From a report of the Charity Commissioners, dated 1819, we learn that twenty pounds was paid to the master for teaching 20 boys on Mrs Legatt's foundation   The first register of the school is still preserved, and among the first batch of boys admitted were many bearing names that are still familiar in Eltham, e g :—

    James Shearing, aged 7
    John Scriven, aged 11
    Thomas Foster, aged 6
    Edward Hand, aged 10.
    William Stevens, aged 6
    Charles Russell, aged 9
    James Kingston, aged 7.
    I Wakeman, aged 6.
    T Wakeman, aged 8

W. Castleton, G Castleton, I. Miskin, S. Norton, I Norton, H Francis, and many other well-known names, are on the interesting list

"The National School referred to in the report of 1819, which was for boys and girls, and an infants' school, established in 1840, appears to have been carried on on a site, the use of which was granted by her Majesty's Commissioners of Woods and Forests " (Report Char. Com , 1895) The site was at the end of Pound-place, adjoining the Back-lane

"By an indenture, dated 18th December, 1851, and enrolled the 22nd January, 1852, a piece of land containing 1r. 8p., situate in East-lane, Eltham, was granted by a voluntary convey-ance, made under the School Sites Act of the 5th Vict , as a site for an infant school for poor persons of the parish, in conjunction with the National School of the parish, and to be in union with the National Society, and for the residence of a school-mistress, and for no other purpose, such school to be under the manage-ment of the governors of the National School of the parish, and to be open to Government in-spection." (Report of Char Com)

The above extract gives the origin and date of the infant school, which still exists in the Back-lane.

The following extract gives the date and origin of the Roper-street Schools

"By an indenture, dated 16th March, 1868, and enrolled the 21st April, 1868, the trustees of Roper's Charity by voluntary conveyance made under the School Sites Acts granted . a piece of land containing one acre, part of a field belonging to Roper's Charity . . . upon trust to permit the premises and all buildings thereon erected or to be erected to be used as a school for the education of children and adults, or children only of the labouring, manufacturing and other poorer classes in the parish, and for the residence of the master and mistress of the school, and for no other purpose. The deed directs (inter alia) that the school shall be in union with the National Society, and shall be open to Government inspection." (Charity Com Report, 1895)

It will be seen from the above dates that the National Schools have been carrying on their educational work for close upon a hundred years. Up to the year 1902 they depended for their maintenance upon the Government grant, supplemented by local subscriptions and dona-tions, and the proceeds of certain endowments They were managed by a committee of twelve, eleven of whom were nominated by the sub-scribers, the Vicar of Eltham being ex-officio chairman

By the Education Act of 1902, the London County Council was made responsible for the educational liabilities, and the managers for the maintenance of the buildings. The com-mittee itself was also reduced in size, being required to consist of four "foundation managers," and two representative managers, one of whom was appointed by the London County Council, and the other by the Woolwich Borough Council During the last few years alterations and improvements in the buildings and drainage system, required by the County Council, have been carried out by the managers at a cost of £750.

POPE STREET SCHOOLS

To provide accommodation for the increasing population at Pope-street, the London School Board opened a mixed school there in April, 1881. The original buildings were those now used as the infants' school, and the accommoda-tion was for 240 children

Six years after, in April, 1887, the main build-ings were opened for boys and girls, 180 each, the infants remaining in the old building.

In 1904, the departmets for the older children were considerably enlarged, to accommodate 298 boys and 298 girls

THE GORDON SCHOOLS

The rapid development of the Corbett Estate, upon the northern side of the railway, necessi-tated the provision of further school accom-modation in the parish In the year 1902 the London School Board erected temporary iron buildings in the Grangehill-road, for a mixed department and infants

This was followed by the erection of the Gordon Schools in 1904. These schools consist of three departments—boys, girls, and infants, to accommodate 380, 380, and 382, respectively

DEANSFIELD ROAD SCHOOL

Under the impression that the rapid increase of population would continue, the London School Board, just before it went out of exist-ence, completed the arrangements for the build-ing of the Deansfield-road Schools, for a mixed department and infants As the contracts were signed, it devolved upon the County Council, in taking over the educational liabilities of the Board, in 1903, to carry out the work that had been arranged by the defunct School Board So the Deansfield-road Schools were built, and opened as elementary schools

But at this time there was a cessation of the building operations, and it was found that there was no immediate need for the schools for elementary education purposes The Lon-don County Council, therefore, closed the school as an elementary school, and opened it in 1906 as a Secondary School for Girls, in which capacity the main portion of the build-ings is now being used.

Other portions have been transformed into a hostel for the accommodation of some of the students of Avery-hill Training College.

AVERY HILL TRAINING COLLEGE

The London County Council, having acquired the mansion and park of Avery Hill, threw them open for the use of the public. In the year 1906 the house, after undergoing a great deal of necessary alterations, to fit it for the purpose, was opened as a Training College for School-mistresses. There are 360 students.

THE MOTTINGHAM COUNCIL SCHOOLS

Previous to the year 1875 there does not seem to have been any attempt to provide a school for Mottingham, under the Education Acts. In May of that year, as a result of a notice received from the Education Department, a Vestry was held at the Porcupine Inn, pursuant to notice, for the purpose of considering the best means of providing the school accommodation required under the Education Act. At this meeting it was decided to inform the Department that the necessary school accommodation should be provided out of the rates.

On February 3rd, 1876, the Chairman drew the attention of the Vestry to the notice respecting the election of members to the School Board of Mottingham, and the ratepayers present nominated the five following gentlemen namely Mr. Alfred Alexander, Mr. James F Redgrave, the Rev Arthur J. Law, Mr Horace Hammond and Mr. Henry Maeers

The second School Board election, in 1879, was very keenly contested, Mr Thomas Chester Haworth, whose name was also closely associated with Eltham history at the time, being the leader of the discontented section against the old Board. Mr Haworth was elected at the head of the poll.

The first Board School was in Devonshire-road, where Mr G Turner now has a bakery. The present schools were opened September, 1877. The first master appointed was Mr D H. Waters, who still holds the position. In 1894 a new infants' department was erected on the Dorset-road

THE ROYAL NAVAL SCHOOL

Although the Royal Naval School does not come in the same category as the educational institutions we have mentioned, its removal to Mottingham is a matter of local interest, which must be entered upon the records of our village history

Established in the first place at Camberwell, in temporary buildings, the school was removed to New Cross in 1843, where it continued till 1889, when it took up its permanent abode at Mottingham. Upon a stone in the south-east corner of the present building is found the following interesting, and in some respects remarkable, inscription —

"This stone was laid 1st June, 1843, by H.R.H Prince Consort, K G, as the foundation stone of the buildings at New Cross, and placed in its present position by Lieutenant H.R.H Prince George of Wales, R N, on the 17th July, 1889"

The historical interest of the school is in some measure heightened by the fact that its present premises comprise what was once known as Fairy Hall, formerly Fairy Hill, at one time the residence of the Right Hon. Henry, Earl Bathurst, Lord High Chancellor of Great Britain, 1771 From "The Lives of the Lord Chancellors," we learn that he retained the first magistracy in the kingdom longer than More, Bacon, Clarendon, or Somers, and "to his credit be it remembered that he reached such a height without a dishonourable action."

CHAPTER LXXV.

SOME ELTHAM WORTHIES OF THE NINETEENTH CENTURY.

We will now give some brief records of the more prominent of the public men of Eltham during the latter part of the nineteenth Century

ROBERT JOHN SAUNDERS

Mr R J Saunders was a co-worker with the Rev. J K Shaw Brooke, whose biography is given in a previous chapter He took a keen interest in the National Schools, as long as he lived in Eltham Mr Saunders held a commission in the Royal Artillery during the Peninsular War, and was present at Waterloo, but was not in action on the day of the battle

He married Miss Isabella Nicholson, daughter of William Nicholson, Esq, of St Margaret's, Rochester, and came to Eltham with her in 1820, and for a time occupied the cottage opposite the Moat Cottage, as it was then called In this house Frederick Grove Saunders was born on the 24th December, 1820, and Mr Saunders shortly after moved into what was then known as Court Farm, now, Eltham Court, and farmed the land attached to it For some years he held an appointment as Inspector of Factories He left Eltham in 1850, and died in 1852.

RICHARD MILLS

Mr. Richard Mills, who died at The Moat on the 21st April, 1880, in his 95th year, settled in Eltham, in what was then called the Moat Cottage, on his marriage in August, 1818, to Miss Sarah Wilgress, daughter of the Rev Dr. Wilgress, who lived in the house in the High Street now known as Ivy Court

Mr Mills during his long residence in Eltham took an active part in all parochial matters, and succeeded the Rev J K Shaw Brooke as Treasurer of the Eltham Endowed Charities, and Secretary of the Eltham National Schools He was also Churchwarden of the Parish Church He was one of the "Six Clerks,," a Chancery appointment, which he held till the abolition of the office, when he was made Taxing Master in Chancery

THOMAS LEWIN

Mr Thomas Lewin was a distinguished member of a family which has been associated with Eltham for upwards of two centuries. He was born at the house called Merlewood, in the High Street, now the residence of Mr J. Roselli, in the year 1798, and died in 1873 By profession, Mr Lewin was a Barrister, and he took a keen and active interest in the welfare of his native place He was a magistrate of the Blackheath division, an Eltham Guardian for many years at the Lewisham Board, a Warden of the Parish Church, and a Trustee of the New Cross Turnpike Trust

Mr Lewin was always a friend and benefactor of the working class of Eltham The Eltham Friendly Society, which he was the means of establishing as far back as 1830, and which still exists as a flourishing institution in Eltham, is a standing memorial of the interest he took in social problems Another memorial of the kind is the volume of "Brief Essays on subjects of Social Economy," which were published from his pen by Messrs Simpkin and Marshall, in 1856 These essays, upon such topics as "Civil Government," "Capital and Money," "Wages," "Endowments," "Taxation," etc, etc, deal with problems that are of vital interest in the present day, and the masterly way in which the writer discusses them reveals an acquaintance with the evils of the social condition of his time, such, perhaps, as could only have been obtained through his experience as a magistrate, poor-law guardian, and other offices he filled.

Mr Lewin lived at the "Barn-house," and the well-known clock which for so many years has proclaimed the hour to that part of Eltham, was erected at the Barn-house by him

FREDERICK GEORGE SAUNDERS

Mr. F G Saunders, the son of Mr R J Saunders, was born at the "Court" in 1820, and died on New Year's Day, 1901. He married the third daughter of Mr Richard Mills, in 1846, and resided for some years after in Eltham He was exceedingly popular as the first Captain of the Volunteer Corps When the Parish Church was erected, he bore the entire cost of the south aisle as a memorial to his father and other members of his family He also gave a donation of £500 towards the erection of the Cottage Hospital

RICHARD BLOXAM

We have already referred in another chapter to the work of Mr Bloxam in connection with the enlargement of the "Court," and the re clamation of Palace precincts, which had got into delapidation and decay. But Mr Bloxam was also a parochial worker He was a member of the Committee of the National Schools for many years, and was the Secretary of the Build ing Fund of both the Parish Church and Holy Trinity Church He also took a keen interest in the local Corps of Volunteers, of which he was the Captain, and the memory of him in this capacity is still cherished by the old rifle men, whom we may call the old guard, and a good number of whom are still left to recount the glories of the early volunteering days.

THOMAS CHESTER HAWORTH

Mr Thomas Chester Haworth was a well-known figure in the Eltham familiar to the last generation, and many stories may be gleaned from the old inhabitants of his characteristic methods of life and business. He first settled in the village as a tailor, and that he worked his way to a position of considerable import-ance and influence, so impressing the imagina-tion of his contemporaries that the mention of

his name never fails to give rise to vivacious comments, even at the present day, is some evidence of the individuality of the man and the forcefulness of his character. He has left his mark upon Eltham history of the Victorian times His disregard of convention is shewn by the fact that in order to avoid burial in the Eltham Churchyard, he constructed for him-self and family a tomb by the wayside in a line at Mottingham Here they were buried, and the structure, until quite recently, could be easily seen by the passers-by During the pre-sent year, however, it has been walled in

Among the numerous enterprises of Mr Thomas Chester Haworth was a newspaper called " The Eltham Journal," which appeared somewhat irregularly for a number of years In some respects it was a unique journal, and was regarded as the "organ" of Mr Haworth.

DAVID KING, M D.

Amongst our portraits, on another page, is that of Dr David King He is well remembered by the older inhabitants of to day as the popu-lar doctor who practised in Eltham for fifty years, covering the middle part of the Nine-teenth Century. He lived at King's Dene, which stands at the corner of Sherard Road, where it joins the High Street

HENRY WILLIAM DOBELL

We have already alluded to Mr W H Dobell's work in connection with the Congre-gational Church, a work which has left its impress upon our parochial history Mr Dobell's family came originally from the North of France at the time of the Huguenot perse-cutions, the Sussex and Cheshire branches of the family dating back to the early part of the Seventeenth Century The father of Mr. Dobell was intended for the Navy, and was present at Lord Howe's action on the 1st of June, 1794, off Cape Ushant He was then twenty years of age In that memorable action the French were defeated, six of their ships being taken and one sunk.

Young Dobell was subsequently introduced to George the Fourth by Lord Howe, and the King, taking a fancy to him, assigned to him a place at Court Afterwards he became State Page to their Majesties, George IV., William IV , and Queen Victoria, in succession.

The original warrant for lodging at St James's Palace, now in the possession of Mrs Dobell, is dated January 28th, 1822, the third year of his Majesty's reign. One of his daughters was born at St James's, in January, 1807

Henry William Dobell was the fourth son of John Dobell, and was born on August 8th, 1813 He was educated at Christ's Hospital Afterwards he proceeded to a post at the Custom House, London In 1854 he was appointed Comptroller General of Customs, retired in 1874, and died on March 2nd, 1895 His widow still resides at Sherard House

THOMAS JACKSON

Mr. Thomas Jackson came to reside at Park Farm Place about the middle of the Nineteenth Century, and for upwards of forty years was a prominent figure in the village history The story of his life, as revealed in the remarkable book entitled, "Industry Illustrated," is an example of the triumph of self reliance, diligence, and integrity. The many incidents in the career of a man who had started life as a plough boy when eight years of age, and eventually became one of the most eminent and successful civil engineering contractors of his generation, read more like a romance than the records of a real life.

It is not possible to give these incidents here, as they would occupy too much space We can do little more than record some of the great works that he carried out. We will, however, give one almost tragic circumstance, which occurred after he had relinquished the work of plough boy and taken up that of canal boy It occurred on the Birmingham Canal, called "The Cut"

"I found this work," says Mr Jackson, 'very different to my plough driving The boats being very old and leaky, I was constantly wet and had to remain so till I went to bed, when my clothes were put to dry by the fire till morning"

While engaged at this work he had a narrow escape from drowning He says

"I was leading the horse under a low bridge, and had got on the wrong (or canal) side of him, when he happened to strike his head against the arch and knocked me backwards into the water I recollect gradually sinking, when I felt the towing line rub across my chest; I clutched it, but remember no more till I found myself on the bank of the towing path My mate then placed me on the back of the old horse and sent me home to my lodgings alone. On the way, I had to pass some cottages where one of my father's workmen lived, and just as I was passing, this man happened to be standing at the door, who, seeing how pale and ill I looked, said 'Tom, lad, what's th' matter, thou looks pale?' I told him the horse had knocked me into the 'Cut' He quickly had me off the horse's back, but I had become unconscious, and remained so till next day, when I came to again, and found myself in his son's little bed, very ill, in which condition I remained several days, but was at length able to go to my work again"

Mr Jackson was often heard to express his deep sorrow at never being able to find out this man in after years, when it was in his power to reward him handsomely for his humane act—which, in all probability, was the means of saving his life

A deep sense of gratitude prompted Mr Jackson to go to the house where the poor man had lived, hoping either to see him or someone belonging to him, but he had left that part of the country, and though Mr Jackson made diligent enquiries after his benefactor, he was never able to ascertain his whereabouts, much to his grief and disappointment

He was associated with George Stephenson in Railway Construction, and the great engineer has left on record his high appreciation of the work of Mr Jackson

One of the greatest works was that of the completion of the Caledonian Canal It was originally commenced in 1803, but the work was found to be extremely difficult In 1822, it was opened before the work, as originally designed, was completed The result was a failure The Government, in 1843, decided to do something towards its completion, but stipulated that the cost should not exceed £150,000. The tenders of an Aberdeen firm ran into £239,000 Mr Jackson's was £136,000 By a stroke of genius, Mr Jackson fulfilled the contract Another of his great works was the construction of the

"Harbours of refuge in The Channel Islands," and, yet another, not mentioning the many railways, was the "Harrogate Waterworks"

During his residence at Eltham Park, Mr Jackson associated himself with many works of Charity, and his death in the early nineties was greatly mourned

COLONEL NORTH.

Colonel John T North, who, during the latter half of the Nineteenth Century had acquired a world wide name and fame, and may be fairly classed among the nation's celebrities, resided at Avery Hill from 1882 to 1896, when he died suddenly in London, occupies a prominent place in our village history

He has left his mark upon the face of the parish in the great work which he accomplished at Avery Hill, which locality he may be said to have transformed Having purchased the estate of Mr Boyd, in the year 1882, he pulled down the greater part of the old house and erected the present mansion and winter gardens with which the public are so familiar He laid out the park and diverted the course of the old road which ran much nearer the house than the present one, removing in the operation the old farm house formerly occupied by Mr Grace, and constructed at great cost the fine piece of road which runs in a direct line from the bottom of the Lemon-Well Hill to the junction with the Bexley Road, at White's Cross

And the name of Colonel North will long be remembered by the parishioners of Eltham His bountiful hospitality, his thoughtful consideration for his poorer neighbours, especially at Christmas time, when it was his annual custom to provide every cottage with the good things needful for the season's festivity, his generous patronage of local sport, and his readiness to give of his wealth towards the maintenance of local institutions, charitable and otherwise, are memories that will long be associated with his name and with Avery Hill

Among his public offices the one with which Eltham folks are perhaps most familiar, is that of the Honorary Colonelship of the Second Tower Hamlet Engineers, for it was one of the annual events of the neighbourhood, when, as was his custom, he invited the regiment to a

week under canvas in his park Here the regiment were regally entertained at their host's expense

"The Colonel," by which epithet he was known by his friends and associates in the City, was never happier than when contributing to the enjoyment of those about him His hospitality was of the generous, old-world kind, and many tales are still told of these military celebrations and of the open house which was kept on the occasions, recalling in some degree the conditions which prevailed at the other end of the village, centuries before, in the days of "Merrie England"

No less than four foreign nations conferred Orders upon Colonel North, in recognition of his public services The Khedive of Egypt, in 1894, made him "Commander of the Imperial Order of Osmanich." The King of the Belgians awarded him the "Order of the Lion, First Class," a similar Order to that conferred upon Sir Henry Stanley, the Explorer France gave him the "Order of Merit" (Agriculture), and from the late King of Italy he received "The Second Class Order of Umberto"

His keen interest in the welfare of national sport is illustrated by the fact that he was one of the originators of the national testimonial to W G Grace, the veteran cricketer On the dedication page of W G.'s book, "A Hundred Centuries," we find the following —

"To Colonel John Thomas North, a thorough all-round sportsman, and the first subscriber to my national testimonial fund, I dedicate this book (Signed) W G Grace July, 1895"

The sad news of Colonel North's death came as a surprise and shock, not only to Eltham, but to the whole country, and his loss was followed by genuine sorrow Commenting upon the mournful circumstance, one of the great daily papers wrote at the time "Colonel North was a prominent figure in the crowded canvas of English life. The news of his sudden end will be received with sorrow in many and varied quarters He had a niche for himself in the popular imagination The most rabid Socialist had a good word for "the Colonel" He was so thoroughly human in all he did that envy of his riches was lost in a sense of the good

fellowship with him.   Idolised at
Leeds as a typical Yorkshire man—bluff, hearty,
hard-headed, and successful—he was held in regard throughout the country as a general
favourite

"He spent his wealth in regal fashion,
not only in the entertainment of his hosts of
friends and acquaintances, but also in public
purposes and in charity. His name will be perpetuated in Yorkshire by his princely gift of
Kirkstall Abbey and grounds to the town of
Leeds The turf had no more generous and
sportsmanlike patron His horses ran straight
He trained and raced them because he had the
true Yorkshire man's instinct for sport. We
deplore his death A man of ideas, enterprise,
and financial daring—thoroughly English in his
frankness, breadth, and variety of character—
can ill be spared "

The funeral of Colonel North was a singularly
impressive demonstration of the esteem and
regard in which he was held The interment
was in the Parish Church-yard. Some 800
wreaths and floral designs, requiring six vehicles
for their conveyance, were sent by friends and
societies from far and near The procession was
of such dimensions that when the Church was
reached the last carriage had not left the keeper's
cottage in the Bexley Heath Road Every shop
and public-house in the village was closed upon
the occasion, and the blinds of every house in
the High Street were lowered Among the dis
tinguished visitors at the grave was the Belgian
Ambassador, representing the King of the Belgians ; while the Khedive of Egypt sent a letter
of condolence to Mrs North

In December, 1905, His Majesty, King Edward
VII , conferred the honour of Knight-hood upon
the Colonel's eldest son Sir Harry and Lady
North reside in Eltham, at Lemon Well, their
house and grounds adjoining the Avery Hill
Estate

ALEXANDER GEORGE MILNE

The following note is extracted from the Log
Book of the Eltham National School, in which
the entry was made on June 16th, 1903 .—

"Mr A G Milne, who for nearly thirty
years has been a member of the Committee of
Managers of the Eltham National Schools, died

on Saturday, June 13th, at his residence in the
Court Yard, after a long illness. He was within
a few days of completing his sixty-seventh birthday.

"Mr Milne was born in Eltham, where his
father and grandfather had both resided, and
he lived here nearly all his life He was a great
reader, and was well versed in all matters relating to the Antiquities of Eltham, upon which
he was a recognised authority He was the
author of a pamphlet on " Eltham Palace and
those who visited it in by-gone years," which
was read to the members of the Kent Archæological Society on the occasion of their visit to
Eltham in the summer of 1899.

" Throughout his life he took a great interest
in all parochial matters, especially those connected with the Parish Church He also filled
the office of Secretary to the Schools, and for a
time, after the death of Colonel Gordon, was
Treasurer He was also for many years a
trustee of the Eltham Charities "

In the compilation of this " Story of Royal
Eltham," the writer would like to acknowledge
his indebtedness to the research work of Mr A
G Milne The little pamphlet alluded to is
not only a mine of information most accurately
set forth, but its foot-notes, indicating authori
ties, are most valuable to the student It is
possible that much which has been written in
this book would not have found its way into
the pages, but for the "finger posts" pointing
the way, which are contained in the notes of
Mr. Milne

A POST-SCRIPT

Happily there are with us yet many who were
public workers of the Parish from the sixties
of last century and onwards Some of these
have earned a well-deserved repose, others are
still in harness.

Of the former are Dr Jeken, who for the
greater part of the last half century practised in
Eltham, Mr George Pritchard, Mr. Walter
Richardson, and Mr W. P. Moore, who have
occupied important positions in connection with
the Church, the Charities, the Schools, and
Hospital.

Mr T W Mills succeeded his father, Mr.
Richard Mills, as the Treasurer of the Eltham

Charities, a position which he still holds. He has also been Secretary to the Hospital, a Churchwarden of Holy Trinity for 39 years, and a member of the Committee of Management of the National Schools.

Mr. W. J. Mortis has, perhaps, held more public offices in Eltham than anyone. At the age of 22 years he migrated from Woolwich and settled in Eltham. In 1854 he was appointed Parish Clerk, and fulfilled the duties of the post for 46 years. In the same year he was made Vestry Clerk, and the Registrar of Births and Deaths. In 1858 he was appointed Assistant Overseer, Collector of Rates, and Secretary and Manager of the Eltham Gas Company. In 1856 he was Clerk to the Eltham Committee of the Plumstead District (afterwards Lee) Board of Works. In 1900 he was Co-opted as Alderman of the Woolwich Borough Council.

In 1903 he was elected a Borough Councillor for the Eltham Ward, and in the same year was elected a Guardian of the Eltham Ward of the Lewisham Union.

In the old days, he was Colour-Sergeant in the local Volunteers. He has also identified himself with the work of the Cottage Hospital; has been Chairman of the Committee of the same, and contributed largely towards its fund. He has been also a Manager of the Eltham Council Schools, and for many years a member of the Committee of Management of the National Schools. Of the latter body he is Correspondent and Treasurer.

Mr. Mortis's knowledge of the Eltham of the last half-century is quite unique, and the writer is indebted to his store of knowledge for much that has been written in these pages concerning that period.

Mr. W. B. Hughes has also filled many public offices. He was a member of the Plumstead Board of Works, afterwards of the Lee Board of Works. He was one of the Councillors of the Eltham Ward on the Borough Council for six years, and has been a Guardian for the last 12 years upon the Lewisham Board. On this body he has been for six years Chairman of the Works Committee, and the representative upon the Committee of Management of Anerley Poor Law Schools.

"THE STOCKS."

No. 162.

Mr. J. HAYWOOD   (Parish Beadle).

(1909).

APPENDIX.

The following notes, some of them accidental omissions from the body of the book, and others of matters connected with Eltham history, are here submitted in the form of an Appendix.

JOHN OF ELTHAM.

The following details, extracted by Mr. A. J. Sargent, from the Archives of Westminster Abbey, and kindly sent to the writer since the chapter on John of Eltham was in type, are very interesting, and reveal a circumstance, connected with that Prince, which seems to have been passed unnoticed by all our local historians.

"Warrant for the removal of the body of John of Eltham.

"Edward par la grace de dieu Roi Dangleterre Seignour Dirlande et Duc Daquitaine, As noz cheres en dieu Abbe et Covent de Westmonster salutz. Nous avons prione cherement que selone la esleccion et le devis de nostre tres-chere dame et miere Isabel Raine Dengleterre, vueilletz ordiner et suffrir que le corps de nostre tres-cher frere Johan jadis Counte de Cornewaill peusse estre re-muez et translatez du lieu ou il gist jusques a autre covenable place entre les Roials.

"Faisant toutesfoitz reserver et garder les places plus honourables illoeques pour le gissir et la sepulture de nous et de noz heirs, selonc ce que reson le voudra droitement demander. Les choses avantdites ne vueilletz lesser en nulle manere. . . . .

"Donne souz nostre prive seal a Brusselles le xxiiij jour d'August, lan de nostre regne treszime."

(Endorsed) Littera Domini Regis de sepultura sua seservanda, et remocione fratris sui concedenda.

TRANSLATION.

"Edward by the Grace of God King of England, Lord of Ireland and Duke of Aquitain, to our beloved in God, the Abbey and Convent of Westminster.

"We lovingly pray you that according to the wish and instruction of our dearly beloved lady mother, Isabella, Queen of England, you will ordain and suffer that the body of our beloved brother, John, Earl of Cornwall, may be removed and translated from the place where it lies to another and more suitable place among those of the royal lineage.

"Notwithstanding which that more honourable places shall be reserved there for the interment and sepulture of ourselves and our heirs according as propriety would justly require. Do not fail in the things authorised in any manner whatsoever.

"Given under our privy seal at Brussels the 24th day of August, the 13th year of our reign."

(Endorsement). "Letter to His Majesty the King, concerning the reservation of a place of sepulture and granting space for his brother's body."

THE ELTHAM MOTION.

In a previous page of this book allusion is made to the "Eltham Motion," or the "Eltham Thing," a subject about which there have been many conjectures but very little information of a definite character.

There is, however, a very scarce work at the British Museum written by Thomas Thymme, "A Professeur of Divinitie," and published in 1612, under the title of "A Dialogue philosophicall, wherein Nature's secret closet is opened. . Together with the wittie invention of an Artificial Perpetuall Motion, presented to the King's most excellent Majestie."

23

The King was James I. The invention was what we know as the "Eltham Motion.". The inventor was one Cornelius Drebbel, a German scientist of the day who had won fame at the various European Courts as a genius at invention, and who was given rooms at Eltham Palace to set up his "Motion." It seems that Drebbel's list of inventions is a very long one. He

patterne of the Instrument itself, as it was presented to the King's most royall hands by Cornelius Drebble of Alchmar in Holland . . . to make plaine the demonstration unto you that the heavens move and not the earth, I will set before you a memorable Modell and Patterne, representing the Motion of the Heavens about the fixed earth, made by Art in the immitation

ELTHAM MOTION.

invented them all without the "aid of the black art," but by natural philosophic alone, and by his experiments he so gained the King's favour, that his Majesty granted him a pension of 2,000 guilders. He died in London in 1634.

In the preface to his book, in reference to the Perpetual Motion, Thymme says : " And for that rare things more much, I have thought it pertinent to this Treatise to set before thee a most strange and wittie invention of another Archimider, which concerneth Artificiall Perpetuall Motion, imitating Nature by a lively

of Nature, which instrument is perpetually in motion without the means of steele, springs and waights."

The picture we give is from an etching of the original in the book referred to.

JOHN EVELYN AND THE VICAR OF ELTHAM.

In his " Diary," Evelyn has made numerous references to Dr. Owen, the Vicar of Eltham, with whom he was on intimate terms. These entries are so interesting, and present the conditions of life at the time so vividly, that we venture to reproduce a number of them It is this Dr Owen, who is referred to in the short life of Thomas Doggett, in this book.

" 1649, January 31st

I went through a Course of Chymistry, at Sayes Court Now was the Thames frozen over, and horrid tempests of wind

The villany of the rebels proceeding now so far as to try, condemn, and murder our excellent King, on the 30th of this month, struck me with such horror, that I kept the day of his martyrdom a fact, and would not be present at that execrable wickedness, receiving the sad account of it from my brother George, and Mr Owen, who came to visit me this afternoon, and recounted all the circumstances "

" 18th March, 1649

Mr Owen, a sequestered and learned minister, preached in my parlour, and gave us the blessed Sacrament, now wholly out of use in the parish churches, on which the Presbyterians and fanatics had usurped "

" 18 March, 1652.

That worthy divine, Mr Owen, of Eltham, a sequestered minister, came to visit me "

" 2nd Sept , 1652

Mr Owen, the sequestered divine, of Eltham, christened my son by the name of Richard "

" 1st January, 1653

I set apart in preparation for the Blessed Sacrament, which the next day, Mr Owen administered to me and all my family at Sayes Court, preaching on John vi., 32, 33, showing the exceeding benefits of our Blessed Saviour taking our nature upon him He had christened my son and Churched my wife in our own house as before noticed "

" 11 October, 1653

" My son, John Stansfield, was born, being my second child, and christened by the name of my mother's father, that name, now quite extinct, being of Cheshire

Christened by Mr Owen, in my library at Sayes Court, where he afterwards Churched my wife, I always making use of him on these occasions, because the parish minister durst not have officiated according to the form and usage of the Church of England, to which I always adhered "

" 25 October, 1653

Mr Owen preached in my library at Sayes Court on Luke xviii , 7, 8, an excellent discourse upon the unjust judge, showing why Almighty God would sometimes be compared by such similitudes He afterwards administered to us all the Holy Sacrament "

" 29th March, 1654.

That excellent man, Mr Owen, preached in my library on Matt xxviii , 6, a resurrection sermon, and after it we all received the Holy Communion "

" 3rd December, 1654 Advent Sunday

There being no Office at the Church but extemporary prayers after the Presbyterian way, for now all forms were prohibited, and most of the preachers, were usurpers, I seldom went to Church upon solemn feasts , but, either went to London, where some of the orthodox sequestered Divines did privately use the Common Prayer, administer the Sacraments, etc , or else I procured one to officiate in my house , wherefor, on the 10th, Dr Richard Owen, the sequestered Minister of Eltham, preached to my family in my library, and gave us the Holy Communion "

" 26th June, 1658

To Eltham, to visit honest Mr Owen "

" 22nd August, 1664

I went from London to Wotton, to assist at the funeral of my sister-in law, the Lady Cotton, buried in our dormitory there, she being put up in lead Dr Owen made a profitable and pathetic discourse, concluding with an eulogy of that virtuous, pious, and deserving lady It was a very solemn funeral, with about fifty mourners. I came back next day with my wife to London "

MRS OWEN'S TULIPS

The following letters between Mrs Owen, the wife of the well-known Vicar of Eltham, who was sequestered in the days of the Commonwealth, and John Evelyn, the famous diarist, are very interesting, revealing as they do in a realistic way, not only a little local incident, but also illustrating agreeably the habits and intercourse of John Evelyn with his neighbours and friends

Mrs Owen to John Evelyn
Eltham   June 25, 1680.

Honoured Sir,

I am heartily sorry that I forced you to buy tulips for your fine garden.   I must confess your guineas look more glorious than now these tulips do, but, when they come to blow, I hope you will be better pleased than now your are

I have sent you some of my ordinary sort, and, sir, when mine are blown, if you please to come and see them, Mr Evelyn shall buy no more, but have what he pleases for nothing I am so well pleased with those that I have, that I shall neither buy more, nor part with any, unless it be to yourself

I cannot, sir, send my husband's service to you, because I don't acquaint him of my trading in tulips   Sir John Shaw I cannot speak with (being taken up so much with visitors), as to know his mind about a gardener.

Sir, I now beg your pardon for my rude lines, and desire you to assure yourself, that my husband and I, upon any occasion, shall be always ready either to ride or go to serve you or yours Thus having no more, but desiring to have my service to yourself, your lady, and Sir Richard Browne, and your beloved progeny, I shall take leave, and subscribe myself

Your most humble servant, to command,
AMY OWEN

John Evelyn to Mrs Owen
June 26, 1680

Mon Amy (that is, My Friend),

I am not so well pleased with Mrs Owen's letter as with her tulips, because I am assured there must needs be some mistake, and that my gardener (who, perhaps, does not care that I should purchase anything but through his hands and in the common manner), as was to tell you that I would come myself and make friends with you, did leave that out

Can you ever imagine that I looked on your kindness as an imposing on me?   Sure, you know me better than to think so; and when I told you flowers of less value would better become my poor garden, it was neither to save

your money nor reproach your merchandize But I assure you that I not only thank you for [them], but shall condemn you for a very unwise woman if you should forbear to continue a traffic which is so innocent, so laudable, and so frequent even among very great persons You and I, therefore, must come to a better understanding upon this chapter

In the meantime I had a good mind to have sent your last present back again, till all this had been cleared, for I do not love to be overcome in point of generosity, though I see that for this present I must be   You seem to think I complained I had not full measure, and think now to make it up by overwhelming me with your kindness   This is a revenge I cannot long endure, as you shall be sure to find, the first opportunity I can lay hold on.   In the meantime I thank you most heartily for all your good intentions, and the kind offices which both you and the Doctor have ever been ready to do me   Sir. Jo Shaw did us the honour to visit us on Thursday last when it was not my hap to he at home, for which I was very sorry   I met him since casually in London, and kissed him unfeignedly.   I chided myself that I was not there to receive him   Two of our coach-horses are still so lame, that we have not been able to stir out this fortnight, but so soon as they are in very tolerable condition, my wife and I will not fail of kissing your hands, and repaying this civility to Sir John ; and so with our best respects to you and your Doctor,

We remain, etc ,

AN EARTHQUAKE AT ELTHAM
Extracted from Philosophical Transactions (Royal Society), Vol 46

" On Thursday, the 8th Feb , 1749 50, at about half-an-hour after 12, as I was sitting reading with one elbow on the table, on the ground floor in my house at Eltham, Kent, I felt two shocks from East to West, which I immediately thought was an Earthquake, as I had felt something like it once at Naples ; and was confirmed in my opinion, by my wife's running down stairs frighted, and declared it was an earthquake, she having felt one in the West Indies   She was in the room over me, in which room there was China standing on a Cabinet, which, she says, shook in such a manner that she expected it to fall   My children, who were in the room over her, seem to have felt it stronger, as they say, they apprehended a chest of drawers in their room was falling The servants that were in the kitchen, which has no room under it, seem to have felt little of it One that was writing says he felt the dresser move, and the wall, but thought it was only the shutting of a door Other servants in the same room felt nothing at all of it My gardener, who was at work in the garden, felt nothing of it.

" The wind was at S W and had been high in the night and morning, but was much abated, and after this, for some time, it was quite calm, which I believe it is generally observed to be, in those countries where earthquakes are more frequent. A flight of pigeons I have, seemed to be much frightened

" Eltham is about 8 miles S S E from London Bridge, and stands on a hill.

" This account was written before I had heard anything from London "

The above is " An account of the shock of an Earthquake felt Feb 8, 1749-50," by William Fanquier, Esq , F R S.

AN EARL OF ELTHAM.

Frederick Lewis, son of George II , was created Earl of Eltham, and was succeeded in the title by his son, afterwards George III When the latter became King his titles were merged in the Royal dignity, and that of the " Earl of Eltham " has not since been revived

As students of history know well, a pretty strong Jacobite feeling existed in the country through the earlier reigns of the Hanovarian kings, and it was probably to such a source that the uncomplimentary epitaph upon the prince, which found circulation at the time, owes its origin

Epitaph.

" Here lies poor Fred, who was alive and is dead,
And so there is no more to be said
Had it been his brother, 'twere better than another,
Had it been his sister, no one would have missed her
Had it been his father, we would rather.
Had it been the whole lot, no one would have cared a jot

But as it's only Fred, who was alive and now is dead
There is no more to be said "

WHY " KING " JOHN'S PALACE?

The origin of the error of calling Eltham Palace " King " John's Palace is discussed in an interesting manuscript note left by the late Mr Alexander Milne After showing that the name could not have come from the Associations of the English King John with the place, he says :—

" The following, I take it, is most probably the origin of the error After the Restoration, Sir John Shaw (there was a succession of them) was the great man in Eltham, and, practically, with other remains of the Palace, owned the Banqueting Hall, which was used as a Barn, and this became to be known as Sir John's Barn, which title in the course of a couple of hundred years, slipped into King John's Barn

" In illustration and part proof of this theory, it is known that Sir Tregonwell Frampton, a great racing man of the seventeenth century, laid out part of the Park as a racecourse, or training ground, for the first Sir John Shaw This bit of land, a long straight field, south of the House, running nearly parallel with the Green Lane, in my recollection was always spoken of as " King John's Race-Course," an obvious mistake for " Sir John's Race Course " It is curious, however, that the name of King John is often traditionally connected with old buildings with which he really could have had nothing whatever to do "

THE UNDERGROUND PASSAGES

The following additional notes on the Subterranean Passages have been kindly given the writer by Miss Edith Anderson :—

"The existence of a series of underground passages, running westerly in the direction of Lee, and in connection with this Early Palace, had long been popularly believed; but nothing certain was known on the subject till 1834, when Messrs Clayton and King explored these military stratagems of the Middle Ages, and cleared about 700 feet of the passages, which were partially filled with rubbish.

" They descended a ladder, below a trapdoor on the South side of the Hall, and entered a subterranean room, whence a narrow arched passage, about 10ft in length, conducted them to a series of passages with decoys, stairs, and shafts, some vertical, and others on an inclined plane, which—so they suggest—were once used for admitting air, and for hurling down missiles or pitch-balls, with deadly effect, in case of attack

" The remains of two iron gates, completely carbonized, were found in the passage under the moat

" There is a tradition that at Middle Park, through which the passages are believed to run, there are underground stables, sufficient in extent to accommodate sixty horses

" The date of these several passages is assigned to the reign of Edward III or commencement of the 14th century. They were more probably passages of escape in the case of unsuccessful attack from without or from treason within the walls "

THE COTTAGE HOSPITAL

The Cottage Hospital stands in Park Place It's first home was near the Parish Church, where it was opened in 1880 As the original building was found to be of inadequate size, the present buildings were erected in 1889, at a cost of nearly £4,000, the whole of which was defrayed by voluntary contributions In 1906 an addition was made to the structure in the form of the Children's Ward The Hospital is doing a great work in the parish and is one of the most cherished of the parochial institutions.

THE PUBLIC LIBRARY.

The Public Library, opened on the 23rd October, 1906, stands upon ground purchased by the Municipality for the purpose of erecting thereon a Public Hall, District Offices, Electricity Sub Station, Public Library, and Public Baths Only the Sub-Station and the Library, have as yet been put up The latter has a frontage of 80 feet and a depth of 68 feet, and forms an imposing feature of the High Street It was built by " direct labour " under the supervision of the Eltham Buildings Committee of the Council, and of the Borough Engineer, Mr. J Rush Dixon, M.I C E , from the designs of Mr. Maurice B Adams, F R I.B.A The

total cost of the buildings and fittings was about £7,000, of which £5,000 were defrayed by Dr Andrew Carnegie The public part of the building includes, the Library which is on the open access system, a Reading Room, a Magazine Room, and a Reference Reading Room

HOLY TRINITY CHURCH

Since the note on Holy Trinity Church, which appears in an earlier chapter, was written, important alterations and improvements have been made in the building, the work being carried out during the tenure of office of the Rev Henry A Hall, M A , the third Vicar, who was instituted on December 23rd, 1907.

In 1908, a new Choir Vestry was erected, the gift of Mrs A C Latter, in memory of her sister, Miss Agnes Elizabeth Plevins A new ventilation apparatus was also applied

In 1909, the Nave was extended two bays The new Narthex and Baptistery, with nine windows and handsome west window, are the gift of Mrs North, in memory of her late husband, Colonel John Thomas North The Chancel has been extended westward, a low retaining wall separating it from the body of the Church, and upon this is a low iron screen, the gift of Mr T W Mills, who for thirty-nine years had filled the office of Vicar's Warden. The Choir Stalls have been lengthened, Priests' Stalls added, and the whole Chancel paved with black and white marble. A new East window has also been put in, the anonymous gift of two ladies, and another smaller window, representing " The Flight into Egypt," the gift of Mrs Latter, in memory of her aunt, Miss Plevins

All the windows added in 1909 are by Mr. Tower (Messrs Kempe and Co), and are among the finest examples of stained glass art in the South of England

The turret, which contained the historic bell alluded to on a previous page, was condemned by the architects as unsafe, and consequently removed The whole Church has been cleaned and distempered, and the roof repaired

The architects were Sir Arthur Bloomfield and Sons, and the total cost of the work of 1909, is about £3,000

ARCHERY ROAD.

Since the paragraphs were written upon "Woolwich Lane," in the Chapter on "Landmarks Old and New," it has been transformed into "Archery Road," during the present year (1909). The foot-path, which afforded a short cut across the fields to Well-hall Station, has also been closed to the public.

The Authorities at first proposed to name the new road "Batang Road." A local protest was, however, lodged against this name, and ultimately the name "Archery Road" was adopted. As the new road crosses the "Eastfields," so often alluded to in the Parish Records, where the butts were set up for the practice of archery in the days of Merrie England, the consistency of the name "Archery Road" will be at once seen.

AN OLD ROAD MAP.

The accompanying map, which has been kindly copied by Mr. W. H. Browning from an old map of 1790, shows the Eltham portion of the Coaching road from New Cross to Maidstone.

It is interesting as showing the position of the various country houses and the names of those who resided in them. The guide lines show points of the road from which views of the houses marked could be obtained.

SOME BOOKS AND AUTHORITIES CONSULTED IN THE COMPILATION OF THIS VOLUME.

Lambarde's Perambulation of Kent.
Philipot's Kent.
Hasted's History of Kent.
Domesday Book.
Lyson's Environ's of London.
Buckler's Account of the Palace.
Drake's "Hundred on Blackheath."
Pamphlet on Eltham Palace, etc., by Alexander J. Milne.
Records of Eltham (Rev. E. Rivers).
Dictionary of National Biography.
Archæologia.
Archæologia Cantiana.
Abel's History of Kent.
Records of Woolwich (W. T. Vincent).
The Church Bells of Kent.
Chaucer Society's Records.
Froissart's Chronicles.

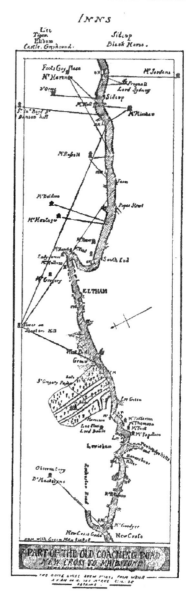

Stow's Chronicles.

Evelyn's Diary.

Pepy's Diary.

Reports of Charity Commissioners.

Reports of Proceedings of Woolwich Antiquarian Society.

Sir William Roper's Life of Sir Thomas More.

State Papers Domestic.

Rymer's Fœdera.

Issue Rolls, Devon.

Holinshed's Chronicles.

Privy Council Records (Nicolas).

Order of the Garter (Nicolas).

Reports on Old Wills belonging to the County of Kent (Leland L. Duncan).

The Golf Club House (Rev. R. N. Rowsell).

And many others whose names are already alluded to in the text.

INDEX.

A

B

LIST OF OLD PRINTS.

LIST OF SUBSCRIBERS.

——•••——

A

Mr Alex Abrahams — West Hampstead
Mr. A P Adams — Eltham
Mr E Adams — Eltham
Mr E W Akhurst — Canada
Mr H Akhurst — Streatham
Mr R. Akhurst — Canada
Miss Akhurst — Catford
Mr C H. Aldred — Plumstead
Mr J H Allchin — The Museum, Maidstone
Mrs E Anderson — Budleigh Salterton
Mr W Anderson — Eltham
Miss Anderson — Eltham
Mr W Andrews — Blackheath
Miss Andrews — Eltham
Mr F D Annesley — Lee
Mr H P Atkins — Eltham
Mr John R Ayres — Balham
Mr T Arundell — New Eltham

B

Mr G Leslie Bannerman, K C , — Lee
Mr John Baines — Eltham
Mr Archer Baker — Eltham
Mr A E Baker, M A , D Litt — Eltham
Rev S Martyn Bardsley, M A — Greenwich
Mr C W Barber — Eltham
Mr R Barber — Eltham
Mr F Barnes — Plumstead
Mr W E. Barnes. (Public Library, Greenwich)
Mrs Barrett — Eltham
Mr H. J Barry — Eltham
Mr R G Bassett — Sidcup
Mr Thos Batterbury, F R I B A., F S I — Eltham
Mr J Baxandall — Eltham
Mrs Bayley — Middle Park, Eltham
Mr C W Beamstead — Plumstead
Mr Herman Becker — Mottingham

Mr E P Bell . — New Eltham
Mr A Evelyn Benbow — New Eltham
Mrs A Evelyn Benbow — New Eltham
Rev Canon Benham — Finsbury Square
Mr G F Benjafield — Eltham
Mrs Randolf Berens — South Kensington
Mr F J. Bevis, B A , B Sc — Eltham
Mr. S. Biddle H M I — ... Catford
Mr T Bilbe — Eltham
Miss Birss — Birkenhead
Mr. Geo. Bishop — Eltham
Mr Blacknell — Eltham
Mr Blakiston — New Eltham
Mr Hubert Bland — Well Hall
Mr E F D Bloom, H M I — Lee
Miss Bloxam — Eltham
Mr Victor Blyth — Eltham
Miss L E Boakes — New Eltham
Mr Edward Bolus, B A. — Stamford Hill
Mr Henry Bond — Public Library, St Pancras
Mr E W Borrajo — Guildhall Library
Mr E Borthwick — Greenwich
Mr H. Boult — Orpington
Mr A Bowden — Blackheath
Mr A S M Bowers — Eltham
Sir Edward Brabrook, F S A — Bedford Hill
Mr W C Brake — Eltham
Mrs Bramley — . Eltham
Miss Bramwell — Eltham
Miss E Brand — Eltham
Mr C E Brandram , — Eltham
Mr F Brandon — Plumstead
Mr C Brinsley Marlay — Regent's Park
Miss A Brookes — Eltham
Mr J Brookes — Eltham
Mr J W Brookes — Lewisham
Mr H Broughton — Plumstead
Mr E D. H Brown — Lewisham
Mr J T Brown — Eltham
Mr P Boswell Brown — Eltham

Mr W Bruin	Eltham
Miss M Buckley	Eltham
Mr C Burford	Eltham
Miss R J Burgess	Lower Clapton
Mr W H Burman	Eltham
Mr Gavin J Burns	Blackheath
Mr W F. Burrows	Basinghall Street, E C
Mr P C Bursill	Woolwich
Mr R Bussell	Bromley
Mr Albert Butcher	Welling
Mr F. E. H Butler	Eltham
Mr. A E Butterworth	Sidcup

C

Mr James Cabban	Lewisham
Miss S Cabban	Bexley Heath
Mr Sydney W Cackett	Dartmouth Park
Mr J. A. W Campbell	Eltham
Mr Thos. Cannon	Mottingham
Mr S. R Carr	Eltham
Miss Carter	Eltham
Misses Carter	Eltham
Mr T V Cater	New Eltham
Mr. H S Cavell	Eltham
Mr. W. Chaffey	Greenwich
Mrs. Chalmers	Eltham
Miss Chalmers	Eltham
Lieut Henry Chamberlain	Epsom
Mr J A Chamberlain	Brixton
Mr W Geo Chambers	Plumstead
Mrs W G Chambers	Plumstead
Mr T D Chandler	Blackheath
Rev E H Chappel	Eltham
Mr. Francis Chappell	Lee
Mr. C. Childs	Rushey Green
Mr. C. Churchill	Old Charlton
Miss A. E L. Clark	Derby
Mr. A E. Clarke	Mottingham
Miss A Clark	Eltham
Miss E Clark	Eltham
Mr. Stanley Clay	Eltham
Mr. H P Clay	Eltham
Mr H C Clifford	Blackheath
Miss A N Clifford	Charlton
Mr J H Close	Eltham
Miss E Cobb	Sidcup Hill
Mr R A Cocks	Eltham
Mr H Cole	Well Hall Parade
Mr R A Collingwood	Eltham
Mr A Collins	Eltham
Mr. J. J. Collins	Woolwich

Mr. C E. Collyer	Morden College
Mr. F J Colson	Eltham
Mr. G Cooling	Chislehurst
Mr J. Coomber	Eltham
Mr G H Cooper	Eltham
Mr J Corps	Eltham
Mr W C Cory	Eltham
Mr. J. H. Cossins	Catford
Miss Cottingham	Eltham
Mr C. Coulter	Eltham
Miss Evelyn Court	Eltham
Mr. H. Cowland	Eltham
Mr. F. J. Cox	Lee
Mr W A Crapp	Eltham
Mr H W Crapp	Eltham
Mr W B Creighton	Godalming
Miss A Crocker	Blackheath
Mr T R Croger	Wood Street, E C
Alderman H Cuff	Eltham
Mrs Cuff	Eltham
Mr D. Cunliffe	Lewisham

D

Mr F Day	Lee
Mr H Day	New Cross
Mr J E Dando	Stoke Newington
Mr T W Dannatt	Blackheath
Lieut.-Col Davies, R.A.M.C.	West Park, Eltham
Mr W E Davis	Eltham
Mr J W Dean	East Greenwich
Miss Winifred De Lisle	St John's, S E
Miss Denning	New Eltham
Mr H C Digby	Eltham
Mr Thos Dinwiddy, F R I B A, F S I.	Blackheath
Mr W. D Diplock	Eltham
Mrs Dobell	Eltham
Mr F A Dodson	Eltham
Mr A. W Dover	Charlton
Mr Arthur Dryden	Bedford Court Mansions
Rev Canon Duckworth, C V O, D D	Westminster Abbey
Mr. G Duggan	Eltham
Mr Leland L Duncan, M V O, F S A	Lewisham
Miss Duncan	Eltham
Miss A Dunn	Eltham
Mr. W Dyer	Eltham
Miss Dyke	Lullingstone Castle Eynsford
Mr. Thos. Dyke	Eltham

Mr H. P Hollis .	Blackheath
Mr A J Hone .	Eltham Road
Mr C H. Hopwood	Fenchurch Street, E C
Mr J R Howe	Eltham
Mr W B Hughes	Eltham
Miss Hughes .	Eltham
Mr W S Hunt	Eltham
Mr G R Hunter	Woolwich
Mr W Hunter	Eltham
Mr R. R Hutchings .	Wincanton
Mrs Hutchinson . .	Eltham
Miss Hutchinson	Plumstead
Miss E Hyde	Eltham

I

Mr H. Icongh	Eltham
Dr T A Ingram, L L D , M A	Woolwich

J

Mr A Jackson	Eltham
Mrs F S Jackson	Eltham
Mr. R J Jackson	Woolwich
Dr Jeken .	Eltham
Mr M Jenks	Eltham
Mr P M Johnston, F S A , F R I B A ,	Champion Hill, S E
Mr. E J Jones	Eltham
Mr Herbert Jones, F S A	Blackheath
Mr T. H Jones Inspector of Schools, L C C	
Mr C H Jordan, M I N A	Eltham
Mr S E Joyce	Burnt Ash Hill

K

Mr F A Kebbel	Eltham
Mrs A Keeble	Greenwich
Mr. A J Keeble .. .	Eltham
Miss F. Keeble .	Greenwich
Mr H. Keeble ..	Rochester
Mr. A. N Kelly	Blackheath
Mr A. Kennedy	St John's, S E
Mr W J Kenny .	Eltham
Mr F C Kenward .	Eltham
Mr S W Kershaw, F.S A	Lambeth Palace Library
Mr H. Kitto	Lee Green
Miss Kibble	Catford
Mr A Kidd	Plumstead
Mr A Killick	Eltham
Dr C W Kimmins	Chief Inspector of Schools, L.C.C.

Mr E C. King	Eltham
Mr Sidney King	Eltham
Dr H D R Kingston	Eltham
Mrs G Kitson .	Mottingham
Mrs. H J Knight	Sidcup
Mr. J Knight . .	Eltham

L

Mr. A C Langley .	Eltham
Mr A C Latter ..	Eltham
Mr C E Lawrence .	Hammersmith
Mr H. E Lawrence	Blackheath
Mr A R Layman .	Eltham
Miss Leaver	Eltham
Mr W H Lee	Lee
Mdlle Therese M Leroy	Lewisham
Mrs A Letchford	Derby
Miss Lewin	Eltham
Mr D J Lewis	Eltham
Mr T Lewis .	Eltham
Mr H J Lindeman	Eltham
Mr S W Lister	Woolwich
Mr W K Low	Eltham
Mr C P Lucas	Mottingham
Mr E Luke	Woolwich
Mr A E Lund	Eltham
Mrs Lush	Plumstead
Miss M Lys	Eltham

M

Col M F. H McCausland, R A ,	Blackheath
Mr John McGregor L C.C ,	Clerkenwell Close
Mrs McGregor	Eltham
Mr F W Machen	Plumstead
Mrs Maddocks	Eltham
Mr G J. Mansfield	Blackheath
Mr G C Marks, M P .	Lincoln's Inn
Mr T D Marsh ..	Eltham
Mrs F A Marshall ..	Eltham
Mr J Marshall	Eltham
Miss C Martin .	Eltham
Mr W Martin .	Eltham
Mr G F Masters	Eltham
Miss Matthews	Clapham Common
Mr W Maud	Blackheath
Mr W J Mercer	Margate
Alderman J J Messent .	Woolwich
Mr G. A T. Middleton, A R I.B.A.	The Strand, W.C
Messr T Miles and Co .	Islington

25

Miss Miller New Eltham
Mr A E Miller Lee
Miss H Mills . . Eltham
Mr T W Mills Eltham
Mis Milne Courtyard, Eltham
Mr John Milton Fulham Palace Road
Dr. W T Milton, M D , M S Lond Eltham
Mr C. L Miskin Blackheath
Mr A W D Moore . Eltham
Mr L J Moore Eltham
Mr W P Moore .. Eltham
Mr A E Morran Eltham
Mr G Morris . . Eltham
Mr. W J. Mortis Eltham Road
Mr H C Mott Lewisham
Mr H Muller West Park, Eltham
Mr A Mulley Eltham
Mr W E Mullins, L C C Hampstead
Mr J R S Murphy Eltham
Mr W C Musquin Old Charlton

N

Mr W A Narbeth Eltham
Mr F F Nash Eltham
Mr G Neves . Woolwich
Miss B N Newbould Eltham
Miss Newman Russell Square, W.C
Mr A. Nicholl Fenchurch Street, E C
Sir Henry Norbury, K C B , R N Eltham
Mr. W Norman Plumstead
Mr P Norman, F S A South Kensington
Mr C North Blackheath Press
Mrs North Eltham
Major Sir Harry North Eltham
Mr. J North Elmstead, Chislehurst
Mr. E. Norton Eltham
Mr F. W. Nunn Lee

O

Mr H Ockerby Queen Victoria Street, E.C
Dr F. O'Leary Eltham
Mr M. C Outtrim Eltham
Mr Edward H Oxenham Town Hall, Catford

P

Mr G L Paine Chester Square, S W
Mr R Pallett . Wallington
Mr W H Pannell, F C A , J.P. Eltham
Mr J W Parker Eltham
Mr J C Perniby, J P New Malden

Mr Geo Payne, F S A
Public Library, Rochester
Mr A G Peace ... Sidcup
Rev R Peake Sidcup
Col M B Pearson, C B . Lee
Mr. A. G Pembroke Eltham
Mr Sidney Pembroke Eltham Road
Rev E. J. Penford . Eltham
Mr S J. Penny Eltham
Mr F. J. Peplow Public Library, Deptford
Mr H N. Perrett . Eltham
Col Sir Herbert Perrott, Bart , C B
South Kensington
Mr. C P Phillips . Sevenoaks
Mr F Phillips Eltham
Mr H L Phillips Kennington Park Road
— J R Phillips, R N H M S Dido
Mr W S Pillans Mottingham
Mr W D Pink Newton le Willows
Miss L Pitman Castle Cary
Mr C Poland Blackheath
Miss Pocknall Eltham
Mr J Poland, F R G S Seal
Mrs Polkinghorne Clapham Common
Mr A G Potter Eltham
Mr. H D Poulter . Eltham
Mrs Powell . Eltham
Mr J Powell Cheltenham
Mr F H Preston . Plumstead
Mr W R B Prideaux, Reform Club, Pall Mall
Mr S Priest, F G S . Stone. Kent
Mr G N Prior Eltham
Mr G Pritchard Eltham
Mr T H Pritchard Eltham

Q

Mrs Quaife Eltham
Mr W Quilter Blackheath

R

Mr F Raby . . Eltham
Mrs Rawlinson . Eltham
Miss Read Eltham
Mrs Relf Hastings
Mrs Relph Eltham
Mr J Rennie Clapton
Mr S Renton Eltham
Mr J S Reynolds . Lee Green
Mr Alfred Rhodes Lambeth, S E
Mr E W Rhodes, M A Eltham College
Mrs M J. Richardson Plumstead

Mr. H. Richardson, J P.   Mayor of Greenwich
Mr. W H. Richardson   Eltham
Mr F A Richardson   Eltham
Mrs B Rickman   .   Mottingham
Mr. C H Roberts   Sidcup
Mr E Roberts, I S O., F R A S   Eltham
Mr F Roberts   .   Clapham
Miss Robertson   ...   Wareham, Dorset
Dr T L Rogers   .   ...   Eltham
Mr E Roswell   ..   ..   Eltham
Rev W. P. Rowley   .   ...   Eltham
Mr. T Rule   .   Eltham

S

Mr F Sadler   Lewisham
Dr St. John   .   Eltham
Mr A. J. Sargeant   .   New Cross
Mr A G Sargent   ...   London Institution
Mr. F. Saunders   ..   .   Eltham
Miss Sceales   .   Eltham
Mr. J G Schmidt   Eltham
Mr F. Schmidtz   Eltham
Mr A Scott   .   Mottingham
Mr W H Scriven   Eltham
Miss R Scrutton   ..   Eltham
Messrs Seager and Sons   ,   Poplar
Miss E M Sharpe   Beckenham
Rev Sir C J M Shaw, Bart
    The Vicarage, Margate
Mr S C Shearing   Eltham
Rev G Shebbeare   .   Lee
Mr A D Shepherd   Eltham
Mrs M A Silvey   Plumstead
Mr A. E Simpson   Eltham
Mr E Simpson   .   Eltham
Miss M G Skinner   Charlton
Mr W. Small   .   ...   .   Eltham
Mrs. W Small   .   .   Eltham
Miss Ethel Small   ..   Elmstead
Mrs Colin Smart   Eltham
Mr W Smart   ...   ..   .   Eltham
Mr E Smith   .   ..   Blackheath
Mr H Smith   Sidcup Hill
Dr Sandford Smith   Eltham
Mr. Whittaker Smith   Eltham
Mrs. P Smithers   ..   Greenwich
Mr J M Somerville   Ladywell
Mr J Spicer   ..   Eltham
Mr. C Spon   ..   St Albans
Mr F Spires   Frederick Street, W C.
Mr J Spry   .   Eltham

Mr S. T. Stafford   ..   .   Eltham
Mr E W Stahlsmidt   .   .   Eltham
Mr F C Stainton   Eltham
Mr J Stanley   Eltham
Rev W E Stebbing, B A   ..   Eltham
Miss M Stefansen   Eltham
Miss S M Stephenson   Plumstead
Major-Gen Sir John Stevens, K C B   Eltham
Mr H Stevenson   Eltham
Mr Steward   .   Eltham
Mrs F M Stiles   ..   ..   Eltham
Mrs Stodart   Mottingham
Mr E A Stone   Old Charlton
Mr. Edward Stone, F S A   Blackheath
Mr J M Stone, M A.   Lincoln's Inn, W C
Mr H de Struve   .   Eltham
Mr W T Sturton   Woolwich
Mrs Swan   Eltham

T

Mr H W. Taffs   Eltham
Miss Taylor   South Petherton
Mr E R Taylor   .   Sidcup
Miss S M Taylor   Sidcup
Mr W R Taylor   Orpington
Lieut.-Col H B Tasker, V D   Eltham
Mr. W G Thame   Eltham
Mr S L Thomas   Eltham
Miss F Thomasset   Eltham
Mr F. G Thompson   Eltham
Mr L C Thomson   Blackheath
Mr C. H Tibbs   Eltham
Mr E D Till   Eynsford
Mr. J Tolhurst   Beckenham
Mr R Tomlinson   ..   Old Kent Road
Mr A. Treliving   .   .   Lee
Messrs Truslove and Hanson
    Oxford Street, W
Mr R. Turner   Eltham
Mr H E Turner   ...   Plumstead
Mr Twidle   .   Sidcup
Rev A C Tyler-Taylor   Eltham

V

Mr Veasey   Eltham
Mr Kenneth D Vickers, M A   Gray's Inn
Mrs Vickers   Sidcup
Mr J Villesia   Eltham
Mr W T Vincent   Woolwich
Mr G W Vincent, F S A   Mottingham
Lady Vyvyan   ..   Shooters Hill

W

Councillor R B Wakelen .   ...   Eltham
Mr. D W Wakeford   .   Greenwich
Mr. J. O Wale .   .   Bexley Heath
Mr. Allen S. Walker .   London Institution
Mr F C Walker ..   .   .   Eltham
Mr H Wallis .   ..   .   Eltham
Councillor R. A M. Walters   ...   Eltham
Mr. G. T. Ward   ..   Eltham
Miss Warner ..   ..   ..   Eltham
Mr E. Warner ..   ..   Eltham
Mrs. Warmington   ..   Bromley
Mr M Warren   Bexley Public Library
Miss E Waterhouse   Avery Hill
Major General J Waterhouse   Eltham
Mr F. J. Waters   .   Northfleet
Miss E. J. Watkin ..   ..   ..   Eltham
Mr. H. Watkin .   ..   ..   Lee
Mr. J. Watkinson   .   .   Herne Bay
Hon. Mrs. Watson   ..   Clonmel, Ireland
Mr J. N. Watts   .   Brockley
Mr. T R Webber   Plumstead
Mr Herbert J Weise   South Norwood
Mr W F Wenyon   .   Eltham
Miss Westbrook   .   Yeovil
Mr. J. Westwood   .   Eltham
Mr. George Whale, J P   Mayor of Woolwich

Mr A. T. Wheeler ..   .   .   Catford
Rt. Rev. Abbot White   .   Eltham
Mr H. Whistler   .   .   .   Eltham
Mrs White   ..   .   .   Sidcup
Mr F White ..   ..   Eltham
Mr G H Wiggins   ...   ..   The Minories
Mr T. P Wiggins   ...   The Minories
Rev T B. Willson, M A.   ..   Shooter's Hill
Mr. C. D. Wilson ..   Eltham Palace
Mr. W. T Wise   Eltham
Miss Wood   ...   .   ..   Eltham
Mr W. W Wood ...   Lee
Mr H W Wood ..   ..   ..   Eltham
Woolwich Library (Kent Collection)
Mr. J Worters   .   ...   Eltham
Mr A E Wren   ..   .   Bexley
Mr. W Wren   .   Plumstead
Mrs J. J. Wright   ...   ..   Eltham
Mrs. James Wright   .   .   .   Eltham
Mr Ernest H. Wright, P A.S I. ... Woolwich

Y

Mrs Yeatman   ...   ...   Eltham
Miss E V Yeatman   ...   ..   Eltham
Miss Yeatman ..   .   Eltham
Mr. C Youens   .   Dartford
Mr. W B Young   for Erith Public Library

Lightning Source UK Ltd.
Milton Keynes UK
UKHW050133070223
416581UK00005B/311

9 781016 724333